WARREN HASTINGS

WARREN HASTINGS, 1790, BY THOMAS BANKS

WARREN HASTINGS

BY

KEITH FEILING

'Who, rowing hard against the stream,
Saw distant gates of Eden gleam,
And did not dream it was a dream.'

LONDON
MACMILLAN & CO LTD
NEW YORK · ST MARTIN'S PRESS
1954

MACMILLAN AND COMPANY LIMITED
London Bombay Calcutta Madras Melbourne

THE MACMILLAN COMPANY OF CANADA LIMITED
Toronto

ST MARTIN'S PRESS INC
New York

PRINTED IN GREAT BRITAIN

TO
CAROLINE FEILING
IN REMEMBRANCE OF
INDIA AND THE
COTSWOLDS

PREFACE

THE life of any man in great place, like Warren Hastings, is three-dimensional; the State he serves, his own life, and a third area where these two meet and interact. This book is mainly concerned with the second and third arenas, and is based primarily on Hastings' own papers, the three hundred volumes of which have still left much that seems untold. It does not attempt any fully documented account of his manifold policies, the content of which must embrace intricacies of revenue and land tenure, diplomatic relations ranging from Egypt to Tibet and from the Sikh confederacy to Pondicherry, military campaigns over vast theatres, and problems of Brahmin and Moslem learning. Many more special studies must, I think, be written, before one hand could grasp and judge the whole.

In a book which seeks original authority throughout, precise reference would involve a numeral and a footnote every four or five lines. I have therefore given in an appendix a classified list of the manuscript sources used, together with the chief printed authorities; followed by a series of notes, to provide exact reference on a number of points which seemed specially significant or controversial, or sometimes ignored.

Unless the context shows a clear indication to the contrary, quotations come from Hastings' letters and despatches, and since his power and historic legacy were largely the achievement of his pen, quotation must be substantial. In spelling Indian names, I have conformed to recent practice; adopting the forms of standard authorities such as the *Imperial Gazetteer*, except in the case of words which long tradition has made part of our common history.

The names of those who have allowed me to use or reproduce original manuscripts, pictures, or busts in their possession will be found on pages xi and 402. To all of these I acknowledge my very grateful obligations; and especially to Miss Vansittart Neale, who gave me the use of Hastings' letters to his familiar friend,

George Vansittart. I have also to thank the staffs of the British Museum, of the India Office Library at the Commonwealth Relations Office, and of the Indian Institute at Oxford, Bodley's Librarian, Sir Arthur Knapp, and Mrs. Wilkinson of Daylesford Rectory, for much kindness and assistance.

K. F.

1953

CONTENTS

ix

LIST OF ILLUSTRATIONS

Youth: 1732-50

WARREN HASTINGS, last and greatest of his immediate line, never saw his parents, for his mother died in giving him birth and his father, leaving Warren and his sister Anne to the care of others, vanished and died in exile. It was from his grandfather Penyston Hastings, Rector of Daylesford, that he first heard of the glories of his race.

They had come over with the Conqueror. Domesday Book found them on the upper Thames and its Cotswold tributaries, Windrush and Evenlode, taking root both at Eaton Hastings on the Berkshire bank, which property left their hands after a century, and at Yelford near Bampton on the Oxfordshire side, which they kept till the ruin of the Civil War. By the middle of the twelfth century, moving west again, they had acquired yet another manor at Daylesford, one of those islands of Worcestershire which, by a freak of history, are lapped round by the four shires meeting on the eastern Cotswold slopes.

In the Middle Ages the house of Hastings shone with lustre, quartering its arms of the 'maunche', or sleeve, with those of the greatest barons, until it reached the steps of the throne. This was especially true of the main line, originally seated in East Anglia, to whom the Daylesford branch stood for some generations in the relation of vassals. So, in virtue of descent from William the Lion's brother David, John first Lord Hastings was an unsuccessful claimant to the throne of Scotland, while his grandson Lawrence in 1339 became Earl of Pembroke, taking title and lands from his marriage to a Valence heiress. After that earldom failed in the male descent, a cadet branch rose up as Earls of Huntingdon, who intermarried with the Staffords, Dudleys, and

Greys during the Yorkist and Tudor revolutions, so that they nearly won a claim to the Crown, and fought in the Civil War as the fiercest of Cavaliers.

Over all these centuries, however, there seems nothing to record of the Yelford and Daylesford family, except poverty, trouble, and insignificance. Sir Miles Hastings, who died in 1305, had been 'out' in his youth as a rebel with De Montfort, nearly lost his lands a second time for 'enormous trespass' on Edward I, and mortgaged the Buckinghamshire fief he acquired by marriage. By that date they had parted with Eaton Hastings and, after a minority, Daylesford itself was once in others' hands, but was recovered in 1408. When Yorkist followed Lancastrian, we hear little save that Edward Hastings is a debtor of long standing in King's Bench. All the time the Tudors were making a new England, no Hastings of Daylesford emerges as member of parliament, or even in the commission of the peace. We know only that one John died in 1545, presumably a Catholic still, leaving his second-best gown to 'master parson', who was bidden 'pray for my soul', while a later John was thrice summoned at Elizabethan quarter-sessions for killing pigeons with a bow.

For though their coat-of-arms and ancient blood were commemorated in many Oxfordshire churches, and though they lived in a rich countryside of wool and cloth-making, they did not win, or certainly did not keep, this new wealth. No great profit could be made out of the bleak downlands rising behind their Daylesford house and stretching north towards Chipping Norton, the jurors of 1305 thus reporting only a dovecot, an 'old and frail' water-mill, a little valley pasture and eighty acres of arable, with six tenants paying among them but 21s. a year and a pound of pepper.

So small was the scale. A century later the parish had not ten householders capable of paying subsidy. From Elizabeth's reign onwards the Hastings sometimes married into the families of small squires like the Penystons of Cornewell, but as often made more plebeian matches with yeomen and merchants.

The worthy Simon Hastings, who reigned from 1585 to 1628, and whose praises were rehearsed by Habington, the Worcestershire poet and antiquary, pushed his family nearer to the gulf by leaving eleven children from his two marriages. His widow, *née* Susan Dobbins and mother of nine, died at Daylesford just as the Civil War began, bequeathing a hundred sheep and an inordinate quantity of sheets and feather-beds. But the heir, her stepson John, carried further still the dispersal of property, which his father's last testament began in order to provide for all his children. Three younger brothers were set up in Daylesford with houses, orchards, and sheep walks, the youngest took holy orders and the advowson of the rectory, and marriage portions were raised for all the daughters. John sold thirty acres along the river, where the first house had stood and had been burned down, he rented out to two brothers-in-law the water-mill, with hill pasture for 400 sheep. He himself, it seems, went to live at Yelford, part of which was leased also. And then, having barely completed these arrangements, he died in July 1629, only a year after his father, leaving from his three marriages two daughters and one son John, aged one year and five months.

This infant John grew up into the supposed 'Cavalier', whose sacrifices for the royal martyr were depicted by his grandson the Rector, both to his own grandson, Warren, and to Nash, the Worcestershire historian. Yet John was only eighteen when fighting in the first Civil War ended on the neighbouring hill at Stow on the Wold, and not a line survives about his property in the Commonwealth accounts of sales and confiscations. Perhaps he took part in the later campaign of Worcester. At least we have no ground for disputing the family tradition that under the Protectorate he took refuge at St.-Jean-de-Luz, whence he brought back sainfoin, the earliest grown in the Cotswolds. Somehow or other he parted with the Yelford lands to that cautious profiteer, Speaker Lenthall, whose descendants held them through the next century. Little else seems discoverable of this John, save that his wife, born Elizabeth Penyston of Cornewell, had died during the troubles, leaving him two sons and two daughters.

After him followed three successive Penystons Hastings. The first married a Creswicke, from the manor-house at Moreton in Marsh, ran deep into debt, and in 1715 sold Daylesford to a Bristol merchant, Jacob Knight, who soon demolished the Hastings home. Within three years the squire's eldest son died in Jamaica, intestate and childless, leaving as head of the family his brother, Penyston the second, Rector of Daylesford for a half-century from 1701. Quarrelling, the story runs, with

3

Mr. Knight over his tithes, the Rector lived most of his life at Churchill, the village 600 feet up on the hills three miles north-east. He was a Balliol man, with the pleasant antiquarian interests of that age, but though he married a Gardiner of Temple Guiting, descended from that rich Sir William who is thought to be the original of Justice Shallow, she can hardly have come to him well endowed. For he sold the advowson of Daylesford for 800 guineas and in 1752 died a bankrupt, leaving no assets to his then only surviving child, Elizabeth. Of his other children, the second son, Howard, had done well in the Customs service; Samuel, the youngest, died a midshipman and childless. Of Penyston, the heir, there is more to be said, but nothing good.

After leaving Balliol without a degree, this third Penyston took holy orders and in July 1730, now a man of twenty-five, married Hester Warren, that autumn being also inducted as Vicar of Bledington, a hamlet in the Evenlode valley midway between Daylesford and Churchill. A daughter, Anne, was born next year; a son, Warren, was born at Churchill in his grandfather's house on December 6th, 1732, and baptized there on the 15th. But on the same day his mother was buried at Daylesford. Seven months later Penyston married again, this time the daughter of an Oxford tradesman, Mary Dandridge. A little later still his brother-in-law, John Warren, presented a petition in Chancery, alleging that Penyston was 'withdrawn from his habitation', leaving his children unprovided for, and that he was diverting their small trust funds towards payment of his own debts. When next we meet Penyston, it is as Rector of Christ Church, Barbados, where he married yet a third time. There he died in the winter of 1743-44, calmly leaving by will to his third wife, Jemima, the property of which he was said to have robbed his children by his first. This story considered, and remembering that sixty years later Warren Hastings was being dunned by a supposed grandson of Penyston's second wife, he rather naturally told would-be biographers 'there was not much in my father's history worth repeating'.

For forty years, until they heard of his fame and wealth, an iron curtain fell between him and his mother's family. Perhaps his parents had made a runaway marriage, for it took place at Worcester, not the home parish of either of them, and it is certain the Warrens were much lower in the social scale. Hester's father held a little yeoman farm at Stub Hill, Twyning, in Gloucester-shire, and her sisters respectively married a Birmingham surgeon and an unprosperous Gloucester grocer. Her brother Thomas, the inheritor of Stub Hill, who had been accused of conniving at the bad dealings of Penyston, grew old as a local original character, though hardly one which the Hastings pride would appreciate. During the general election of 1774 John Walsh, member for Worcestershire, came across him while canvassing, revealed his nephew's high position, and wrote out to India about this uncle; to which the Governor-General replied, 'I was even ignorant that such a person existed'. Uncle Thomas, it seemed, had planned and engineered the Worcester and Tewkes-bury roads. Though Stub Hill was mortgaged, he had planted fine oaks and made water-ways, taking out a licence to open his grounds for the sale of cider. He was shocked to hear, he wrote to his 'nevieu', that he had passed through Cheltenham on his last furlough, without communicating either with him or with 'sister Turner' at Gloucester; 'I hope you have no dislike to the family'. At this point the Governor's old aunt, Elizabeth Hastings, weighed in heavily, to put him on his guard against these Warrens; 'they are an artful designing set of people . . . your mother never had sixpence either from her father or mother, and you and your sister are some pounds the worse for Mr. T.W.' But no claim of kindred ever appealed to Warren Hastings in vain, and very soon Indian shawls were going to Twyning, and hints from Twyning to Calcutta that Stub Hill would be his, 'if you deserved it'. Finally, the commander of the Governor's body-guard, when on leave, arranged that Thomas should give up his public garden in return for an annuity from Warren. So this family story closed in 1782 with Thomas' will, bequeathing Stub Hill, and the care of an impecunious niece, to his nephew.

Years later still, making some jottings of autobiography, he wrote that one 'peculiar uniformity' had attended on his life, the character of 'a solitary insulated wanderer'. That began in 1733, with his mother dead and his father disappeared, when he was put in charge of a village foster-mother, Mary Ellis. She was illiterate, for she could only make her mark, and very poor, for in old age she was getting 2s. 6d. a week from the parish, when in her last year of life Warren, on hearing of it, assigned her sixteen guineas a year. Her son, however, was literate enough to send a begging letter from an Oxford slum many years after, 'as we both sucked at one breast and were playfellows together'.

After that infancy he grew up in his grandfather's house, probably in the care of his aunt Elizabeth. When he saw the house again, in 1791, in the occupation of a shoemaker, he noted 'once a good house and still in a decent condition'. Though now sub-divided, it still stands solid and foursquare, close to the ruined church where he was baptized, looking south-east towards the distant line of the Fosse way, along which Roman empire-makers had marched with the eagles. Here he attended the village school and survived an attack of smallpox. Though his dates and facts might go astray, the old man might truthfully record what he suffered as a child, and of what he had dreamed. That recollection was, first, of a home hardly above 'the pressure of absolute want', and then of his dream, 'one bright summer's day', as he lay in his favourite haunt by the Kingham brook in the plain below, that Daylesford, the lands he could see a mile away, should one day be his again. It never, he says, faded away. And the first step in its slow fulfilment was, in fact, taken in 1740 when, at eight years old, he was taken off to his uncle Howard Hastings' house at Westminster.

Whether he was happy there can hardly be judged from a note sixty years after, that to his uncle he owed his education, and 'every care which good principle, unimpelled by natural affection, could dictate'. Nor does he ever seem to mention his uncle's wife, daughter of a Lincoln cleric; perhaps they had differences over his refusing dancing lessons, having 'insuperable aversion', a later letter says, 'to masters of all kinds in the holidays'. Alone in a childless household, it is probable that a new stamp and a new reality were imposed on the dreams and ambitions first nurtured by his poverty-stricken grandfather. For Howard Hastings, having broken out of the rustic mould, had 'a genteel place' in the Customs House, prospering so far that he owned horses and fowling-pieces and a diamond ring. He took Warren into the fringes of a world of wealth and leisure, which belonged to ancient blood, and why not to a Hastings of Daylesford? His chief occupation, rather than the Customs House, was to be companion or business adviser to William Vane, Duke of Cleveland, and when he went down to the Vanes' lovely house at Fairlawn near Tonbridge, he would sometimes take his nephew, who there got to know the weird poet Christopher Smart, son of the Vanes' steward. Indeed, Howard staked his future on the Vanes. His will, stating he was entitled to £200 a year from the Duke and £2000 at death, recommended Warren to the protection of the Duke's heir Henry, later Lord Darlington, and Warren's sister Anne to Vane's wife. But the Vanes belied his hopes. Harry Vane, 'toad-eater and spy to all parties', as Horace Walpole described him, renounced probate and repudiated liability, which the Governor-General was exploring even in 1780. And it was Harry's daughter Anne who, as wife of Colonel Monson, then member of Warren Hastings' Council, spread the story that he was only a natural son of her father's steward.

His uncle saw faithfully to his education, sending him first to a boarding-school at Newington Butts, where the teaching was good, but the food so poor that he thought it accounted for his small frame and digestive weakness. In May 1743 he moved on to Westminster, boarding as a town boy with Mrs. Gibson in Great College Street. Four years later precisely, he was elected into College, heading the scholars' list for the year, and so became 'liberty boy', exempted from fagging; a certain Elijah Impey, son of a Hammersmith merchant, came in fourth, who two years back had been in the form above Hastings. Under the benevolent headmaster, Dr. Nichols, the school was flourishing, with about 350 boys, and teaching some of the best young minds in England. Vincent Bourne the great Latinist, with his greasy wig, was on the staff. The second master was James Johnson, whom sturdy Whigs accused of Jacobite leanings, as the bosom friend of the two men they most detested, the silver-tongued lawyer Lord Mansfield and the Duke of Newcastle's *éminence grise*, Andrew Stone. Two future Prime Ministers were there with Hastings, Shelburne and Portland; the two poets, Cowper and Churchill; Peter Beckford, the historian of hunting; Gibbon, the historian of empire; the dramatist George Colman, the elder; and Francis Hastings, tenth Earl of Huntingdon, whose arms he claimed to share. He complained later that 'English was never taught there', but Lady Anne Monson remembered he was nicknamed 'the classical boy', and he retained all through life a taste for Latin poetry, and for scribbling English verse on the Horatian model.

All the hints we have picture him a normal and happy boy.

Cowper remembered him as gentle and popular, he kept recollections of rowing and cricket with Impey, while from his nephew Stormont, another schoolfellow, Lord Mansfield had a story he told in another, and more serious, connection. Hastings, he was heard saying to Lord George Germaine, was not a man to despair : 'I remember, when he was a boy, he took it into his head that he could fly, and made a very ingenious pair of wings. It is true he broke his nose, but that is nothing to the purpose.' Anyhow, broken nose or not, there was never a more devoted old Westminster. In his days of supreme patronage in India, countless recommendations arrived 'from your old schoolfellow and friend', or on behalf of a schoolfellow's son ; he sent his nephew there, and encouraged his friends to send their sons. And the common case against the eighteenth-century public schools is weakened, when we scan — to say nothing of Gibbon or Cowper — Warren Hastings' reading in India.

These good times ended in February 1749, when his uncle died. His will dealt lavishly, indeed, in annuities to his old father the Rector and his sister Elizabeth, left some South Sea stock to his niece Anne, and to Warren £40 a year, besides whatever he could get from the little Cheltenham property which his mother had owned, but which his father Penyston had tried to dispose of. But the will was largely founded on his expectations from the Vanes, who proved obstructive, and the remaining executor, who now became Warren's guardian, accepted defeat. At Whitsun he took Warren away from Westminster, to the indignation of the headmaster, who offered to pay for the boy himself, and boarded him out with a Monsieur Deprez.

This guardian was Joseph Creswicke, of that Moreton in Marsh family into which Penyston the first had married, and a colleague of Howard Hastings in the Customs service. He lived in comfort at Streatham, rising later to become an East India Company director, but we detect in the Hastings and Penystons a sub-acid note on his peevishness, and his lack of zeal in protecting their interests. Anne Hastings was off his hands, for this year she married John Woodman, a steady industrious attorney. No doubt, however, Mr. Creswicke found it a thankless business. Only a Chancery suit secured to his wards the Plow Inn property at Cheltenham, which Warren made over to his sister, while at the very end of the century he was being plagued by an alleged debt of his uncle Howard, incurred in fitting him out for India. He repudiated the bare idea of such a thing. 'My uncle never had the most distant intention of such a destination. It originated with myself, from a consideration of the destitute state in which I was left.'

This was written in 1799, but in 1749 Creswicke must have had a hand in it, considering that in November Warren finished 'a regular course of merchants' accounts' under Mr. Thomas Smith at Christ's Hospital, and that his guardian got his nomination as a writer in the Company service and stood as his security. Early in December he was assigned to Bengal, kept Christmas at Streatham, and sailed from Gravesend in the *London* on January the 27th, 1750. Of his voyage we know nothing, except that half a century later he was glad to think he had climbed to the masthead, 'without crawling through the lubber's hole'.

On August 25th he reached Fort St. David on the east coast of India, which was then the seat of that Presidency, for Madras had been in the hands of the French in the late war, and was not set up again as capital till 1752. A fortnight later the *London* put in at Madras, where news was circulating of the unofficial fighting which had continued without paying attention to the peace signed in Europe; how Dupleix had routed Mahomed Ali, the Nabob of the Carnatic supported by the British, and how Bussy had gone on to storm the mountain fortress of Gingee, which Mogul armies had found impregnable. On September the 12th the *London* left this war zone, beat up the coast, and so into the Hugli, where she anchored at Kalpi on October the 9th.

9

CHAPTER II

The Indian Scene: 1750-56

AGED 18-24

THE native boat that took him up the river had fifty miles to sail. By banks covered with low woods down to the water edge, past Fulta on the right in feverish swampy ground, where giant bats flew by night and the jungle behind was full of tigers, past coconut groves to the small town of Budge Budge. There were many corpses floating downstream, but otherwise little to see, save the country boats bringing down salt, or taking up lime and cement. At last, as they bent eastwards, they saw the Indian fort of Tana on the west bank and then caught their first sight of Calcutta, the shipping, and the tall flagstaff of the Fort.

It was only sixty years since Job Charnock had founded the settlement, indeed his daughter-in-law was living there still, and the position of the English had made little progress. If their fortifications and wharves straggled for some three miles, 'the white town' where they lived covered only about a mile from north to south, by a quarter of a mile eastward from the river, a thin ribbon of England against which strained a 'black town', of perhaps 200,000 souls. For the Company's imports of bullion, broad cloth, and fire-arms, their demand for Indian goods to export, the protection and employment they offered, and the ransom for which they could be squeezed, had brought together a great mixed population, of Moslem officials and Hindu or Jain bankers, Armenian traders, Portuguese, half-castes, Dutch pilots, with swarms of labourers and servants and slaves. Inland, east and south-east of the Fort, they had made their pocket edition of English life. St. Anne's church overlooked it, a few steps on were the Mayor's court, the play-house, and the jail. Beyond the great tank, their chief source of drinking water, and the park were the comfortable houses, with gardens and wide verandahs, of members of Council and senior officers, among them that of the doyenne of society, Lady Russell, widow of Sir Francis, late chief at Kasimbazaar and grandson of Oliver Cromwell. South again lay the hospital and, conveniently near it, the burial-ground. For life was apt to be short in this swampy settlement. East lay a feverish jungle; west, an unbanked river a mile wide and liable to high floods. Such drains as existed lay open to the sun, orders still issued to clear the streets of scrub and undergrowth, dead bodies lay unburied on the river-bank, *pariah* dogs plunged into the great tank, adjutant cranes and vultures acted as scavengers. Every year an enormous rainfall undermined some Company building; each hot weather, with the assistance of heavy drinking and incompetent doctors, bore off a large crop to the burial-ground. Small wonder, though we forget it too often, that the Presidency was ruled by young men. When Roger Drake, governor from 1752 to 1756, was appointed, he was thirty; William Watts, chief at Kasimbazaar, when Hastings went there, was thirty-four, while boys in their middle twenties were third or fourth in every factory, and coining fortunes.

Here for nearly two years, till August 1752, a boy even then under twenty, Hastings worked as a writer in the Company's junior grade, learning his business in the secretary's office. His official salary was £5 a year in cash, with 20 rupees a month for his board and a trifle for his washing. His inner life and thought in those years have left not a rack behind. Its discipline he had acquired at Westminster, and a little more, maybe, on the voyage out, when Company servants must salute the captain on his quarter-deck, appear at meals to the roll of drums, and put out their cabin lights by ten at night. And now, we must suppose, he achieved the mastery of Urdu and fair competence in Persian which, in the next few years, distinguished him from the ruck of young Englishmen.

In all Bengal, even including the military, there were hardly a thousand Britons, and he was a humble unit of their inner circle, the Company's sixty or seventy 'covenanted' servants. Though recent Governors had taken to living outside, their life was concentrated in the Fort. Here was Government House, with a long pillared front facing west and a colonnade down to the water gate; armoury and laboratory, and 'the long row' where the young writers lived. Southwards stood the huge godowns, heaped with silks and cotton goods waiting for shipment; eastwards, the curtain wall and gate confronting the native city, with barracks for the guard, and a cell for offenders christened 'the Black Hole'. But the Fort had been shamefully neglected, and might fall to any serious attack. Eight years before, in a sudden alarm, the Indian inhabitants had dug the 'Mahratta ditch', but when four miles of its crescent curve were done they wearied, and left it unfinished. Though its gun line would protect the river front, everywhere else the Fort was defenceless. It was overlooked by the church and some large houses, the warehouses masked the fire from its southern bastions, walls had been cut through to make passage for goods. One officer after another had pointed out that most of the walls were too shaky to bear a gun, even if guns and gun-carriages had been forthcoming and the powder were not damp.

If he knew little of this, even the boy Hastings may have grasped the weakness of the Governors and the sixteen senior merchants who composed the Council. Two Governors were dismissed within these two years, a third died of dysentery, and so the office came to the youthful Drake, whose marriage to a deceased wife's sister apparently gave more offence than his character of straw. The *zemindar*, or magistrate, — for in the Mogul system the Company ranked as *zemindar* of Calcutta — was Holwell, once surgeon on an Indiaman, an older and more forceful person than most of them, but conceited and ill-liked. Heat and tedium and alcohol made them quarrelsome; we shall hear again of an angry and corrupt McGuire, who attacked the chief engineer with a sword. At least a babe in arms might have reflected what an easy hostage the city was to fortune, through what hands passed its volume of wealth, and in what 'slavish dependence', as Hastings wrote afterwards, they rested for its safe passage on the native government. Every day boats were bringing in silks from the mulberry trees of Beerbohm, saltpetre from Patna, muslins from Dacca, lacs and gums and cotton, or from far Sylhet the iron, which women had first loaded in baskets held by a belt over their forehead. Each season country ships carried out Bengal rice for Madras, or sailed in with betel from Malacca, teak from Rangoon, Mocha coffee, or China tea.

The Company's wealth had been a prize in British politics from the latter days of Charles II, while since Godolphin had patched up their internal feuds in Queen Anne's reign it had rapidly increased. In 1744, in return for a loan of a million to government, its charter was extended until 1783, its sales and payment of customs in that year totalling about £2 million. In sale of tea alone it cleared about half a million a year. Its issued capital was £3 million, and for some time past it had paid a dividend of 8 per cent. Yet these riches were won, and must be maintained, in a sub-continent which was quivering in war, anarchy, and revolution.

Aurungzebe's criminal half-century as Emperor had ended at last in 1707, leaving in ruins the great realm which in our Tudor days the Moguls had extended from Kabul to Delhi, and from Kashmir to the Indian Ocean. This harsh ascetic, fanatical in the orthodox faith of Islam, had spent years of his life and millions of treasure in wars to master southern India. He had torn down Hindu temples and crushed the peasantry with poll taxes, steepening also the land revenue till it sometimes took half the produce of the soil. His predecessors had made friends of the Rajput chieftains south-west of Delhi, who had given the dynasty some of its finest soldiers, but he sacrificed that alliance to his bigoted religion. So from his cruelty sprang forth, what must in any event have happened sooner or later, a universal revival of Hindu India. For over a hundred years already in the Punjab the Sikhs had defied death and torture, they had their martyrs, their sacraments, and their holy place at Amritzar. Repudiating caste, they defined their military brotherhood as the *Khalsa* or 'the purified', distinguished by their daggers and their long hair, and eschewing the comforts of wine and tobacco. But their great day was still distant. The imminent menace came from the Mahrattas.

The western Ghauts, separating the coastal strip of British Bombay and Portuguese Goa from the Deccan uplands, were thrown wildly up into rocky hill-tops, spaced between by deep clefts, where the trees waved below. Here an aboriginal people had lived apart from Aryan and Mogul conquerors, worshipping their own fierce gods and goddesses of fertility and sacrifice, and perpetuating their racial identity in heroic ballads. From these hill men came, when Cromwell ruled Britain, the mighty conqueror Sivaji, the epitome of his race in endurance, soldierly discipline, and treacherous craft. He had resisted Aurungzebe, and broken south into the Carnatic; his descendants had doubled their efficiency by taking as their ministers, or Peishwas, a line of Brahmins, who made a capital at Poona just east of the Ghauts, and reduced their nominal masters to the role of a figurehead. Mahratta raids had already crossed the path of the English. In 1739 they took Bassein, just north of Bombay, from the Portuguese, while one of their race made himself Rajah of Tanjore, near the British Fort St. David. Under Ballaji Rao, the third Peishwa (1740-61), they often raided Bengal, from whose Nabob they wrenched the province of Orissa, and had lately plundered a convoy of British salt boats from Kasimbazaar. The Moguls had granted them the right of taking *chouth*, or a quarter of the land revenue, in the Deccan, the control over which, and over the Carnatic, they henceforth contested with Moslem princes. One of their ruling families, the Bhonslas, made themselves Rajahs of Berar. They tore away from the Empire most of central India, where three Mahratta chieftains were settling in those areas which became the great States of Scindia, Holkar, and the Gaekwar. Their ambitions were rising towards Delhi itself.

Moreover, the once great Moguls had dug their own grave. Civil wars, depositions, blindings and murders, made a rapid succession of weak Emperors whose dominion fell into fragments. In the 1720's Asaf Jah, Vizier and strongest of their councillors, departed to his government of the Deccan, to found an independent line of Nizams of Hyderabad. A little later the Nabob of Oudh, by origin a Persian Shiah, set up for himself also. Northwest of his State an Afghan clan, the Rohillas, entrenched themselves north of the Ganges. Just south of the Jumna, the sturdy Hindu Jats from the Punjab were making a power near the Imperial city of Agra. In 1739 Nadir Shah of Khorasan, having made himself King of Persia, overran Afghanistan and swept on to Delhi, where he looted and massacred at will, carrying away untold treasure and the peacock throne made for Shah Jehan. On his assassination one of his Afghan officers, Ahmad Shah Abdali, advanced from Herat to seize the Punjab, which he achieved by 1748, and left a Rohilla to command the Mogul armies. In 1741 Aliverdi Khan, a Tartar adventurer, having slain the heir of his benefactor, established himself as Nabob of Bengal with his Pathan troopers.

This welter of revolution and new principalities naturally

14

went to its extreme in the Deccan and the far South, where Mogul authority had been stretched to its weakest. Here the spray of many waves of conquest, Hindu and Moslem, thrown over areas made impregnable by great rivers and mountains, had left behind a shifting formation of rival claims and upstarts. And here it was that the European settlements first engaged deeply in Indian politics. For if they wished to strengthen their thin forces by enlisting sepoys, to hire Mahratta horsemen or Hyderabad Pathans, to buttress Madras or Pondicherry by a more defensible frontier, here was raw material ready to their hand.

During the war of the Austrian succession, there were signs that the undying strife between Hindu and Moslem would drive some of them to seek protection in the walled European cities, or to buy European help by ceding territory. And when that war officially ended in 1748, the remarkable governor of Pondicherry, Dupleix, seized his opportunity with both hands. The 'constitutional' ruler of the Deccan (if such a word can be used of Mogul India) was the Nizam, but in this year the able and experienced Asaf Jah died, leaving many sons, the eldest of whom was preoccupied in the factions at Delhi. The territory east of Hyderabad, between the Ghauts and the sea, was ruled by the Nizam's subordinate, the Nabob of the Carnatic, at this date one of his own soldiery, whom he had chosen to suppress the anarchy left by a previous Moslem dynasty. But at this very moment, aided by French money, the ablest man of that dynasty, Chanda Sahib, who had long been a Mahratta prisoner, reappeared and claimed the Carnatic. Great French triumphs filled the years from 1749 to 1751. The few hundred Europeans with whom they stiffened their allies' forces destroyed the legend of Indian power; both the new Nizam and the Carnatic Nabob were killed in battle, in whose stead ruled the claimants set up by the French. The Nizam declared Dupleix governor of all India south of the Kistna. The fearless Marquis de Bussy marched 900 miles inland with disciplined sepoys, to install himself as the power behind the Nizam's throne. Grants of territory along the coast would enable French traders to finance this new supremacy.

Official peace covered Europe, but the British in India could do nothing but resist this suffocation. They recognised as Nabob of the Carnatic Mahomed Ali, a son of him slain by the French. Saunders, the resolute governor of Madras, had with him an admirable soldier in Stringer Lawrence, and discovered in the ranks of his writers a heaven-born fighter in Robert Clive. From Clive's capture of Arcot in 1751 onwards, the English wore their enemies down. Bussy was pinned to the Deccan by Moslem hostility to the foreigner, and in 1754 the French admitted the title of Mahomed Ali and recalled Dupleix. Yet since Bussy still ruled indirectly at Hyderabad, and directly over the Northern Circars, lying on the coast between Orissa and Madras territory, the British were considering an expedition from Bombay which, with Mahratta assistance, might disperse this French menace.

Thus all over India power had disintegrated, new men and fragments of old races redoubling the historic hatred between Hindu and Moslem. Sometimes the Mahrattas compromised their claim on Deccan revenues with the Nizam, sometimes insulted his weakness, and rode to protect the Hindu Rajahs of Tanjore and the South from the Moslem ruler of the Carnatic. On their path thither lay the small Hindu State of Mysore, whose military strength was being revived by an illiterate Moslem officer, Hyder Ali, the grandson of a Punjab dervish, whose sword was drawn in the 1750's first for the English, and then for the French. In 1754 the reigning Emperor was blinded and deposed, the great Ahmad Abdali might at any time reappear in the centre of India, and in fact he ruthlessly pillaged Delhi in 1756. Oudh and the Rohillas alternately fought each other, or combined against the Mahrattas, one of whose warriors, the Peishwa's brother Ragoba, invaded Rajputana. And if either the Afghans or the Mahrattas were to master Hindustan, what would be the future of the British handful in Bengal?

But meantime individual Europeans made hay while the sun shone, on a scene where wealth meant power and power came by corruption. Bussy had his native councillors, deserters and adventurers of all countries were selling their skill in artillery or their strong arms in the Deccan or at Delhi, even mates of East Indiamen turned mercenary soldiers. The pagoda tree was being shaken for its fruits, clustered on many spreading boughs.

In this India, Warren Hastings was in 1752 ordered up from Calcutta, to learn the detail of trade at Kasimbazaar.

CHAPTER III

The Fall and Recovery of Bengal: 1752-57

KASIMBAZAAR was one of the senior trading posts, going back to Cromwellian days. For silks made a large item in the 'investment', the basis of the Company's homeward cargoes, and this was a famous silk-producing region. The Ganges, flowing towards Eastern Bengal, some three hundred miles north of Calcutta, threw off two side-streams which, after separate lives of about a hundred miles, looped together at Nuddea to make the Hugli. Between that point and Calcutta, though on the other or western bank, intervened the important French settlement at Chandernagore and the Dutch at Chinsura. Thus the inter-looped area above Nuddea made a broad island, where early in the century the Nabobs had transferred their seat of government; to Murshidabad, now a city of several hundred thousand people and as large as London, lying on both sides of the shallow Bagi-rathi river. The royal palace lay on the east bank, while a mile or so away, downstream, were the British, French, and Dutch factories.

In every sense this was an important centre, always entrusted to one of the Company's rising men. For here the British must have their ear close to the ground, whether to thwart the Nabob's newest scheme to squeeze more extortions from their trade, or to disarm the next threat from Mahratta raiders. And here accordingly we find them providing 'curiosities' for the Nabob's *zenana*, or bribing his officials with gifts of pistols, snuff-boxes, and musical clocks. In Queen Anne's time they had paid dearly for the privilege of fortifying their factory, which on paper was defended by a garrison of two officers, four drummers, and fifty-two 'centinels'. But, like Calcutta's, their defences were hopelessly inefficient. Their artillery were a few venerable nine-

17

pounder guns, and when the crash came it was found that the counter-wall was undermined by rats, the Fort overlooked from all sides, and the European half of its garrison mostly Dutch deserters.

In this circumscribed life of petty trade we must imagine Hastings learning his business, hardly a word of his own remaining which could help us. A few yards each way measured the area of the day's work, from the Chief's counting-house to the 'great hall' where they met for a weekly 'consultation', and to the Treasury, which was apt to be pilfered by their own lascars. In the godowns they stored the taffetas of local make which, Calcutta insisted, must have a proper variety of 'stripes and sprigs'. From a terrace verandah they looked out on the river, which on nights of Moslem festivals was alight with floating lamps, while a mosque next door was heard at prayer through the trees of their garden. When they could, they would ride to their garden-house at Mandipur, where they kept hounds for coursing.

As to his company, the Chief was William Watts, an active, courageous, but perhaps ingenuous person, too often deceived by Indian politicians, yet with a sharp eye for the main chance. His wife Frances was more remarkable. She had already had two husbands in Bengal before Watts, returned to India when he died, and took as her fourth the Presidency chaplain, William Johnson. When he, wearied either of matrimony or of India, left for home, she went on at Calcutta till her death in 1812, a show-piece of society as the 'Begum Johnson'. Incidentally, her daughter by her third, or Watts, husband formed an important link in British-Indian politics by marriage to Charles Jenkinson, head of the 'King's friends' and later first Earl of Liverpool. Second in command to Watts was Collet; another councillor, still under twenty-five, was a bad-tempered Stanlake Batson. But Hastings' real friends were two of the young writers, a jovial Randall Marriott and the Yorkshireman Francis Sykes who, as one of Clive's 'Nabobs', speculator, and member of parliament, long continued a power in Company politics. Other civilians and soldiers would come and go, one Captain John Buchanan for instance, who once commanded the escort bringing bullion to the royal mint, and of whom Hastings was to hear much again.

Their business which, though incidentally political, was primarily to trade, was subjected to the danger and abuses always involved in European trade within an Oriental State. According to the loose wording of the Imperial *firmans*, all goods covered by the Company's *dustuk*, or permit, could pass by road or river duty-free. But at the customs-posts or *chokeys*, every few miles, Indian officers and revenue farmers claimed fees, or a duty; as well they might, for the *dustuk* was monstrously abused. The average young Briton, often with a bare smattering of the language, was entirely in the hands of his *banyan* or general factotum, who exploited the *dustuk* to pass goods for themselves, their friends, and English adventurers. There were already signs of another evil, which in after years became a giant growth. The Company's privilege only applied to goods imported from, or to be exported to, Europe; not to the 'inland trade' in the common necessities consumed in Bengal, such as salt, betel-nut, tobacco, and grains. And as their servants' private trade must not compete with their masters' for Europe, individual profits could only legitimately come from exporting Indian goods to ports not in Europe but within the Company's charter, whether the Cape, Manila, Sumatra, or China. Yet without any doubt many Englishmen were already encroaching on the inland trade, so much so that all British India was a network of investment. Thus Robert Orme, the historian of Hindustan, now quartered at Madras, left money for speculation in pearls in his old station in Bengal, while Hastings had 6000 rupees of his in his hands to employ in the silk-weaving villages.

Late in 1754 we find Hastings' round hand transcribing the factory consultations; in October 1755 he was promoted to its council with the posts of secretary and storekeeper, and the next month was sent to open up a market east of the island area, just beyond the main Ganges. In those remote and easily flooded villages he stayed well into 1756, with Marriott as his companion, who remembered long afterwards what good laughs they had together. He carried 10,000 rupees for the 'investment', for money had to be advanced for stock to these poverty-stricken people. Altogether the factory employed about 1400 silk-winders. There were two alternative methods of agency, the one through salaried *gomastahs*, who were apt to rob both Company and weavers, the other by contracts with *dadni* (that is, 'advance') merchants. The factory had to forbid contracts going to their own *banyans*, and the first system was now tending to prevail, much to the annoyance of a rich class in Calcutta. So we have our earliest Hastings official reports, dealing with 'prime costs' or 'contingent charges', and forwarding specimens of raw silk. Prices ranged very high, which he put down to phenomenal rains which had killed the silkworms, and to crushing taxes.

When some years later he was defending himself against a charge of being too much on the side of the Indians, he recalled how, in this 'inferior station', he had met among native officials 'the greatest indulgence and even respect'. And how often his later letters dwell on the gentleness of Indian character! He had some claim to judge. For, though so young, he was already selected for work where knowledge of Indians and their languages was indispensable. This very February of 1756 he was detailed to the *durbar* at Murshidabad, representing the Company in one of the chronic trade disputes. From there he seems to have rejoined Marriott in the *aurungs*, the village centres where their silk was collected.

It may be that, in the City of London, Mr. Joseph Creswicke sometimes thought of his ward, though as a business man his mind more probably revolved on the outbreak of the Seven Years War; his aunt Elizabeth, we may be sure, thought and wrote often. But what each read in the London papers of June 1757 was startling news: that Calcutta had fallen, that 123 Britons had been killed in the Black Hole, and that Warren Hastings, Esq., had a year earlier been taken prisoner by the Nabob.

The old ruler of Bengal, Aliverdi Khan, sage and determined, died in April 1756, having chosen his heir with undiscriminating affection in his grandson, Siraj-ud-Daulah. The omens were unfavourable. Except that he had sworn on the Koran to his grandfather to stop drinking, his subjects agreed that the new Nabob was vicious and irresponsible, while against the British he nursed several grievances. There were rival candidates for his throne, and possibly our Resident Watts had momentarily backed the wrong horse. There were some difficult incidents, such as British protection extended to Indians on whose wealth the young Nabob wanted to lay his hands, and some feeble refortification of Calcutta, which he called aggressive.

Certainly the British and French conquests in the Carnatic

and Hyderabad, and the Bombay government's attack this spring on the pirates of Gheriah, alarmed and offended Indian rulers. But such alarums had passed over in Bengal before, with no more consequence than a few extra *douceurs* to the Nabob and his courtiers, so that it came as a thunderbolt when, in May, Siraj-ud-Daulah demanded the razing of the Calcutta fortifications, and the surrender of the British trading privileges. On June the 1st, with thousands of men and 500 elephants, he blockaded the Kasimbazaar factory; by the 3rd Watts and Collet were entrapped and prisoners, and the Fort surrendered. Calcutta gentlemen were critical, — Mrs. Watts, they said, was expecting a baby and made her husband nervous — but they refused to send reinforcements, and the Fort, ill-conditioned as we have seen, was quite defenceless. Batson and Sykes escaped to other European factories. Rather than endure days of insult, of threats to cut off ears and noses, unhappy Lieutenant Elliott, commanding the surrendered garrison, blew out his brains.

Meanwhile Hastings was caught out in the *aurungs*, plundered of all he had, and taken as a prisoner to Murshidabad. But he quickly found protectors. One Indian friend already was Cantoo, famous in after-years as *banyan* to Sykes, and then to himself. He owed most, however, to the kindness of Vernet, head of the Dutch factory. And he never forgot it. When Vernet had died in Batavia and his widow returned to India, the Governor-General paid her a pension of £300 a year, and this he continued till her death in 1793, when he was a ruined and impeached private citizen. So now he remained at Kasimbazaar, the Dutch giving bail for his appearance. There he presumably saw the arrival, in irons, of Holwell and the survivors of Calcutta. And there heard that story of disgrace, of the flight of the Governor and commanding officer, the deaths in the Black Hole, and how the remnant, without arms or money and with bare clothing, had gone down the river to refuge at Fulta, the wretched hamlet where the Dutch ships called.

He was at any rate left so free that he could visit the prisoners and do them some kindness, whereby perhaps it came about that Holwell and Watts were freed, and in August reached Fulta. He himself, however, stayed on under instructions, to watch and report. To this, he noted half a century later, 'I owe my first consequence in the service'.

At Fulta the refugees were just a mass of recrimination. Watts and Calcutta were blaming each other for the disaster, and Holwell blaming both, each inflamed by a contingent who had fled from Dacca, with several men of later note among them, — John Cartier, one of Hastings' shipmates in 1750, Luke Scrafton, and Richard Becher. Most of them lived on shipboard, for there was no accommodation ashore, they were scrounging for food from Dutchmen and Indian villagers, they doubted whether to depend wholly on the help they had begged from Madras, or to creep back into Calcutta by pleading with the Nabob. So they approached all sorts of intermediaries: the sinister Sikh merchant Omichand whom they had imprisoned during the siege, the wealthy Armenian Khwaja Petrus, the great Jain banking family of the Seths, and the Nabob's *diwan*, Rai Durlab. Hastings, it seems, did not approve of these rather grovelling approaches, and held back several letters he was told to deliver. On the contrary, he reported a growing resistance to Siraj-ud-Daulah, who was nervous of hostile moves from Delhi or the Mahrattas. He appears also to have procured some food supplies for Fulta through one Nobkissen, his teacher in Persian.

However, such hopes as ever existed of a conspiracy against the Nabob had evaporated by October, when his army marched to attack his cousin, the Rajah of Purnea, and killed him in battle. On the 10th of that month Hastings escaped to the Dutch at Chinsura, and thence made his way to Fulta.

That sad place was full of gloom and peril. True, they had word that Admiral Watson and Clive were on the way to their relief, but if the Nabob attacked before it arrived, they were doomed. The few hundred troops sent in advance from Madras were decimated by malaria and dysentery, and had barely fifty rounds of ammunition a man. If the food supply was getting better, drinking the water was courting death. Old Lady Russell and a good many women had died, some perchance not wishing much for life, whose husbands had died in the Black Hole. Among those war widows, in these two months before the Madras squadron dropped anchor at Fulta, Hastings found and married his first wife.

Mary Elliott had married Captain John Buchanan of Craigieven, just before they sailed for India in 1753. He had seen active service before this transfer from the royal army, was respected (Hastings wrote) for his 'fair character', and showed conspicuous courage in the fall of Calcutta. But he was trampled to death at Holwell's feet in the Black Hole, his money chest in the Fort was pillaged, and his wife with two infant daughters escaped to Fulta. She had little time with her new husband now, for before December was over he marched with the expedition to retake Calcutta. 'I carried a soldier's musket', says his note in old age, 'and served in the ranks in the character of a volunteer.'

With the fleet guarding their left, Clive's soldiers and the volunteers, Hastings and Sykes among them, had a tough march of sixteen hours to cover the ten miles to Baj Baj, wading breast-high through water, or stumbling in jungle and marshy paddy fields. While the fort there was attacked and fell to the enterprise of a drunken sailor, the volunteers kept west of the Calcutta road, driving the enemy into the arms of Clive, and beat off a sortie from the city. On January the 2nd Fort William was recaptured, and on the 11th the combined fleet and land forces stormed the fort at Hugli.

They found themselves in a ruined Calcutta, renamed by the Nabob as Alinagor. Everything vital in the Fort was gone, from Government House down to the wharves; a mosque had been made in the east curtain wall. Mat bungalows had to be run up, to house the young writers; even the furniture of the English houses had been used as firewood, and as their own St. Anne's church was burned down they took over one from the Portuguese, turning out its priests as sympathizers with the French. But it was hardly worth while rebuilding anything till they had a more assured future. What was to be their relation to the Nabob? If war with France had broken out again in Europe, did that necessarily mean war in Bengal? What would Bussy's strong force in Hyderabad do, would it march on Bengal or attack Madras? And if the last, how soon would Clive be recalled to the Coast?

In the next decisive six months there is little personal record of Hastings. First acting as assistant in the *zemindari* office, he was soon employed in that diplomatic work for which his capacity seems to have been now accepted, so that when the Nabob's army threatened Calcutta again in February, he was one of two emissaries who took to him the Company's demands. Once again he bore arms, in that rambling costly skirmish on a foggy morning round the Mahratta ditch, which brought Siraj-ud-Daulah to terms, and in which one volunteer, William Ellis, of whom we shall hear much, lost a leg. Early in March he went back to Kasimbazaar as export warehousekeeper and second to Watts, finding all the records destroyed and their old silk-winders scattered.

In effect he was acting Chief, since Watts was entirely occupied at the *durbar* in pressing the Nabob to carry out the treaty, with restitution for British losses and acceptance of their *dustuk*, and all the time in a day-to-day struggle against Law, the very plausible French resident. There, within Hastings' hearing a mile or so away, but with no direct share of his that we can trace, the great game was being played; of Clive against Admiral Watson, Clive's man Scrafton jeering at Watts as a simpleton, Madras tugging against Calcutta, and believers in moderation against those who would cut these knots by the sword. There they were battling with some of the least scrupulous of Indians, — Omichand, Rai Durlab, and the *foudjar* of Hugli, a certain Nuncumar who, after taking bribes in the English interest, denounced them to the Nabob.

Violent and irresolute, Siraj-ud-Daulah swung between all the extremes. Sometimes he threatened to impale Watts and turned him out of the *durbar*, sometimes gave him robes of honour. Sometimes he begged Clive's help against Ahmad Abdali, but at the same moment appealed to Bussy. On March the 20th, taking advantage of one of his favouring moods, the British seized the French fort of Chandernagore, refugees from which joined Law at Kasimbazaar. Repenting too late, the Nabob gave ear to Law's promises, so adding new grievances to those the British had over the treaty, and in April they embarked in the conspiracy to dethrone him.

The plot originated with those Indians whom he had outraged, or who hoped to profit by a change. The *diwan*, Rai Durlab, had been overruled by palace favourites. The Seths, who could meet bills for a million at sight, and whose wealth had made Aliverdi Khan, had been locked in their houses and menaced with circumcision. Mir Jaffir, Aliverdi Khan's brother-in-law, had lost the command of the army. Omichand hoped for a gigantic commission. Khwaja Petrus, the Armenian, was pro-British throughout. So the intrigue matured till the burning days of June, when Watts, hidden in a woman's litter, reached the palace by night and signed a treaty with Mir Jaffir. This pledged him to close alliance and joint action against the French, promised ample restitution for our damages in the past year, and would extend the Company's *zemindari* over the 800 square miles of the twenty-four *parganas* south of Calcutta. Keeping up the mask till the last safe minute, on the evening of June the 12th Watts left the city, on the pretext of hunting next day from the factory garden-house at Mandipur; he had with him Sykes and Collet, whose later recollection was that Hastings was with them. Thence they rode to the river, took boat, and met Clive's advancing army.

On the 23rd Clive won the battle of Plassey, his troops reaching Kasimbazaar four days later. Siraj-ud-Daulah was betrayed within the week by one victim of his cruelty, and murdered by Miran, the new Nabob's son; only some mullahs paid by his faithful Begum henceforth annually mourned his death. Mir Jaffir was seated on the throne at Murshidabad by Clive in person, to whom he made a gift of some £240,000, with corresponding lesser sums for Watts and Scrafton, Clive's secretary Walsh, Drake, and members of Council. Two hundred boats, with flags flying and music blaring, carried treasure to Calcutta, while Clive wrote to his old father, telling him to repair the family home in Shropshire and get him a seat in parliament, in the Duke of Newcastle's 'interest'. Both for him, and for the British in Bengal, a golden age seemed to have dawned.

CHAPTER IV

Trial and Error: July 1757–October 1760

AGED 24-27

BEFORE Clive sailed home in 1760 and his successor Henry Vansittart took office, Bengal went through three years of uncertainty, misrule, and bloodshed, at the end of which we come appreciably nearer towards deciphering the authentic Warren Hastings.

It was a hot unhealthy summer when he settled down again at Kasimbazaar, where half the garrison were dying men. In October Watts, being promoted to Council, left him in charge as provisional Chief; in August 1758 his work was doubled by appointment to follow Scrafton as resident at the *durbar*. In fact, only Sykes' help in the factory allowed him to get through it. One and the same man could not be at the same time pricing silks and watching the factions at Murshidabad. Among other things it meant he was often separated from his wife.

One of her daughters by Buchanan, perhaps both, had been sent home to their grandmother in Ireland, but Hastings' own son, George, was born in December 1757; a daughter followed the next autumn, but did not live a month. He certainly did his duty by his stepchildren, sending money home for their education and trying to recover their father's estate, and it is hardly fair to judge of his affections from some rather stilted letters to his old guardian, Mr. Creswicke, whom he told, 'as every man would upon the same occasion', how happy his marriage made him: repeating it later 'with much greater confidence . . . having, besides a great similitude in our dispositions (which I think must principally contribute to the happiness of the marriage state), experienced every good quality n my wife which I always most wished for in a woman'.

At first her health was the better for coming up-country, then we find him getting a carriage from Calcutta, and early in 1759 both mother and son were ill. Perhaps she never got over the birth and death of the little Elizabeth. She lived to see George baptized in June, but, while Hastings was away up the river, died on July the 11th and was buried at Kasimbazaar. The blow, he wrote to Clive, asking some relief from the *durbar*, had been 'too severe for me to recollect myself in an instant'. And though he thanked God, he told Holwell, he had 'strength of mind sufficient' to bear it, and 'submit myself to the will of Providence', 'it has fallen to the lot of very few men so early in life to be forced to so cruel a trial'. He kept George with him another year, but no discoverable letter seems to mention Mary again. Only a regular payment of a pension to Peggy, her Goanese maid, shows he had not forgotten.

He must have missed her the more, since many letters reveal him as a sensitive, proud, irritable being, easily cast down when disillusioned or deceived. As these were the only years when he was in the same continent with Clive, — except for eighteen months in England later — it could only be from this contact that Clive deduced the shortcomings against which he warned the younger man when, rather loftily, he congratulated him on appointment as Governor. 'Integrity and moderation with regard to riches' was high praise indeed from Clive, but he had diagnosed, he said, a diffidence in his own judgement, too much attention to the views of 'the natives', and a certain pessimism. Much of this was true. In this young Hastings we undoubtedly find inconsistencies of opinion, a thin skin, and an attitude to 'the natives' very different from that of the Clive circle.

What that circle thought of him, and he of them, comes out in his correspondence with Scrafton, now at Calcutta, and in after years Clive's best adviser in India House politics. He was a hot-tempered man, who once most gratuitously challenged Vansittart to a duel, and held a robust view that Indians must be ruled with a 'rod of iron'. When Hastings' infant daughter died his manner of consolation was to say he had no doubt 'you will soon replace it', and he plainly thought him too gullible and easy-going. 'Your reputation is at stake', he wrote, let him threaten another Plassey and throw some 'God damns' into his rejoinders. However, while he did some worldly errands for Hastings, such as buying him a scarlet coat, he gave him some sound worldly advice. He warned him to remember that Clive saw his letters; that Murshidabad was a valuable training whatever its vexations. His letters are more affectionate than we should gather from Hastings' later tepid description of him, as 'neither ill-natured nor hard to manage when he has no troublesome people about him'.

Through Scrafton he received offers of promotion to Calcutta, which he apparently declined; perhaps to move so soon would be an admission of failure, much though he hated some of his work. He loathed being the whipping-boy between English corruption and a corrupt and factious *durbar*. To Clive he complained that his remonstrances against the Englishmen's *gomastahs* were 'slighted', while to his intimates he wrote that our perpetual grumbles to the Nabob made us 'little and mean'. 'I am tired of complaining to people who are strangers to justice, remorse, or shame.'

He had one brush with Clive over the appointment of a surgeon at Kasimbazaar, as between Clive's friend Hancock, one of his Madras importations, and his own choice of the doctor who had attended his wife in her last illness. It was then that the Colonel declaimed upon the ingratitude of the Bengal folk, 'for never did you enjoy such indulgences . . . and perhaps never will again'. For Clive, who so much enjoyed making money himself, encouraged his subordinates to do so — within limits — setting an example of private trading which Hastings, like all around him, followed. So while he was buying silk for the investment, he got a request to allot 200 maunds to Clive for the Guzerat market, with an offer of a share in a cargo the Colonel was sending to China. In fact, Hastings was trading far and wide. He went partners with Sykes in one concern and with Hancock in another; he was selling imported coffee, on commission no doubt, on behalf of a young fellow-Westminster, Richard Barwell; and by the Nabob's leave he was dealing in salt. Not as yet, probably, with much profit; remittances home of £200 at a time for his sister, his aunt Elizabeth, and his step-children do not sound like riches.

The English appetite was growing. He wrote in 1760 we had spent our blood and treasure 'to little purpose, if we are to be bound by precedents drawn from the abject state in which we remained before the battle of Plassey', claiming that Company servants had always traded in betel. But he allowed that salt was different, requiring the Nabob's licence, and sharply reproved Sumner, Chief at Dacca, for allowing others to set up monopolies and to question the Indian officials' 'undoubted right' to inspect *dustuks*. There are other signs that he doubted the whole future of the Clive régime. Fundamentally it was a failure, only held up from collapse by Clive's sword, and the memory of the heavy naval guns which since 1757 reverberated in Indian minds.

The sword was needed at this moment, with all Clive's self-assurance and his gay response to danger. North and South, Indian and European were rocking amid war, murder, and catastrophe. Afghans on superb Khorasan horses traversed the country, offering five rupees for every Hindu head. In 1759 the barbarous Ghazi-ud-din, grandson of the first great Nizam, murdered the Emperor he had set up at Delhi, and then disappeared, to emerge only forty years after as a pilgrim to Mecca. While another phantom Emperor reigned, the dead man's son, Shah Allum, fled with a thousand horse to Oudh, where he was hatching plans to overrun Bengal. The Mahratta Ragoba had taken Lahore; the great contest of Moslem and Hindu for the control of Delhi was nearing its peak, and in it Ahmad Abdali, Oudh, the Rohillas, and all the Mahrattas would be involved, the powers whose victory or downfall would shake Bengal. Meanwhile the Seven Years War of Europe complicated this Indian strife. Early in 1758 Lally, with his Irish regiment and French warships, reached Pondicherry and swiftly captured Fort St. David. Recalling Bussy from Hyderabad, over the next winter he laid siege to Madras, planning to turn on Calcutta after it had fallen. He failed, however, at Madras, and with a master's eye Clive seized on Bussy's absence from Hyderabad, despatching a resolute Colonel Forde to take the Northern Circars.

Early in 1760 Eyre Coote sallied from Madras to crush Lally in the battle of Wandewash, and took Bussy prisoner; the end of French India was in sight. And their puppet-Nizam was speedily murdered by a much abler and long-lived brother, Nizam Ali. Clive and Forde had also broken to pieces a wild mismanaged effort of the Dutch, to assert their commercial equality by force of arms.

If Clive thus held danger at bay, revolution at Delhi and in Bengal had ended the Mogul system, leaving nothing to replace it. For one more generation salutes would be fired in every British barracks on the Emperor's birthday, for another half-century the coins they struck would bear his image. Yet when Shah Allum appealed to Clive for help and offered the Company the *diwanni*, or revenue collection, of Bengal, appeal and offer were alike rejected. Sometimes Clive alarmed Sulivan, the Company chairman, by vowing that with 2000 Europeans he could conquer India; once he wrote to Pitt that the nation, not the Company, should declare its sovereignty, holding forth visions of Indian wealth with which to reduce the national debt. But the Company would have none of this. 'You seem so thoroughly possessed with military ideas', they wrote, 'as to forget your employers are merchants'; denouncing a whole 'chain of irregularities' in private trading, 'plunder' taken from the Nabob and never accounted for, a drop in the investment, and costly fortifications. It was this letter which Clive and his Council answered so fiercely in 1759, that their diction was unworthy of any relation, 'either as masters to servants, or gentlemen to gentlemen'. But long before that he had wearied of his employers, and of Bengal.

He often spoke of a quick return to England, once he had put our defences in order and received the Nabob's promised money. He despised most of his Council; Drake was 'lost to all shame', Holwell had 'no heart', and he pressed on the Directors the urgent need of young men of character. They ought to promote Vansittart and Du Pré from Madras to the Bengal Council. Indeed, Bengal was already full of his Madrasis, the soldiers Forde and Caillaud, Dr. Hancock, Brohier as engineer to design a new and stronger Fort William, and the missionary Kiernander. For he felt public problems in terms of persons, and measured persons in terms of force. So Mir Jaffir, 'old fool' that he was, must be shown who was master, and not allowed to obstruct the flow of money which kept up the British sepoy army. His orders to Hastings rang like sharp blows on a bell. Omichand has left Calcutta without leave; arrest him. 'Be a little severe' in revenue collections; 'ten sepoys or chokeys now and then will greatly expedite the payment of the money'. 'Avoid extremities', but let our power be realized, even by bluff; 'instil into the Nabob high notions of the great force which is coming out, huff away, and assure him Pondicherry will soon be in our possession'.

And as he had proved to his own satisfaction that a swift blow and refusing to admit the possibility of defeat always succeeded, he could not pardon a failure such as the surrender of Fort St. David, asking 'had they no bayonets?' He was confident all would go well with his reorganized brigades, his new Fort William, and more European ranks, especially if Vansittart succeeded him in the chair, with Forde and Caillaud commanding the army. And his final recommendation was that each Presidency governor should receive a general's commission.

He did not believe it possible, nor did he try, to conciliate Indian goodwill. Moslems and Hindus, he held, were equally 'indolent, luxurious, ignorant, and cowardly'. The Moslem ruling caste did not know what gratitude meant; we could depend on nothing but 'such a force as leaves nothing to the power of treachery or ingratitude'. He preached this doctrine to the young Hastings. 'You may lay it down as a maxim, that the Mussulmans will never be influenced by kind treatment.' Nor must he ever sink to play their game; 'leave all trickery to the Hindus and Mussulmen, to whom it is natural'. But in the resident at Murshidabad we find, increasingly, a very different mood; less consistent but less satisfied, less racial, less prepared to put up with bad men, and looking for a system that would endure. There was something about the Colonel's star that swept you off your feet, something about his large and affectionate side, his invincible legend, and his power with men. But this comet had its dark and sinister tail; moreover it was plunging homeward, and what then?

The scene in Bengal, as our revolution had left it, was a murky hateful business. Mir Jaffir, once a good soldier against the Mahrattas, had not been installed four months before Scrafton was writing 'I could not have believed him such a bad man as I find him'. The beastly revenges of the seraglio still continued. A young son of Siraj-ud-Daulah was the first to disappear, then some leading soldiers, while a bevy of the royal family were kept prisoners at Dacca. Miran, Mir Jaffir's heir, was violent and butcherly, a natural focus for the Moslem soldiers whose supremacy had been destroyed by the British, and whose pay was ever in arrears. Conceivably a military *pronunciamento* might raise him up against his father. The third important member of the reigning family was the Nabob's son-in-law Mir Kasim, no soldier but an able, scholarly, and ambitious man, whose immediate objective was to become Naib of Bihar. As for those whom Mir Jaffir and Miran suspected, they were the very men who had first served Aliverdi Khan and then overthrown Siraj-ud-Daulah; that is, the Hindu magnates, notably Rai Durlab the *diwan*, Ramnarrain the present Naib of Bihar, and the Seths, whose wealth might be extorted to keep the army in contentment. There were other Hindus, however, ready to bargain for power, especially Rajballabh, whom Miran had taken as his *diwan*, and the *foudjar* of Hugli, Nuncumar.

On this ugly stage Clive acted forcibly, in ways peculiar to himself. He was a magnate of the Empire, by a patent given him by Delhi after Plassey, and asked for a grant of the *jagir*, or landed revenue, attached by custom to such a command. In 1759 he received it, but in a most anomalous and undesirable shape, that the Company's rent for their *zemindari*, of about £30,000 a year, should be paid to him for his life, instead of to the Nabob. This would scarcely assist to extricate Mir Jaffir from the quagmire in which the immense sums taken by the British had plunged him. The Colonel was clear that Mir Jaffir was 'weak beyond conception', destined to fall to a revolt but for British arms. He must be humoured, of course, to keep him away from the French and the Dutch, the Vizier and the Empire, and honourably entertained. So that we meet him as the British guest at Calcutta, poor Scrafton complaining to Hastings he was never in bed till four in the morning, organizing a ball and a theatre party for the Nabob, and gifts of waxwork figures of Venus; 'he has led me a hell of a life here by the constant attention I have been obliged to pay to him and his wenches'.

But this velvet glove covered an iron hand. Clive took pains to see that our army's pay was assured by an assignment of the revenues of Burdwan and Hugli. He had, further, determined that this puppet-Nabob could only be propped up with the help of Hindu bankers and officials. After once thinking of arresting Ramnarrain in Bihar, he decided to support him, even describing him as 'universally beloved', and though he could not prevent Rai Durlab being superseded by a Moslem, British troops saved him from Miran's executioners and he was given refuge at Calcutta.

In Hastings, ground every day between these factions at Murshidabad, we seem already to find two sentiments that marked all his Indian life : a sympathy for individuals who were the victims of a bad system, and respect for constituted authority. Three years after Clive had gone, he testified that his favour to Rai Durlab and Nuncumar had 'justly' offended Mir Jaffir. He had, indeed, taken the same line with Clive himself. Even before he was resident, he suggested some presents to the Nabob, 'to take off the bitterness of their treaty with us', and was severely snubbed for his pains. When the Nabob complained of English 'insults', when he thought of bribing the Mogul prince Shah Allum and encouraged the Dutch foray on the Ganges, Hastings reported every move. Yet he begged Clive to encourage any signs of repentance ; 'I still cannot see any just cause to ascribe it so much to actual treachery . . . as to his timorous and irresolute disposition'. If Mir Jaffir were left to himself, 'I am and always have been of opinion' that he would continue staunch.

So he stood at the very centre of this corrupt, hand to mouth, dual government. He carried through one important piece of business, the securing of the British *zemindari* title in perpetuity, irrespective of the reigning Nabob. He it was who had to effect the rescue of Rai Durlab's family from the vengeance of Miran, to question Scrafton's 'bits and scraps' of accounts, to answer Clive's everlasting calls for money. And here Clive's arrangements brought him face to face with the one person whom this amiable, proud young Englishman hated. Thirty years later he wrote, 'I was never the personal enemy of any man but Nuncumar, whom from my soul I detested even when I was compelled to countenance him'. For to Nuncumar Clive made over the revenue collections in Burdwan, Hugli, and Nuddea.

When the Colonel dwelt on Nuncumar's 'known attachment to the English', his subordinates violently disagreed. Scrafton blamed Watts for first bringing forward 'the necromancer', whose double-dealing was held responsible for the downfall of Rai Durlab. Hastings' letters breathe a sort of frozen anger, next door to insolence. Was he to take this appointment, he asked, as a censure on his own incapacity? He would suppress his 'mortification', and endure Nuncumar's 'daily indignities'. Indeed, considering the Brahmin's proved contacts with the French, a suspicion he had been bribed by the Dutch, and that he was already accused of forgery, there remains something mysterious in Clive's indulgence.

In February 1760, when Clive embarked for England, the crisis began, as Hastings had predicted. True, the defeat of the Dutch, our capture of the Northern Circars, and Coote's victory sent the Colonel home in a blaze of glory. But he left a desperate situation behind him. Shah Allum, now proclaimed as Emperor and recognized as such by Ahmad Abdali, advanced to attack Bihar, in alliance with the Vizier of Oudh. His prestige unsettled some Bengal landowners, officers whom Mir Jaffir had insulted joined him, Mahratta raiders rode through the northern frontiers and prevented collection of revenue. Every Indian politician was re-insuring with these powerful invaders; Rai Durlab was suspect of inviting the Mahrattas, Nuncumar was certainly writing to Shah Allum. While the Nabob and Miran poured out money, Hastings wrote, 'on idle schemes of luxury', Caillaud bore witness that their sepoys were starving and would not fight. Bihar was half lost, and Ramnarrain might go over, even in self-defence. Obstructed by Miran's sulks and moods, Caillaud dashed against the enemy from point to point, but how was his army to be maintained? On Clive's rosy advice, the Directors had stopped export of specie to India, but now the treasury was empty and the investment dried up. Mir Jaffir had taken back the assigned areas and would grant no others, a year of war and building the new Fort had drained the revenues, the Seths refused a loan. The siege of Pondicherry was at a decisive stage, Madras was beseeching Bengal for money. Caillaud had to post guards to save Mir Jaffir from his own subjects, and a single sentence of his gloomy despatches from the north is enough for our purpose, 'the present system is rotten to the core'.

The Councillors whom Clive left in power were equally rotten in their way, yet they might be excused if they looked for new remedies. Holwell, acting President pending Vansittart's arrival, was abrupt and prejudiced; by May he was putting forward a violent solution. Had not Mir Jaffir betrayed us to the Dutch? Was he not bargaining now with Shah Allum behind our back? His oppressive government and Miran's barbarity were a reproach to the English name, and a perpetuation of this no-system would ruin the Company. Let us come to terms with Shah Allum, the legal sovereign, and acquire Bengal for ourselves.

A year earlier Shah Allum had offered Clive the *diwanni*, which he refused, since we had not enough military force to carry it through. Yet his letter to Pitt showed that this vision, perhaps even the sovereignty of the province, had sunk into his mind. Even in defending Mir Jaffir, one of Hastings' last letters to Clive argued that only 'an interest properly established' at Delhi could make a solid basis for the British title, and by the summer of 1760 he was clear on the alternatives. Though still a subordinate with no voice in policy, as resident at the *durbar* he spoke with knowledge, while in this self-seeking quarrelsome community he was friends with men of all sorts. With Caillaud he had one sharp breeze over some gossip, barking out 'I have been little accustomed to severe censures', but soon cemented what was to become a very long loyal friendship. As things stood, the views of the army commander were all-important and, negatively at least, we find Hastings in full agreement with his objections to Holwell's proposal, which was to depose Mir Jaffir without delay.

For the rest, his letter of June to Caillaud shows him in two minds. 'Let the Nabob be ever so bad, we are bound, if not in justice, in honour and policy to support him through these troubles. . . . Neither his tyranny nor rapaciousness are to be vindicated, tho' I cannot think him in his nature cruel, but where are we to meet with a better man?' There was no proof that Shah Allum had any plan, except to squeeze wealth out of Bengal. 'A change of the system which we have with so much blood, costs, and pains established, without the most evident necessity and provocation, would destroy one of the greatest advantages to the influence which the English have ever possessed in India, their reputation for an inviolable attachment to their alliances. . . . But should the Nabob's behaviour ever drive us to such fatal extremities, as we have (most assuredly have) the means in our hands, why should we not take possession of the government for ourselves? Every individual of the province almost would rejoice in the exchange, and our own country would reap a considerable benefit from it, — only perhaps the Company would not gain so much from such an acquisition, which would be too great for the narrow basis on which their constitution was originally founded.'

A fortnight later the provocation he spoke of was given, of a sort to impress a mind like his. He learned that the Nabob had ordered two Begums of the late royal family to be drowned; as they were, with weights fastened to their legs and beaten off as they clutched at the gunwale. A whole catalogue of other murders was rumoured; if true, he broke out to Holwell, nothing could excuse our supporting such a tyrant, and to Caillaud, 'God forgive me for attempting to vindicate him from the charges of cruelty and barbarity'. Yet another fortnight, and decision was forced on them, when on July the 3rd Miran was killed by a stroke of lightning. While minute guns and flags at half-mast signalized official grief at Calcutta, Hastings wrote that the sepoys at Murshidabad had blockaded the palace, besieged the *zenana*, and were only momentarily appeased by the Nabob's son-in-law, Mir Kasim, disgorging from his treasures. Mir Jaffir was stricken into lethargy; there seemed no hope for him, Hastings reported, in the next inevitable crisis. On the 26th, as a later memoir in his hand tells us, he set out for Calcutta on 'affairs of the greatest moment'; in fact, to meet Vansittart, the new Governor.

If the army was to be paid, elementary law and order preserved, invasion repelled, and Madras assisted, something must be done at once. Holwell's dreams of the *diwanni*, or of sovereignty, would not fill the treasury, and might involve us in the warfare of Moslems and Mahrattas. Amyatt, Chief at Patna and senior member of Council, supported Caillaud in arguing against a revolution of system, and Vansittart agreed. They hoped to stop what Holwell once called 'this royal game', of hunting Shah Allum to and fro, and to strike a bargain with him. But if they were agreed to keep a Nabob of Bengal, then someone must replace Miran as army commander, and someone (else?) as heir; someone, too, who would yield territory to the Company as a solid fund for military pay. Amyatt and Caillaud, surrounded by rebellious sepoys at Patna, put forward an earlier recommendation of Clive, that Mir Kasim should replace Ramnarrain there, the man so distrusted by the Nabob, while Miran's young son should be adopted as heir, with Rajballabh as his *diwan*. However, before Vansittart appeared, Holwell adopted the rival view; the Nabob should put his trust in Mir Kasim, and recall old Rai Durlab from his disgrace at Calcutta. Hastings agreed with him. The essential, he wrote, was to decide at once on one or the other, and not waste the next cold weather, but he vehemently denounced Rajballabh, saying that to his 'aspiring and rebellious temper we owed the loss of Calcutta'. On the other hand, he held a high opinion of Mir Kasim, 'not founded on prejudices but facts'. He wanted to be made *diwan*, and would be made desperate by exclusion.

By September Mir Kasim's wealth and diplomatic address had won over the principal figures who had made the previous revolution, — the Seths, Rai Durlab, and Khwaja Petrus — and he came to Calcutta for conversations, where on the 27th a treaty was signed. Mir Jaffir should continue as titular Nabob, but should admit Mir Kasim as his deputy and heir. The British troops would defend Mir Kasim, who in return would discharge all balances owing, grant the Company a share in the rich cement trade of Sylhet, and make over in perpetuity the provinces of Burdwan, Midnapore, and Chittagong. In their private conferences the Select Committee favoured alliance with Shah Allum, but the treaty merely declared he must be removed from Bengal and a settlement with him arranged in concert with Mir Kasim. The meetings ended by Mir Kasim offering twenty lacs to the Committee for themselves. For the time being they were declined, Vansittart returning his bond with the note that, if he renewed his offer when the country was at peace and all payments satisfied, they might accept this token of friendship.

Holwell, it was believed, had made his own bargain, he was sailing home soon, and declined responsibility. The mission of persuading the old Nabob was therefore committed to Vansittart and Caillaud. Mir Kasim warned them that force might be wanted, so they took with them 200 Europeans, a battery of artillery, and a sepoy battalion. Vansittart foresaw Mir Jaffir might refuse the terms, but both his immediate attitude and his later apologia proved that he hoped to carry out only their professed programme, of getting rid of evil ministers and leaving Mir Jaffir on the throne, with Mir Kasim holding the reality of power.

On October the 4th Hastings met the Governor's party at Chinsura, including the soldiers Caillaud and Ironside, and Henry Lushington, a survivor of the Black Hole, as interpreter. Travelling by easy stages to give the troops time to arrive, they reached Kasimbazaar on the 14th, where Hastings immediately went off to persuade the Nabob to see Vansittart next morning. He then saw Mir Kasim, who said the Nabob was taxing him with his Calcutta conversations, discussed other details of what he calls 'the great plan', and so back to Kasimbazaar at ten at night.

The two following days went in useless evasive conversations. Amyatt wrote from Patna he expected an army mutiny, while all-day conferences on the 18th at the British headquarters showed the ineradicable suspicion between the Nabob and his son-in-law. On the evening of the 19th, hearing he was in Darbar with his worst counsellors, Vansittart decided to act. Between three and four the next morning Caillaud and his men entered the palace courtyard, with orders to arrest the ministers and install Mir Kasim as deputy and successor. Being the night of the Holi feast, it was hoped the Hindu leaders would be too fatigued to resist.

Two or three hours passed, amid furious reproaches and refusals from Mir Jaffir, who incidentally had become an opium addict, while Hastings and Lushington tackled the ministers; Vansittart said he must have his answer by sunset. Then resistance collapsed. The Nabob swore his life would be unsafe from Mir Kasim, even for a day; the standards were raised and the drums beaten in his successor's name, and with some sixty women and a load of jewels the old man boarded his boats, which would take him to the safety of Calcutta.

This bloodless revolution over, Vansittart received congratulations from the Select Committee, presided over in his absence by a newcomer, William Ellis (he who had lost a leg in the battles of 1757), and in November returned to the Presidency. Great events were proceeding in India. Coote and Monson were finishing off the siege of Pondicherry, where Lally's men were starving on rations of dogs and cats. Ahmad Abdali was on the Jumna once more, preparing to join Oudh and Rohillas against the Hindus, and had cut one army of Scindia's to pieces. A vast Mahratta host, with hordes of elephants, silken tents, and splendid horses, took the fort at Delhi and were now entrenched at Panipat. Shah Allum, for whose throne they were contending, still threatened the British army in Bihar, now commanded by Carnac, for Caillaud was ordered down to Madras.

So whether the revolution would save Bengal and its British masters was still to be seen; so, also, was what view would be taken of these doings by the Directors, and what by Colonel Clive.

CHAPTER V

Henry Vansittart and Mir Kasim: 1760-64

AGED 28-32

HENCEFORWARD Hastings' destiny was caught up in the play of two interlocking wheels, the British government in Bengal and the Indian 'interest' in British politics. Formally unrelated, but yet clashing, jarring, emitting dirt and friction as they revolved, at the end of four years they seemed to have crushed him, returning him to England as a man branded with failure, partisan of a fallen cause.

We know little of his personal life at this stage, though in February 1761 he was brought down to act as the President's assistant, and in August took his seat in Council. He was, however, much on the move, for Mir Kasim had taken a liking to him and was always asking he should return to his court; he was also very much alone, for his small son had gone home in care of Francis Sykes. We have letters telling of long journeys in the hot weather, with replies that show him the same likeable human being. So Samuel Staveley thanks his 'dear chum' for his 'long, friendly, agreeable letter', assuring him 'my soul thirsteth to see thee, my dear Hastings, skin and bone though thou art'. In general he kept his health by an hour's ride at dawn and then a cold shower, in some idle hours strummed the guitar, yet assiduously kept up his Persian. Of his old circle Watts and Sykes were in England, and Marriott at Benares, but he was making new friends, and lasting ones.

Of these the nearest now seems to have been the surgeon Tysoe Saul Hancock, whom Clive had brought from the coast, and his wife Philadelphia, who was born an Austen and aunt of the immortal Jane. Hastings was godfather to their one child, Elizabeth. For some time his own son George lived in the care of Philadelphia's brother George, father of Jane and vicar of

Steventon in Hampshire, where he died in 1764, of what sounds like diphtheria, just before his father reached England. Besides, Hastings and Hancock were partners in a whole series of trading ventures, in salt and timber and carpets, Bihar opium, and rice for the Madras market. But infinitely more vital and lasting was the affectionate friendship he achieved with the new Governor and his family.

The Vansittarts made a close-knit and highly individual clan. Dutch by remote origin, they had reached England by way of Danzig a century before, amassed large fortunes in Baltic trading, and struck their roots deep in Berkshire, in part through the Governor's mother, a Stonhouse heiress of Radley. They were likeable, intelligent, and rather feckless people. The Governor's elder brother, Robert, was distinguished by winning the affection of Dr. Johnson, Goethe, and Hogarth, and yet, though regius professor of law at Oxford, was a member, as Henry was too, of the Hell-Fire club at Medenham Abbey, where John Wilkes and Francis Dashwood practised their blasphemy and obscenities. Henry had made a name for himself at Madras as a good colleague and commercial expert, and held a strong position in the Company. His wife was Emilia Morse, daughter of an ex-governor there, a brave warm-hearted woman who had lately been a French captive. His sister Anne was just going to marry Robert Palk, Governor of Madras from 1761 to 1767; another sister was a favourite of the Princess of Wales, the King's mother; his younger brother, George, who for years was to be Hastings' dearest friend, was just beginning service in Bengal. Though Clive's nominee, the Governor was much more akin to Hastings, being like him an ardent Persian scholar and, like him, ready to trust Indians. 'Amiable and gentle', 'beloved by everyone acquainted with him', such was Hastings' later word to his widow, and he always remained a man of 'Van's' school, with the causes that ruined Van ever in the forefront of his mind.

According to the then agreeable custom, these official colleagues helped on each other's private fortunes. Hastings suggested George Vansittart might succeed him at the Nabob's court, where he might lay a foundation for riches. The Governor in turn assisted Hastings to get the government contract for supplying bullocks for transport. In fact, he was becoming a man of substance, with a town house in Calcutta and another at Belvedere, Alipur, where his garden was the pride of his heart. He was certainly prospering enough to be able to lend money to others, and to invest £950 for his sister in Bank annuities. As with all his contemporaries, his money affairs were largely in the hands of Indians. Cantoo, whom Burke made so famous and who had befriended him in the troubled days at Kasimbazaar, was already his *banyan*, while he had borrowed much from the rich Armenian, Khwaja Petrus, who had played a leading hand in the Bengal revolutions.

If there was danger here, what distinguished him from the other young Englishmen round him, all suddenly become sovereigns, was a hatred of the callous force and injustice with which they drove their race for profits. And the private papers of 'Hancock and Hastings' show it was genuine. Their instructions forbade the use of sepoys, the beatings, and the usual oppressions, 'many so scandalous', he wrote of one agent whom they dismissed, 'that I can no longer put up with them without injury to my own character'. This gives us confidence in the argument he used repeatedly in a hostile Council; that substantially the rights were on the Indian side. He had already reached the view of a memorable paper he wrote in 1765, as regards 'a fierceness in the European manners, especially among the lower sort, which is incompatible with the gentle temper of the Bengalee'. It was a lifelong conviction, emphatically repeated forty years on to the Marquess of Hastings, one of his successors as Governor-General.

The scene of turmoil on to which he stepped, high in office for the first time, promised well for the British. On January the 7th, 1761, the Mahrattas broke out of their blockaded camp at Panipat, near Delhi, dense with starving human beings and poisoned by the stench of dead animals, and under their high yellow banner were annihilated by the Moslem army of Ahmad Abdali. Having there lost his heir and 100,000 men in battle or massacre, the Peishwa Ballaji Rao died broken-hearted, and for a time at least Bengal could afford to ignore the Mahrattas. On the 16th of the same month, the French in Pondicherry surrendered to Coote. In January also Carnac defeated the wandering Emperor Shah Allum, bringing him back to Patna. Given friendly relations with the new Nabob of Bengal, the British future looked to be excellent.

Mir Kasim, it must be remembered, had been particularly the candidate of Hastings on whom, when disaster came, he laid the responsibility for inducing him to accept the title and entrust himself to our good faith. And in Hastings an opinion once formed was rarely shaken. 'I never met', he wrote after their long interviews in 1762, 'with a man of more candour or moderation than the Nabob . . . was there but half the disposition shown on our side which he bears to peace, no subject of difference could ever arise between us.' A character of Mir Kasim he drew up, in or before 1765, argued that his business habits and notorious timidity in war made him an ideal choice. But any spirit 'superior to that of a worm' would turn at the injuries heaped on him by 'a violent party' among the English from the very beginning, breaking out in that 'hoarded resentment' which caused such tragedy. Twenty years later it was still enough to mention the poverty of the Nabob's sons, starving exiles in central India, to enlist the Governor-General's sympathy.

At first everything seemed to justify this good opinion. The British quietly took over the ceded districts, money was forthcoming for our sepoys, and enough to spare some for Madras. The Nabob's economies were so drastic that he sold off the royal menagerie, while he had to be compelled to pay Mir Jaffir an allowance sufficient for his large harem. He put down the rebel *zemindars*, centralized the revenue collections, and restored some discipline to his redundant army. Vansittart on his side adopted a settled policy that, if assured of solvent finances and security, the Company should drop Clive's perpetual interference, and leave full control of internal administration to the Nabob. He was punctilious in insisting that Chiefs of our factories must pay the first call on the Nabob's representative, and not vice versa. Such an attitude, however, would grate not only on the arrogance of the Clive school but on more honourable feelings. For Mir Kasim, this Louis XI of Bengal, interested in scholars and swayed by astrologers, was as cruel as Mir Jaffir, had proposed to 'remove' his predecessor in the time-honoured way, and by execution or murder disposed of some suspect officials. Was the British uniform to be tarnished by championing this despot? Yet in fact the experiment was doomed by more fundamental causes, implicit in the Mogul collapse, the structure of our Bengal government, the temptations to which its servants succumbed, and their relation to factions in London.

The President at Calcutta was merely chairman of sixteen Councillors, having neither a veto nor final powers. Ordinarily some leading members were absent, since the plums of the service were the chiefdoms of factories, at Patna, Dacca, or Kasimbazaar, which were combined with a seat in Council. And though a Select Committee had been set up after Plassey, its relation to the Council as a whole was undefined. If ill-will were present, all this could be exploited easily enough. The mere fact that Vansittart had been imported from Madras was enough to condemn him, especially with the senior Councillor Peter Amyatt, who stood high in Clive's favour. There were also some adequate grounds for disapproving the revolution of 1760, and even more pretexts. Unhappily it is impossible to acquit the opposition of much baser motives.

Nothing was a secret where Indians acted as intermediaries, and the Council majority were convinced that the Select Committee had already pocketed the £200,000 offered them by Mir Kasim. Holwell, who had gone home, had pretty certainly cleared some of his bargain. Sumner took £28,000 during 1761 ; McGuire was promised the same. 'Van', however, it seems, had as yet taken nothing, and made the revolution without stipulation. In any case, minutes of disapprobation were lodged by Councillors outside the Committee like Verelst, by the disappointed Amyatt, and by William Ellis, who had wanted the rich post at Patna which Van had given to McGuire.

This feud was much inflamed by two hot-tempered soldiers, John Carnac, Clive's special favourite, now commanding in the field, and Eyre Coote, Clive's *bête noire*, who in 1761 came from his triumph at Pondicherry to command in Bengal. Carnac was vociferating that 'English forces, while I have the honour of commanding them, shall never be employed as instruments of violence and oppression'. He was not on speaking terms with the Nabob, and on no terms at all with his civil superior, McGuire. As for Coote, Clive deplored that 'such a mercenary man' should be appointed, — a view taken, we must admit, some twenty years after, by the very different mind of Philip Francis. However that may be, it was an extreme provocation to the Nabob when Coote chose as his *diwan* a partisan of Mir Jaffir, the notorious

Nuncumar, whose letters to rebels had been intercepted. Angry scenes at Patna ended by Coote posting his own sentries on the city gates, and entering the royal tent armed with pistols. After complaints from Mir Kasim that these insults destroyed his authority, in July — though only by a majority vote — both Coote and Carnac were recalled to Calcutta.

For other reasons, galling or alarming to the Nabob, the opposition Councillors were deeply committed. Ramnarrain, Naib of Bihar, so long his rival, still firmly gripped that province, hotly supported by British soldiers who swore Clive had pledged him our permanent protection. After months of charges and counter-charges, Vansittart withdrew this shield. The Nabob's payments to us, he argued, depended on his clearing off Ramnarrain's arrears, and he must be allowed to choose his own servants. In August the defaulting minister was thrown into prison and stripped of his wealth; victim, cried the opposition, of our broken pledges, — the tool, replied Van and Hastings, of a clique who were bent on overthrowing the Nabob. Counter-revolution was in the air, the very boys in the service, says Holwell, being incited to toast 'Mir Jaffir for ever'.

There was a larger matter still. Shah Allum, the titular Emperor, after his defeat by Carnac promised mighty things. In return for his restoration to Delhi the British might take over the *diwanni*, or revenue powers, of Bengal; an offer which Council declined to proceed with for the moment, and were commended by the Directors for so doing. But Holwell's old dream, that we might be sovereigns of Bengal, was not dead. The soldiers declared the march to Delhi was easy; news from the North, filtered through a Lucknow Jesuit to a Capuchin at Patna, coloured the airy violent views of Ellis. Hastings was indignant at our weakening the Nabob's prestige with his subjects, and at the notion of paying the Emperor tribute for Bengal.

In August, while they sweltered in these controversies, orders from the Directors upset the balance of power. They summarily removed from Council the three surviving (McGuire, Sumner, and Holwell's son-in-law, Playdell) who had signed Clive's impertinent despatch of two years ago. And as a fourth member resigned, Vansittart was left in a permanent minority. Of the new appointments involved, he could count entirely on Hastings, little on Cartier, and not at all on Hay and Johnstone, who were members of a bad trading combine with an able and rascally William Bolts. Such men would join hands with Coote and Carnac, with Ellis now promoted to Patna, Batson once with Hastings at Kasimbazaar and now Chief there, and the more upright but limited Verelst. Their tone was shown by a letter to the Directors of March 1762, which attacked the revolution of 1760 as a breach of treaty, accused Van and his friends of being bribed to carry it through, deplored the rejection of the *diwanni*, called out for a march on Delhi, and predicted that Mir Kasim would revolt.

The crisis began with Ellis' arrival at Patna, under instructions (carried only by Van's casting vote) binding him to non-interference in the 'country' government. He threw them to the winds. He defended subordinates who imprisoned Indian officials, sent one of the Nabob's high Armenian officers in irons to Calcutta, and on the ground he was harbouring our deserters invested the royal fortress of Monghyr. A flood of complaint reached Council that Indians were ignoring the Company's *dustuk*, with counter-complaints that Englishmen and their *gomastahs* were making a corner in salt and betel, oil and rice, forcing peasants to buy at monopoly prices, and beating and imprisoning at their sweet will. Declining all further dealings with Ellis, Mir Kasim withdrew far up-stream to Rajmehal; conspiracies threatened his life, stimulated by rumours of his coming deposition. In these circumstances Hastings, as one 'in whom the Nabob has great confidence', was deputed on a mission of reconciliation. But the new majority added a rider to his instructions, at once a threat to Vansittart and an insult to the Nabob, demanding payment of the twenty lacs he had originally offered the Committee, which Amyatt and Carnac openly hinted had already been received.

Evidence before and after this time proves to the hilt the reality of Mir Kasim's grievances. Mir Jaffir had already protested to Clive; in 1766 Mahomed Reza Khan, Naib under his second government, reported the peasants were in flight and the revenues ruined. In 1772 Verelst, Governor after Clive and one of Van's former opponents, wrote that here was the immediate cause of war, that our *gomastahs* 'trampled on the authority of government, binding and punishing the Nabob's officers whenever they presumed to interfere'.

In all this long journey, in burning heat which reduced him to 'extreme weakness', Hastings' letters to Vansittart blazed with indignation. His part was taken, without doubt, and indeed without scruple. Batson's charges against the Nabob, he said, were indecent, 'every man that wears a hat, as soon as he gets free from Calcutta, becomes a sovereign prince'. He derided the suggestion that the Nabob would invite a powerful rival like the Vizier into Bengal. When he reached the wide prospect at Monghyr, where thousands of duck clustered on the marshes and women harvested the shells left by the retreating waters, together with Colonel Ironside he inspected the Fort, where Ellis accused the Nabob of harbouring British deserters. But they found none. It was in vain that he tried to conciliate Ellis by recalling his own opium agents, — 'though I abhor all monopolies, especially those founded in violence'. Ellis, he concluded, and all the majority were 'inveterate'. They had used every means 'to ruin yourself and everyone who held the same principles with yourself'; 'I cannot think calmly on the unprovoked injury which has been done to my own character'. He therefore was careful to let Mir Kasim know that Vansittart had not signed the impudent demand for twenty lacs, and advised the Governor to see the Nabob himself, but to conceal his visit from Coote until it was definitely arranged.

These letters also looked anxiously towards the India House. Hastings noted that the Directors seemed 'barely to approve' the deposition of Mir Jaffir. And he agreed with the Governor that Ellis, Carnac, and their group were trying to upset Mir Kasim in England, though they had not as yet entirely persuaded Clive.

As he described the 'beautiful prospects' on his march, his anger heightened against the men who were treating this fair land so vilely. Their agents, and impostors posing as such, were 'a disgrace to the English name'. Hardly a boat passed that was not sporting our flag, while our sepoys behaved so abominably that he found shops shut and villages abandoned. 'Were I to suppose myself in the place of the Nabob, I should not be at a loss in what manner to protect my own subjects or servants from insults.' Our trading privileges must be precisely defined and, going beyond Vansittart's instructions, he suggested that *gomastahs* guilty of violence be left to the Nabob's jurisdiction. But for the time being he found a deadlock. Mir Kasim refused to produce the twenty lacs and demanded a formal treaty; the Council majority rejected all his complaints. Hastings therefore returned to Calcutta in July, sick of a bad business. He had had to 'sit like a criminal and hear my fellow-servants taxed with oppressions . . . to hear our government charged with countenancing such proceedings . . . without a reply but what would make my conscience fly in my face'. But Vansittart took his advice in deciding to see Mir Kasim himself. Meantime Hastings was busied in exploring the latest devilry of Nuncumar, who was trying to incriminate Van's *banyan* by forged letters. Even the majority found him guilty of acting as go-between with Shah Allum and the French, and put him under house arrest.

Late in October he went up-country with the Governor, reaching Monghyr again on November the 30th. There, in almost daily conferences with the Nabob, they drafted an agreement. Rightly they laid down that the Imperial *firmans* had never been intended to allow the Company the inland trade, duty-free, which they sharply distinguished from their privileged commerce, 'imported or exported by shipping'. They proposed that, while this last should continue to be covered by the Company *dustuk*, inland traders must receive a pass from the Nabob's officials; the duty payable by the British on such goods being only 9 per cent, a rate well below that levied on the natives. Disputes arising with British *gomastahs* should be referred to the Indian magistrates, who, however, must furnish copies of the proceedings to aggrieved parties. Final settlement, if required, must be left to discussion between the Nabob and the Governor. Mir Kasim gave fair warning that, if this concordat was rejected, he would fling open all trade free of duties. In January 1763 Vansittart returned to the Presidency, persuaded that Mir Kasim, who had gone off to attack Nepal, could not be designing war with the British.

The majority instantly made it clear they would never swallow this agreement. And unhappily they were presented with good pretexts. Mir Kasim precipitately circulated the new scheme to his officers, with orders for the expulsion of British *gomastahs* who violated it. But he exempted from this order the private agents of Vansittart and Hastings. There was something worse. While at Monghyr Vansittart accepted the five lacs offered him two years before, so giving colour for Carnac's violent

47

letter to Clive that concessions, 'so evidently shameful', would never have been made 'except by persons who were bought into them'. Before Van reached Calcutta, the majority admitted Carnac to the Board, and summoned the 'out' members from the factories.

Long fierce meetings of Council filled the first quarter of 1763. Amyatt denounced Van's usurpation of power, Johnstone spoke of his 'black dependants', Carnac asked for the Patna command as 'the post of honour', Batson sneered at the 'constant artifices of the President and Mr. Hastings'. The ground which Hastings took was wide and lofty. Nothing in the new regulations could damage the Company, with which individual interests were 'too much confounded'. As to the Indian magistrates' powers, which he alone defended to the end, 'if our people, instead of erecting themselves into lords and oppressors', confined themselves to a fair trade, 'the English name, instead of becoming a reproach, will be universally revered'. Against any temporary inconvenience, let them weigh the Company's paramount interest, 'the duration of their acquisitions and influence'. Let them not destroy their necessary union with the Nabob, by creating this 'abhorrence of the English name'.

All in vain. When their inland trade came in question, even moderates like Cartier or Hastings' old friend Marriott lined up with the Batsons. So Amyatt and Hay were deputed to make another agreement, to claim reparation for losses, and the admission of a British resident to the *durbar*. By March there was talk of war. Ellis asked powers to seize the city of Patna, whose people were shouting abuse from its walls. Mir Kasim came back sore from defeat in Nepal, convinced that the English meant his downfall, and forthwith executed his threat of abolishing all customs duties whatever. This, the Council majority voted, was beyond the power of a Nabob, 'raised and supported by us'. Only Vansittart and Hastings minuted, 'it is not to be expected the Nabob will join with us in endeavouring to deprive every merchant of the country of the means of carrying on their business'. In April a move of Batson and Johnstone for immediate war was narrowly defeated.

The Amyatt-Hay mission reached Monghyr in May, but any chance spark might touch off the explosion. Council had authorized chiefs of factories to 'clear' our trade, if need be by force; they were swallowing wild rumours that the Nabob was moving troops, and cutting down mulberry trees and cotton plants to wreck our profits. Mir Kasim on his side, certain he was to be attacked, seized British boats carrying arms, and demanded removal of troops from Patna. Yet though he roughly told Amyatt the British were only concerned with their private profits, there were signs he did not want a break; thus he asked that Ellis be replaced by Amyatt or Hastings.

In long discussions on June the 9th and 10th the majority refused all his requests. Hastings alone voted that, if our boats were released, Amyatt and Hay should continue negotiation. To break off without more ado might 'ensnare the Nabob into a rupture', nor did he believe he would deal treacherously with our envoys, while he altogether declined to trust Ellis with discretionary powers. His argument roused Batson to fury, who, calling him and the Governor the Nabob's 'hired solicitors', struck Hastings on the face in Council.

On June 20th Council had got so far as to be discussing how best to replace Mir Kasim, whether by restoration of Mir Jaffir or by taking all power for ourselves. Hastings predicted the bloodshed such a change would bring, with a warning they must save the Company 'from sinking with the weight of their own acquisitions'. On the 21st Amyatt reported that he and Hay were effectively prisoners, Mir Kasim took fire at messages that Ellis was preparing scaling ladders, and moved his troops. On the night of the 24th Ellis stormed his way into Patna, but his sepoys scattered to plunder, the Indians retook the city next day, and captured all his party as they were escaping towards Oudh. Kasimbazaar was taken too. Hay was left as a hostage at Monghyr; Amyatt was cut off near Murshidabad, and his severed head sent to the Nabob.

Much worse was to come. In July the British declared war and restored Mir Jaffir, Adams' gallant force occupied Murshidabad and marched on Monghyr. Before he fled thence to Patna, taking his British prisoners with him, Mir Kasim drowned Ramnarrain and many more Indians in the Ganges, and had the Seths shot by the famous 'Samroo', — that is, Walter Reinhard, his Alsatian soldier of fortune. And lastly, at Patna, on October the 5th he fulfilled his threat that, if the British advanced further, he would kill his captives. Samroo saw to it. So were massacred in cold blood Ellis and Hay, Lushington whose memorial hangs in a peaceful church at Eastbourne, and nearly fifty more Company servants, defending themselves with chairs and bricks, knives and forks.

Would not this be the end of Warren Hastings? All his predictions had been falsified; the Nabob of his choice, after thus glutting himself in British blood, had fled to ask help from the Emperor and Oudh. Amyatt, but lately married, Ellis and Hay, whose last message bade the army advance and not think of them, these men whom he had criticized had died like heroes, and their bodies were heaped in wells at Patna. And a counter-revolution reopened the feuds of Bengal. His client, Khwaja Petrus, was under arrest: his bitterest enemy, Nuncumar, was given high authority by Mir Jaffir. His private fortunes were imperilled, already one salt boat belonging to him and Hancock had been seized. Home and happiness were gone at Calcutta. 'Mrs. Van' had sailed for England, promising to see his son George. And though Van had written of him to Sulivan 'I know but one person here that I can recommend as fit for the charge of this government', all hope of promotion must now have vanished.

But he sat in Council dour and unyielding. Like Vansittart he would not vote on the restoration of Mir Jaffir, agreeing to stay only for the duration of war, now become 'the common cause'. His minutes still refused to endorse 'past measures of which I disapproved . . . I still abide by the sentiments which I have all along expressed'. He dissented from the extortionate terms imposed on Mir Jaffir as 'manifest injustice', especially the demand for a duty-free inland trade. He joined Vansittart in denouncing Nuncumar as dangerous; nine years later he recalled that 'when Mr. Vansittart and every other person was reconciled to him, I refused it even in the presence of the Nabob'.

This war against Mir Kasim did not end until Hector Munro's victory at Buxar in October 1764, after a year that justified Hastings' forebodings and proved that a change of ruler would not mend a rotten system. All the ambitions were aroused of the neighbours of Bengal, from Delhi to Benares. Nuncumar was convicted of contact with the Vizier, but Mir Jaffir would not dismiss him; Council were pushing forward a rival minister in Mahomed Reza Khan, Naib of Dacca. Mir Jaffir's old incom-

petence disordered the army's pay and supply; Carnac, bickering
with Council as usual, would not or could not take the offensive.
The very grievances of which Mir Kasim had complained were
repeated by Mir Jaffir. Batson, now resident at his Darbar, was
making high-handed arrests, English traders in grain or betel
oppressed the poor. On paper, indeed, all European agents
were recalled. But settlement of the trade question was postponed
till the arrival of Clive, of whose reappointment they had just
heard, and Mir Jaffir's dying days were cursed by demands for
more payments for our sepoys, and indemnity for our losses.

'Hastings and Hancock' were winding up their opium transactions, for any price they could get; he told his diamond-dealing
friend at Benares, Motte, that he had neither money nor credit.
In November 1764 Vansittart sailed for home, having refused a
donation proffered through Nuncumar. And on December 20th
Hastings resigned the service, 'to come to England', sailing on
the *Medway* in January. He left behind most of his trading
capital, as most Anglo-Indians did, to be looked after by his
friends. He was still only thirty-two, but had been out of England
fourteen years, his wife was dead, his fortune precarious, and his
reputation tarnished. Cartier, his shipmate in 1750, was in
Council and would shoot ahead of him; men he despised like
Johnstone were in their glory. As he left the Hugli, Clive was
leaving the Cape for Madras. How would he stand now with the
'Colonel' and the Company?

Had he known the full facts, he would have realized that
never again would he serve the Company he had known. For
its factions were fast tied to ministers and parliamentary groups,
who would henceforth twist and divert his fortunes. It was torn
by jealousies between three Presidencies, and made disreputable
by the corrupt fortunes and battles for patronage of returned
'Indians'. But it was, above all, the prestige and megalomania of
Clive which merged it in British politics. The quarter of a
million he had accepted from Mir Jaffir roused criticism, while
the *jagir* he received, making the Company his tenant and worth
£30,000 a year, was indefensible. His airy assertions of the ease
of conquest, with suggestions that the Crown ought to take over
the territorial revenues, offended a trading body who prized
their charters. His favouritism to Madras men, his jealousy of
Coote, and prejudice for Carnac and Forde, injured many private

interests. And with this corroding ambition he coupled high notions for saving this jewel he had won from France.

Such causes brought him into collision with Laurence Sulivan, whose election as chairman he once had championed. Unlike most directors, Sulivan had local knowledge, having served some years in Bombay, and in a sense he makes the central figure in all this story. For down to his death in 1786 the politics of the India House largely turned on his sincere zeal for peace and reform, his inextinguishable love of power, and his financial misfortunes. Since no director could serve continuously over four years, in 1762 he was out of office, and it was now that his differences with Clive turned to open war. His last letter during Clive's first governorship had never been forgiven, — 'you seem to have acted like men divested of your understanding' — nor was Clive's furious reply — 'unworthy of yourselves . . . as gentlemen to gentlemen'. His merchant's sense revolted at this language of conquest and expansion. The two men disagreed over the Peace of Paris, as regards the restoration of the French factories and the guarantees given to the rulers of the Deccan and the Carnatic, so that Clive voted, with the followers of Pitt and Newcastle, against the peace preliminaries.

Ever since Plassey, the Colonel had determined to prolong his Indian supremacy through parliament and the India House. By steady pressure on Newcastle he came in as member for Shrewsbury in 1761, and from him received, without much enthusiasm, an Irish peerage. He found seats also for his father and his former secretary Walsh, who as brother-in-law to a well-known 'Indian', Joseph Fowke, was his 'contact' man in these arrangements. In the next parliament of 1768 his group in the House rose to seven. With backing like this he could measure swords with this ungrateful cheese-paring Sulivan, and having rejected Lord Bute's approaches, counted on the Newcastle Whigs to support him.

He had to move gently at first, since Sulivan held one deadly weapon against him, the wealth and the reproach of his *jagir*. But, having joined hands with those whom Sulivan's directorate had dismissed and losing his temper under press attacks, he staked everything on stopping Sulivan's re-election in the spring of 1763. Though he spent £100,000 on winning proprietors' votes, the combined weight of the Bute-Fox government and the

Sulivan interest defeated him with ease; promptly the new Directors instructed Bengal to suspend payment from his *jagir*. While he impartially canvassed Grenville the new Prime Minister, Pitt, and Newcastle to get it renewed, he was further divided from Sulivan by those matters of Indian policy in which, we have seen, Hastings was involved.

Vansittart had, indeed, been his friend and his nominee. But he was indignant at his surrender of Ramnarrain, he resented the supersession of Amyatt as Van's successor by one of Sulivan's men from Bombay, and Van had become the Directors' favourite. Under Sulivan's lead they endorsed his refusal of the *diwanni*, issued orders for prohibition of inland trade, and in January 1764 were considering his reappointment for a further term. Then this prospect changed overnight. Early in February news reached London of the Bengal war and the Patna massacre, and instantly the proprietors pleaded for the services of Clive.

He was thus in a position to dictate at least a compromise. Refusing to return to India if Sulivan were in authority, he got his way with the proprietors and his candidates into the 'chairs', though Sulivan won half the directorate. With Grenville's support he received the red ribbon of the Bath, with a guarantee of his *jagir* for another ten years, and though not allowed all the powers he asked, was given a Select Committee (Van's opponents Carnac and Verelst, together with Sykes and Sumner), whose powers were large or vague enough to overawe the Council in Bengal. His pronouncements on past mistakes were dogmatic. Of Van's ideas and his own, he declared that one or the other must be wrong. The Nabob's independence was incompatible with our safety; 'it is impossible to rely on the moderation and justice of Musselmen'. When he reached the Madras coast a year later, he wrote back of the 'Augean stable there is to be cleansed'; by the same ship sending Walsh cipher orders, to invest in India stock all his holdings in the funds and anything he could borrow.

Such were the changed ingredients of the Anglo-Indian world which met Hastings when, on June the 16th, 1765, he reported to the Directors his arrival in England.

CHAPTER VI

Unemployed: 1765-69

A HEAVY blow awaited him as he stepped ashore in this new half-known world. He was told that his son George had died in the previous autumn, at George Austen's rectory. But on this grief, and on all else during these four years at home, not a line in his own hand survives. We have to stumble along by the faint glimmering light of his household bills, chance allusion, or some backward glance of later times.

Wife and children being gone, his near circle was diminished to what remained of his youth. Aunt Elizabeth still lived, probably already settled at Kensington. His sister Anne and her husband, the cautious John Woodman, had two children, Elizabeth and 'Tommy', with whom he made great friends. Perhaps it was because their home was in Cleveland Row that we find him first living in St. James' Place, bringing him near his chief, Vansittart, in Burlington Street. Uncle Howard Hastings' widow had lately died. His old guardian — Joseph Creswicke — had just become a director, but was withdrawing nowadays to his Cotswold home at Moreton in Marsh. Of his mother's folk, the Warrens, we know from their later complaints that he saw nothing. Finally, there were his two stepdaughters, presumably with their grandmother in Ireland.

He drifted about, with no settled home. From St. James' Place he moved to Golden Square, then to Essex Street, Strand, which would bring him close to the Hancocks in Norfolk Street, who had travelled home with him, and last of all to Piccadilly. Once he was in treaty for a country house at Ewell, but nothing came of it. For his heart was in two places only, India and Daylesford, and in the first as the avenue to the last; if he was to make another Indian fortune, to live in London near the India

54

House was wiser. But to buy back Daylesford, he told his brother-in-law, was 'my first wish'.

He thought at first enough money would be forthcoming. He had left behind, he reckoned, about £30,000 invested in India, and for a watchful eye on that looked to Francis Sykes, now one of Clive's Council, who took over some of his interests. With both principals in England, and the effects of war in Bengal, the accounts of Hastings and Hancock were in a tangle. But he began spending as if they concealed a gold mine. He settled an annuity of £200 on his aunt. He made many small loans to needy friends. And though his own tastes in dress and food were plain, — liking best, says Woodman, a leg of mutton and apple pie — he was bent on living as a Hastings of Daylesford should, and hated poverty. He liked soft toothbrushes, which he bought in the Haymarket, loved pictures and was buying landscapes from Anthony Devis, and preferred claret to other wines. His coachmaker's bills tell us that his post-chariot was chaste and expensive, its body being painted 'a pleasant pompadour', while his crest and arms were embraced within green and gold wreaths.

Of his life and movements we know only enough to say that his standard cannot have been thrifty, and that he picked and chose his company. Orme, for instance, historian of Hindustan and a central Anglo-Indian figure, never saw him in these years. On the other hand, he made some eminent acquaintances. Joshua Reynolds painted him. He paid one visit at least to Samuel Johnson, who wrote later 'I had too much pleasure from it to forget it', and sent him a copy of his *Journey to the Western Islands*. Mansfield, the brilliant and sinister Chief Justice, he probably knew of old, having been at Westminster with Stormont, his nephew and heir. What did they make of this young, most reserved, but experienced 'Nabob'? He suffered all his life, as he put it afterwards, from a sort of 'mental malady', an intense lassitude when the pressures of work were taken away, as now they were, while he had plenty of other reasons for depression. Yet so many different human beings became attached to him that, outwardly perhaps, he lived up to the temper he once commended in an East India chaplain, as 'a man of society, of decent manners and without guile, pride or reservedness, hearty and benevolent', — 'a good composition, better perhaps than richer ingredients'.

When he returned to India, all his clothes were too small, for the London tailors had measured him when 'reduced by sickness'. By fever or dysentery, it seems; a chemist's bill (only paid seven years later) running up formidable lists of emetics, sudorifics, and 'stomach drugs'. Perhaps this illness brought about his friendship with Percival Pott, leading surgeon at Bartholemew's Hospital, and father of the rascally Bob Pott who shines in the Hickey memoirs. Before this sickness of 1767 he received yet another blow, in hearing that his Indian fortune had broken like a bubble. One message after another from Sykes to Creswicke rubbed it in. 'I never saw such confused accounts', he must get Hastings sent out again. Hastings' finances, he told Clive, were 'more to the credit of his moderation than knowledge of the world. He is almost literally worth nothing, and must return to India or want bread.'

Hastings himself seems to have come very quickly to the same conclusion. The longer it was delayed, the heavier his debts. There was a mortgage on the Cheltenham property that had come from his mother, a bond of £6000 to William Sumner, another for £1000 to one Grimstead, and a third of £1500 to William Mackett. Of which last he wrote afterwards that Mackett had been 'a little shy of trusting me even so long as to my arrival in India; indeed, there was some reason for it'. But with the help of one Indian remittance he reckoned his English debts in 1770 at not much over £4000.

A good many stories sprouted after his death about his desperate search for employment; how he would furbish up his classics and turn schoolmaster, or with his knowledge of Oriental languages find work in the universities. He did, in fact, circulate a scheme for founding a chair of Persian at Oxford, for which Dr. Johnson promised to draft regulations, but his note in old age says 'it met with no other encouragement, and therefore dropped'. But there is much more solid evidence that India was never out of his mind. Fragmentary notes among his papers say we must arm the Nabob against the Mahrattas, and have yearly revisions of land revenue; there are sardonic comments that 'we have been scrambling for power', or that Clive's success came to nothing but 'specious ostentation of ideal wealth'. But he was writing in earnest too. One of his friends, William Hirst, a considerable astronomer and chaplain at Calcutta, sent out to

WARREN HASTINGS, 1766–68, BY SIR JOSHUA REYNOLDS

India an unknown pamphlet by Hastings, which Richard Barwell praised as the best by any East Indian he had read. It is more important that in 1766 he drew up a full programme of reforms, comprising all he felt to be essential, now that Clive had accepted the *diwanni*, and every major point for which he struggled himself when Governor. A Governor who was also Commander-in-Chief, and with a veto in questions of war and foreign affairs, a wholly resident Council and not one part-composed of Chiefs feathering their nests at Patna or Dacca, abolition of the *dustuk* and trade freed from duties, fixity of land revenue for terms of years, revenue collections in the hands of Indians only, Indian magistrates to rule through native law, — in short, a government for a people 'whose ease and welfare we are bound both by justice and policy to preserve; to make their laws sit as light on them as possible, and to share with them the privileges of our own constitution'.

Whether or not these proposals were circulated at the time, he plainly meant to take a hand in Company politics and return to the East. He took out his stock qualification as a proprietor, but surrendered it to a friend when seeking employment, in case he was 'disagreeably called upon for a vote'. His first application was turned down. Though Sykes might call him 'a very honest deserving man', something more than that was needed when the Company was split by faction and under parliamentary fire. For at midsummer 1767 'the Colonel' came home again, after a whirlwind administration of eighteen months. He was more imposing and more heavy-lidded than ever, and more given over to opium. Preceded by men whom he had expelled, he was perfectly satisfied that he had left behind a system which only corruption or incompetence could destroy.

His actions, though built on the work of the predecessors he so loudly despised, were indeed decisive. He had accepted the *diwanni*. He had arbitrated between rival princes, surrendering to the Mogul the tribute of Bengal and the fortress area of Allahabad, but restoring to the Vizier all the rest of Oudh, which he might well have forfeited by warring against us. He had broken a mutiny of British officers. He enforced the covenants against taking presents. He had carried out, though not as they wished, the Directors' prohibition of inland trade.

57

But he had governed as an autocrat; like Henry VIII, wrote Rennell, the geographer of Bengal. He made his Select Committee absolute, ignoring his Council, three of whom were dismissed with ignominy, while the arch-rebel Johnstone hastily resigned; vacancies which he filled up with Councillors from Madras. When his civil servants boycotted him, he broke their spirit by dismissal or refusing *dustuks* for their trade; and one ringleader was George Vansittart.

What maddened his victims was the contrast he liked to draw between his own integrity and their corruption; between the fortune Mir Jaffir had heaped on him for great service, and the sordid haggling of Johnstone and his circle on the accession of Mir Jaffir's son. Having exacted the covenants and reduced private trade, he organized a monopoly in salt for his senior colleagues and himself, arranged he should receive a commission on the revenue to the tune of about £30,000, in addition to the other £30,000 from his *jagir*, and if he saved little for himself, sent his staff home with comfortable fortunes.

Every blow at the Vansittart régime was a blow to Hastings, and the reactions in England and India could not be separated. On Van's departure, and after a competition in bribery, the Council had got Nuncumar dismissed and installed Mahomed Reza Khan as Naib. When Clive returned, however, he appointed two Hindus as colleagues to the Moslem and freed Nuncumar from arrest, who carried litigation even to England against Burdett, one of those whom Clive evicted. And we note that if Nuncumar was Hastings' old enemy, Mahomed Reza Khan had done his best to look after Hastings' financial interests. Again, Vansittart had now become in Clive's eyes — for he was the friend of Sulivan — 'the meanest dirtiest rascal', and as he found Hastings 'a dupe to Vansittart's politics', his request for employment must be rejected. At least he should not return to Bengal. For four successive years the Directors' majority faithfully reflected the Colonel's wishes. Yet when in July 1767 he reached England, he found the Company impotent and his own position half-undermined.

The great boom in India stock had begun eighteen months before, when his agents began buying lavishly. At the news that the *diwanni* was ours, the stock jumped from 165 to 263, and against the Directors' advice the proprietors clamoured for higher dividends. Clive's numerous enemies saw and seized their opportunity. The Vansittart interest and that of Palk, his brother-in-law; Hastings' old friend, General Caillaud, and his brother-in-law Pechell, a power in the Company; a Madras contingent headed by the much respected Du Pré, and even the Colonel's oldest admirer Robert Orme, who vowed he could write no further of Hindustan since 'those cursed presents'. Most vindictive of all were the Johnstones; John, the dismissed, George or the 'Governor' (having once ruled West Florida), and William, heir by adoption to the great wealth of Pulteney, Lord Bath, whose surname he had taken. John Johnstone led the ring of dismissed Councillors, against whom the Company had begun a lawsuit for recovery of their presents, and who were naturally working for a change of Directors. From Madras and Calcutta letters of denunciation were streaming in. Barwell wrote that in this second governorship Clive had netted another £200,000, and that behind the screen of a puppet-Nabob his tools like Sykes were running a lucrative private trade.

Sulivan was in the centre of this storm, for he was the link between Clive's enemies in the Company and national politics. From the patronage of Bute and Henry Fox, which had first given him power, he had kept a legacy in the friendship of Shelburne, from whose house in Hill Street he conducted this anti-Clive campaign. And while Clive had anchored himself to George Grenville, choosing as his voice in parliament one of Grenville's most impudent followers, Alexander Wedderburn, Sulivan had another and stronger alternative in contacts with the Rockingham Whigs, who dominated the government of 1765–66. In particular, he was working closely with Rockingham's under-secretary William Burke, and his cousin, the illustrious Edmund. But in July 1766 the Chatham-Grafton ministry was formed, with Shelburne as a Secretary of State. His under-secretary was a college contemporary of Burke at Dublin, one Lauchlin Macleane, an extraordinary gambler alike in India stock and in political combinations.

That autumn Sulivan joined hands with the Johnstones, who were said to have put up £125,000 to win over the proprietors. A vote by the General Court for an increase of dividend from 6 to 10 per cent was followed by a Cabinet warning, that the Company's affairs were to be considered in parliament, though

Sulivan hoped, by deferring to the dividend-seekers, to win backing enough to let him strike a good bargain for the Company. His former ally Shelburne, however, followed his leader Chatham and would claim the new territorial revenues for the Crown. Over against them Charles Townshend, Chancellor of the Exchequer, was manœuvring to admit the Company's claims in return for a cash subsidy; all with an eye to remodel the Cabinet to his own advantage. In this state of confusion, crowned by Chatham's mental collapse and absence from Cabinet, the rival parties in Leadenhall Street washed each other's dirty linen for the public: the Directors in the *India Observer*, answered in good Eatanswill style by the *India Examiner* for Sulivan. Early in 1767 Clive's representative Walsh carried a resolution, though only by twenty-nine votes, that his *jagir* be extended for a further ten years. And this half-defeat was turned to disaster in May, by two votes of the proprietors, that the prosecution of Johnstone and his fellows be suspended, and that the dividend should again be increased, to $12\frac{1}{2}$ per cent.

If these half-censures on Clive pleased his enemies, they were also quite irrelevant; the real question was how far the Company were prepared to defy parliament. The Commons summoned before them for examination the principal Company servants now in England: Vansittart and Holwell, Coote, Munro, and McGuire. Hastings was heard at length in March, though no detail of his evidence survives. In the debate that followed, the Chatham group advocated State sovereignty in India, while Grenville and Burke defended the Company. But Townshend's tactics prevailed. By going direct to one section of the proprietors, he evaded Sulivan's proposals for a lasting settlement, preferring to meet the requirements of his Budget and, he hoped, his own political future by a compromise, in the shape of two statutes with merely temporary effect. By one the Company's rights to their new revenues were admitted in return for an annual subsidy of £400,000 to the Exchequer, while by the second the rate of dividend was restricted to 10 per cent.

Clive's star was sinking. He exclaimed furiously that even this friendly Board of Directors were 'mean and sneaking', nor could he adjust his fortunes to the prevailing current of politics. Chatham was buried in apparent madness, Shelburne was on the eve of retirement, hopes that his ally Grenville might come back in the stir over Wilkes and the Middlesex election were disappointed. Grafton, on the contrary, strengthened himself by taking in the Bedford group of Whigs, and Sulivan turned towards this apparently stable Cabinet. He and Vansittart were borrowing money right and left to make sure of re-election, buying £100,000 of India stock at the desperate figure of 268. Indeed, only Van's return to India could save both of them from ruin.

Hastings was helping Vansittart with the 'Narrative' of his government, which would vindicate them both, and any retrieval of Van's fortunes must help him. As it chanced, the Directors were particularly anxious about Madras, which had fallen into a squalid and unsuccessful war with Hyder Ali of Mysore and was beseeching assistance from Bengal, which itself was nearly bankrupt. In 1768 they chose Du Pré, one of Clive's chief opponents, as next Governor of Fort St. George, and late in the year nominated Hastings as his 'second', and presumed successor. Clive waived his opposition at Sykes' request; it would at least keep this 'dupe to Van' out of Bengal.

So Hastings was off East again, and set about his preparations. Woodman undertook to see to his aunt's annuity; to pay £20 a year for his stepdaughters to Mrs. Forde, who would manage their welfare; and to keep his ears open about a purchase of Daylesford. Hancock had already returned to Bengal, so Hastings left some money for his wife Philadelphia. He sallied out to buy silks in Covent Garden, an epergne in Fleet Street, and a compass box in the Haymarket. Messrs. Warren of Cecil Street had a standing order to send him annually three chests of claret and one of hock. For a long tedious voyage he bought some solid reading from his bookseller, Charles Bathurst; Hume's *History* and *Essays*, Robertson's *Charles V*, two volumes of Diderot, James Macpherson's *Fingal*, and Dow's *Hindustan*. Caillaud promised to send him lists of the newest books.

After a last dinner with Scrafton in Grosvenor Square, on March the 26th, 1769, he sailed from Dover on the East Indiaman *Duke of Grafton*, 499 tons, Captain Samson. She carried troops and stores, besides ten guns for the Madras artillery, reported on arrival as highly inferior. She carried also a good many young military cadets and writers, among them Frederick Stuart, a son of Lord Bute, with whom he made friends. As the pilot boat cast off, he sent a last line to his sister that he had a good 'apartment' and a fair wind; 'my love to my dear Tom, my aunt, and all friends . . . may every blessing attend you, and a few years unite us again'. He wrote next a month later, after a gale in the Bay, saying he had no sea-sickness, and 'never enjoyed a better state of health'. But that summer at sea all his life was changed.

Being the leading Company servant aboard, he occupied the round-house, probably not seeing much of fellow-passengers except when the drums called them to meals, and they buttressed their plates or dishes with the sand-filled baize cushions as the ship rolled. There were few women, though his eye was caught by a rather sprightly 'Mrs. Thompson', going to join her husband, a Company marine officer. But the state cabin below him was taken by a Baron Carl von Imhoff, with his young wife and their little boy Charles. Though they barely spoke English, Hastings knew French, and their story was short and not unusual. The Baron came of a good but impoverished Nuremberg family, — one kinsman had been Governor-General of the Dutch East Indies — and while serving in the Württemberg army had married Anna Maria Chapuset, descended from French Huguenots settled at Stuttgart. Money was short, but the Baron had another gift besides his sword, that of painting in miniature, and not long before had migrated to England, encouraged by some acquaintance with Madame Schwellenburg, Queen Charlotte's mistress of the robes. The Baroness had enough charm, or her husband enough social or artistic status, to get her portrait painted by Pine, but though he exhibited one picture in London, they could not live. Through his Windsor influence he then contrived to get a cadetship in the Madras army. They had left behind another little boy, Julius, not six months old, in the care of a Mrs. Touchet living at Chiswick, of whose sons at Westminster School Hastings had probably heard.

We have nothing but the family tradition, given to Gleig, his official biographer (though given when Marian Hastings was just alive), for the story of how love first arose. How Hastings fell ill after they passed the Cape, and how the Baroness nursed him, sitting in the round-house when he was barely conscious. 'That day we read no more'; though whether by sea, or at Madras, we shall never know; whether some night as they watched the lanterns in the mizzen shrouds of the ship to windward, or in some garden-house, under the ironic indigo curtain of Indian darkness. Heart-stricken or fancy-free as yet, in August he saw the low Coromandel coast, the surf, and palm trees beyond, and on the 29th landed at Madras in excellent health.

CHAPTER VII

Madras: 1769-72

WHEN he took his seat in Council next day, or looked out of his exorbitantly rented house in the Fort, all the world was different from his familiar Bengal. Life should be more peaceful here, among the palms and tulip trees screening the dazzling white houses, and moved at a slower pace, nearer to the Company's original factory existence. Lines of women were carrying drinking water and horse fodder into the Fort; country bullock carts crawled over the causeways with charcoal, and that *chunam* or lime which made the houses so white. Indeed, half their military problems seemed to turn on these half-starved bullocks, a full dozen of which were needed to drag a six-pounder gun, at two and a half miles an hour. Council, he found, dealt much with the petty things he had known at Kasimbazaar but long forgotten, — damage done to cloths by white ants, sales of 'red aurora' or 'popinjay', or the share-out of the 'concession' wine of the Company, thirty-four pipes of which, vintage '67 and rather fiery, had just come in from Messrs. Scott, Pringle, Cheap & Co. of Madeira.

And if individuals were rich, the Presidency was poor. The war with Hyder had drained their finances, a low rate of exchange gave an advantage to the French, while for some essentials, rice and gunpowder for example, they were dependent on Bengal. Besides, the structure of society surprised him. Not just the 'rancorous bigotry' of caste divisions as compared with Bengal, but the half-Indian, half-foreign strains among Europeans, and the power of the free merchants. There were families of Portuguese descent from St. Thomé, whose dark daughters captured many English husbands, a colony of wealthy Jews, and some old-style British merchants who lived and died on the Coast. One of their leaders was Nicholas Morse, Governor himself far back in the '40's, and father of Mrs. Henry Vansittart. Another clan were the Powneys, large creditors of the Nabob, and in latter days pillars of George III's pocket borough at Windsor and creditors to the Prince of Wales.

Hastings' reputation had reached Madras before him. Even Joseph Smith, the best soldier of the Presidency, who was disgruntled by the Council's incompetence, admitted 'Hastings is a good man and sensible'. For all that, he was a Bengal importation, whose high place superseded, among others, the chief engineer John Call, whom Clive had run for the governorship against Du Pré. The outgoing Governor, Charles Bourchier, was also displeased but went off to England with Call in 1770; however, he smuggled with him some ruffled shirts for a friend of Hastings, who wrote, 'I have desired Mr. Bourchier to conceal them among his foul linen'.

Here too was the identical conflict of powers which had troubled Bengal. Directors' orders gave a large discretion to a Select Committee, to consist of Du Pré and Hastings, Joseph Smith, and Alexander Wynch. The last was a bad-tempered elderly mediocrity; Smith was a capable fighting soldier, whose good qualities were discriminately praised by Du Pré as not 'fit to govern Yahoos', — and 'men, my friend' (this to Orme), '9 out of 10 are Yahoos'. The Colonel concluded later that Hastings, though 'the best man at the Board', had 'dropped all his Bengal notions, at least those he was so much praised for', and like Du Pré showed 'no mercy on the military'. As for the ruck of the Council, all seem to have been corrupt by modern standards, and some of them villainous. The pearl perhaps was 'Black Jack' Whitehill, uncle to Sterne's 'Eliza', and in his middle age a temporary protector of the brainless beauty who ended life as Princess Talleyrand. There were two decent men with whom Hastings made friends. One was 'Billy' Goodlad, secretary to government, a great lover of claret (which maybe helped to kill him young), but a real reconciler amid these factions. And the other was a much-loved doctor, Gilbert Pasley, on whose tomb at Madras is inscribed 'the common friend of mankind', and whose nephew, the illustrious Sir John Malcolm, continued his virtues.

Government, in fact, turned on good relations between Du

Pré and Hastings; which did not fail. They were easier because both belonged to the school of 'Van', and had a mutual friend in Robert Palk. Hastings' 'mildness', Goodlad hoped, would temper Du Pré's 'rigour'; the Governor's only fault, said Hastings, was a little jealousy, which was natural enough, perhaps, when his second in command was intimate with powers in the Company like Sulivan, and very soon Governor-designate of Bengal. But at the close of his Madras years Hastings gave Du Pré thanks for his 'sincerity' and 'gentleness' as 'the best endowments in the gift of heaven', and many years after quoted the judgements of this 'wise man'. On his side the Governor enlarged to Palk, how it was 'a great comfort in my distress to have such a man as Mr. Hastings'.

Before looking at their joint problems, which, as Du Pré said, assuredly gave Hastings a good 'seasoning', we may bring together what is discoverable of his private life. He liked his colleagues, as hitherto he liked most men, and was loud in praise of Goodlad. As time went on, we find him owning a house in Church Street by the Fort, and though he rarely left the town, kept his health which he attributed partly to the dry air and in part to his temperance. He still got his claret, at £52 a hundred, from Peter Warren of Cecil Street, yet thought it very bad, — 'fortunate that I drink but little wine even when it is good, or I should be sick with drinking this out of pure economy'. He kept horses, a pair of which he gave to Dr. Pasley when he left, and hawked now and then, though complaining the Carnatic only boasted paddy birds, kites, and crows, that 'will not be caught'. In general, it sounds as if he kept much to himself, for he would not drink, one young Palk grumbles at his 'superciliousness', and he read widely. He begged Caillaud to send him more French books, and asked Woodman for regular despatch of the *Annual Register*, and 'if Junius continues to write', all his letters. Thanks from Colonel Egerton of Bombay, for an ode in 'true Horatian style', shows he was still scribbling his verses.

Old bills and letters let us see his width of interests. Silver-spangled buttons and embroidered coat-loops were details, if compared with the £73 spent on pictures in 1770, or the £39 on Rennell's Bengal atlas. Woodman had to consult the great engineers Smeaton and Brindley, whether something like Margate Pier could not get over the dripping landing in the surf at

Madras. A questionnaire goes to Motte at Benares on land tenures; if a *ryot's* title is hereditary, or whether *zemindars* have judicial powers.

When he became second in Council, export warehousekeeper, and commissary-general he drew in salary and allowances £2400, and early in 1770 sent home bills for over £4000, with instructions to pay off his debt to Sumner. Most of it came, no doubt, from private trading. He went on experimenting in all directions, investing his spare capital mostly in Bengal, and when he left Madras told Sykes 'you will stare when I tell you that my books were balanced'. He had one venture in a ship to Manila, and was member of a syndicate for marine insurance. He got Bengal silks for sale at Madras from Hancock, who for that matter supplied his table with Bengal poultry. But he was not optimistic in his correspondence with his old partner. He vowed his god-daughter 'shall not be under the necessity of marrying a trades-man', but lamented it would take some years for him 'to get much above the world', their capital being so locked up that they were missing chances. He resented pressure for repayment from his old creditor Khwaja Petrus, whom he had helped to affluence in the teeth of angry English feeling. He heard too that Cantoo was juggling with his Bengal accounts, and that his Alipur garden was a jungle; ending on a gloomy note, 'it may soon be too late'.

Flowing parallel with his life was that of the Baron and Baroness Imhoff. After ten months at Madras and painting half the settlement, the Baron decided to try his luck at Calcutta, where Hastings asked Hancock to find him a house. In September 1770 the obliging Council gave this military cadet leave to pro-ceed to Bengal, to practise 'one of the liberal arts'. Marian did not follow till October 1771, living meantime, according to Hancock, in a house belonging to Hastings. While cordial letters passed between the two men, Marian plainly reigned in Hastings' circle, as later messages show from the good Pasley, or cruder allusions from John Macpherson to 'your fair female friend'. If Hastings confesses in these years to his experience of tambour-work, we must notice also that he remained on excellent terms with the new-married Mrs. Du Pré.

Certainly he now acquired that knowledge of Carnatic politics, and predilections about them, with which we meet later.

Nowhere, and at no time, were exposed to a harsher light the anomalies in the British position, the corruption of Company servants by a rotten system, the Directors' incompetence, and the rank ignorance of parliament. Here too was proved to the hilt the fatuity of Clive's advice 'to take no open part with these Hindustan princes', but let them quarrel 'to all eternity'; here also was demonstrated the impossibility of three Presidencies pursuing three foreign policies.

On this original scene of the Anglo-French duel for supremacy, the great questions were forming which beset the last years of his public life. By the date he reached Madras four causes had given them a new colour. One was an article in the Peace of 1763, whereby France and Great Britain acknowledged as Subadar, or Nizam of the Deccan, Salabut Jung, who in fact had already been deposed by his brother Nizam Ali and was murdered that very year; and both Powers also recognized, as a sovereign and Nabob of the Carnatic, Mahomed Ali, who in Mogul law was only the Nizam's deputy. The second lay in the treaty of Allahabad of 1765, imposed by Clive on Shah Allum. This not only freed the Carnatic Nabob from dependence on the Nizam, but transferred to Britain a part of the Nizam's possessions, the five Northern Circars stretching between Madras territory and the Bengal province of Orissa. A third was the disintegration of Mahratta politics since the defeat at Panipat, the Peishwa's decline before the great feudatories Scindia, Holkar, and Bhonslay of Berar, and then the effort of a distinguished but short-lived Peishwa, Mahdoo Rao, to reassert his power and free himself from the ambitions of his uncle, Ragoba. And the last came with the rise of a new power, in the uplands where the claims of the Carnatic, the Mahrattas, and the Nizam ran into each other. This was the soldier of fortune Hyder Ali who, having mastered his nominal master the Hindu Rajah of Mysore, by his prestige was turning the area between Bangalore and Seringapatam into a citadel of fighting men.

If even two of these States combined to invade the Carnatic, the Nabob was doomed, and with him the riches, perhaps the existence, of Madras. Though sometimes a panic of war drove thousands of peasants to crouch, without food or covering, under the walls of Fort St. George, for some years fortune favoured us. Round baked clay towers and in deep wooded passes, Hyder was

struggling to make a northern frontier line against the Mahrattas;
simultaneously he was striking down the western Ghauts to the
Malabar coast, where his flag waved above Mangalore. The
Nizam, dipping deep into the internal feuds of the hated Hindu
Mahrattas, once burned the outskirts of Poona. In 1766, however, urged on from Calcutta, the Madras government reached a
momentous decision. Influenced by the Carnatic Nabob's
inveterate hatred of Hyder, they made a treaty with the Nizam,
promising military assistance if required, and to admit his title
to the ownership of the Circars. One group in the Presidency
were prepared to go even further, notably John Call and a
French adventurer, St. Lubin. Though well aware that the
Company's policy was to keep on good terms with any enemy
of the Mahrattas, they gaily embarked with the Mahrattas and
the Nizam in a war for the obliteration of Mysore. Within a
year their adventure ended in utter disaster.

While the Nizam watched his enemies destroying each other,
the Mahrattas at once detected the callow Machiavellian scheme
of the Call faction, which was to use them and then turn against
them, and the Madras military dispositions were as weak as
their diplomacy. The Council, which had quarrelled with
Joseph Smith, its best soldier, confided its fortunes to a showy
and corrupt Colonel Wood. Our sepoy infantry, which could
beat any comparable force, was invariably robbed of its victory
by break-down of transport and dearth of cavalry. And while
we insanely rejected Hyder's offers of peace, and dispersed
tiny garrisons over boundless granite hills, everywhere Mahomed
Ali's extortionate tax-gatherers recruited sympathizers for the
enemy. 'Mr. Hydro', as old Mrs. Morse called him, could
well cope with foes like these. Avoiding frontal battle, he
moved freely with his scarlet-clad lancers, and in the last months
of 1768 struck hard. In six weeks he recovered the losses of
two campaigns, swept south-west almost to Tanjore, and then
moved forty miles a day until in March he reached St. Thomas'
Mount, eight miles west of Madras. His men plundered the
pleasant garden-houses, whose doors and window frames went
into their camp fires; Goodlad reported 'not a hut nor an
inhabitant to be seen for sixty miles'. Hyder's ultimatum, sent
to Du Pré and ignoring the Nabob, brought a collapse, and the
Madras government accepted a mutual restoration of territory

F

and a defensive alliance. The effects at the India House were calamitous, Company stock tumbled sixty points, while the Directors sent a mass of contradictory despatches; sometimes refusing to act as 'umpires of Hindustan', sometimes declaring the Nizam and Hyder necessary bulwarks against the Mahrattas, but always accusing their servants of twisting public policy to private gain. In this fog of recrimination Hastings found his new colleagues.

Their last orders from home were to wind up the debris of war, to investigate Smith's charges against Colonel Wood, and make a settlement of the Nabob's debts. They were also to examine the question of Tanjore, always a Naboth's vineyard to the Nabob, whose Rajah we had guaranteed provided he paid his tribute to the Carnatic, but who was accused of default and of contact with Hyder. To all these matters the key was the Nabob, of whom Du Pré wrote 'I believe no devil has a blacker heart', though Clive had said 'the best Mussulman I ever knew'. It was never in Hastings' temperament to think like that, or make an individual responsible for a system. Mahomed Ali, he told Sulivan, 'is a polite man, of a very agreeable address . . . and the worst man in the world to transact business with'. But the frame in which we had set him explained it. By treaty, we had made him a sovereign prince; indeed, George III had lately sent him one of the royal lions from the Tower, which to the Company's indignation consumed £100 worth of food en route. In law the Company ruled the Northern Circars as vassal of the Nizam, but held Madras as a *jagir* from the Nabob. All revenues and troops were formally his, but in fact all power was ours. Except that his sepoys had tunics with facings of green and ours with blue, or that he habitually took into his service officers dismissed from ours, there was no difference in the employment of the two armies. We made him pay for the French war, and then for the war with Hyder. The result was he was driven to loans, and was now heavily indebted to the Company, but infinitely more to British civil servants and merchants, the interest on which he sporadically paid by the poisonous device of an assignment, or *tuncaw*, on his land revenue.

Here was the root of all evil; loans to the Nabob at 20 or 30 per cent from every leading Englishman now or lately in the settlement, from General Richard Smith and Call up to the

Councillors and Du Pré himself. 'Every member of the Committee except myself', wrote Hastings, 'is a creditor'; vowing thirteen years afterwards that he never received anything from the Nabob, except 1000 pagodas for a ring, thinking it 'infamous to plunder a plundered man'. So grew up, and not by stealth, what history knows as 'the Arcot interest'. A band of Britons preyed on by the Nabob and preying on him; encouraging his aggression on Mysore or Tanjore, as bringing them more profits; setting up, within the Company, a body in conflict with the Company's honour and interest.

In time these creditors included all sorts of innocent parties, — heirs and widows and transferees. But at the heart of Carnatic politics in Hastings' day were two first-class scoundrels. Paul Benfield was the first, native of Cheltenham and most spectacular of civil engineers, at present engaged on a contract to fortify the 'black town'. He was just seeing daylight in the money-lending which was in due course to make him the Nabob's paymaster, the destroyer of Governors at Madras and maker of Cabinets at home, taking him by way of parliament and Grosvenor Square at last to a bankrupt's death at Paris. His rival, or in certain circumstances his confederate, and the first to discover what could be made out of the Nabob's 'sovereignty', was a future Governor-General, John Macpherson. Beginning life in Skye as a son of the manse, his initial advantages were that he stood six foot three in his socks, and possessed a head so strong that it equipped him in later years to live in the circle of the Regent. Like his kinsman James, translator or maker of the Ossian poems, he had a gift of tongues, and could sing his ballad songs with equal brio in Gaelic, Spanish, and Hindustani. He came out first in 1767 as purser of an Indiaman, scraped an acquaintance with the Nabob by interesting him in electricity and the magic lantern, and went home next year as his agent to the Cabinet. There he saw Grafton and his Treasury secretary Bradshaw, before whom he brandished hopes of Carnatic loans to the Exchequer, and induced them to send out a representative of their own to Madras. A few months after Hastings' arrival this bright spirit turned up again, so much impressing Du Pré that he finally recommended Hastings to get him on his Council in Bengal.

For many weary months Council wrestled with what Hastings

called 'the dirt of the late war', especially the case of Colonel Wood. The court-martial proceedings, he added, would 'frighten any man who sets a value on his time'; comprehensive charges of disobedience and incapacity, profits from sale of arrack and seizure of grain, frauds over cattle subsequently sold by Mrs. Wood. The court-martial acquitted the Colonel; Council, however, dismissed him the service. But Hastings wrote forebodingly that he was a relation of Sulivan, and sure enough the Directors restored him. Then came the Nabob's accounts, necessitating many hours of conference with him at the Company's garden-house, even on Boxing Day. But everything paled before his debts. Their orders, that the debt to the Company had priority, were blatantly defied both by Nabob and creditors. It was found that some Councillors had a grip even on the tribute due from Tanjore. Hastings complained to both sides in Leadenhall Street; to Clive's ally, Crabb Boulton, that the Nabob was incorrigible; to Sulivan, that 'the sacred rights of self-interest will never be invaded without great clamours in a people like those of the British government'. From such dealings John Call, an engineer officer who began by trading in tea and candles, went home to found the banking house of Pybus, Call & Co., and a seat in parliament. Hastings added he heard with 'unspeakable pleasure' that Van, Scrafton, and Forde were coming out as supervisors with overriding powers, which were as sorely needed in Madras as in Bengal.

In July 1770 two of the stormiest petrels alive blew in on them, in the person of Commodore Sir John Lindsay, the King's plenipotentiary, and Eyre Coote, Commander-in-Chief for all India. The Cabinet's intentions may have been excellent, but their execution was unspeakable. Lindsay, a fighting sailor in his early thirties, was a nephew of Lord Mansfield, and therefore *persona grata* at Court, but Macpherson, the author of this appointment, had not bargained to see all influence at the Darbar pass out of his own hands into the Commodore's; all the parties concerned being Scots who, Hastings said, had 'a very powerful bias to politics and a most unconquerable aversion to those who have more power than themselves'. So, on the strength of a secret royal commission, Lindsay demanded admission to the deliberations of Council; when that was refused as degrading them in Indian eyes, and setting up a dual power unknown to their charters, he suggested a judicial enquiry into the late war. Hot words simmered in the summer; he begged them not to 'dispute over words', and this at least, they replied, promised a 'seasonable relief'. His memorandum for the Cabinet swallowed whole the Nabob's version of events, while George III invited the Nabob to deputize for him in investing the Commodore with the ribbon of the Bath.

In comparison with this, the Coote business was trivial. Though his commission subordinated him to Council, he claimed it superseded that of the President as Commander-in-Chief, and made military promotions without further reference. But his temper was always ungovernable, and after four months he went home overland, where in due course the Directors approved his side of the quarrel. The episode sunk deep in the mind of Hastings, who wrote 'God forbid he should ever return'.

These matters, with the reversal of their decision about Wood, first lighted up that indignation against the Directors' weak inconsistencies, and their betrayal of their own servants, which was later to consume him. His health would hold out for years, he told his brother-in-law, 'if the people at home do not make me sick'. At the height of the Lindsay battle he sent Sulivan one of his fiercest letters. The Directors' 'undiscriminating censure' and their 'partiality to the military' were suicidal; 'can you expect steadiness, resolution, or confidence or dispatch, from men whose power you have weakened?' He had drafted several letters in 'more guarded style, but they bore so little a resemblance of my thought that I was ashamed of them'. If Council must spend their energies in resisting 'factious cabals of the Company's dependants', or 'pretensions of the officers of the Crown, armed with plenipoteniary and inquisitorial powers . . . no human abilities ever were or will be equal to such a task'.

These royal creatures, Lindsay and his successor Harland, blindly subscribed to the Nabob's version of external policy. Hyder was again battling with the Mahrattas in a war of shocking atrocity, and the King's ambassadors clamoured for our intervention on the Mahratta side. They ignored some details. As, for example, that it would violate our treaty with Hyder; that the Mahrattas were our most dangerous enemies; and that funds for a war were non-existent. Left without instructions from home, the Council maintained neutrality, though clear, as was the government of Bombay, that if we came in at all, it must be against the Mahrattas. They were equally unwilling to back the Nabob in arms, as Lindsay urged and the Directors half-heartedly suggested, against the Mahratta Rajah of Tanjore. Whatever his financial lapses, it would be 'impolitic and unwarrantable' to plunge into new expenditure, and reawaken Hyder's jealousies. In the long run, late in 1771, the Nabob's pressure and some valid argument, — for Tanjore was dangerously near French Pondicherry — persuaded them to contribute some troops to a mild siege of Tanjore. But the Nabob, fearful of Mahratta attack or suspecting the British might keep the fortress for themselves, soon dropped the enterprise for a cash indemnity. On this wretched background Secretary Goodlad depicted Du Pré as 'harassed to death, Hastings knows not which way to turn'.

Against such odds they were doing their best to rebuild prosperity, and pushed through some refortification, a new water supply, and a general hospital. Hastings sat some time too on a board of police, dealing with small essentials like street lamps, paving, and the extermination of pariah dogs. Officially he was more concerned, and no doubt more interested, in radically reforming the investment. The Board having decided to end the use of Indian contractors, and to employ our own *gomastahs* as in Bengal, his main work during 1771 was to put this in operation. His recommendations were to give full-time control to some servant, not on Council; to remunerate him by a commission on sales; to earmark certain weaving villages for work on the investment, leaving the rest open to private trade. He opened up some much larger considerations. Any 'privileges and humanities' for the peasant weavers could only be maintained if the Company had complete mastery of its *jagir*. Without that we should always be 'at the precarious will of the Nabob', and never be able to make the improvements that meant 'command of a numerous and contented people'. But when he signed this document, Madras and its interests were fading away.

He was a Bengal servant, and all the accounts of Bengal were bad. Trade was languid, they were financing the investment out of revenue, the Directors grumbled at poor quality, and flared up at the exorbitant bills on the Company remitted by their servants. Clive's dual system had destroyed the Nabob's executive and law courts, without putting anything in their place. Yet individuals were making gigantic fortunes. Thomas Rumbold, the envious Barwell said, had cleared at least £200,000; Governor Verelst himself had some money dealings with the Naib, Mahomed Reza Khan. Becher, our resident at the Darbar, testified 'it must give pain to an Englishman' to know that the people's condition since our taking the *diwanni* was worse than ever. In 1770 Nature added to the ruin done by man. A famine carried off some millions, perhaps one-third, of the inhabitants. The survivors lived on roots or leaves, and sold their children; the dead lay heaped in the streets of Calcutta, and epidemic followed famine. Both Englishmen and Indian ministers were accused of profiting by the shortage of food. The very honest soldier, Colonel Pearse, declared that, though Verelst's successor Cartier was innocent, 'there never was a Governor less capable, less active, less resolute'.

Hastings hoped for a remedy from home, and his first English letters delighted him. In April 1769, with the help of the Grafton government and Shelburne as against Clive and the Grenvilles, Sulivan and Vansittart were elected directors, their hope being to recoup their fortunes by getting Van reappointed as Governor. Clive's group, however, forced them to a compromise, the despatch of Van with Clive's old friends Scrafton and Forde, as supervisors with full powers. Yet Hastings hoped it meant that in time his old chief would succeed Cartier. In September the three sailed on the *Aurora* frigate, which left the Cape just before Christmas, — to be heard of no more. For many months of 1770 rumour kept some hope alive, — that *Aurora* had been blown to Rio or Batavia, — only to die away. Van's brother Robert wrote from the Cotswolds that hope was gone. So ended three makers of British India. With them perished the sailor poet Falconer, the midshipman Pitcairn who gave his name to a lonely islet, and Hastings' friend, the chaplain-astronomer William Hirst.

For another year the British in India were left in suspense, while the India House rocked in panic and faction. 'The Colonel's' statue, disguised in a Roman toga, stood in their hall; besides his own homes in Shropshire and Berkeley Square, he had bought Chatham's house at Bath and Newcastle's at Claremont. But his health had broken, press attacks pierced his heart, and George Grenville's death demolished his political hopes. Yet Sulivan, his enemy, was in a desperate pass. All efforts to boost India stock were unavailing in the panic over Hyder, the Bengal famine, and threats from Delhi; he owed many thousands, and dared not unload at ruinous loss. Hastings' correspondents warned him that at the elections of 1770–71 the Sulivan group were badly beaten.

Though the investment was being financed by borrowing, with reckless folly the proprietors raised the dividend to its legal maximum of 12½ per cent. One solid man, John Purling, was gaining influence, but the leader of Leadenhall Street in these feckless days was Sir George Colebrooke. This dapper little man, who, Mrs. Thrale tells us, in his green coat and white waistcoat looked like 'a leg of lamb and spinach', belonged to a firm of government contractors who had enlisted in the Newcastle following since South Sea Bubble days. When the supervisors were given up for lost, he took Clive's recommendation for a Council of five; Hastings as Governor, Clive's follower Wedderburn, the soldier Amherst, and two more. But when that idea lapsed on Amherst's refusal, the Directors took a course of which Clive entirely disapproved. In the controversy which, as in his own day, divided Bengal, they came down on the side of the Council against the Select Committee, sent two of his nominees back to Madras, and decided to appoint a Governor at the head of a large Council. For some time their favour hovered round Thomas Rumbold, one of the most rapacious of Nabobs. But Sykes 'split' £30,000 of stock to make additional voting qualifications, Palk was active, Sulivan came to a working alliance with Colebrooke. So Hastings was chosen, the official news reaching Madras in December 1771. 'Much joy it has given me', he wrote to Sykes, 'to learn that I am indebted to *you* for my late appointment; you are the friend that you have always professed yourself to be.'

His Indian friends sent home gloomy predictions of what he must expect; 'a crown of thorns', as Hancock wrote to his 'Phila'. He showed none of this pessimism himself. He was glad to be going back to Bengal, but equally assured that more people at Madras would be sorry than glad at his going, as indeed they were. All sorts of goodwill followed him. Secretary Goodlad wrote home he would be 'much regretted'. Mrs. Powney promised to supply him with coffee. George Stratton, member of Council, entrusted him with diamonds to dispose of in Bengal, — on a 5 per cent commission. A Hindu merchant thanked him for a present of diamond rings. The father of two Madrasi servants he took with him sent thanks for his kindness to his sons. And in his first letters after this great change the original Warren Hastings reappears. That to his sister and her husband runs like one written on the eve of battle; 'my dearest brother and sister, aunt, Tommy, Bessie, may God bless you and protect you'. To Mrs. Hancock, 'my dear and ever valued friend', he held out hopes that now he could help her husband; adding a word for his godchild, 'make my Bessie remember and love her godfather'. He wrote to Marian Imhoff too this January, making only a bare note of the fact.

He was writing against time, often at night; already the petitions and temptations that beset the holders of power were at his ear. Sykes must recommend a young writer, Jonathan Duncan, destined to be an illustrious servant of the Company. Dr. Pasley pursued him with the praises of young Alexander Elliot, Sir Gilbert's son of Minto. Messages reached him purporting to come from Mir Jaffir's widow, the Munny Begum, and attacking Mahomed Reza Khan, which turned out to be forged by Nuncumar. He was literally besieged by letters from a personage who was to cut deep into his life. This was Joseph Fowke, brother-in-law to Clive's confidant John Walsh, and who, having been disappointed of high office, had gone home and gambled away his fortune, but had lately come out again, aspiring as ever. His interest, he instantly pointed out on news of Hastings' appointment, was all-powerful with Clive and Colebrooke; surely he might help in this 'fog of misrepresentations', perhaps as his second in Council? Hastings' friend Motte was his rival in the Benares diamond trade, so could not Motte be suitably moved to Bengal? and by the by, his nephew William Hollond was doing very well at Dacca.

He was a different man, they noticed in Bengal, from the Hastings they had known before, with 'his former reserve' markedly increased. The hot temper he had shown as a boy, even with the great Clive, was under a curb, yet edged out abruptly now and then in these last Madras letters; in the curt words that write down one man as 'improvable', but another as 'troublesome and fawning'. The keynote of those written to the powers in England was a frankness amounting to audacity.

The Directors' censure of their servants, he told Sulivan and Colebrooke, was unfairly harsh; his own reform of the Madras investment had proved they could be influenced by better motives than private profit. Let them rather blame the King's ministers, who had done untold harm in that Presidency, and let them give him loyal support, for his own interest would never be strong enough to survive misrepresentation.

On February the 2nd he sailed in a small country ship, which gave him 'an uneasy stomach and confused head', reaching Calcutta on the 17th; well, Hancock reported, but 'thin and very grave'. The northern news was that the Emperor had at last returned to Delhi, but only with Mahratta assistance, with whom he was attacking the Rohillas, and that the Vizier of Oudh was entreating our aid. Simultaneously, in England, the royal speech threatened more intervention in India. Henry Vane, name of ill omen for Hastings, in seconding the address attacked the crimes of the Company's servants, while Horace Walpole was telling Horace Mann 'we have outdone the Spaniards in Peru . . . we shall lose the East before we know half its history'.

CHAPTER VIII

Bengal: 1772-74

AGED 39-41

MUCH had changed in the seven years since he had seen Calcutta last, and much more in the twenty-one since he saw it first. Clive's new Fort, south of the earlier settlement, was nearly complete. The old Fort held some oddments, even the circulating library, but its ramparts were crumbling. There was still a waste gap where Siraj-ud-Daulah had blown up St. Anne's church, nothing being available for official worship except a so-called chapel, given up on week-days to sorting piece goods, next the ruined Black Hole. But the Dane Kiernander's red mission church, flanked by Selby's club where they gambled deep, made God and Mammon close neighbours. East of the old Fort, the same Court House and the same theatre were in use. Pariah dogs still plunged in their principal water supply; bush and undergrowth still encroached on the streets. Yet the city was expanding with a great activity in real estate and mortgages, in which those who looked ahead, George Vansittart and Barwell among them, were large investors.

On the Esplanade, looking south towards the new Fort, stood the new Council House, built in 1764-65, where Hastings took up his residence, as Cartier had before him. His offices were housed at present in a former Council House by the old Fort, but so fast becoming ruinous that within a year or two he had a house rented for them, near his own. He also kept some nucleus of his old country property at Alipur, and at Alipur incidentally were lodged for the time being the Baron and Baroness Imhoff. New dignity and greater wealth, but little real change, come out in his first instructions to England; for hats, 'not too much in fashion', for a dozen pairs of black silk breeches and many silk stockings, a bill of £4200 to pay off Macket's bond, half a dozen cheeses to be picked up by Aunt Elizabeth at the Castle Inn, Marlborough, on her way from Bath, and for claret 'as many chests as the Company will allow me'.

Some few familiar faces were there to greet him. There were a much-disgruntled Hancock, his old *banyan* Cantoo, his old creditor Khwaja Petrus; George Vansittart and his old chief's son, another Henry; Playdell, whom he had known as a Councillor dismissed but now returned as a merchant, with his jovial singing voice and a new young wife; and Ironside, with whom he had searched Monghyr Fort in the days of Mir Kasim, and whom he now made his military secretary. But his fellow-Councillors, on whom all depended, were new to him, either men lately ascended in their early thirties, or else survivors of those brought by Clive from Madras. He got on well with Samuel Middleton, resident at the *durbar*; better still, perhaps, with the acting senior, Aldersey, whom he found a better man than many 'clever fellows'. So that, when on tour, he bade him open all his letters, — 'I expect none sealed with bleeding hearts nor thimbles'. Dacres, though he helped Francis later over revenue questions, and Lawrell and Lane, are shadows to us, but there were a few more sticky characters, and a considerable tussle before the young Governor made them a working team.

One obstructionist, needless to say, was the Commander-in-Chief, for the Company army was hopelessly undisciplined and corrupt, and this particular officer, Sir Robert Barker, was a dim product of Clive's school. Like Carnac before him, his troop movements on the frontier interfered with policy. Indeed, if Joseph Fowke can be trusted, 'the General is Nabob of Oudh', and not least through his private trade in saltpetre and opium. He was also Fowke's rival in the diamond market and made another fortune by clothing the Vizier's army. There was a first breeze over his appointment of one Captain Harper to the Vizier's troops; the Governor objected not so much to Harper's trading in sugar, but 'because all his ideas are military, and all our paths ought to be peace'. There was another when Council cut down the native cavalry, on which Hastings drily deplored Barker's 'style of emotion', — 'surely you went too far in predicting the Company's ruin from the reduction of 300 troopers without your consent'.

But Barker's grumpiness did not commend him to Council,

opposition from whose civilian members would be much more crippling, and Ironside testified that by the autumn he had conciliated nearly all of them. It was a considerable thing to make a confidential friend of their leader, John Graham the chief of Burdwan, a revenue expert who was freely said to make a good revenue for himself too. More important in the long run, and more revealed to us, were his relations with Richard Barwell. For here was the most typical of all the Bengal Nabobs, 'Nabob' in a sense that Hastings never was one, in all their naked corruption and some of their quite certain virtues.

Barwell was only thirty-one when he entered Council, in his gross and unpurged youth. In Philip Francis' innuendo, that he was 'in every sense a native', there was this grain of truth, that he was born at Calcutta, where his father was at one time Governor. In fact he came of a decent Leicestershire family, members of which had been trading in the East since Charles II's time. His reading tastes, for we find him sending home for Dryden, Otway, and Locke, and some very sensible minutes, show the educated citizen of his day, but his spirit was not elevated, and his view of life candid and cynical. 'A moderate share of attention and your not being quite an idiot', he thought, were all that was needed to make your way in India, and to get rich quickly was his golden rule. No man had criticized Clive and his 'Madras gentlemen' so angrily, or the 'screen' of the dual government, behind which he alleged Sykes and Cantoo had made lacs. His own transactions were flung wide, even to things prohibited to Councillors, like salt fleets and revenue farming, while he still held a watching brief for some notorious Nabobs who had gone home, and taken their wages. Batson, for instance, who had struck Hastings, and Leycester, whom Clive had dismissed. His father being frequently a director, he pulled many strings in Leadenhall Street, having besides a most devoted agent there in his sister Mary, who followed stock prices and elections like a growling lioness. Meantime his Calcutta life was loose and expensive, as he gambled heavily and feasted friends lavishly in his Alipur garden-house. He was shocked to find that a little half-caste he sent home was being taken too literally; 'whether he is my natural child or not is apocryphal, — most probably he is not'; he insisted the child must be rebaptized as 'Richard Hunter', not Barwell, and that £50 was the limit for educational

charges per annum. For some time he had been housing at
Belvedere that detrimental Sarah Bonner, who called herself 'Mrs.
Thompson' and had travelled out with Hastings and the Imhoffs,
and was using Hastings' influence to buy off the troublesome
merchant-mariner, Mr. Thompson.

It took a full year for the Governor to win and overcome
Barwell. The fat youth was fighting Aldersey to get hold of a
house of Munny Begum's, and contesting every item of patronage.
The new British residency in Oudh would be a rich market.
Barwell managed to prevent Hastings appointing a young
protégé of his own, William Hosea, nephew of Orme the historian,
but equally he failed to get this plum for himself. So they went
on with what Hastings called their 'literary war', and with
Barwell's minutes full of 'doubts, dissents, replies, and rejoinders'.
All this being so, Barwell's developing view of Hastings, given in
casual letters to his sister, is of great interest. He complains of
'duplicity of character', 'excess of jealousy', or 'centering the
whole minutiae of business in himself'; as to this last, Hosea
made the same point to Orme, — the Governor 'carries all before
him' but has 'undertaken or already done too much'. And yet,
Barwell continues, what 'very extensive abilities' and how many
'great and valuable qualities!' It was the same with Hastings.
From his first complaints of 'talents for opposition', we move on
to his matured view; that Barwell had 'solid judgement, much
greater fertility of official resources than I have', and agreeable
manners, 'which I am sometimes inclined to consider as the first
accomplishment of a man of business'.

They were all young men, as the British world went, but
Hastings liked to pick them young and make them his own.
Hosea was in the early twenties. Alexander Elliot was rising
high, though not yet of age. Nathaniel Halhed, newly arrived
in 1772 and eminent in after years as an Orientalist, was another
of this kindergarten. Was it because, in this welter of jobs for
'sons, cousins, or élèves of Directors, and intimates of the members
of the Council', he hoped to find glad confident morning again,
or merely that he disliked opposition and selected obedient tools?
Perhaps a piece of both. A touch of the later autocrat, more than
a hint of anger, meet us in this first heavy crop of letters as
Governor. And anger, notably, against British ignorance and
injustice. What, pray, he asked Sulivan or Colebrooke, did

'gentlemen of Cumberland and Argyllshire' know of this great possession? who took their facts from the libellous travesties written by William Bolts and Alexander Dow. It was lamentable to think that even the Directors could be seduced 'by each paltry scribbler of the day'. He was not, therefore, in a mood to welcome news that parliament was once more remodelling the government of India. That was 'a melancholy prospect for the service', he told Graham, — meaning 'hypocrisy, rapine, and corruption', while he wrote home to Palk that the House of Commons was equally ignorant 'of the laws in being, of the manners and customs of the inhabitants, or of the forms of government'.

Later on Barwell often noted the tireless patience of Hastings, 'this very impatient man', who indeed freely admitted his irritable temper. Once convinced of his case, he held it remorselessly, listening, Hosea tells us, 'with seeming impatience', but rejoindering 'with a particularity that amazed me' of detailed fact. In measured reproof he was grave, but satirical. One gentleman who was unwise enough to decline assisting the Mayor's court, on the double ground of no time and small knowledge of the language, was told 'the duties of your station are not so great as to prevent your bestowing the time, — I hope you have under-valued your knowledge of the country languages, as such a plea would equally disqualify you for the office which you at this time hold'. Or again, no doubt the collector of Hugli wanted a house, but 'it was certainly out of form to build one and then apply for permission'. To Ironside he once blazed out at an evil he always detested, when soldiers beat an official serving a warrant on a British officer, — 'it is my duty to require of you a most diligent and rigid enquiry'. Hancock, his oldest Bengal friend, who moaned over his innovations, soon got an intimation of where the Governor drew the line, — 'as to my friends, I shall be glad to serve them, but as to my friends' friends, I neither can nor will serve them'.

From April 9th, when he took over from Cartier, he was pressed down by business till midnight, even on his Sundays at Alipur. A flood of the Directors' despatches launched him on nothing less than the total reconditioning of the government, but what chance had he, he asked, of 'the tranquil mind, an uninterrupted chain of close reasoning'? His temper was 'almost fermented to vinegar' by trifles, by petitioners 'halloing me by hundreds for justice as often as I put my head out of the window', and 'the cursed encouragements of patronage'. Except for one bout of dysentery he kept his health, and when a year had passed had not missed three meetings of Council. But 'I slave but do not move forward', he told George Vansittart, and it was not till the spring of 1773 that he got Vansittart promoted to Council and felt he could delegate 'without the same hazard of sacrificing my own authority'. Barwell's complaint of his over-centralizing was probably just. We find him employing Hosea to make a rough census of Calcutta, even to rename the streets, detailing the virtues of Indian silk-makers' ovens as against 'a more showy mechanism', devising a supply of transport bullocks, reviewing court-martial sentences, and assembling Brahmin pundits to codify Hindu law.

He longed to begin the reforms that could not wait, growling against over-deliberation and palaver. 'We have no time to talk,' he tells Sulivan, 'the whole day is too little to act, and it is infinitely better to proceed even to error than to procrastinate.' They must be allowed to risk making mistakes, to work 'as an arithmetician does with his Rule of False'. Ruin must follow 'if your servants are made responsible for every stumble', or for straining the law. 'Too much stress laid upon general maxims at home' might do terrible damage on Indian frontiers, where sometimes they must do things 'not to be justified on such principles as the public can be judges of'. The Company's position as regards the Nabob 'can neither last as it is, nor be maintained on the rigid principles of private justice'. Right or wrong, he would press ahead, telling Graham 'if we suspend our own operations on the notice of every project to which the weather-cocks either of St. James' or Leadenhall Street may point for the moment, we must stand still altogether'.

He had not worked under Henry Vansittart nor digested 'Junius' for nothing, and never thought Lord North's House of Commons entitled to point the finger at Indian iniquity. Nor was he prepared, as he told Barwell, to be 'the general reformer'. As at Madras, so now he found the fault lay in the system, not the men. Doubtless Mahomed Reza Khan, in his seven years' supremacy, had not neglected 'the due means' of influencing Englishmen. But who was to blame for that? It was all very well for folk at home, who 'live and die in the bosoms of their families'; India was 'in the hands of a few, and the whole wealth of it at their disposal', yet all tied down to antique charters framed for a humble export trade, or measuring silks and muslins. Men would not keep to rules that meant 'perpetual penury', or 'begin the work of reformation on themselves'. Still these boys, profiteering through their 'devils' of *banyans*, were potentially the hope of the country. Meantime, 'how should it be otherwise? . . . most of them young and inexperienced, and some totally ignorant of the languages of the country'. 'But in the name of God what English *banyan* ever possessed so unbounded a sway, or did so much mischief with it, as Rajah Amrut Sing, the detestable favourite of Mahomed Reza Khan?'

Looking back on these years when the Directors loaded him with invidious enquiries, he confessed his own practice to his old friend Sumner, — not to look back but forward, and not to be extreme to mark what was amiss. 'I disdained such dirty work . . . it has always been my line to do whatever I thought my duty required of me, to check with rigour actual offences against the service, but to show tenderness to those who were absent, whose conduct was not committed to my enquiry, and whose inclinations for the service were perhaps as good as my own.' He was an old-style Company servant, and made no bones about it. If a senior servant was given a starvation salary and government suppressed his private salt trade for its own monopoly, 'I should not scruple to have winked at the Resident's being the contractor for it'.

And if he believed the English power should be openly proclaimed and the character of its servants encouraged, it was always in order to rule India for the Indians. His remedy, he wrote before taking the chair, was 'to restore the Government to its first principles', to make regulations familiar to 'the original constitution of the Mogul Empire'. As he went on tour this summer, he tells Aldersey 'it is an exhausted country and has been much oppressed'. For everywhere he saw marks of the great famine, when dogs and vultures had fed on the million dead, and whole villages had gone back to jungle. To sell up defaulting *zemindars* would be 'infamous oppression'; our *gomastahs* had often reduced the village weavers to 'absolute and irredeemable vassalage'. He had noted, when on furlough, the hard case of the proprietors in the twenty-four Parganas, ejected when their land fell to the Company, whose 'name and credit has suffered much', and pressed their case for years to come. His orders were to axe the Nabob's pension list and cut down his household; through the official language his own sentiment shone clearly, when he found among 'the ancient nobility of the country', whom we excluded from all honourable service, 'under all the pride of Eastern manners the manifest marks of penury'. His heart was hot against English oppression. His first instinct was to have no resident in Oudh, who would just monopolize its trade, 'which I would not allow even to my dearest friend'. To subject Indians to our legal code, he told Lord Mansfield, would be 'wanton tyranny'; we must, rather, 'found the authority of the British Government in Bengal on its ancient laws'.

In such a spirit he opened the pile of despatches that lay before him. His honourable masters, who had hitherto ignored the very meaning of the word, airily announced they meant to 'stand forth as Dewan', and 'take upon themselves the entire care and management of the revenues'. Mahomed Reza Khan was to be deposed, and new arrangements made for the charge of the young Nabob. They threw in some details, — each in itself a revolution — such as abolition of the *dustuk*, and creation of new law courts. Personal letters to Hastings directed him to arrest Mahomed Reza Khan, and to use Nuncumar to provide evidence against him; he was, further, to investigate frauds and monopolies of trade by Company servants.

No wonder that he broke out privately, though officially dumb. It would be 'arming my hand against every man and every man's of course against me'. To use the remedies he really believed in was not in his power. 'What can the Directors expect', he asked Sykes, 'from a Governor to whom they have given only a casting vote, and yet made him the only responsible person?' His staff realized it well. Ironside wrote that 'if resolution and intellectual qualifications could ensure relief', all was well; but though Scripture required much where much was given, 'here nothing is given and everything required'.

So, conciliating the Grahams and Barwells as he went, he set about cutting new channels for government. He held fixed Council meetings four days a week; for some months it met every evening at six also, as a Board of Inspection, to review each department in turn and enforce economies. And from the autumn it took on another role as a Board of Revenue, sitting twice a week. The secretary to Council was one John Stewart, a follower of Shelburne who was appointed from home, against which Hastings protested as a slight to the service. But as ever he made the best of it, and got on easy affectionate terms. In fact, judging from Stewart's letters on leaving India, the reserved Governor unbent with the secretary, who could remind him of 'a pretty black foot that used to play out and in, like a little mouse, from under certain petticoats'. His choice of a private secretary might be more important. Dr. Hancock, still hopeful of contracts for making gun-carriages, cement, or anything in reason, had aspirations, but the man appointed was John Belli, who had served with him at Madras. And as Belli came from the well-known financial house of Belli & Fonnereau, the Leghorn agents of Colebrooke the chairman, that presumably helped his appointment.

Before he is plunged under an ocean of work, let us grasp what hints we may of his life and being. His scale was as grand, his generosity as great, and his interests as wide as ever. If his own brown coat were plain, his horses had silver-plated bits with his crest engraved ; he was building his new house at Alipur, begging Motte to send him Benares marble for its staircase. Captain Price was getting him porcelain and tea from China. Then there was his large book-bill running with Charles Bathurst of Fleet Street, successor to Dean Swift's printer Benjamin Motte, for books on India like Bolts and Verelst, William Jones' Persian grammar, Eden's essay on the poor laws, Dalrymple on the revolution of 1688, Goldsmith's poetry and many plays. If we wonder where the money came from, a part-answer comes from his private trade. He shipped fifty chests of opium on his own account in his first year as Governor. He tried to sell jewels to the Nabob on behalf of Madras dealers. Sykes consigned him emeralds and rubies to sell as turban ornaments. He had Spanish dollars invested in the China market, and like most Anglo-Indians remitted his savings home in diamonds, for one of which, experts told him, he ought to ask £10,000. Gosling, Clive, & Gosling were his London bankers ; Sykes and Woodman held his letters of attorney and put out his remittances in sound mortgages. Daylesford was always in his mind, though unhappily the owner,

Mr. Knight, threatened to live long, and had a lunatic brother. 'I will give as much for it as it is worth,' he told his brother-in-law, 'and if you give something more for it, I shall not be sorry.' As for his English budget, his old guardian Creswicke died in 1772 and his son next year, — not that he expected much from them. But his annuity to his aunt went on, while there was serious trouble with one of his stepdaughters who, though prepared for India by dancing lessons and every other genteel accomplishment, ran off and married a corporal.

This was meagre, if put against his Indian benefactions. On that list, after the widows of a coachman and a coolie, we find £250 a year to Mrs. Vernet, widow of his Dutch friend of 1756, and £350 to the Imhoffs. There was £100 advanced to the Nimrod of the Calcutta padres, the Reverend William Johnson, who was about to become the fourth husband of Hastings' old Kasimbazaar friend, Begum Watts. He could not do much for poor Hancock in person, but planned great things for his god-child, having already made over a bond on China, estimated to be worth £5000.

If his letters sound like those of a happy man, perhaps it did not spring only from his pleasure in seeing the soil turn under his ploughshare. Possibly he foresaw, perhaps had realized, the fulfilment of a dream. 'His principal favourite among the ladies', Hancock wrote rather sourly to his 'Phila', was Marian Imhoff, who 'has been very pretty, is sensible, lively, and wants only to be a greater mistress of the English language to prove she has a great share of wit'. But her husband was 'truly a German'. In October a severe letter from the Directors part-cut the knot; if Imhoff declined the military service under cover of which he had proceeded to India, he was to be sent home by the first available ship. Pictures have been painted of a triangular conclave, and a shameful bargain. We can only assemble the few ascertainable facts. The little boy Charles was sent to England in December, his father followed in February 1773, and it was given about that he would be returning to India. Rather earlier, a Madras jeweller was ordered to send eighty mother-of-pearl drops for Mrs. Imhoff. By the November following, Woodman has met the Baron in London and is arranging to pay him £1000 in two instalments; the Baron's portrait of the Governor has been presented to Mrs. Woodman. Only later was it rumoured that a divorce was being negotiated in the German courts on grounds of incompatibility, and that one Richard Johnson was managing the details.

He was away in northern Bengal from June 1772 till late September, during which time no romance or passion tinges his letters, but an indignant purpose and a political fear. He was resolved to end masks and shams. Before taking office he protested to Cartier against paying more 'tribute' to the Mogul, and to Purling against draining Bengal to keep up 'the pageantry of a mock King, an idol of our own creation'. If then we rejected Delhi, must we leave power to the Nabob of Bengal, this pageant's nominal vassal? Trade was gone, justice non-existent or an engine of corruption, the common people hideously oppressed. On this 'wild scene', — and how he recurs to this image! — 'wild as the chaos itself', nothing but the open assertion of British power could restore a constitution. The Directors left him without specific orders; very well, he would act as 'the evident spirit of their orders required', and take the golden chance of the Nabob's minority. We must habituate the people to our rule; 'it is our duty to suppose a total change of government by degrees', substituting for an illusion 'the real power which protects this country'. This would at least give the Company freedom of choice, when the minority was over.

As for the inverted pyramid of our government, where young supervisors were coining fortunes and Councillors drew meagre salaries, and the Governor had no power, Cartier had been recalled for fighting it, 'and I will be turned out too rather than suffer it to continue as it is'. Yet he might be stabbed from behind in Leadenhall Street. Time and time again he reiterated this fear of being 'sacrificed in a party accommodation', or undermined by private letters. Indeed, not a year passed before India was full of rumours that Sulivan had fallen, and that Hastings would follow him. He had a prophetic instinct that what was brewing in London would devastate his life's work.

At the Directors' election in 1772, his friends were again triumphant, for Colebrooke was once more chairman and Sulivan just scraped in as deputy. But Colebrooke's firm, ruined by crazy speculation, stopped payment, and Sulivan was broken. He owed £17,000 to the Vansittart estate and Palk, while he would be lucky indeed if he recovered anything from the equally ruined Lauchlin Macleane, and the syndicate of Lord Verney and the Burkes. In this warfare against Clive, the Sulivan group had over-driven their vessel and wrecked it.

The subsidy to government weighed on the Company, war and famine cut down their investment, they were furious at the heavy bills drawn on them from Bengal. For all that, they voted a record dividend, and early in 1772 brought the searchlights blazing on India by attacking their servants past and present. Clive above all. 'The Colonel' was being consulted by the North Cabinet, who were frightened by a threat of war from France. To head him off, the Directors threatened an enquiry into defalcations. The royal speech spoke of intervention, Clive audaciously cast back their charges with praise of himself and denunciation of their incapacity, Sulivan's effort to reach safety by a reforming bill of his own was swept away. In April, on the motion of the showy careerist Colonel John Burgoyne, the Commons appointed a Select Committee, and all the summer things went from bad to worse. Fordyce's bank went crash, the Nabob Richard Smith was said to have saved Drummonds by depositing £150,000 in notes, many members of parliament were hard hit by India stock falling sixty points in a month. Though the Bank of England refused advances, in August the Directors told the Prime Minister they must borrow a million at least.

Yet they still hoped to stave off parliament. Colebrooke, so Burke reported, was 'in a flutter of expedients'. Once more they hoped to get 'supervisors' of their own choice, and invited Burke, Amherst, Barré, and others. All alike declined; in desperation they fell back on another list chosen from their own body, whom Hastings would apparently be asked to join. In November the blow fell. North moved for a Committee of Secrecy, composed of his nearest supporters, and months of debate began to determine the whole Indian future. The King bade North be 'stiff' with them; only the Burkes and a handful of 'Indians' were on their side.

While such reports reached even the native courts of India, Hastings' papers show how fast he was clutched by these colliding forces. The root of all evil, he told Samuel Middleton, was that 'every Company's servant of whatever rank is either connected with present authority, or rising into power'; he had not 'the courage' to handle the collectors as he wished. And in the matter of presents; what should he do, for instance, with Clive's protégé, old Joey Fowke, writing so plausibly from Benares about the Rajah's generosity? 'I find it absolutely impossible to return it upon his hands without wounding him deeply'; and so gracefully accepting diamonds, shawls, and flowered silk. Worse still, the fight to the death between Mahomed Reza Khan and Nuncumar, the first of whom he had orders to convict on the evidence of the second, a hateful task which went deeper than a Moslem-Hindu struggle for power. For behind each there was a rival group of Company servants, bound to one or the other by revolutions arranged in common, or riches shared. Respected men, now comfortable in their English habitations, were involved. The English courts were about to give Nuncumar heavy damages in a suit against Burdett (who, by the by, lived on into Victoria's reign, last survivor of the Black Hole); those accused of corruption in 1765 were being haled before the House of Commons. Sykes, Hastings' oldest friend, was in an agony. Nuncumar, he reported, sent news regularly to Clive's friend Carnac and the director Gregory, — 'everything which happens and something more'. When the enquiry opened against the Naib, he appealed piteously to Hastings to see he was not implicated; protesting he had never robbed the Company, — the only question had been 'whether it should go into a black man's pocket, or my own'. The Governor reminded him later that, if he had given a free rein to the 'inquisitorial powers' for which Nuncumar asked, seven ignominious years would have been exhumed and Sykes would not have been spared.

With these harsh things in mind he sat down to thank Clive, a trifle ironically, for his 'good advice' on his appointment. 'General licentiousness', he said, had prevailed since we had accepted the *diwanni*, and given power to our servants, 'without any fixed system'. If he was to endure, he had told Sulivan, he must be given a support greater than that springing from 'the bare consideration of the public service'. He must receive 'kindness and confidence'.

CHAPTER IX

Reform of the State: 1772-74

ON April the 27th, 1772, four companies of sepoys surrounded the palace of Mahomed Reza Khan at Murshidabad; the next day Hastings announced in Council he had thus executed the Directors' secret order, and that the Naib was on his way to Calcutta, under a guard. The same steps were taken against Shitab Roy, the much-respected Naib of Bihar.

For seven years Mahomed Reza Khan had been not only Naib, the Nabob's deputy, but agent also for the British in their capacity of *diwan*, exercising therefore sovereign powers over police, justice, royal household, and finance. If his abilities were described by Hastings as 'scanty but imposing', his studied phrases and masked expression enhanced the impression of a formidable personage. Royal blood, a large Calcutta house, a library of Arabic law, and a private doctor who was alleged to have blinded a Mogul Emperor, these were other trappings of his power. Intercepted letters showed he was counting on a change in the Directorate for his restoration. Against Hastings' protest, Council deputed Graham, one of his champions, to give the Naib a deferential welcome.

What Indian then would dare to give evidence against him? Nothing would come of these retrospects, Hastings felt, they were 'death' to his plans of action, and could wait while he turned to the things that could not, — the *diwanni* and the revenue, justice, and readjustment with the Nabob and with Oudh. In May Council appointed a Committee of Circuit, with himself at its head, who in June left Calcutta to settle these fundamentals at Murshidabad. The enquiries, held up till their return in the autumn, dragged on through the next year. After fourteen months' confinement, the Naib was relieved of his guard: Shitab Roy, a dying man, was released and indeed consulted on revenue administration. Yet from Hastings' point of view this foolish prosecution had one decisive advantage.

If he so chose, he told Sykes, he could acquit Mahomed Reza Khan, and put himself 'far above the Company's resentment by making my own terms with him; but I will not forfeit my character'. Without enmity, but not thinking solely of equity, he took his resolutions. He would not choose another Naib, as the Directors recommended; the office should come to an end. To uproot every vestige of the old régime he would employ the sinister agency of Nuncumar, as he was ordered to. But not to restore the power Nuncumar had wielded under Mir Jaffir; on the contrary, he would bring about an 'entire revolution' and make Britain 'all in all'.

Moving up-country with Dacres, Lawrell, and Graham, in intense heat only slightly relieved by an earthquake, at the end of June he began a two-months' stay at Murshidabad, where Samuel Middleton reinforced them. Following the Directors' order, the Nabob's privy purse was halved and the structure of his government remodelled. As guardian and head of the household they selected, unanimously, not any rival Prince of the blood and not his mother, but the Munny Begum, another wife of Mir Jaffir. As she was an inveterate enemy of the late Naib, and as her power would end when the Nabob came of age, no other plan, Hastings argued, could give us 'so passive an administration'. Formally, though with no sepoy escort, the Committee visited the Nabob to announce their decision, which was accepted with unexpected calm. Gifts of pomegranates, ice, and melons reached the Governor, who used his arts to reconcile the two Begums.

The Munny Begum, if she had begun life as an Agra dancing girl, had a masculine sense and could distinguish friends and foes. Her vitality carried her comfortably into the next century, smoking her hookah and talking volubly to Englishmen from behind her scarlet purdah. As part of a routine which Clive and Verelst had followed before him, Hastings now accepted at her hands some £15,000 as 'entertainment money'.

There was more danger in the second part of these rearrangements. The Directors had advised him to use against the Naib his 'jealous and penetrating rival' Nuncumar, who, however, must not be allowed any serious degree of authority. He took them at their word, proposing to his Committee the name of Nuncumar's son Guru Das as *diwan* to the household, with his brother-in-law Jugath Chund, who was on bad terms with Nuncumar, as his deputy. But Middleton alone supported him, and he only got his way after a month of argument by appealing to the Council at large.

For Nuncumar's record was black as pitch. Graham and others revived the charges on which he had been arrested in 1765, of intrigue with Oudh and Benares. Two years later Verelst had censured him for conspiring with the notorious English adventurer Bolts against the equally corrupt Nobkissen. In 1770 Ducarel, collector at Purnea and an intimate of Clive, reported he was once more corresponding with Oudh, and inciting Bengal land-owners to join the Mahrattas. In his own way, no doubt, he was a patriot, forever trying to get Delhi *sunnuds* in favour of Mir Jaffir's sons, and instigating Munny Begum against English encroachment. Hastings had convicted him of forgery ten years ago; the Begum asserted that 'her' letters recently addressed to him at Madras were forged too; in 1773 the Company's seal-cutter deposed on oath he was at the same old game.

Unwilling to disclose the Directors' secret order, Hastings could only repeat that he acted, against his private instinct, on public grounds alone. 'Recollect', he told a member of Council, 'that for many years I was not only engaged on an opposite interest to Nuncumar, but was a principal instrument of detecting his intrigues'; while from the Directors he claimed, and received, approbation for thus sacrificing his own feelings. 'Under other circumstances', he minuted for his dissenting Committee, he would have agreed with them. But to Sulivan he wrote it was the one measure which could break the power of Mahomed Reza Khan, which was so great that the Directors would be 'mad' if they ever allowed him, whether innocent or guilty, to regain it.

So Guru Das was solemnly seated by the Committee in Darbar, and presented with an elephant and a pearl necklace. Hastings was confident that Nuncumar could do nothing serious against our now established power. He alluded almost kindly to his enemy, in Scrafton's phrase, as 'the old necromancer', with some sympathy for his difficulties in bringing the ex-Naib to book. He did still more. Nuncumar was being sued by one Mohan

Persad in a civil court, the president of which, a younger Robert Palk, committed him for contempt. The Governor intervened with Aldersey to stop the proceedings, bidding him tell Nuncumar 'I was much concerned at what happened'. He believed, besides, that his insistence on this appointment had been of real value, showing he could stand up to any vested interest, however strong. Now he could turn with relief to what he called his 'real business'.

He had long ago decided that revenue reform was his first duty. He would have to learn it from the rudiments upwards, for his métier had been diplomacy, and since his first days at Kasimbazaar he had spent nearly all his service in capital cities. But even in his memorandum of 1765 he had seen the fundamentals. Namely, that as compared with a territorial revenue of two million sterling, the Investment had become 'a secondary object'; the *zemindars*' 'natural and just rights'; and the necessity of long leases. On the land revenue, he perceived, hung not only the Company's solvency and payment of its armies, but the entire welfare of the common people. The famine had swept away a third of them, and for recovery he must get 'a few years of peace and quiet population'. Peace for the village where cattle might wander at will, the pigeons fly over the well, and the acrid columns of smoke ascend from each hovel at evening. That was the great matter, to be made clear to ignorant directors and greedy proprietors; somehow to be torn out of a system in ruins, and the interminable jargon of *zemindars* and *kanungoes, awdaluts* and *foudjaris, jama* and *hustobud, parganas* and *talikdars.*

They had inherited a chaos. The assessment was two centuries old, and surcharged with a jungle of arbitrary additional taxes; the peasant's exact liability was unknown, except that in practice it was infinitely more than the sum reaching the *khalsa*, or exchequer. The profits of government were intercepted by tolls and customs, or cut down by rent-free grants to temples and nobles; on any pretext, Ducarel reported, the last penny was squeezed from the cultivator by 'a chain of rogues and plunderers'. Every area had its own peculiar system of accounts. Between the *zemindars*, with a quasi-hereditary claim to act as revenue collectors, and the hereditary caste of *kanungoes* or registrars, who kept records of title and rentals, there was a conspiracy of evasion

95

which had so far baffled every British attempt to ascertain the true value, or true ownership, or true liability, of the holdings.

Working out his principles while waiting to replace Cartier, in May Hastings got them endorsed in Council, and reduced to regulations for the Committee of Circuit. Lands were to be farmed out for a five-year term. Additional 'cesses' were forbidden. As to the agency of collection, his first desire was to recall the British supervisors entirely, who had certainly falsified Verelst's hope they might become 'a nursery of administrators', and turned out, instead, trade monopolists and in Hastings' words 'sovereigns, heavy rulers of the people'. But though he felt bound to retain them under the style of 'collectors', he pointed a whole battery of prohibitions against them. An Indian *diwan*, appointed from Calcutta, would be joined with each collector. No collector might trade in grain or lend money; his *banyan* might not farm revenues; he might not employ sepoys except under rigid conditions; he should normally stay only two years in one place. The Governor might have to wait long for his ideal, of centralizing control and leaving collection wholly to Indians. But meanwhile Council itself continued as the supreme revenue Board, while he transferred from Murshidabad to Calcutta both the courts of appeal and the *khalsa*, or exchequer of accounts. This last was to be directed by an Indian on a high salary, the Roy Royan; the man chosen being Rajballabh, a rival of Nuncumar, and son to that Rai Durlab who had worked for Clive. So the symbols, like the reality, of sovereignty would be concentrated in Calcutta which, he wrote, 'I do not despair of seeing the first city in Asia'.

They had been ordered to 'stand forth as Dewan', using the agency of Company servants but, as his Committee noted, 'by what means this agency is to be exercised, we are not instructed'. It was Hastings' choice of means to fill this blank which made his work so decisive; the creation of British India by the blend of Indian forms with British aspirations. By Mogul custom, government in each province was shared between the Nabob or Nazim, with powers political and military and covering criminal justice, and the *diwan*, controlling civil justice and revenue. Through delegation, Moslem-Hindu divisions, and usurpation a mass of minor jurisdictions had grown up, in the hands of *zemindars*, registrars, Moslem muftis, and Hindu pundits, every

officer in fact doing justice who had the force. The British
acceptance of the *diwanni* had deepened this anarchy, for their
power inhibited the courts of the *Nizamut*, their young supervisors
were so powerful that justice became a matter of buying the
favour of their *banyans*, while the Company forbade the taking
up of the *diwanni's* proper province of civil justice. Only the rich
or the vagabond reached the supreme courts at Murshidabad;
armed force, beatings, and kidnappings terrorized every village.

Hastings drew a firm line through this welter. His Committee's plan of justice, compiled in August, set up in each district
a civil (*diwanni*) and a criminal (*foudjari*) court, the first presided
over by the collector attended by his *diwan*, while in the second
the judges were Indians, though the collector had a power of
review. *Zemindars* and revenue farmers were left only the right
of settling petty disputes, without punitive powers. At Calcutta
he established two corresponding *Sudder* or appeal courts, the
civil presided over by a member of Council, and the *Nizamut*
under Indian judges, yet leaving the last word to the President
in Council.

Here, he confessed, was an encroachment. But while he
opened this *Nizamut* court with all ceremony and made it his
practice to leave to its judges a free choice of their subordinates,
his intention was firm and his expression of it ruthless. Ancient
forms were decent, but 'no treaties nor casuistical distinctions'
should deprive the people of protection by 'the sovereign power'.
Though 'the popular current' at home might pounce on this
stretch of authority, he insisted on keeping this power of review,
above all in capital cases. From a careful study of Moslem law,
he found much of it 'barbarous'. He bade Middleton tell the
Begum that, though he had 'as much of the milk of human
kindness as she can have', he meant to crush murder. His
legislation on this head, in fact, smacked of ancient Rome, or
the Russia of Peter the Great. Murderers, if not executed, were
to be sold as slaves. Dacoits should be executed in their home
villages, all the inhabitants of which should be fined. After all,
dacoity had come as near Calcutta as Hugli, where their leaders'
bodies could be seen hanging on trees.

While from June till September he stayed at Kasimbazaar,
we see in his Committee's measures the revelation of their
ignorance, the sheer limitations on what they could achieve, and

their conception of what things came first. Now, and for ten years to come, every expert, Middleton or Vansittart or Dacres, made the famine the radical cause of revenue decline. Inflated grain prices encouraged the farmers to set their tenders too high; survivors had been mercilessly taxed to keep up the total. Yet they themselves unquestionably made too severe an assessment. If it were 'unavoidably arbitrary', as Middleton said, since they had no time to get at the facts, he also spoke of our 'unrelenting rigour' in collection. Hastings, again, had every intention of giving the old landowners a priority, the *zemindar* being on his view 'the natural guardian of the people's rights'. And in the frontier province of Midnapore their loyalty to the Company was well rewarded. But elsewhere, confronted by collusive low bidding and with one eye on their honourable masters at home, the Committee introduced auction of the revenue farms, with dire results. Old families outbid their means in order to avoid disgrace, while speculators ran prices up in prospect of profit and social status.

Long leases had already worked well in Burdwan, and in the next years Vansittart and others pleaded for leases for lives, or even for a permanent settlement. But the Board decided it was too hazardous, there must be a period of experiment to find the 'medium rent', on which a permanent settlement could be built.

Whatever their mistakes, and they were serious, the foundations were truly laid. Longer leases, even if in the wrong hands, were better than the Mogul annual assessment. With suggestions from Sulivan from his Bombay experience, they rearranged areas in manageable collectorates. They abolished taxes on marriage and a host of other extortions. They routed out a mass of lands made 'rent free' by sheer usurpation. They avowed at least the principle that neither Europeans nor their *banyans* should hold farms. By every device in their power they would protect the peasant. In his *pottah*, or agreement with the farmer or *zemindar*, his liability was to be precisely defined. A box for petitioners hung outside every collector's office. They formally invited allegations of wrongdoing in Company servants.

Almost imperceptibly the spirit of what Hastings always called 'the service' was changing. These profiteers in salt or opium, ardent as ever to retire in affluence, are found pleading for the man on the soil. 'My ryots', wrote Thomas Pattle, were greedily using the new district courts. Rent remissions should have been made immediately after the famine; drought and great floods in turn had broken down the frail margin between subsistence and starvation, our drain of money 'without proportionable returns' was deadly; so spoke the 'Nabobs', Ducarel and Dacres and Hosea.

These springs set in motion, and leaving his colleagues to finish the settlement, Hastings came back to Calcutta late in September, staying there until in June 1773 he left for a momentous visit to Oudh. There were all the final touches to be put to the new revenue schemes and law courts. One of his protégés, Charles Croftes, was made accountant-general; young Alexander Elliot, with his good knowledge of Persian, became superintendent of the *khalsa*. Very resentfully, when he had a spare moment, he attempted the 'endless researches' the Directors ordered; whether, for instance, the very able collector of Hugli, Lushington, had misbehaved in the famine, or their calls for the production of papers, already 'either regularly transmitted, or which are not in being'. The case of Mahomed Reza Khan dragged on; cross-examining and interpreting himself, the Governor only missed one day of all the hearings, listening to Nuncumar's 'multiplied but indefinite suggestions'. Yet his private sympathies might be guessed by his inviting the accused's family to his Christmas party. Of Shitab Roy's innocence he never had a doubt, restoring him to office on his acquittal. When the old man died immediately after, Council named his son as successor, and minuted their defiant tribute, 'that he ever served the Company with a fidelity, integrity, and ability which they can hardly expect to experience in any future officer of government'. All this time the Board of Inspection pushed on departmental economies and a more severe audit of collectors' accounts, so much so that young John Shore, in after-days the most religious of Governors-General, wrote home that Hastings was making a lucrative career impossible.

He was well aware that his measures must be given time and years of peace, constantly warning his correspondents they must expect a temporary drop in revenue. The long-term remedy, he argued, was to open the pores of trade, so making up for reduction in taxes and loss of specie; for, if encouraged, Bengal was 'capable of supplying the markets both of Europe and Asia'. Many times he denounced the 'vassalage' of the country weavers, telling Barwell that he would like to throw open the country trade to all, Indian or foreign, 'were I sovereign of this country'. But 'I am fortunately curbed, and prevented from carrying my evil designs into execution'.

As it was, he was under orders to abolish the *dustuk*, which he did with alacrity, and to return from the *gomastah* or agency system for the investment to competitive contracts, which he much disliked. In Madras he had arranged precisely the opposite, believing that rings of Indian merchants would turn out just as pure monopolists as collectors' *gomastahs*. He put much more stock, plainly, in his reform of the Customs service, drawn up for him by the accused Lushington. A Board at Calcutta in sole control, and five customs houses only instead of the countless *chokeys* which had blocked free movement both by road and river, this was the framework. Excepting the two special cases of opium and salt, all goods, the Company's investment included, would pay a uniform duty of $2\frac{1}{2}$ per cent. Freedom might mean temporarily higher prices, but this 'most rational way', he predicted, would enhance both customs and land revenue, and make Bengal the mart of the north.

As to salt, he had come round to Clive's way of thinking, though then 'the dose was too strong', and returned to the Mogul system of a government monopoly, giving five-year leases to farmers. But though he made an increasing profit, salt was to have a long, contentious, and harsh history. No industry was more easily abused. The producers, the Molungis, were a low and ignorant caste, work was scattered in the innumerable creeks and waterways of Bengal, while the cash advances and book balances involved made ideal avenues for fraud.

Years after he claimed that his early regulations embraced 'every department of the service', a boast which the astonishing array of 1773–74 fully supports. He created a postal service, running as far as Patna north-west and Dacca to the east. He backed Rennell's completion of his geographical surveys, himself sending in detail of rivers and by-ways. He set about restoring trade relations with Jedda and Egypt. He was discussing precautions against famine, public granaries for example, which came to life later. Currency troubles were more arduous. A deluge of many coinages from many mints, — sicca rupees, Delhi rupees, gold mohurs, — without alloy and annually produced without control, confused all values, and allowed every rascal shroff to jockey with brokerage and commission. Gresham's law, that bad money drives out good, and the Indian love of hoarding silver for rings and bracelets, exhausted the specie. Government had to bring down its provincial revenues 'with the destructive parade of military escorts', merchants' remittances requiring peons and boats and guards against dacoits. As a palliative, he therefore established a Bank to receive collections by bills on Calcutta, fixed a standard rupee, and confined coinage to the Calcutta mint. He stopped the issue of notes to pay for the investment, and in two years almost extinguished the bonded debt; the rate of interest was reduced from 8 to 5 per cent, though characteristically he demurred to this as taking advantage of individuals' necessity.

A second stage in his reforms was marked by the Directors' orders of April 1773, on which he took action that autumn. True, they approved the changes he had made in the Nabob's administration and gave him almost *carte blanche*, — 'we now arm you with our full powers to make a complete reformation'. But the austere gentlemen of Leadenhall Street were shocked at their servants' extravagance; 'even youths in our service expend on equipage, servants, dress and living infinitely more than our stated allowances can afford'. Which was not surprising. Still, it was the heyday of the lovely and amiable Miss Sanderson, in whose honour sixteen admirers, each thinking himself the happy man, attended a ball in her 'livery', of a pea-green French frock with pink silk trimmings. So now the Directors ordered all collectors to be withdrawn, telling Hastings to substitute 'some other plan', pending receipt of their final regulations, — which never materialized.

This, he wrote to the chairman, opened 'a scene for great improvements', a plan for 'a length of years to come'. But though his own ideal was unchanged of withdrawing Europeans from the districts entirely, to which end Council outlined a permanent plan, after many meetings they agreed that this ideal must wait: time must be allowed to get the law courts and accounts system into better shape, and to train Indian subordinates. They had suffered too much already in his view from innovations, for 'every habit of longstanding naturally becomes rooted to the constitution, and cannot be parted from it without some danger'. Ordering, therefore, the collectors to withdraw on winding up their accounts, they grouped their districts in six Provincial Councils, each headed by a member of Council, which would be responsible for the revenue and hear civil appeals. Each Council would have an Indian *diwan*, while an Indian *naib* would control collections and civil justice in each previous collector's district.

It is plain how much Hastings disliked this temporary plan, which he had positive orders to produce. He predicted it meant tyranny; to restrain collectors had been hard enough, and how much more to curb members of Council! His regulations therefore forbade any covenanted servant to engage in trade in grain, betel, and other necessities of life, and prohibited the new chiefs of the Councils from trading at all. But he took this opportunity to rub in his familiar moral, 'the servants of the Company are not exempted from the frailties and wants of humanity'. To free them from temptation and incite them, each chief was to have a yearly salary of 36,000 rupees; with 'that respectful reliance which we ought to repose in your justice', he declared that only lack of authority from home prevented him from recommending higher salaries for junior servants also. Enough money would be available, since he had decided to take over opium as a government monopoly. That his work was effectual was proved by officials grumbling, that the compensation was inadequate: 'a severe loss to all us Patna folk,' wrote Robert Palk, 'for there is not one article of trade left us but salt and Europe articles, which barely bring us the full interest on our money'.

The collectors' withdrawal, and the violence of dacoity, impelled him to a further change, an experimental restoration of the Mogul *foudjars*, or local officers of police. His own reforms, demanding conviction by two witnesses, made it nearly impossible to sentence dacoits, who worked by night and took regular black-mail off many villages. Though 'repugnant to the equity and tenderness of our own constitution', he consequently recommended that we should convict dacoits on mere notoriety of character, as had the Moguls, — and for that matter, the Angevins.

Through such encumbering detail, amid dubious experiments

and inconceivable obstruction, he persisted in his ideal of restoring the best in Indian custom. Ten leading Brahmin pundits were called to Calcutta, to codify in Sanskrit their legal principles, thence to be translated into Persian, and then into English under direction of Nathaniel Halhed. In sending the first extracts to the Directors and to Lord Mansfield, he referred with alarm to persistent reports of 'an unadvised system' of law for Bengal being compiled at home. The way 'to rule this people with ease and moderation' was to leave them what 'time and religion had rendered familiar to their understandings and sacred to their affections'; this was the right of 'a great nation', not any 'superior wisdom' imposed from outside.

Men must be given time and shown mercy, and he felt his own integrity unimpaired. He bade Vansittart tell his *banyan* Cantoo either to quit his service or wind up his financial transactions. Yet Cantoo did neither. Miles of dusty rolls in offices riddled by white ants, the most subtle race on earth juggling with figures in local dialects, rival legal systems played against one another, concealed contractings and commissions, how could a Governor cut through them all? Perchance he could, were he given the power.

After eighteen months of office, he wrote to his honourable masters in firm, almost defiant, proud but ingenuous tones. He was 'at a loss for words' to express his sense of their 'applause'; 'if I know my own heart', no bias should divert him from their interests. Yet he must tell them they had laid on him a fruitless task in the prosecution of Mahomed Reza Khan on unprovable charges; it 'can do no real good', it might expose them both in India and England to 'the ruinous consequences of personal malevolence'. The Naib must go free, but let him not ever be restored to power.

'There can be but one government and one power in this Province.' The Nabob, he tells Sykes, 'is a mere name'; and to Sulivan, the Company's authority is fixed in 'every branch of the State, unshakeable if your administration is well supported at home'. For all that, government was loose, and his own control 'accidental'. Had he forgotten, he asked Colebrooke, the fate of Henry Vansittart? Powers of peace and war must be vested in the Select Committee, but the President should be enabled to go direct to Council on these or any other subjects. He must be given a 'discretionary power', to act in 'urgent and extraordinary cases', against both Committee and Council; with a veto and right of recall, 'even without a reason assigned', on civil appointments. His reasons, much the same as those Strafford had once given in Ireland, were not likely to be commendable to his countrymen. Their own 'distant and slow' action could not cope with disorder. 'A principle of vigour, activity, and decision must rest somewhere', but in a body it lost force, and most of all in a small body. Only by being 'fixed to a single point' could it ensure 'continuity'.

He laid his cards on the Directors' table even more boldly. At some period, 'not far distant', such powers would assuredly be given. He asked them for himself, for he hoped to hold office 'for years to come'. It was 'an honourable ambition' ('a chaste ambition', Strafford had called it); he too could make quick money like his predecessors, but hoped 'the constant tenor of my conduct' would free him from such a suspicion. 'I feel my mind expand to something greater. I have catched the desire of applause in public life.' Were there not grounds for a longer term? The Vizier had asked how, with frequent changes of Governor, he could pledge the Company's faith. And 'innovations of real use' demanded time, 'the unremitted application of their original principles'. 'Who that looks only for present applause, or present credit, would hazard both for remote advantages?'; moreover, 'no man can have an equal interest in the success of any new system with the author of it'. To Sulivan he added a still more daring word. 'I do not know a man who may be more safely entrusted with extraordinary powers than myself.'

So he thought, while with Marian he watched his new house at Alipur take on its white polished surface, or with Charles Croftes took his leisure up the river in the bungalow at Sooksagur, where they experimented in silk-making, coffee-growing, and other fancies. He was still the English exile, getting honeysuckle and sweet-briar from home for his garden, yet his philosophy of motives seems to be changing. A respect for realities, a loathing of force, a benevolent belief in an upward path for men and nations, passion overruled by purpose, these were making him the enlightened but determinate eighteenth-century ruler. Things must be kept in ordered proportion. The French, he thus reports, were asking for their factories 'unreasonable and distressing' pretensions, asserted in 'very provoking' ways. And how he abominated militarism! He told Bogle, whom he was sending to explore Tibet, there were 'thousands of men in England' who would listen to the story of an expedition 'in search of knowledge', with 'ten times' the interest they would take in 'victories that slaughtered thousands of the national enemies'. Despite his championship of Indian law, he allowed that they lacked our advantages of 'a free exertion of the understanding, and an opposition of opinions'. As in private life he treated Indians with the same courtesy as his own people, so his papers never apply a different standard, or speak of 'black agents' like Clive. On and off in these first two years, he had to conduct a little frontier war against the Bhutanese, yet found this primitive enemy 'much more sincere, liberal, and polite' than they all expected.

He had revolutionized the character of Bengal. 'The eyes of the people will be turned to Calcutta', his Committee of Circuit claimed, 'as the centre of government, and to the Company as their sovereign.' The 'mother country' would open up new channels of trade: Indian civilization 'will by degrees assimilate with ours, and breed a kind of new relation and attachment to us'. Nothing could be done, however, if there were instability at home. He was aware of Colebrooke's fall, and feared 'the quiet unimportant issue' over Mahomed Reza Khan might raise a new clamour. But the despatches arriving early in 1774 brought tidings much worse than this, announcing in effect that the Company's control of India had been destroyed.

Lord North's legislation of 1773 sprang from the reports of Burgoyne's Select Committee and the Secret Committee of his own choosing, followed by furious debates when Clive and Sulivan attacked each other. 'A few envious and resentful individuals', Clive wrote loftily to Hastings; in actual fact, the King was severe on his 'rapine', and though he escaped a censure, most ministers voted against him. But the Company and its elections were become matters of party. At the April election Sulivan was thrown out; 'Sandwich erected the standard', he wrote, and Boulton was brought in as chairman by ministerial and Clive interest. Only the appointment of Lauchlin Macleane as commissary-general in India lightened the Sulivan horizon. True, he was borrowing money off Miss Barwell, but much might be hoped from a commissary's opportunities. If the Opposition, led by the Duke of Richmond, Dempster, and the Burkes, were defending chartered rights, Hastings gathered from his friend Caillaud that it was only a mask for party purposes.

So the Company got their large loan, but at a ruinous price. Their dividend was limited to 6 per cent till the loan was repaid, their surplus receipts were earmarked for the Exchequer, their territories were guaranteed only for six years. The Regulating Act doubled the qualification for a proprietor's vote, raising it to £1000 of stock; instead of annual elections, one-fourth of the Directors would retire each year. It appointed a Governor-General of Bengal on a salary of £25,000, with four Councillors at £10,000 apiece, with powers of 'superintending' Madras and Bombay, save in cases of 'imminent necessity' or special orders from the Company. It appointed also a Supreme Court in Bengal, with jurisdiction of all sorts over 'all British subjects', and a power of approving the Council's legislation. It gave the Governor-General only a casting vote. It wholly forbade taking of presents or inland trading. Despatches from India were to be submitted to the Treasury or a Secretary of State.

There were several competitors for the post of the first Governor-General. At one moment Sykes reported that Rumbold, once Clive's aide de camp at Plassey, would get it, having come down handsomely with loans to Colebrooke. Lord Pigot, most oriental of ex-Governors of Madras, had his pocket members; there was some support for Du Pré. But it seems quite soon to have been settled for Hastings. Sulivan saw to it that his letters reached the ministers who, having got their way, would not reject Sulivan votes. North praised in debate his abilities and application, and as a man who had 'resisted the greatest temptations'. The pillar of the Select Committee, and leader of the Court members, Jenkinson, admitted afterwards he had been much impressed and 'contributed greatly' to the result. Everyone who knew the facts, loyal Caillaud wrote, was pleased, though 'I know that praise is painful to your nature'.

Perhaps he got an early hint from a fever-stricken Lauchlin Macleane, who reached Bengal late in 1773, armed with Sulivan's introduction, as formerly 'under-secretary of State, Lieutenant-Governor of St. Vincent's, member of parliament, and in affluence, — alas, what a reverse!' But Macleane had his own aspirations, even to be a member of Council. Even in March 1774 Hastings knew nothing except that he was to be Governor, and his old school-fellow Impey to be Chief Justice. His letters sound ill at ease. What with the new provincial councils and the recriminations about Mahomed Reza Khan, intrigue and compromise were blowing up an ill wind.

He was troubled most, baffled it would seem, by Nuncumar, 'whose gratitude', he told the Directors, 'no kindness can bind', persistent in 'the crooked politics which have been the study and practice of his whole life'. In the civil courts a case was dragging on, which Hastings tried to accelerate, and in which Nuncumar was accused of forgery. Our resident wrote that Guru Das would get on all right with Munny Begum but 'for that old fox, the father', and the Governor ordered that Nuncumar's letters to Murshidabad should go through Middleton's hands; 'one consideration alone (you know what I mean) prevents my securing him effectually'. But what did he mean? Perhaps his refusal of Nuncumar's request, to be allowed 'a personal and local inquisition' into his rival's accounts.

It was not a clear sky, then, when he told Sulivan that, being left without authentic news, he would continue 'as I have always done, to act as if no alternations were expected'. And in it one dark cloud, of the Rohilla war.

CHAPTER X

Northern India and the Rohilla War

BOTH the historical fame of Hastings and the darkest charges against him depend, in great part, on the British relation to Indian States. The problem was new and arduous, but nowhere was the weakness of the Company and parliament so glaring, or so disastrous their compound of ignorance and faction. And nowhere were his own qualities so vividly revealed, or so fast matured. Here he showed, on a canvas that all the world could see, his resolution, his unmeasured resource, and clear vision of the future. Here also, however, appeared that strain of living dangerously, an autocracy in his use of agents, and an obstinacy in representing the picture as he wished it to be.

Formally, till the Regulating Act took effect at the end of 1774, and in practice long after, the three Presidencies had different policies and some conflicting interests. Happenings at Delhi had little or no importance for Madras or Bombay, whereas to Bengal they were paramount. Mahratta aggression was held out by the Company as the greatest of dangers; yet they had instructed Bombay to negotiate with the Mahrattas for the acquisition of Salsette and Bassein, while at Madras the royal agents had done their utmost, aided by the Nabob and his creditors, to push that Presidency into a Mahratta alliance against Hyder Ali. Formally, again, the Directors had enjoined strict neutrality as between Indian States, and forbidden all offensive war. But recent despatches allowed that emergencies might arise, demanding some discretionary power for men on the spot, and promised to send their matured decision. Which, as was their habit, they never fulfilled.

Since the great battle of Panipat in 1761, the primary events had been the collapse of the Mogul Empire and the astonishing recovery of the Mahrattas. Though fears of new invasions over the Himalayas died away, Delhi had been fighting for its life, both against rebel Moslems such as the Rohillas, and against its Hindu enemies, Jats and Mahrattas and Sikhs. Imperial rule had dwindled to a fragment. Afghans had come as far east as the Sutlej; northwards, the Sikhs hemmed in Lahore; Rohillas lined the north bank of the Ganges, and were contesting with the Mahrattas and Oudh the rich plain of the Doab, between Ganges and Jumna. Look out from Delhi Fort south across the Jumna, and to the west the Rajputs had made themselves free, while eastwards the Jats had taken Agra, the second city of the Empire. Nadjif-ud-Daulah, the Rohilla left by Ahmad Abdali as custodian of Delhi, died in 1769, when the Emperor had been four years an English pensioner at Allahabad.

His Madras experience had persuaded Hastings that the Mahrattas were the enemy to dread. In November 1772 the heroic Peishwa Mahdoo Rao died of consumption, aged twenty-eight, and his widow burned herself on his pyre. His much weaker brother was assassinated within the year and succeeded by their uncle Ragoba, in whose interest this military conspiracy had been made, and who for thirty years past had led forays over central India, a chivalrous impulsive soldier, dominated by a hateful vindictive wife. But when Hastings reached Calcutta, things had looked very different. Mahdoo Rao had stripped Hyder Ali of half his conquests, even of Bangalore, and brought the Mahratta frontier to march with the northern bounds of the Madras Presidency. He had humiliated a rebel of his own race, the Bhonsla Rajah of Berar, whose descent from Sivaji gave him some claim to the supremacy. He defeated the wiles of the treacherous Nizam. Then he renewed the Mahratta drive to the North.

There were no nations in India and, except for the penniless exile Shah Allum, nothing left in existence, whose title went back much over fifty years. The Persian family ruling in Oudh only dated their power to 1720; much about the same time as the territory west of them was seized by the Rohilla chiefs, who were Pathans from the region of Kandahar. The Oudh rulers were Shiah, but the Rohillas orthodox Sunnis; religion therefore as well as ambition divided the first from the Rohillas and from other Afghans settled in the Doab. For many years now these rival Moslems had played the dangerous game of enlisting Mahrattas to fight one another.

The new Mahratta surge to the North was led by great warriors, the experienced Holkar and Mahdoo Rao Scindia, whom Hastings was to find the most subtle of Indian princes. Though illegitimate, he alone survived of his house, going lame from a wound received at Panipat, which he was sworn to revenge. After plundering Rajputs and Jats, they expelled the Rohillas from the Doab, and in February 1771 captured Delhi, to which Shah Allum returned the December following, against English advice. Early in 1772 they attacked Zabita Khan, son of the late Rohilla minister of the Empire. Since the Ganges' upper reaches were no barrier in dry weather, they crossed the fords with 90,000 men and ravaged Rohilkund. Nothing now separated them from Oudh, whose Nabob was thinking of a bargain with them, and if Oudh collapsed they would reach Bengal. The captive Emperor empowered them to occupy Allahabad and Korah, which Clive had assigned to him.

All Hastings' actions must be determined by the manifest failure of Clive's treaty of 1765. Were his grant of the Allahabad area and an annual tribute from Bengal to stand, when both had passed out of the Emperor's hands into those of the Mahrattas? Hastings instantly protested to Cartier against the tribute. This 'mock King', this 'idol of our own creation', should not bleed Bengal of £325,000 a year. We did not hold the *diwanni* by his 'piece of paper', but by 'the best of all titles, power'. And 'this King of shreds and patches' was trifling with us like the Nabob of the Carnatic, sending in 'insolent propositions' through a British adventurer, to transfer his friendship from the Company to the Crown.

It was even more urgent to get a better relation with Oudh, our immediate neighbour. Shuja-ud-Daulah, Nabob since 1754, like his father was also Vizier or minister of the Empire; though he had a hereditary feud with the Rohillas, he had saved them once from the Mahrattas and, after some hesitation, had come out on the Moslem side at Panipat. Despite his profligacy and his harem of eight hundred women, this handsome courageous prince was a shifty active politician. He had taken his fling in backing Mir Kasim, but Clive had wisely restored all his territories, except for the grant of Allahabad to the Emperor. If his artillery and growing army alarmed some English soldiers, Hastings thought it needless; 'the sure way to make a man your enemy, whether in public or private life, is to believe him one'. On the contrary, the Vizier could not stand without us, and if he fell Bengal was in imminent danger. Yet in practice this valuable alliance was in all ways unsatisfactory. Our military men treated the Vizier with suspicion and took large profits for themselves. Almost every year he asked help from our troops, but by treaty he was only obliged to pay their 'extra' expenses, which meant a heavy loss. And the clause of Clive's treaty allowing the Company to trade duty-free had been a dead letter, the Vizier realizing from Mir Kasim's tragedy what 'freedom of trade' meant with British agents.

These were good grounds for treaty revision. But what immediately faced Hastings was the fear that the Mahratta torrent might overflow into Oudh and that an appeal might come from the Vizier for our assistance, as bound by treaty. If we failed him, he must either accept the Mahratta offer of partitioning the Rohilla lands, or fall to a Mahratta-Rohilla combination.

There was nothing sacrosanct about the Rohillas. They had entered the Empire, said Akbar's chronicler, 'like ants and locusts', numbering it seems less than 50,000 souls, who ruled several million Hindus by the sword. Their present leader, Hafiz Rahmat Khan, had won his place by usurping the rights of a young kinsman, Fyzullah Khan, whom he was sworn to cherish. The sad confusion among Whig partisans between this Hafiz and the famous poet of Persia was no better grounded than their panegyric on Rohilla arts and civilization. Burke called them 'the most honourable nation upon earth', — Fox, 'the only free people in India', and all this was nonsense; much truer was Hastings' picture of a military tribe who 'quartered themselves upon the people'. His predecessor Verelst dwelt on Hafiz' cunning and deceit, and certain it is that in any scene of blood in this expiring Mogul society the Rohillas took a natural lead. Shah Allum had this year turned the Mahrattas on to attack Zabita Khan, who had debauched his sister; sixteen years later, it was Zabita's son who blinded Shah Allum.

It is thus not surprising that Hastings' early attitude was to listen unconcerned to reports of a proposed partition of Rohilkund between the Mahrattas and Oudh. His first measure was to stop Barker pushing forward troops to support the Vizier, and plainly he was displeased at his assuming the role of mediator. This treaty of June 1772, which Barker countersigned, was no work of his; binding the allies to expel the Mahrattas, and the Rohillas to pay the Vizier forty lacs for his assistance. In later days he was to argue that Barker's signature committed the British as guarantor; at the moment, however, he wrote to Barwell that 'the General and his coadjutor' were imperilling our political system, and that step by step the Vizier was leading us into 'an unnecessary breach with the Mahrattas'. That would mean financial strain in Bengal and grave embarrassment to Madras; he would have no hand, he told Du Pré, in an offensive war.

Meantime Zabita Khan was reconciled to the Mahrattas, the Vizier feared Hafiz would follow suit, and by the autumn the Emperor had promised the enemy possession of Allahabad, the key of the Ganges line and portcullis to the Doab. Yet the same reluctance marked the British counsels. In November the Select Committee informed the Directors that the Vizier was being tempted to 'extirpate' his old enemy Hafiz Rahmat Khan, which would be 'little consistent with prudence or equity'. At this date Hastings was even unwilling to fight for Korah, believing the Mahrattas' internal troubles would tide over this crisis.

Oudh, however, was our outer guard, and the Vizier was behaving well. He had made over to us, with good grace, the important fort of Chunar, and promised to dismiss his foreign soldier of fortune, Gentili; not an insignificant matter, when a more famous Frenchman, Madec, had just joined the Mogul under instructions from Chandernagore. And as the Mahrattas were once more on the fords of the Ganges, in February 1773 the Council decided to defend Korah, and to include Rohilkund in our 'defensive line'. Yet nothing could be more guarded than Barker's instructions. After arranging for the defence of Korah, he was to offer our alliance to Hafiz but, whether he was friendly or hostile, to protect Rohilkund against the Mahrattas. Under no circumstances was he to move south of the Ganges.

Sulky under instructions which he vowed lost us a golden chance of routing the enemy, the Commander-in-Chief reported that the Vizier offered fifty lacs 'on the nail', if we would help him to take Hafiz' country, while his next despatches, when the Mahrattas had dispersed, certainly proved the Vizier had something on his side. Hafiz had sent the Mahrattas money and nearly joined them in the field, only force would make the

Rohillas disgorge the subsidy they had promised to the Vizier, 'neither promises nor oaths have been able to bind this treacherous sect of people'. Officially he was told it was 'not discreet to create new enemies', nor should we dream of giving Oudh help, except for a valuable equivalent. But Hastings wrote privately he would like to see it done, sooner or later, 'on grounds of public justice', and to Colebrooke in England spoke of 'tempting offers'.

The same week of April he replied to the Vizier's appeal: that he had 'long thought' it essential to bind the Rohilla country to Oudh, whether by permanent treaty or by war, to make the Ganges throughout its length a defensible frontier. But it could not be held by occasional punitive expeditions, or at the ruinous cost to the Company hitherto involved. To find a solution he proposed an early meeting, and on June the 24th left Calcutta.

By road and river he made a slow progress, held back by 'foul winds, violent currents, and separation of our fleet'. He had to meet the young Nabob of Bengal at Plassey, whom he found much improved by Munny Begum's care, his 'awkward and unpolished' manners almost gone. There was the Begum herself to see at Murshidabad, and her petulance to endure on a hint about her jealous treatment of Guru Das. And so, after inspection of Monghyr Fort, revenue collections round Patna, and Dinapore cantonments, at last to Benares, reached only on August 19th. Of his Council, George Vansittart and Lambert were with him, while by flooded roads and slow-moving budgerow General Barker came to join them.

The General, in fact, was his worst stumbling-block. Inheriting the Clive outlook, he suspected the Vizier's loyalty and believed a bargain could be struck with the Emperor; putting in a claim, too, to be present at every meeting, as Carnac had been with Clive. All this was anathema to Hastings, who told Sulivan 'I wish to make the Vizier depend on government and not on the military power, and I want to open a free trade with the Vizier's dominions, which are now subject to a military monopoly'. And this he made clear to Sir Robert, who after much silence announced he would resign before the next campaign. Generally speaking, then, Hastings conferred alone with the Vizier, whose 'very clear and easy elocution, and an uncommonly quick apprehension', made it easy. Duly they exchanged their gifts; he noted giving, as 'not charged to the Company', a string of pearls, Chinese carpets, and 2000 yards of velvet. When Shuja-ud-Daulah pursed his lips or stroked his whiskers, it denoted a crisis, but they parted friends, — the Vizier requesting an exchange of one of the Governor's hats in return for his turban.

Many years later, defending himself before the House of Commons, he spoke of a 'natural gradation' of events, entangling us in what was essentially a defensive war. 'Natural' was perhaps hardly the right word. The wording of his diary in 1773, many expressions to his Council, and protests against the new Councillors of 1774, converge to one overriding conclusion; that originally he cared nothing for the Rohilla war, — though equally nothing for the Rohillas — and used it only as a means to greater ends. He accepted it, his diary says, rather for 'the indirect advantages which were to be drawn from it than from any great opinion which I had conceived of the expedition itself'. It was 'the means of purchasing the Vizier's compliance in . . . the principal object of my commission', — this in November to his Council; it was 'the allurement', 'the instrument', for getting the Vizier's consent to pay the full expenses of our troops, and his words 'encouraged it' must be taken as the language of negotiation, not as 'my real sentiments'. And indeed his letter to Hafiz stands on record, urging him to pay the Vizier what he owed.

The Benares conversations seem to bear out this view of his original motive. When the Vizier promptly raised the subject, Hastings replied he saw no objection except the expense. When the Vizier, again, pondered whether he could not stir up the Rohillas to attack the Mahrattas and then intervene when both were weakened, he 'commended the project'. Asked if he would advise some financial compromise with the Rohillas, he answered 'take what he could', but reserve the deficiency 'as a fair pretence for any future design'. Such notes in his diary hardly entitle him to be acquitted in morals; they are certainly some way removed from the emphasis developed under later attack, that the war was just, waged against a 'perfidious leader', and 'for recovering the rights of nations'.

His instructions, he rightly noted, were not 'fixed to any specific terms', but put in the forefront our relations with Oudh, the Emperor, and Benares. When he accepted in principle a

Rohilla war, the first two problems made little difficulty. As the Emperor was asked to send a representative and failed to do so, he was disregarded; Hastings entirely refusing to allow Company troops to fight south of the river, to win for him some compensation in the Doab. The major question was the future of Allahabad and Korah. And as the Vizier passionately wished to recover them, and the Company as ardently wanted to save them from the Mahrattas but would find them burdensome to garrison themselves, an agreement to restore them to Oudh was quickly reached. But for what equivalent? He was instructed to ask in exchange for the rich lands of Benares and Ghazipur on our frontier, but seeing the Vizier's repugnance, — 'I knew the pain it would give him' — he concentrated instead on a massive equivalent in money, and an advantageous military treaty.

So it became a fortnight of strenuous Oriental haggling. Shuja-ud-Daulah contested every revenue estimate, stressed his danger from Mahratta and Mogul resentment, and even more his forty-nine expensive children. The Governor held his own stoutly; finally getting fifty lacs for the Allahabad area, a doubling of the subsidy whenever the Vizier called in our brigades, and another forty lacs for the Rohilla war, if it materialized. This last was to be paid, whether the expedition ended in a conquest or an 'accommodation'. As to free trade with Oudh, he could not overcome the Vizier's horror of our agents, but by arranging with Benares that our cloth and metals should be sold duty-free at Mirzapur, achieved much the same result.

On Benares itself he stood firm. 'Rajah' Chait Singh was really a *zemindar*, illegitimate son of a self-made Brahmin official from the Bihar frontier. In the troubles of Mir Kasim, and the war ending at Buxar, the father had played a tough unscrupulous hand, and Clive confirmed his title, the interposition of a Hindu magnate between us and the Vizier making a better balance. But now the Vizier wanted to make Benares his own, or at the lowest to increase its tribute and seize its strongest forts. Hastings would not hear of it. He confirmed Chait Singh's status in return for a fixed revenue, arranged that he should hold 1000 cavalry ready for the Company's service in need, obtained his assent to the free market at Mirzapur, and ordered all Englishmen out of Benares except three approved diamond merchants, two of them being our old acquaintances Thomas Motte and Joseph Fowke.

Before they separated, the Vizier declared that on financial grounds he must postpone a Rohilla war. Hastings undertook to support it, when and if he brought it forward again, but said he felt a repugnance, 'both on account of its distance, the uncertainty whether such a plan would be approved by the Company, and the uncertain duration of it'. It was therefore not mentioned in the treaty. Not that Hastings concealed it. The conference proceedings were daily communicated to the Councillors with him; this was followed up by private letters to Sulivan and Colebrooke, a full minute for his Council, and finally by a copy of his journal sent to Palk, to be seen by Sulivan, Colebrooke, and Du Pré. But not by others; 'unless you judge it may do me service, which I do not think it will, except with those who wish me well already'.

He came back to Calcutta in October, well pleased but perfectly aware he had taken 'a great risk'. Even on the way up his diary noted the rumours of 'national clamours' against the Company's servants, and the 'virulence of popular odium', adding 'it is now too late to retract'. To his first Board meeting he emphasized all they had won, — repudiation of the Delhi tribute, a safe frontier, financial salvation, and alliance between Oudh and the Mahrattas made 'morally impossible'. He asked power to name, and recall, a resident at Lucknow, selecting Nathaniel Middleton as the first. As to the Rohilla war, he was 'pleased' that it was dropped, yet the Vizier had just complaints, and 'there are powerful arguments to recommend it'. He proceeded to trample on some of Sir Robert Barker's objections. Our hold of the *diwanni* and the question of Allahabad were not connected, nor did we require Imperial *sanads*; 'the sword which gave us the dominion of Bengal must be the instrument of its preservation'. For all that, a school of thought existed, Graham among them, which argued that, if war broke out, the Emperor should be given his share of the Rohilla lands.

In mid-November the Vizier claimed the fulfilment of the understanding. After long debates the Select Committee were unanimous for acceptance, but the Council on balance for rejection, and Hastings summed up the argument with candour and dexterity. As a barrier against the Mahrattas, the Rohillas were useless; conquest would give the Vizier 'a compact State', while a third of our army would be employed at his expense, though in our own interests, and with advantage to their discipline. In return for this commitment, they were aware of the great advantages we had received, and a refusal would be 'unfriendly', perhaps dishonourable. 'This is the predicament in which I now stand.' Yet 'at present' he opposed the project, fearing the Vizier's inability to fulfil his obligations and the 'popular clamour' at home. His suggestion therefore was a draft reply, so rigidly insisting on the meticulous timing of every payment that the Vizier would draw back, 'and that I verily believe will be the issue'.

The Board agreed and, when in due course the Vizier acted as predicted, reported to the Directors at the new year of 1774 that all was 'happily terminated'. Even in March, when the Vizier had swung round again and Hastings' pledges were actually being implemented, his nearest friend, Vansittart, wrote 'it would carry us to too great a distance, and besides I am a friend to the Rohillas, and look upon them as a part of the balance against the Mahrattas'.

Only facts convert politicians in dealing with marginal emergencies. When the war was over and under fierce criticism, those of this Council who survived into the new régime repainted their self-portrait. Left without instructions, they pleaded, and aware of attacks at home and their coming supersession, 'we considered ourselves as acting for the national benefit, and assumed an extraordinary but a dangerous degree of responsibility'. Only one consideration had prevented their following a forward policy, 'the personal hazard we ran', when public opinion was inflamed against the Company. But when at length they found the Vizier's resolution 'coinciding with our opinions', they brushed aside 'the checks of self-interest'. So their gladness of January at the project being dropped had vanished by October. In December Hastings' pen took on the final and majestic note. By standing aside and giving the Mahrattas a free hand, he and his colleagues might have protected themselves against 'legal imputation'. But it was 'not by such cold and prudential cautions that the British name has acquired such a lustre in India, nor that the British Empire in Bengal is likely to be perpetuated'.

In February 1774, then, the Vizier decided on war, moved doubtless by the Mahratta internal dissensions, and having privately negotiated for the neutrality of Delhi and its Rohilla minister, Zabita Khan. The war was soon won. Our forces entered Rohilkund on April 17th, and on the 23rd Hafiz and some 2000 of his warriors were killed in battle. Fyzullah Khan, whom he had kept suppressed, fled with the surviving fighting men into the mountains, the Hindu landowners rose against their oppressors, and before two months passed the peasants were again peacefully tilling the soil. But the barbarity of Indian warfare damaged the good name both of Hastings and his country.

In the controversy that followed, it is certainly clear that this war was repugnant to many British officers. Young Palk at Patna called it 'hiring the troops to the country power', while one testimony must weigh very heavily, that of Colonel Pearse, commanding the artillery in Bengal, and always one of Hastings' most passionate champions. 'My consolation', he wrote, 'in not being with the army was that the war was un-British.' Yet that it could be represented as one of wholesale atrocity we may ascribe mostly to the peculiar character of our commander-in-chief.

Colonel Alexander Champion had some of the defects that marred all British soldiers in India in this age, together with a self-righteousness very much his own. Joseph Fowke had written of his brigade, 'whenever they move, they move for destruction and devastation', the Vizier complained of his sepoys looting, there is much evidence against his corrupt *banyan*. The Colonel, moreover, was displeased at being refused general's rank, and even more at finding that all political business was to be managed by Middleton. From the first, therefore, he was disposed to quarrel with the Vizier, the cowardice of whose 'banditti' he upbraided in his despatch written when, 'with beat of drum and fifes playing', the army 'passed in glory through the Rohilla camp'.

As for the atrocities, his sense of evidence was nil, and his picture of 'the merciless Shuja' much over-coloured. Barwell told his sister, and the testimony of field officers supports him, that the people at large suffered little, and that the Vizier's treatment of Hafiz' family was rather 'penurious' than barbaric. They ran short of food, while some of the *zenana* were robbed of their jewels. But there was none of that 'extirpation' with which the new Councillors, and Burke after them, made such play, the very word being a mistranslation admitted by the civil servant who made it. Actually the fighting men, to the number of perhaps 18,000, were either expelled south of the Ganges, or took service with Fyzullah Khan.

Hastings did, indeed, lose patience when Champion lamented
he had been forced to turn a deaf ear 'to the cries of the widow
and fatherless', retorting that if the whole Board had been present,
they could not have used 'coercive power' over an independent
ally. But he complimented him on his 'humane counsel', while
he ordered Middleton to insist on decent treatment for Hafiz'
family; 'I shall publicly exculpate this government . . . and
shall reserve it as an objection to any future engagements'. He
asked for the whole truth, 'neither glossed by favour, nor
blackened by prejudice'. Middleton's report in substance came
to this, that, though there had been 'much distress and inconvenience', the reports of outrage were baseless, and due in some
part to our army's soreness at being deprived of any share in
the spoil.

On this point Champion was even more eloquent than on
atrocities, and by his large promises worked up the army to
something like mutiny. Hastings officially refused to hear of prize
money, which must be avoided 'like poison', and sent up Lauchlin
Macleane to smoothe things down. The question of a donation
from the Vizier, referred to the Directors, dragged on till 1787,
when an old and broken Champion received his £10,000, and
others survivors grants according to scale.

Champion had also political ideas of his own. The Vizier
was at loggerheads with his wealthy and fiery mother, who
threatened to go on pilgrimage to Mecca; Middleton writing
gloomily 'I have endeavoured to inculcate the most dreadful
notions of sea expeditions'. There were rumours of Sikh and
Mahratta moves. The Emperor had bought the sword of
Samroo, the butcher of Patna, and was believed to be in touch
with the wanderer Mir Kasim. Fyzullah Khan was holding out
in his fastness. But, instead of pushing forward, Champion
plunged into private negotiations both with him and the court
of Delhi.

Was the commander-in-chief, Hastings asked, to become 'the
arbiter of peace and war'? Even if Fyzullah Khan could produce
the money he offered for Rohilkund, which he disbelieved, money
was not our objective, but the security of Oudh territories, 'which
is in fact the security of ours'. At length, in early October, a
reasonable settlement was brought about, whereby Fyzullah Khan
kept some lands round Rampur and became the tributary vassal

of Oudh. The war was over, but not the paper war. While Champion was confident the Vizier's complaints had been manufactured at Government House, Hastings was brewing charges that the atrocities had been 'methodized' at Calcutta.

It was typical that out of this inglorious frontier war he was already conjuring a daring political future. Though he had spent his Madras period in perpetual protest against the Crown's intervention in the Carnatic, he now suggested through Middleton a settlement with Oudh on those very lines. Would it not give British dominion a duration far exceeding the life of the Company if we could win the Indian inherent deference to Royalty?

The same question might arise in other quarters. It was in August 1773, while he was at Benares, that Ragoba on the palace terrace at Poona heard the conspirators cutting his nephew down. Instantly the Nizam was in arms; the Mahratta dynasty in Berar was divided between rival claimants; Hyder Ali's kettledrums were beating, he drove into Coorg and on to the Malabar coast, while his son Tippu recovered most of the ground lost in the last Mahratta war. Meantime, helped by British sepoys, the Carnatic Nabob won his goal, the fortress of the Mahratta Rajah of Tanjore.

Early in 1774 Ragoba's power suddenly collapsed. His evil wife, who had brought about his nephew's murder, attempted but failed to murder that nephew's widow, who was found to be with child. A band of conspirators, headed by a remarkable figure, Nana Phadnavis, safely immured her in a fortress, where her son was born. In April the child was recognized as Peishwa, and Holkar and Scindia abandoned Ragoba, who appealed to the British at Bombay.

That government, at present under a Governor of some decision, William Hornby, had long been looking for better defences for their harbour and for larger revenues, in which the Directors encouraged them. In 1772 they had sent one Thomas Mostyn as their envoy to Poona, to explore the possibility of acquiring the port of Bassein and the island of Salsette, which would protect their northern approaches and open up a secure market for their goods. Ragoba's misfortunes gave them their opportunity. In the autumn of 1774, while negotiating with him for the cession of Salsette and Bassein, they learned that a Portuguese fleet from Goa had designs on those places, which they

had lost to the Mahrattas forty years before. They determined
to strike out for themselves.

The Regulating Act, giving Bengal a determinant voice in
peace and war, took effect in August, though no official confirmation had reached Hastings. Problems much nearer than
Bombay were pressing on him, and what was right for Bombay
might be very wrong for Bengal. Already the Berar Rajah had
sent an agent, asking our friendship. Again, if Hyder was to be
an enemy, then the Nizam, who hated this parvenu, ought
certainly to be made a friend. Yet he, for one thing, had taken
offence at Clive's occupation of the Northern Circars, and
Hastings' Council seriously considered advising Madras to
surrender them. The Nizam's weak brother Basalut Jung, who
held the Guntur Circar for his life as our vassal, was building up
an army disciplined by Frenchmen, while the wretched
Carnatic Nabob, aided by corrupt Englishmen, hoped to install
his second and favourite son as a sovereign in Tanjore.

Further and further afield Hastings' eye scanned all the loose
scaffolding of British India. The overland route had such great
possibilities that he was anxious to improve relations with Egypt,
to whose Turkish governor he had just sent presents of a hookah
and a gun. Then there was the northern frontier. Skirmishes
with the Bhutanese had brought contacts with Tibet, where this
year he commissioned George Bogle as his envoy. He was to
find out 'what countries lie between Lhasa and Siberia' and the
trading routes between China and Kashmir, to trace the course
of the Brahmaputra, to report in full on climate and roads.
'Leave no means untried, but hazard neither your person nor
your health.' By the end of the year Bogle had seen the Teshoo
Lama, and sent in a report on the exports of musk and gold dust,
on the Kalmucks whose camels brought Siberian furs, the
Gurkhas who sent rice and iron, and the teas and porcelain
from China.

But while such disconnected threads of policy ranged so far,
the Company's economic prospect was bleak; already Bengal had
severely reduced the remittances asked for Madras and Bombay.
His Council registered how urgent it was 'to unite the powers of
the three Presidencies into one manageable system'.

CHAPTER XI

The Conspiracy: I. 1774 and 'The New Gentlemen'

WHAT with the Benares journey, revenue reform, and the Rohilla war, it had been a strenuous year, not leaving much leisure for private life. The Baron Imhoff had been gone a year, but nothing had been heard of a divorce. Where Marian lived there is nothing positive to show, though presumably at Alipur, but in 1775 the Governor leased a house a stone's-throw from his own, where perhaps he lodged her. Just before the new Councillors arrived he changed his official quarters, for his offices were so cramped that he moved them to the Council House, himself taking up residence in another, divided from it only by a garden, and leased from Mahomed Reza Khan. Furthermore, he spent £6000 on buying the garden-house of Belvedere at Alipur, which Verelst and Cartier had held before him, while he was progressing near by with his favourite toy, Hastings House. If we add to this his share in the Sooksagur plantation and an investment in the suburbs of Calcutta, clearly a good deal of his capital was locked up.

He was, in fact, spending, borrowing, and loaning in his usual casual magnanimous way. There was a loan to Lord Bute's son, Frederick Stuart, who had run off from Oxford to Paris and then been packed off to India; and a larger one to his own secretary, Belli. There was a mortgage for one of his Turner kinsfolk, and the standing payments for his unsatisfactory stepdaughter. We note one wine bill of £230, and a large insurance on a diamond traded to Russia; indeed, during 1776 he cleared £25,000 in England by sale of diamonds.

This unconscionable carelessness about money, or anything else he found petty or time-consuming, was notorious, in contrast to his watchfulness over political and personal relations. A declared enemy like James Grant put him down as 'fond of

MRS. HASTINGS, BY ZOFFANY

power but despises wealth', while even Philip Francis drew his distinctions, — 'rapacious, by no means avaricious'. George Vansittart warned him that his 'inattention to trifles' gave offence. As with the younger Pitt, his correspondence teems with laments from soldiers and agents, complaining they cannot get an answer, while when Nesbitt Thompson became his private secretary, he found 'cart loads of papers of all descriptions lay about in heaps, unsorted and unindorsed'. As in duty bound he gave his large parties, at the New Year or the King's birthday, in the assembly-room, amid its busts of the twelve Caesars. But he still hated 'parade', in particular military parade, and was careless of his clothes on great occasions.

He had aged somewhat since Reynolds painted him during his furlough. The dissipated Tilly Kettle, having done the Vizier, was painting him now for John Stewart, a picture which shows him with hair much receded and head a little weary on the hand. But the blue eyes, just a fraction near together, look out firmly, he had no need for spectacles for some years to come, while from Fowke's charming daughter Margaret we learn that his teeth were the finest in the world. In these harsh years he never had an illness; indeed about his health he was never careless, not from what he called 'unmanly attentions', but from long habit and frame of mind.

Though staunch to old friends, like other men in great place he made friends of few on an equal footing. Hancock was becoming very infirm and made Hastings his executor, who in March 1775 instructed his English attorneys to settle £10,000 for the benefit of his god-daughter and her mother Philadelphia. He was not really friends with Barwell, and of his near equals probably only Vansittart knew his heart. Otherwise, he seems to have most appreciated men of action who had their roots deep in India, such as Edward Baber, the excellent Chief at Midnapore, the accomplished Swiss Colonel Polier, now in Oudh service, with his rare collection of Indian manuscripts, or the gunner Colonel Pearse, with his Begum wife and a half-caste son at Harrow. But he was increasingly dependent on the band of quite young men of his own making; Elliot, David Anderson, most versatile of negotiators, his Persian translator John D'Oyley, Toone the enthusiastic Irishman commanding his bodyguard, Halhed the queer scholar who had codified the Hindu laws and later in life lost himself in the Book of Daniel, and Augustus Clevland, who first showed in the Bhagalpur hills what an Englishman could do with a primitive people.

If Calcutta were not yet the first city in Asia as he planned, his rule had already brought about some commercial revival. New residential quarters were rising on ground that had lately been creeks leading to the river. Near the old Fort the Begum Johnson was beginning her historic whist-parties in Clive Street; not far away, the new theatre was opening. Court House Street, leading from Government House northwards, was being developed too, to hold the library and a 'Europe shop', and Englishmen and Indians, Barwell and Nobkissen, were coining money in such speculation. Portuguese and Armenians in their own quarters were building their churches and amassing wealth. But in September 1774 there was a tenseness in the official houses, at the tidings that the new Councillors had reached Madras; until their arrival, Hastings wrote, all would be in 'a state of inanimation'.

He was slowly becoming aware that the basis of his home influence was undermined, built as it was on the Sulivan group, who were down and out. Their one hope in India was Macleane, but Shelburne was asking the Governor's good offices to make Macleane pay his debts. William Burke was entirely ruined, so was their patron Lord Verney, from whom they borrowed to buy Edmund's house at Beaconsfield. A flagrant job to recoup the Burke fortunes in the West Indies had just collapsed, ending in the ruin of Burke's brother Richard, and the ejection from the North ministry of their ally in this hopeful scheme, Charles James Fox. With some complacency Clive wrote to Hastings that he was now 'very strong' with the Company, adding that he was naming as his attorney in Bengal Mr. Philip Francis, with whom he was 'particularly acquainted'.

A year later, in November 1774, Clive killed himself. But nothing arrested the decline of Sulivan. At the elections of that and the next year he could only report to Hastings his 'total defeat', adding 'the ghost of Clive haunts me'. While Palk wrote that Lord North dare not lose 'the Clivites', Sykes absolutely distrusted Sulivan, being convinced that in return for election he would sell Hastings, or anyone else. But, indeed, the Regulating Act was not merely associated with a shifting in the parliamentary groups who were competing for power; it marked the end of the independence of the India House, whose elections henceforward were dictated by the Treasury and Downing Street. The fall of Grafton and George Grenville's death in 1770, the sharp conservative reaction after the upheaval of John Wilkes, the breakdown of co-operation between Chatham and the Rockingham Whigs, — all this had seated Lord North firmly in the saddle, secure in the King's affection and, given external peace, his own conciliating gifts. It was in this new setting, destructive to the calculations of Clive and Sulivan alike, that parliament dealt angrily with the scandals of India, which had infuriated the public and which, by the Company's impending bankruptcy, made such intervention inevitable.

Whatever Clive's sins, and parliament had forgiven them in view of his service, his name was potent. His members in the Commons were one consideration, while he had an unscrupulous partisan in the solicitor-general, Wedderburn, his channel for advices to North. In that proud spirit ambition would only die with physical extinction. Though he did not care for parts of the Regulating Act, still it gave the Crown larger powers and set up a Governor-General, as he always had advocated, and to his last days he continued to lobby the India House and influence the newly appointed Councillors.

There was one other group whose attitude, though unimportant during the passage of the Act, was to be of fated import to Hastings, the party nominally led by the decent dumb Lord Rockingham but inspired by Edmund Burke. While Shelburne, once Sulivan's ally, reluctantly accepted the Act, the Rockinghams stood by the Company. No voice was more voluble than Burke's in exclaiming against this destruction of chartered rights, or the seizure of Indian patronage by the Crown; no one so active at the India House as the Radical Duke of Richmond, in alliance with Clive's old enemies, the Johnstones. But, even as early as this, Burke's meteoric mind shot forth at a new angle. The Crown, he said, was appointing men of the guilty era, whom the Commons had branded, and Hastings among them. In the last resort, however, his political conclusions were ruled by his heart. Poor cousin William, oldest and dearest of friends, — was he not ruined by the harpies of the India House? And was not poor Richard ruined too by North and his pettifogging officials? Alas, when poor William fled to India in 1777 to get money somehow, he collided with this recreant Hastings, mysteriously defiant of, but doubtless secretly sustained by, this fatal government of the King and North. It was still some way to go to the full frenzy over poor William, 'your wicked, your undeserved persecutors'; though poor William was, in fact, hopeful of a rich racket in handling government balances. But here was a volcanic soil which some external spark might rouse to flame.

And now for 'the new gentlemen', as the Vizier called them.

In Lord North's Micawber-like mind there were two ponderables, the King and the House of Commons. George III, who disliked misgotten riches as much as democracy, had taken a hostile view of the Company, and wanted a perpetual parliamentary control. The two seniors of the new men were entirely congenial to him. General John Clavering, a Coldstreamer now aged fifty-one, had been a royal aide de camp, fought bravely at Guadeloupe, and served as resident at Hesse-Cassel. His political connections were most respectable. His brother Sir Thomas was a veteran member, of the Grenville-Clive group, and was firm with the Court against Radicalism; he was related, too, to Grey Cooper, a Treasury secretary, and a crony of Welbore Ellis, most typical of the King's 'friends'. Accepted as a specially royal appointment, Clavering was to be not only second in Council but Commander-in-Chief, a double role much pressed by the King but only just carried in parliament. In the King's mind he was to succeed Hastings, with all convenient speed. For the rest, the General would sail with a second wife, and several marriageable daughters. Though believed to be upright, his temper was pugnacious, — thus he challenged the Duke of Richmond during these debates — and was a stickler for every tittle of authority; writing back, indeed, from Madeira, when eastward bound, to claim some additional salary.

Colonel George Monson was of the same calibre, though with some important variations. A Grenadier, now aged fifty-three, he had served with distinction both at Pondicherry, when he was badly wounded, and at Manila. He had sat in the House where his patrons were supposed to be Clive and Grafton's secretary of the Treasury, Bradshaw, whom 'Junius' attacked as a 'cream-coloured parasite'. He had married Lady Anne Vane, daughter of the Lord Darlington to whom Howard Hastings had been general factotum, and she was telling her acquaintance that

Warren was really Howard's natural son. Otherwise, she was a hospitable lady who, as the Francis circle discovered, played a capital hand at whist.

Each Councillor was to receive £10,000 a year, and for the third place there were a good many candidates, including a son-in-law of Bute, one George Macartney. But late in the day the lot fell on Philip Francis. 'How did you get the appointment?' was the immediate question from a cousin of his in America, and from that day to this no one has known the answer. By his own account it was by pure chance, on the eleventh-hour resignation of the man selected, so that North had to find a name in a hurry. Others later, including some of his descendants, believed it was hush-money to 'Junius', who, the King was quoted as saying, 'will write no more'.

Francis was not quite thirty-three, a Londoner ever since he had been brought as a child from his native Dublin, and a brilliant boy at St. Paul's School. His father, the Reverend Philip, translator of Horace, entered politics in the curious role of chaplain to the Fox family, obtained a pension from George Grenville, and was well placed to plant his much-loved son in avenues leading to fortune. Young Philip began as a clerk under the Secretary of State and, after some diplomatic experience, was appointed by Welbore Ellis as his first clerk at the War Office. Here he made one of his closest friends, Christopher D'Oyley, who was also a near ally of Clive. Early in 1772, however, when Lord Barrington was Secretary at War, D'Oyley resigned and Francis, — declining, or so he said, an offer to succeed him — followed suit. Like his father, he had already dabbled in politics and burned his fingers. He first attached himself to John Calcraft who, after massing a fortune as Henry Fox's deputy as Paymaster, had abandoned Fox for Chatham. Together they banked on the great man's return to office in 1771, when war seemed likely with Spain, in fact the preservation of peace cost Francis £500 on the Stock Exchange; when Calcraft died the next year he left Francis a legacy and the promise of a parliamentary seat at Wareham. But he had decided the Opposition game was played out, and wanted an offer from the government.

When the Indian appointment came about, he had thus been unemployed for a year and was casting about for a job, sometimes thinking of taking up lands in America on which he held an option, and sometimes of the East, having made a little money in India stock. His acquaintance was wide in the City and the press; his reputation for ability stood high, so much so that even at Calcutta Barwell heard that his resignation from the War Office was engineered by the Whigs as a blow to the ministry. This eligibility, and the backing of Barrington and Grey Cooper, presumably got him the appointment, and he lost no time in extending his contacts.

Within two months he was fully established with the Clive family in Shropshire, imbibing the proconsul's grievances and his version of the past, sucking the brains of Strachey, Clive's former secretary, about his Indian supporters, and fraternizing with Lady Clive over their common love of cats. Here too he was first introduced to General Clavering. A Miss Ducarel was *l'amie de la maison*, whose brother was an able Bengal civilian; Wedderburn made a link with the Cabinet. Did they speak of Warren Hastings, in the lucid intervals between county dinners and electioneering? We cannot doubt it. Four years after, Francis wrote to Wedderburn that they had all been mistaken in Hastings' character, except Clive.

But he never believed in having but one political wire. He took pains to keep in touch with North, on whom he impressed the need for giving this reformed Council the fullest powers, and secured a promise that the Wareham seat should be kept open for him at the next election. Yet North might fall. So before he sailed we find him visiting Edmund Burke at Beaconsfield, with an introduction from his kinsman John Bourke, one of his own convivial City friends. This Irish clan was worth cultivating. John had a favourite nephew, George Shee, who was soon living with Francis in Bengal. Edmund was recommending several Hickeys, while Strachey advised Francis to send messages to Edmund in his Indian letters, 'that he may remember you in any opportune compliment in the House of Commons'.

If Francis indeed were 'Junius', satanic in malignant pride and pattern of baseness to Francis' benefactors, little more need be said of his public character. But some few personal facets of mind and temperament illumine the Francis we shall meet in India. He always loved a cosy home, women liked him, he had distinction of speech, an agreeable irony, and soft hands. As almost a boy he had married Elizabeth Mackrabie, to whom he was a kind though masterful husband, and a good father to his small children. But 'Betsy' must stay behind in England and bring them up, and intellectually, poor woman, she could not compete. For Philip had the hall-mark of the late eighteenth century on his bright metallic intelligence. When the vein seized him, of course, he liked a deep drinking bout with his City friend Daniel Godfrey, or exchanged bawdy with his own fire-eating cousin, Major Baggs, whom he congratulated as 'a dangerous man in a seraglio'. He would tell Godfrey he found 'unyielding virtue' unendurable. But though he did not admire mankind, he had read and thought much about them, and his library held Aretino as well as his much-thumbed Tacitus. His note-books were filled with analyses of Bacon and Montesquieu, he had the Whig maxims from Algernon Sidney onwards at his finger-tips, and while he disbelieved Christianity and hated priests, he had studied constitutional law deeply. In the new science of economics he thought himself an adept, freely appealing to the authority of Sir James Stuart or Lord Kaimes. Above all, he gloried in being a man of 'principles', which during the French Revolution effectually alienated him from Burke.

All seemed in order. For his most secret letters he left behind a cipher with D'Oyley, who was to share such information with Strachey, Wedderburn, and Ellis.

Eighteenth-century government being what it was, this implicit conspiracy against Hastings embraced yet other persons. There was a General Simon Frazer in the House, friend of Wedderburn, whose young brother-in-law John Bristow was serving in Bengal. There was another Bengal servant, Charles Goring, with political ambitions, who had promised North to support Clavering. Lord Barrington had his protégés there, and notably Charles Boughton Rouse, a decade later the secretary to Pitt's Board of Control. Wheler, chairman of the Company in 1774, wrote Hastings most pious letters, how 'the British Senate' was bent on succouring the oppressed, but had been active for Clavering, and recommended his brother-in-law George Livius, who shared house with Francis in Calcutta. Widest of all were the radiations from Joseph Fowke, whose brother-in-law Walsh was Clive's right hand in politics, whose nephews the Hollonds were Clive's agents at Madras, and who was an old friend of Barrington.

Conspiracy, or understanding, extended also to the judges of the new Supreme Court. One of them, Lemaistre, was a client of Lord Sandwich, and a convivial gambling spark, who reserved his hot temper for the Chief Justice. His colleague Hyde was proud of office, ceremonious, and hospitable. The Chief Justice was Elijah Impey, Hastings' best friend at Westminster School, and married to a Cotswold neighbour, Mary Reade of Shipton Court. He was intimate with Dunning, Shelburne's friend among the lawyers, and with North's attorney-general, Thurlow, and much consulted in drawing up the Court charter. His family were Hammersmith merchants, his children were numerous, and he was not of a temper to undervalue the emoluments of office.

The nomination had swung between him and the colleague who, though the youngest, was put second, Sir Robert Chambers. This amiable undecided man had already some reputation as Blackstone's successor in the Oxford law chair and as a close friend of Dr. Johnson, who wrote to Hastings, 'that he is going to live where you govern, may justly alleviate the regret of parting'. But Chambers carried something more with him, a promise from North that he should, when possible, be promoted from the bench to Council. He regularly forwarded copies of Francis' minutes to Jenkinson, and claimed credit for never opposing 'those gentlemen in whom the government of these provinces was meant to be lodged'. His old mother sailed with him, and a very beautiful young wife, a famous model of Reynolds, who was to create one corner of charm and natural goodness in the hateful Calcutta of the next ten years.

Something more than instinct, therefore, made Hastings ill at ease, despite the usual blarney from Shelburne, or Sulivan's report on Clavering's high character, or Sykes' view that Francis had no 'depth of understanding'. While he waited, he prepared well-turned letters of welcome, asking for mutual trust, not forgetting to recall himself to the memory of Lady Anne Monson.

It was only in April 1774 that the Indiamen got off, the *Anson* with the judges, and the *Ashburnham* with the Councillors. The ten months since their appointment had been most disagreeable. Directors and proprietors had drawn up rival sets of instructions, while only Cabinet pressure carried Clavering's sweeping claims to appoint an adjutant-general and a bevy of aides de camp. There was another scuffle over the Board of Trade, which was to consist of the senior servants, such as Aldersey and Vansittart, who had sat in Hastings' previous Council, and to which one section of proprietors and the Rockingham Whigs wished to give almost independent powers. And when they sailed, the voyage was marred by the Councillors' growing irritation with the Court, whose charter they discovered gave Impey precedence next to Hastings. Francis' very pleasant brother-in-law Mackrabie declared that Impey had the great seal always paraded about with him, ashore or afloat.

When they reached Madras, Macpherson sent Hastings word that he and Impey and Frederick Stuart (now on his way home) had held 'a little divan', and that Monson was warning the Nabob to drop the Sulivan interest. Clavering penned a diatribe to Lord North against the judges, while Francis wrote of Hastings' 'obliging' letters. On September the 23rd they sailed on again, and as they entered the Hugli were nearly wrecked in a storm, but got safely to the budgerows which would take them up-stream. Before they moved, however, Joseph Fowke arrived for a conclave with Clavering; his plan, Francis wrote later, was hatched with Nuncumar, 'to take possession of us — and through us to govern the country'.

At noon on October the 19th the new gentlemen landed and walked in some heat the few hundred yards to Government House, to be introduced to their predecessors. Though Aldersey, as senior Councillor, had gone to meet them, they were displeased at receiving a salute of only seventeen guns, and 'surely', says Mackrabie, 'Mr. Hastings might have put on a ruffled shirt'. A large banquet at two o'clock did not dispel a suspicion that Hastings meant 'to lower us in the eyes of the natives'. Next day they met in Council, spent some hours wrangling whether proclamation of the new government should be accompanied with the military ceremony Clavering desired, and adjourned at Hastings' request till Monday the 24th, an interval during which, the triumvirate officially complained, they were left 'in the most anxious, not to say disgraceful, situation'.

He asked this delay, in fact, to have time to decide whether he should not resign. He had pondered it a month now, and openly told his new Council that the instructions, and especially the powers given to the Commander-in-Chief, disturbed him. But it is difficult to believe that he hesitated long, or Francis' story that he was only persuaded to stay by Vansittart and Graham. In any event, when they reassembled, he had ready for them a long memorandum on the revenue, and another on our relation to Indian States.

Their later argument was that, till they reached Calcutta, nothing was further from their thoughts than an attack on the Governor-General. It is transparently false. Though they attended church in a body on the Sunday, it was not to the neglect of mundane things, and their procedure was ready in every detail. They would ask what troops were assisting the Vizier, demand a sight of all Hastings' correspondence, public and private, with Middleton and Champion, and if he refused they would recall Middleton. There were other items, including a questionnaire into the employment and salary of every Company servant, British or Indian, but these would serve to begin with. And so it was done. Without examining previous proceedings, on the 26th the majority recalled Middleton, while two days later they instructed Champion to withdraw the British brigade and to demand immediate payment of what sums the Vizier had promised. Their first appeal to the Directors spoke of 'the extirpation of a brave and independent nation', and hinted at a parliamentary enquiry.

To make the Rohilla war their lever was Francis' advice, and one well thought-on, simultaneously involving the Governor's policy, his control of foreign relations, and his personal loyalties. 'Bear with patience', he told Middleton, 'this unmerited return for your services. If ever I am again invested with the power of recompensing them, I will not forget them.' For six months he poured out minutes to vindicate his policy, or to refute the charge he had dishonoured the British name. Much time was taken up with Champion, whose fury with the Vizier threw him into the arms of the majority. His denunciation, Hastings was convinced, was 'either Francis' *aut Diaboli*', in its mixture of rant and malevolence. Was it possible, the Colonel asked, the Governor-General could so 'prostitute the English troops', and leave the innocent Rohillas in 'the iron grasp of Sujah', 'exulting over the pale head of Hafiz'? As for himself, he had stood up for 'a persecuted people'; 'happy he who in such a situation can put his hand on his breast, and say all is quiet, all is serenity within'. Champion, however, did not turn out a strong investment. An examination of field officers by Council blew away his hearsay stories of 'extirpation'.

This field of conflict soon ranged far beyond the Rohilla war. Someone must succeed Middleton in the Oudh residency, but Hastings' candidate, Frederick Stuart, was rejected in favour of Bristow, the nominee of Clavering and Francis. Hosea, one of his own young men, was angling for patronage from Monson. Rival lists were compiled for the Provincial Councils, the chiefs of which were in every case but one chosen against his recommendation. This 'preconcerted opposition', this 'tribunal of inquisition' in Barwell's words, left no room for compromise. In the first week of December he solemnly appealed both to the Directors and Lord North, by whose verdict he would abide, undertaking not to be provoked into resignation, nor copy the Three in 'a warfare of scurrility'. And 'in this blessed state', he told Caillaud, 'I am to continue for eighteen months to come'.

A year or so later Francis set down for his private edification his version of these opening months. Hastings, 'I am assured', was ready to buy them with £100,000 apiece. His conscious guilt was visible at their first meeting. 'The sweat ran down his face, tears gushed from his eyes, he beat his head, and ran about the room in a fit of distraction.' It was the practice of 'Junius' to rehearse this sort of pre-audition. But there was this much truth in it; that Hastings, so sensitive to rebuke and so proud of his character, could not breathe in this air of unrelenting malice. 'Dark allusions, mysterious insinuations,' he told the Directors, 'bitter invective and ironical reflections are weapons to which I have been little accustomed.' He sat at his Council table an 'object of the most illiberal persecution', 'denied even the rights of personal civility'.

Week by week we follow the crescendo of this tactic of insult. They began in November with an almost apologetic statement of principle; that their own conduct could only be justified 'by a strong and deliberate censure of the preceding administration', though hinting at the 'dark and mysterious' transactions in Oudh. When the Governor minuted 'an appeal to the passions is an insult to the understanding', they stored that up for future reference. In December they said that they might have acted in concert with him, 'if it had been possible for us to attribute his conduct to error of judgement'; his 'happy reconciliation' with

Barwell was doubtless corrupt; no man was 'better acquainted with the great leading motive which is supposed to influence' others. They would not imitate Barwell's attack on the Rani of Burdwan; 'we leave it to the mercenary auxiliaries of Suja Doulah . . . to violate the sacred retirements of the zenana'. The facts about the declining revenue would emerge, not to be screened by Hastings' 'everlasting theme' of the famine. By February their style had considerably matured. They would not labour the Governor-General's 'last volume'. He had appealed to the Directors, on the score of past services; 'is this an appeal to the justice of his judges, or is it an insult to their understanding?' For the Governor could not 'offer us a stronger presumptive proof of the weakness, impropriety, or depravity of any political principle or public measure whatsoever, than by telling us it was adopted by the late administration'. In March they perfected the fine flower; 'there is no species of peculation from which the Honourable Governor-General has thought it reasonable to abstain'.

Long before that, however, the delicately masked machine of his creation was running down. The Supreme Court alone he found 'a dreadful clog', only prevented from being fatal by Impey's moderation. Its writs of habeas corpus demolished all the rough-and-ready means by which revenue was collected; the vagueness of its authority, encouraging the Indian passion for litigation, was drying up the Company courts. The Board of Trade, half intended to rival Council, was only saved from doing so through Hastings' friendship with Samuel Middleton, its president. The Bank he had made was promptly abolished. His 'fatal regulations' of 1772 for the revenue were declared to be bringing Bengal to ruin; how could such a State be rescued? 'common men are not equal to the occasion'.

Late in January the Vizier died; 'I have the pleasure of assuring you', Francis agreeably wrote, 'that he died in torments'. He commended his heir, Asof-ud-Daulah, to Hastings, but the uncommon men of the majority saw things very differently. Declaring the treaty of Benares merely personal to his father, they forced on the unhappy young Vizier an increased scale of payment for our troops, and seized the chance to transfer the sovereignty over Benares from Oudh to the Company. Though Oudh payments due to the British were in heavy arrears, and its own troops mutinying for their pay, Bristow barred the Vizier from the great treasures left, contrary to Moslem law, in possession of his mother and grandmother, negotiating a settlement which gave him barely a quarter of the whole, and while their first grievance had been Hastings' refusal to produce his correspondence from Middleton, when he proposed to prohibit private communications from Bristow to Councillors their virtue revolted; it was 'injurious', they voted, 'if they were thought capable of carrying on an improper correspondence with anybody'. Even more alarming was their fatuous outlook on the state of India. It was not just that they declined any liability for defending the Rohilla country. Monson would have made it over to the Emperor, while Clavering wanted to restore Allahabad in return for his remission of tribute from Bengal.

Hastings and Barwell fought every step in this insensate weakness. If Benares were thus unjustly to be torn away from Oudh, Hastings at least wished its ruler treated as an independent ally, and not merely in the capacity of a *zemindar*, to which the majority reduced him. But their policy was a thing of shreds and patches. While Clavering flourished the Mogul letters demanding tribute, Francis already suggested that the King of Great Britain be declared sovereign of Bengal. Even while they plundered Oudh, they condemned any punitive expedition against the raiding frontier tribes as having 'too near a relation to the expressive words so often made use of, "extirpate", "exterminate"', and praised the 'simplicity of manners' of these bandits.

He had vowed in his first appeal not to be provoked to resign, and 'to abide the decision of my employers'. How could he leave the Company's affairs to men like these? Moreover, the mind, he wrote to Graham, 'has something of an electrical property in it, which warms and increases its attraction to the spot in which it receives any hard friction'. Yet he began to think of ways out. Perhaps North would agree to name additional Councillors, in which case he would suggest that of Vansittart. He determined to use Macleane, with his intimate knowledge of home politics, as his agent, while Graham, who was going home too, a very sick man, should share the responsibility. What precisely their instructions were became, later, a matter of controversy. 'An unlimited discretion to act for me as they thought best', so he described them, and by his own account and the separate testimony of Vansittart and John Stewart his line in January came to this; that, though he would not retain office without power, he refused to be exploited by a party, and if his friends found the government decided to remove him, he would rather disappear quietly. When Macleane reached Madras, carrying with him Hastings' correspondence with Middleton which was to be shown to North, he received yet another agency, from the Nabob of the Carnatic. In late September he reached England, where he instantly received £6000 from Hastings' attorneys, with the promise of another £4000 to come.

To be or not to be, to stay or to go, backwards and forwards the Governor veered and tacked about, from February till May. He had George Vansittart by his side, but it was to the memory of Henry Vansittart that he harked back. For proofs were piling up that the same combination, which had destroyed his lost master, had come to life again; of British Councillors with the native powers of Bengal, at their back an underworld of crime, and from their fingers lines of communication leading to Leadenhall Street and the Treasury. Proof, and instinct also, pointed to Nuncumar; 'whom, against my nature, I have cherished like a serpent till he has stung me'.

CHAPTER XII

The Conspiracy: II. 1775: Nuncumar

AGED 42-43

ON January 11th, or thereabouts, Hastings forbade Nuncumar to enter his presence again. On March the 11th Nuncumar brought his accusations before Council. On April the 19th the Governor launched against him a prosecution for conspiracy. On May the 6th Nuncumar was arrested, at the instance of a private suitor, on a charge of forgery. His trial for this began on June the 8th, and on August the 5th he was hanged. On this wise, according to Burke, Hastings 'murdered Nuncumar through the hands of Sir Elijah Impey', a fact which Macaulay thought no one but 'fools and biographers' could doubt. The crisis was packed into eight weeks of the fiercest Calcutta summer, but its origins go back to the cold weather when the new gentlemen arrived, and the old time before them.

How the new gentlemen hated Bengal, and how they had come to dislike each other! Francis was driven mad in a scorching barn-like house, where horns and drums from neighbouring mosques made night hideous, until at the New Year he bought another on the Alipur road, where he could garden in peace. Here he lived with Mackrabie, Livius and his harpsichord, and Collings, who matched him at picquet, often 'tormented with the bile', for which he prescribed mutton chops and water. The climate filled them with loathing. Monson was once given up for dead, Impey reported that Clavering had suddenly turned an old man. They held their rival salons: Lady Anne Monson, whose hoops excited surprised admiration; Mrs. Clavering's fixed Wednesdays, graced by three stepdaughters whom susceptible Colonel Pearse deemed 'divine creatures'; and Lady Impey, who did not approve of Marian Imhoff.

Calcutta society seemed to them perfectly deplorable. The

vast trains of servants, with their licensed robbery and their everlasting refrain 'master must have this, master must do that', — the enormous dinners where the ladies sipped cherry brandy, and bread pellets flew across the table. So we are told by Mackrabie, who adds that Francis 'sighs and grumbles'. For Francis could find nothing good in India. 'The baseness of a Bengali', he wrote, 'is proverbial', while as for the *banyans* and office-holders you could not conceive 'more refined depravity'. His sketches of character flew thick and fast to North, Clive, or Strachey. Hastings had 'some little talents of the third or fourth order'; Barwell was just 'rapacious, tyrannical, and profligate'. 'Mr. Hastings wholly and solely has sold and ruined Bengal'; 'let my Lord Clive look to his *jagir*'. He sang the same tune to his old patron Barrington and to D'Oyley, 'if there be a doubt about the immediate recall of our two colleagues, farewell Bengal!' Yet his different correspondents needed a different emphasis. For Wheler, now chairman of the Company, there must go grave explanations of their revenue measures. But to John Bourke the harp must strike a wilder note. 'This glorious empire, which I was sent to save and govern', on the verge of ruin; corruption not just at the root, 'every twig is putrified'. 'Talk to Ned Burke . . . he is wanted here. . . . I would act with him, or I would act under him.'

But they could have no answer for a year, nor could Hastings know, though he guessed, the content of their homeward mail. He was concerned with something more sinister, and nearer home. All experience in Bengal showed that, though British officers took decisions and moved the pieces, without an Indian following they were helpless. Society was set in a complex frame of land revenue, embarrassed by sub-tenures and masked titles, ruled by an aristocracy of Moslem landowners and Hindu bureaucrats and Armenian money-lenders, each living by the profits of office and retailing government patronage. And over all this a few score young Britons, wholly dependent on Indians for the intricacies of the revenue and tolerable administration of justice, not to speak of channels for the private trading whereby nine out of ten of them must live.

Half a dozen Indians had stamped their power and intrigue on the last revolutionary twenty years. Nuncumar's official history went back to the Black Hole; he was now about seventy, embittered by long exclusion. His rival, Mahomed Reza Khan, deposed as Naib by Company orders but long since acquitted, had a train of Moslem supporters; one Sudder-ud-Din, for instance, *munshi* or interpreter to Barwell, or Ali Ibrahim Khan, of whose integrity Hastings had a high opinion. There was Gunga Govind Sing, *diwan* of the Calcutta Revenue Board, who was to figure in the murkiest circle of the Whigs' inferno, and the rascally Naba Krishna (usually Englished as 'Nobkissen'), well known to Hastings since his Kasimbazaar days, then *banyan* to Clive, alternately enemy and friend to Nuncumar, speaking fluent English, and a large house-owner in Calcutta. And there was Nuncumar's oldest enemy, the Armenian Khwaja Petrus, once money-lender to Hastings and in power under Mir Kasim. Many Englishmen were closely knit in their fortunes to such Indians. Sykes was pleading to Hastings on behalf of Mahomed Reza Khan, who was himself lobbying Sulivan for restoration, while Clive had recommended Nobkissen to the new gentlemen.

Some two years later Hastings named three persons as guilty of the 'first incitements'. These were Nuncumar, Joseph Fowke, and a Madras merchant, Andrew Ross, which takes the origins back to September 1774 when the new Councillors touched there. And Fowke was 'the original incendiary'. Giving evidence at the conspiracy trial, he put it down to 'my not having served him to the extent of his wishes', which we have seen reached to membership of Council, and to a temper 'violent to the last degree'. He certainly was a singular old creature, with a likeable side. Chess and music, he said, were his resource 'in heavy distresses', especially Corelli and Handel's violin concertos; 'noisy unmeaning modern music has destroyed all true taste', the clarinets at Calcutta parties nowadays were like 'the grunting of hogs'. Though a Madras Councillor long before Clive, years later he was reported as 'flirting like a young man', and his letters are those of the connoisseur, 'Mrs. Stuart falls short by daylight, and is every way short of Lady Chambers'. Perhaps a letter from his son Francis tells us the root of the trouble with Joseph; 'you gamed away your whole original fortune', on return to India 'you gamed away between five and six thousand pounds' . . . 'I have been at the expense of about two thousand pounds in sending to India your natural daughter'. Joseph called this letter 'mean and unmanly'. But at any rate through his brother-in-law Walsh he was connected with Clive, and Francis had come out pledged to unite Clive's friends and protect their interests.

Sooner or later, it was certain that the new gentlemen would take their cue from some of these Indians. And sure enough, after several conferences with Nuncumar, Fowke went down to meet them. He struck up a close alliance with Clavering. In November the General traced the complaints of some salt workers back to the *banyan* of a British officer, formerly on the Governor's staff; there was another salt revenue controversy, in which an old acquaintance of Nuncumar, one Kamal-ud-Din, was concerned, together with Hastings' *banyan*, Cantoo. In these activities the General used Fowke, though now only a merchant, to take depositions, and in December Kamal protested to Hastings that Fowke accused him of bribing English Councillors. Brushing aside the Governor's protest against this employment of Fowke, the majority stiffened their campaign against Cantoo. As the Governor's *banyan* he held, by old custom, a court for disputes between men of low caste which, Francis wrote, he had made a Star Chamber. They had a more vulnerable target in his revenue transactions. Nothing could be more easily abused. They showed that Cantoo farmed revenues of over £100,000, and if this was forbidden to a collector's *banyan*, how much more should it apply to the Governor's!

Fowke's apoplectic letters of exculpation had hardly been received when Nuncumar instigated a complaint from the Rani of Burdwan. This princess, 'a vile prostitute' according to Barwell, had been in trouble since Cartier's time, whose sentence Hastings, despite a proffered bribe, had merely confirmed; to remove her son from her custody, and to appoint a *diwan* of our choice. He could quote the collector's testimony, and as exactly the same story was forthcoming in 1780 from Francis' close ally Ducarel, it can hardly be in doubt. However, the Rani now deposed that Graham and Frederick Stuart had taken large pickings from her, and Hastings forbade Nuncumar to enter his presence.

At the same time he became aware that the majority were also sounding the rival quarter, of Mahomed Reza Khan. Carrying out his promise to Lord North, Charles Goring was trying to persuade the ex-Naib of the impossibility of 'one man's following two interests', and flattered himself he had won this 'master key to every secret transaction'. Though the Naib told Goring that Hastings had refused all presents from him except a Persian cat, he was menaced with the loss of his *jagir*, and after some third-degree pressure supplied the majority with more or less suitable replies. Francis, wrongly believing that neither Hastings nor Nuncumar knew of this intrigue, prided himself on it as superior to the deal of Clavering with Nuncumar; in his large schemes for a revival of native rule under the Crown, the ex-Naib might play a useful part.

While such information was being 'raked up out of the dirt of Calcutta', as Hastings put it, there was a pause. One ship after another took home majority minutes, asking publication of their views on the Rohilla war, or justifying their choice of Bristow on the ground of his excellent Persian and his relation to noble houses. Many cheap insults, — such as 'without implicating ourselves in the operations of the Governor's understanding' — and much highfaluting appeal to principle, are enough in themselves to mark the author. Francis' private notes ranted on the 'lenity of the ancient government, and the simple unerring wisdom of its institutions', while he was careful to claim as a mark of confidence 'the readiness with which General Clavering and Colonel Monson signed whatever I wrote for them'.

Till the mine was ready, they must act with caution, for lack of which Clavering sometimes reproached Francis, 'you certainly let the cat out of the bag yesterday with Aldersey'. But the Governor rightly guessed their respective roles. 'The General rummages the Consultations', his part was the strategy, and he was thus already proposing the eviction of Munny Begum. Monson ran the lower tactics, of inviting accusations. 'Francis writes.'

Yet curious cross-currents ran through this Council. As a body, they were affronted by the Supreme Court. Hot-headed Judge Lemaistre was most provocative over revenue cases; Impey complained to Thurlow about the 'insolence, and superior airs of authority' of the new Councillors. But while Clavering would have a frontal attack, Francis thought it foolish to throw the judges on to the Governor's side. He was, in fact, already convinced that Clavering was unfit to be Governor, though by his own account he alone stopped Clavering declining the succession; for who knows ? proof of such incapacity might clear the ground for a better man. Competition over patronage so much divided the Three that Clavering, though warm in Monson's praise, was painting Francis to North as 'a doubtful friend', or of 'no defined character'. In his own egoistic way Francis respected Hastings ; begging the Company chairman, if a choice must be made, rather to recall Barwell, — 'better keep the man who has some parts and considerable experience'. His indignation may thus be conceived when he saw signs of an understanding between Barwell and Clavering.

Twisting in and out of these avenues of accusation, death, and infamy, shambles this tragic comedian Barwell, a more intricate person than Francis perceived. The fuss the new gentlemen made about corruption was, he felt, ridiculous. He had ragged them to their face about taking presents, — all *he* had got was a couple of shawls — and sensible men, he wrote to Sulivan, could surely admit Hastings' eminent service, 'without expecting that his easy chair shall have been wholly useless to him'. Why, he was himself under fire on some pedantic idea that he had profited from the Dacca salt revenues, and he thought this reforming zeal was humbug. In his view, the General would be quiet enough if Hastings would consent to marry one of his daughters.

In spite of his past differences with Hastings, he explained to North that quite unbiasedly, for he had not been in Council when the decisions were taken, he entirely supported him over the Rohilla war, arguing in Council that wise men would accept the fact and the considerable profit accruing. But a wise man, his letters to his faithful sister indicated, must first look after himself. True, he called the majority's steps against Hastings 'base and infamous'. But in any questions for or against Hastings 'made a point of by the Ministry, go implicitly with the Ministry. To you, my good genius, I recommend my fortunes.' So when Nuncumar's charges came before Council, he told Stuart he was grieved to find Hastings so 'vulnerable', and hoped his friends would save him from the same 'charcoal mark'.

In this phase, though he once told Mary 'I shall never marry', he began to speculate about marriage with Miss Maria Clavering. On the whole, he doubted. But the lady was impulsive, he told her his 'expectations', and Francis wrote off furiously of this 'damnable match', which would shatter the confidence of Indians in their new friends. In April, however, this coalition collapsed. The General charged Barwell with peculation, Barwell called him a scoundrel at the Board, the General could never resist a duel. Thus one early morning they met on the Budge-Budge road. 'What distance do you choose, Sir?' says Mr. Barwell; 'the nearer the better', — this dialogue comes down to us through Charles Grant, the well-known and religious secretary to the Board of Trade. The General fired and missed, which Francis found inexplicable, and it ended in apologies. 'I am providentially preserved', Richard wrote to Mary; no more Clavering marriage for him. But that was in mid-May; much had happened to Hastings since the first hint of this matrimony in February.

Nuncumar had reached his hour of glory. Sometimes fifty palanquins stood at his door; he sent for Rajahs' agents, distributing threats and promises; he had 'met with employers', wrote Vansittart, 'who allow full scope to his genius'. Week after week reports reached Hastings of coolies passing Cantoo's house, carrying on their heads gold mohurs for Nuncumar, of sums promised from Burdwan to the Three, or of Francis' *banyan* journeying to the neutral Dutch town of Chinsura to hasten delivery. Zero hour was near, and it was brought nearer by fears of a counter-mine. For in February it was known that Mohan Persad had applied to the Supreme Court for papers which would enable him to prosecute Nuncumar for forgery. The old man, Vansittart said, was 'a little frightened'. But Clavering was hot on the scent; 'at last', he tells Monson, 'we have got Mr. Van's name on the list of culprits'.

They struck in the second week of March. On the 8th Clavering wrote to Francis, 'I hope you have seen Mr. Fowke'; on the 10th Fowke's servant lodged an accusation of bribery from Burdwan; on the 11th Francis brought in a sealed letter from Nuncumar, with the contents of which he said he was not acquainted, though 'I did apprehend' it held some accusations. It did, indeed. Nuncumar hardly concealed his motives. The Governor, he wrote, had cast him aside, ordered him out of his house, and was in touch with his deadliest enemies, his son-in-law Jugeth Chand and Mohan Persad. He had acquitted the two Naibs accused in 1772 against all the evidence, had lavished excessive salaries on Rajballabh the Roy Royan, and given revenue farms to Cantoo. Having thus implicated his own Indian rivals, Nuncumar fired his second barrel direct at the Governor, who, he alleged, had taken bribes from Munny Begum and himself to the tune of three and a half lacs.

On the 13th Monson moved that Nuncumar's offer to give further evidence in person should be accepted. Hastings intervened. 'I will not sit at this Board in the character of a criminal, nor do I acknowledge the members of this Board to be my judges.' All the more, since in truth they were his accusers. He had 'long ago' known of charges taken by Nuncumar to Monson (this Barwell confirmed). From their first day they had aimed at the annihilation of his authority, now they were trying to fix 'a personal and popular odium', 'and fit instruments they have found'. 'The chief of this administration . . . shall I sit at this Board to be arraigned in the presence of a wretch whom you all know to be one of the basest of mankind?' They might form themselves into a committee of enquiry, but he would not have Nuncumar at the Board, and when they rejected a suggestion from Barwell, who wearily remarked it was five o'clock, that the proper tribunal was the Supreme Court, he declared Council dissolved. 'I had no alternative', he told his agents, 'but to do that, or throw up the service.'

When he with Barwell left the room, the Three heard Nuncumar, who produced a letter, which was pretty demonstrably forged, from Munny Begum detailing the bribes she had given. He then elaborated his other charges; how Mahomed Reza Khan had given Hastings money through Khwaja Petrus and Ali Ibrahim Khan; how Cantoo had been his go-between with Shitab Roy in Bihar; what bribes he had pocketed from the Vizier and Rajballabh. Without other evidence, the Three voted the Governor guilty, demanding a refund to the Company of what he had received.

Next day the Burdwan witnesses trooped in, and again he dissolved Council; and once more later, when they threatened Cantoo for refusing, on his order, to appear in an incomplete Council. Clavering moved that Cantoo be put in the stocks, the punishment, he said in his gross way, 'which the Governor inflicts every day upon so many miserable Hindus merely for easing themselves upon the Esplanade'. At this Hastings' native temper flared up; if Clavering attempted this 'by his own authority', he would 'personally oppose it, at the peril of my life'.

The Rani of Burdwan, having given in the due accusations, left for home, restored to power, and rewarded with shawls and an elephant. Finally, an old acquaintance of Nuncumar (seemingly a brother of Mahomed Reza Khan) testified that Hastings had embezzled the salary of the *foudjar* of Hugli; like many others who would not co-operate, the present holder was dismissed and Nuncumar's nominee installed.

'The Triumvirate carry everything before them', Mackrabie wrote, 'but with a high hand.' Usurping the power of judges, they put those they accused on oath, and convicted them on evidence so extorted. Defying any official agenda, they used Council meetings to spring new charges, forcing Hastings to unpremeditated replies, amid a stream of insult designed to warp 'my judgement and understanding; I thank God I have hitherto possessed both undisturbed, at least I think so'. Indeed, while this cauldron boiled, he was busy with Barwell and Vansittart preparing a new revenue settlement, and sent North his proposals for more continuous powers for the Governor, and for some amalgamation of the Supreme with the Company courts. Then he put to the Directors his reasoned case against the Triumvirate. Their last efforts, he said, had 'not even the pretext of a public object'. His dissolutions of Council were in accord with 'the ancient and invariable practice of the service', and his honourable masters well knew the ill fame of Nuncumar. He was charged with rapacity, 'of all others the most foreign from my nature'; what a fortune could he not have amassed if he had consented to maintain the Mogul tribute and the Nabob's privy purse at their old level!

But his endurance was nearly exhausted. If the Three got at the Nabob to ask the dismissal of Munny Begum, then 'Nuncumar, supported by the powers of government, is not so easily to be dispossessed'. Words that fell from him show anguish of mind. 'The meanest drudge', he broke out to North, 'enjoys a condition of happiness compared to mine'; he begged either for immediate recall or power on an honourable footing. Wherever he moved there were bitter tongues and averted eyes, and his good name sunk and hawked about wherever Indians foregathered. 'Little passes now', he wrote to Admiral Hughes, 'that is not known in the Bazaar.' Up through the obscure funnels, by which Indian opinion reached the seats of the mighty, mounted this impression that he was thrown to the kites and vultures. All men, he tells Graham, 'are on the side of my opponents, even the son of Ramchurn [whom he had saved from Nuncumar's clutches in 1762] and Mohan Persad'.

He could bear no more. On March the 27th he wrote to Graham and Macleane that he had decided to sail in the autumn, if the treaty of Benares or the Rohilla war were condemned, or if, as he put it some weeks after, the next despatch bore 'evident symptoms of ill humour against me and portended my fall'. They were to use this resolution, 'as you think proper'.

Meantime that singularly timid creature, Kamal-ud-Din, was wondering on which side of this horrid fence to descend. Nuncumar's stock stood very high. On the other hand, he had heavy revenue balances to meet, and the Revenue Board's *diwan*, Gunga Govind Sing, was a formidable man. Besides, there were followers of Mahomed Reza Khan, and other Moslems like his old friend Sudder-ud-Din, who hated the prospect of the Brahmin Nuncumar in supreme power. All the first half of April he dithered, being given to tears and bowel trouble in emergency. In the middle of the month he was thick with Nuncumar, whom he would induce to present petitions against the brutal Gunga; in return, he was persuaded to recant his accusation of December against Fowke, and to recast it so as to depict Hastings and Graham as compelling him to involve Fowke in a conspiracy. On the 18th a curious scene took place at Fowke's house. By Kamal's own account, he would not admit giving bribes, whereupon old Joey, crying 'God damn you, you son of a bitch', offered to strike him with a folio volume of Churchill's *Voyages*. Kamal also alleged he was made to sign a second document, confessing he had given a large sum to Barwell, and lesser ones to Hastings, Vansittart, and Cantoo. At any rate, after many tears he broke away, vainly begged Nuncumar to intercede, and then consulted Sudder-ud-Din. He tried again next day to get back his petitions but departed after a scuffle with Nuncumar's servants, and then, on the advice of Rajballabh, hastened to see the Governor, who sent him off to be examined by Impey.

Here and there in the evidence we feel the foul reality of this Calcutta underworld, ostensibly so far removed from the decencies of Leadenhall Street, and the 'Nabobs' in their seemly English homes. Palanquins pass in and out of narrow lanes, to attend Nuncumar's *durbar*, where a swarm of *vakeels* are squatting, waiting for what may interest their masters. Kamal passes over the screen, his seal ready on his finger, and his cummerbund stuffed with papers. He passes his hookah to Nuncumar's servant, while he screws up his courage. Joseph Fowke sits on his bed, offering him betel and ottar.

All day long on the 20th, till eleven at night, the whole bench of judges, in their capacity as magistrates, examined the parties at Impey's house, finally agreeing to give Hastings and Barwell four days to decide whether they would prosecute. The next evening the Three in two coaches and a chaise paid Nuncumar a state visit, while the same day, by leave of the judges, Hastings again cross-examined Kamal, as he reported there and then to Vansittart.

'C. o' Din has been with me. He persists in his story. I have begged and entreated him to reveal the whole truth to me, and not to deceive me. I have told him that it must be discovered if the matter is brought to a trial, and will bring shame on him if it is false. He swears that every syllable is true, and has told the whole over again with additional circumstances, and a variation in the manner and expression, but with so exact a consistency that I cannot refuse my credit to it. If you know any way to look into a man's heart, I wish you would take a peep into his, for unless I were morally certain of the fact, I would not for the universe proceed in it. And if I were certain, I would not for the universe drop it.'

It does not read like the letter of a man bent on destroying an enemy by hook or crook. Yet another day convinced him of Kamal's 'undeviating consistency', and on the 24th he, and Barwell with more hesitation, decided to prosecute Nuncumar, his son-in-law Radachurn, and Joseph Fowke for conspiracy,— the case against Joseph's son Francis being dropped.

He was not confident of success. Was it likely this timid Kamal, a revenue farmer who could be ruined on any vamped-up charge, would stand out till the assizes in June? And the Three instantly showed their defiance. Clavering's staff officers went bail for Nuncumar; the revenue authorities issued a peremptory order for payment of Kamal's balances.

But on May the 6th, on the oaths of Mohan Persad and

Kamal, Justices Hyde and Lemaistre committed Nuncumar on the charge of feloniously uttering a forged bond, — 'no doubt of his guilt', Lemaistre stated later, 'remaining in the heart of either of us'. On the 18th Hastings revoked the discretionary powers for his resignation he had given to his agents. 'Besides that no man ever saved himself by jumping out of a carriage when he was run away, I am now determined by many considerations to wait the final issue on our mutual appeals.' Was one such consideration that, as he let fall, Nuncumar was 'in a fair way to be hanged'? John Stewart added a postscript that he doubted whether more accusations would come in, 'till they see how Nuncumar's ears hang in his head'. To this we must add an odd note that day from Hastings to Graham, saying he put 'as much faith in the quick and the dead as Macleane does in the Apostles' creed'.

War was declared now; these were May days with a vengeance. The Three sent Goring up to Murshidabad to depose Munny Begum, and to put Guru Das in her place. Her accounts were ransacked, her servants locked up to prevent their appealing to Calcutta, the resident who defended her was dismissed on a charge of fraud. So was Gunga Govind Sing, so was Nuncumar's hostile son-in-law Jugeth Chand, so also the recalcitrant *foudjar* of Hugli, while Kamal was imprisoned for his revenue deficiencies.

From intimidation they went on to illegality. Clavering, we must suppose, genuinely believed in Nuncumar's innocence. For he proposed a minute to Francis, arguing how dishonourable it was in Hastings to use Cantoo and Sudder-ud-Din to incite Kamal and Mohan Persad, to revive a charge against Nuncumar which 'had been kept alive for four years past on purpose to keep him in dependence'. They questioned the under-sheriff and jailor in Council, and asked Impey to allow exceptional treatment for the accused, who was refusing to eat in prison on account of his caste. They encouraged the old man to hope for release by their notes, and by messages from their wives and daughters. Indeed, rumours filled the city, which they had to repudiate, that they would rescue him by force.

Their violence precipitated the long-threatened breach with the judges. Impey opposed their interference with the courts, which should be 'believed and known to be above all influence'. The hot-headed Hyde and Lemaistre threatened the Three with an action for defamation, who replied they would watch their proceedings 'with an attentive eye'. They then wantonly raised a new controversy by an absurd claim of diplomatic immunity for Radachurn, as the ambassador of the Nabob, whose complaint they forwarded to the Court. That the Nabob's powers fulfilled none of the essentials of sovereignty, the Court had little difficulty in showing, Lemaistre even speaking of 'this phantom, this man of straw'. But their stand for judicial independence was more vital. Where had the Nabob learned, they asked, this doctrine that he could prevent the Court acting? Council had no authority 'to correct or control any acts of the judges, either in or out of Court, be those acts ever so erroneous'. They appealed to the Directors to protect the sole bulwark of impartial justice.

While Nuncumar's comfortable tent became a *durbar*, and his agents scoured the province to suborn witnesses, the machinery of government collapsed. Francis wrote that Clavering had challenged Barwell, and that Hastings would probably challenge the General. Macpherson at Madras told Hastings of a faction there who were sure he was 'under the waters', and begged that some trusty European, perhaps 'your fair female friend', would taste all his food. On the case of Kamal the Board of Trade, led by Vansittart, were at loggerheads with the Revenue Board, which was full of 'Franciscans', such as Goring and Shore. Every factory and Provincial Council was divided. At Dacca, for instance, a Hastings section led by Shakespeare was opposed by another under Fowke's nephew Hollond, who was said to be threatening Barwell with exposure of his crooked dealings there.

Meantime, by every possible channel, the Three called the attention of England to Nuncumar. Their minute of May the 16th commented 'if it be observed that he is the principal evidence against the Governor-General, the measures taken to compass his destruction may be easily accounted for'. To Francis, Nuncumar was worth as much dead as alive. To Clive (himself now dead) he wrote that this violent persecution showed 'how material some people thought it to invalidate the credit of his evidence', while forty-eight hours after the execution he imparted to Admiral Hughes that no man doubted that, 'if he had never stood forth in politics, his other offences would not have hurt him'. A year later, on Strachey expressing the hope they had better evidence than this 'notorious rascal', he let the term pass, 'but by ——

he spoke truth, or why were they in such a hurry to hang him?' The years passed, and he grew bolder, breaking out to North that 'the Judges tried and hanged one of the principal natives, whose evidence would have convicted Mr. Hastings, on an English penal statute, which I affirm without hesitation no more extends to this country than it does to Tartary'. And so thought Indians, good and bad; both the Moslem noble who wrote the last annals of his house, and the unspeakable Nobkissen, who implied that the Governor's revenge for the charges from Burdwan was to revive the case of Mohan Persad.

Here is the darkest mark against Hastings, not making a legal count at his impeachment, but under-scored deeply in history: the moral indictment that he instigated, or connived at, a judicial murder to save his own political life.

We cannot re-try Nuncumar to-day, nor ascertain after two centuries the degree of his guilt. Let us merely recall that, while Hastings was on the high seas in 1769, one Bolaqui Das, 'yellow of colour and old', died at Calcutta, leaving a pious will and commending his widow and family to Nuncumar. This up-country banker had formerly lived dangerously as money-agent for the Nabob Mir Kasim. Slowly, as the law allowed, disputes developed over his ledgers and legacies, till by 1772 his papers were deposited in the Mayor's court. Late that year a claim for moneys due began in a Company court against Nuncumar, whom young Robert Palk imprisoned for contempt but whom Hastings, as we have seen, had released. Over the next two years the case crept dubiously forward.

Vainly we should try to pierce the fantastic mist of evidence that swathed the Supreme Court, as it sat, week-days and Sunday alike, to try Nuncumar from June the 8th to the 16th, 1775; when the judges, stifling in robes and wigs, retired thrice a day to change their linen, and Calcutta society crowded the assembly-room where, on festive occasions, they used to dance. The mist was transmitted inch by inch through interpreters, with Hastings' young favourite Elliot among them, a veil of twisted conversations and of documents in Persian, Urdu, and sundry dialects; a story of papers buried in compounds and dug up again, and of receipts kept in arm amulets. We should be sorry to vouch for the integrity of the witnesses for the Crown; of the sinister Nobkissen, — 'Mahrajah Nuncumar had better not ask me that question',

— or Kamal so plausible and weak in the bowels, or Sudder-ud-Din, once partaker in Nuncumar's forgeries but now so close to Gunga Govind Sing. And still less for the witnesses for the defence, with their remarkable agreement in statistics and their preternatural eyesight for seals. All gone alike from that airless court, repeating to the patient Elliot 'what is in my remembrance I remember, what I have forgot I have forgot'.

We must leave Nuncumar's guilt to the unanimity of the four judges and the jury, or to the private verdict later of Justice Chambers, friend of Francis and sympathetic to the accused, that 'he certainly was guilty of uttering the writing in question, knowing it to be forged'. But that does not dispose of the charge against Hastings.

For that we must go, first, to the evidence of two of his English enemies, emphatically belonging to the camp of Clavering and Francis: Charles Boughton Rouse, at this time chief at Dacca, and Thomas Farrer, Nuncumar's counsel. Both gave evidence at Impey's impeachment in 1788, and unless it is dismissed on the ground of senility (unusual in men in the fifties) or the lapse of thirteen years, the Governor-General was substantially cleared. For Rouse testified that in the civil court, in which he presided, Mohan Persad alleged forgery as early as February 1774; that the court recommended arbitration, in part to avoid that charge in a complex case, and in part because one Indian member of it was thought to be under Nuncumar's influence; and that Nuncumar, or both parties, were still evading arbitration, when the arrival of the Supreme Court gave the prosecution a better opportunity.

Farrer was even more decisive. He deposed that in November 1774 Mohan Persad's English attorney told him he had advised his client to prosecute for forgery, and had actually applied in the previous March for the allegedly forged bond; that the Mayor's court had only offered a copy, which was not sufficient; but that he would advise him now to brief Farrer to ask the original from the Supreme Court, to which all the papers had been transferred. Now the actual facts of 1775 bear Farrer out. In January, and with final effect on March the 24th, the Supreme Court granted the application; it was on March the 11th that Nuncumar, laying special weight on Hastings' interviews with Mohan Persad, brought his charges before Council. Farrer added that in the forgery case he did not put in the previous civil proceedings, in effect because they would damage Nuncumar. If all this were so, a criminal prosecution had been in the air for more than a year, developing naturally out of the civil suit, and the last step to make it possible had been taken six weeks before Nuncumar accused the Governor.

Yet if the Governor and his circle did not inspire, they watched the moves of Mohan Persad. In mid-April, we recollect, Hastings lamented 'even Mohan Persad has left me'; in early May Durham, the Company attorney, was in conference with him. When all is said, our dilemma narrows to a single question, whether or not we accept the word on oath of the Governor-General.

When Nuncumar lay under sentence of death, the conspiracy trial came on in July, and Hastings was examined. 'Did you not say that you would be revenged on him and would ruin him?' 'I am clear I did not mention these words, because it is not in my disposition.' 'Did you directly, or indirectly, countenance or forward the prosecution?' 'I never did; I have been on my guard: I have carefully avoided every circumstance which might appear to be an interference in that prosecution.' And then his minute in September: 'it would have ill become the first magistrate in the settlement to have employed his influence either to promote or dissuade it'.

On August 7th, when Nuncumar had been dead two days, the Governor wrote many letters to England. One was to Dr. Johnson, sending Bogle's account of his Tibet journey, in return for *The Voyage to the Hebrides*; thanking him, too, for his introduction to Chambers, though of late business had deprived him of 'the gratifications of society'. But another went to Francis Sykes: 'Nuncumar has met with a miserable fate, which he has deserved ever since I knew him'. Sometimes in later years that name crops up, and always on this casual and unconcealing note; once alluding to Nuncumar's last petition, 'if the paper delivered by General Clavering to the Board after that unhappy man's death were really his, which I very much doubt'.

Perhaps to sit still was enough, for after sentence had been passed Farrer found no European, except one juryman, who would ask a respite. It looks as if the real forces in Bengal politics, — a rally of Europeans, and of Indians held together by Hastings' long service, popularity, and powers of reward, —

gathered behind the Governor-General. He was never the man to let his Indian dependants down; his accounts for the following year show payments to the unhappy Kamal and the dismissed *foudjar* of Hugli. And he could count on the devotion of his own household. When Farrer, rather rashly, lobbied the foreman of the jury for a reprieve, it was Hastings' secretary Belli who complained of it to Impey. And if it were to be life for Nuncumar, a respite like that given in another forgery case ten years before, it was hardly in human expectation, and not in his nature, that Hastings should move in it.

But Nuncumar's death came about at the hand of his friends. It was their threats and insolence which inflamed the angry obstinacy of Hyde and Lemaistre and the stiff legalism of Impey. Yet Impey's chief arguments were not those of law, but of policy. Apart from an 'atrocious aggravation of the original offence' by perjured evidence, the conduct of the Three made it 'absolutely necessary' to refuse a respite. Clavering threatened the judges with dismissal; offers of a large bribe reached Lemaistre. Every Indian would have put a respite down either to pressure from Council, or corruption. And yet, Impey added on his impeachment, if Council had asked for it on the ground that the prosecution was merely engineered to save Hastings, the judges must have granted it.

As to that, on the evening of August the 1st the tireless Farrer ran down the Three at a party given by Lady Anne Monson, and showed them a petition for mercy. Clavering and Monson refused to hear of it. August the 5th was fixed for the execution, and on the 4th Clavering received another plea from the prisoner; he did not open it, and produced it at his leisure in Council on the 14th. There it was unanimously condemned as a libel on the judges, and Francis moved that the original be burned by the hangman. He did this, he explained in 1788, to save Clavering; 'Colonel Monson started . . . and desired me to go with him into another room', where in grisly tones he said that judges who had 'dipped their hands in blood' would strike at Clavering. How they loved one another! Ten days later Clavering suggested to North that Francis should be recalled.

So it was over. Brahmins burned the body of Nuncumar, addresses of thanks reached the judges, and Tilly Kettle was commissioned to paint Impey for the town hall. Yet it would be mistaken to think that all British opinion was united. In 1777 the Directors condemned the refusal of a respite, and this severe application of English law to a country that lived by a different code. And in 1781, giving evidence before parliament, two illustrious servants of the Company, each a great admirer of Hastings, declared that the execution caused general terror, shocking the Indian mind not so much by the severity of punishment as by the fear it might be extended to other offences. These were James Rennell, the great geographer, and Baber, sometime resident at Murshidabad.

Hastings and Impey, knowing it would make an ill impression, took their counter-measures. Alexander Elliot was immediately chosen as their envoy, armed with Hastings' seal and with his recommendation to the Prime Minister; in due course he received £1000 from Hastings' attorneys in London. He carried with him authority, signed by all four judges, to publish an authentic account of the trial, compiled from their notes. Impey entrusted to him a defence of his impartiality for the Secretary of State; yet, he said, 'I would by no means have my attachment to Mr. Hastings be denied or extenuated. It was founded in friendship for a schoolfellow, and has been confirmed by opinion of the man.'

Three more months' experience of the majority impelled Hastings to send off someone of greater weight, and nearer to himself; his best friend, in fact, George Vansittart. So we read:

DEAR GEORGE,

As you cannot decide for yourself, I will determine for you, — go! All that could be done for the general cause in this quarter is done, and the rest must depend on the weight which is given it in England.

But it was not till January 1776 that Vansittart got off, loaded with documents, and with Hastings' final message: 'remember me kindly to all who ask kindly after me, and tell them I have strength, health, and spirits to hold out nine months longer, and for nine years if I get delivered in that time. Farewell once more, my dear George, remember me, for no one loves you more than I do.'

It was high time. Before he sailed, Hastings was buried under new accusations, and dangers from all India, which he

thus summarized for his old chief Du Pré: 'The pacific government of Bombay has engaged in a desperate war with the
Mahratta State, without men, money, or resources; the Presidency of Madras are at variance with the Nabob and one another,
and this government is in a state worse than anarchy'.

CHAPTER XIII

The Last Year of the Three: 1775-76

AGED 43-44

DEATH spaced out the history of British Bengal, and turned the course of their policies. Nuncumar's in August was soon followed by that of Dr. Hancock, much broken in his fortunes. Lady Anne Monson died in February 1776, her husband soon failed, and in September his death destroyed the majority. The agreeable Mackrabie vanished that November; in the year after, gay Justice Lemaistre and General Clavering.

How infinitely weary Philip Francis grew of 'this cursed country', and how we weary too of his groans, that he was 'worn to a shadow' by this 'slavery worse than the mines'! But his hatreds bore him up. Had he given way to the spleen, he wrote, he would have been stretched beside his colleagues, 'with a damned *hic jacet* upon my heart'. He saw no reason why Barwell continued to live, 'but that death does not think it worth while to kill him'; as for Hastings, 'he is more tough than any of us, and will never die a natural death'. Impey, C.J., was doing his best to avoid it, never in court after one o'clock, and insistent on holidays by the sea.

They met, of course, on neutral ground, at Mrs. Hyde's 'Tuesdays', or the musical Alderseys, or at the Governor's concert party this New Year; where Barwell chaffed Mackrabie, 'and pray what brought you here? Coming over to the majority, I suppose?' They would dance at Colonel Galliez' ball, where poor frail Mackrabie saw with envy Begum Johnson holding the floor, and French women 'dancing *cotillons* as if they had not another hour to live'. There was the other neutral territory of Barwell's gambling week-ends, where Francis and Lemaistre would take their host's money, — Francis with gusto, for 'the blood sucker should bleed'. On one 'blessed day', desperate with melancholy, he staked deep and won £20,000, of which he managed to keep £12,000, and after that played low.

In fact, the reformer was doing quite well. His salary was £10,000, yet in 1777 he managed to remit home that sum precisely, while a year later Hastings heard his total remittances touched £45,000. He believed he was making loans to the wretched Vizier, the Impeys thought he dabbled in opium. At least he moved, with his faithful train, into a fine house near the new theatre, for which he paid £1200 a year, took over the Claverings' capable housekeeper, and rode a fine bay horse from Agra.

Now and then he looked with something like despair towards the Governor who, he allowed, was making 'a surprising battle'. And Barwell felt the same surprise, that this once very irritable man seemed hardened into a prodigy of self-control. He had acquired some new power of reading the mind of others, by which he detected Francis' growing loathing of Clavering. And when mere accusations evaporated, and they had to face up to hard issues of policy, he exulted that, even when outvoted, he alone kept government together. 'Cats and dogs and serpents could easier unite in society than so incongruous a composition as Clavering, Monson, and Francis.'

Yes, Francis decided, Clavering was impossible. Monson was sickening fast, perhaps only hanging on to avoid service in America, but the General would never do. Not so much that he was sticky over patronage, or audaciously disagreed with Francis' sweeping plans for the revenue; it was the blend of violent words and spineless policy that he despised. 'Here am I', he confided to Strachey or D'Oyley, 'harnessed between two of the bravest men in the world, without an atom of political courage in either of them.' Clavering's dominion would be unendurable; 'you might as well hang me at once as make him Governor'. He would accept the government of Madras, but still hoped for Bengal; 'I have a hold on this country which none of them can shake'.

The stout youth Barwell seemed inclined to lie back, he was often an absentee at Council, and courting the famous beauty, Miss Sanderson. To North's man of business, Robinson, he defended Hastings. But to his sister Mary he wrote that they must re-insure, he was a servant of government, not of any minister or governor; he would serve under Clavering, and equally under Rumbold. For he reckoned that his own chances of the succession were dim.

The Governor felt lonely. It took him long to make new friends, or break 'the reserve which it is not in my nature to throw off but by a long and familiar intercourse'. Macleane had long gone, and lately Elliot, — 'I love Elliot as much as his father can' — and in 1776 John Stewart his first secretary, and Vansittart, with whom Marian played chess. Stewart took with him Tilly Kettle's portrait of his chief, and wrote back, 'I am afraid, indeed, the people won't take my word for it, that this same Governor Hastings, whom they have heard so much of, is but a plain-looking man like any of us, with a brown coat'.

When he escaped from work, he was with Marian at Alipur, and with his Arab horses; perhaps she was already on the way to become, as he boasted later, 'the best horsewoman in India'. This time of waiting was hard for her. Some of his friends did not like her influence, some of the women turned a cold eye on her auburn curls and her diamonds. There was still no word of the divorce, but some time probably in 1776 he settled £12,000 upon her, part of the income to go towards educating her Imhoff sons. What with this, and the £10,000 to Macleane, £1000 to Elliot, and a bill drawn on him by Frederick Stuart, he was spending at a rate that worried his friends. 'What are you about with your money?' asked Vansittart, 'your attorneys have not above £20,000 of yours in their hands.' But no consideration interfered with his life's dream; buy any land, he repeated to his brother-in-law, 'near Daylesford or along the Sarsbrooke'.

Having let Nuncumar die without raising a finger, the Three drew breath and began again. Their campaign touched a new low level of insult and unwisdom. Nuncumar, they now said, had till lately been the 'bosom friend' of the Governor, whose first design had been to use him as a spy in their camp. And now he was safely dead, they brought into the full light the charge they had so long covertly hinted, the 'precipitate removal' of Nuncumar as murder. Corruptions, they said, had been 'almost universally practised and connived at'. Vansittart, Thackeray in Sylhet, and half a dozen more, had robbed the revenues through their *banyans*. They accused Baber of taking bribes. Cantoo smuggled salt, in addition to his farms and contracts, and 'our opinion of Mr. Hastings will not suffer us to think, that a participation of profits with his servant would have been repugnant to his principles'. Munny Begum, 'a slave and a dancing girl', was merely the Governor's instrument. He had evaded the Hugli charges; 'provided he can secure himself from conviction in a court of law, he seems to care very little what the Court of Directors or the world may think of him'. No doubt he would appeal to the Indian interest in London, but 'we will not submit our cause to such a tribunal'. What Indians had signed the address to the judges, except 'the famous Nobkissen' and 'black tribe of banyans'? As to policy, the Governor's rejoinders, 'voluminous as ever', could not conceal the collapse of his revenue system, his 'utter disregard of the faith of treaties', or his intention to destroy the native government, subordinating 'the accumulated wisdom and experience of ages' to 'the crude ideas of a few foreigners'. Coldly Hastings noted, 'frivolous and useless debates'.

It had been very much more than a paper war. Goring, with the obsequious Guru Das, had carried through the disgrace of Munny Begum; 'she has been cruelly used', Hastings told Vansittart, 'and unhappily possesses a spirit that doubles the effect of every indignity'. John Stewart was dismissed from his various posts 'on frivolous pretexts', so Impey wrote to Shelburne. Playdell, superintendent of police, and Robinson, the foreman of the jury, were turned out of the service for signing the address to the judges. They were digging far back into past history in order to destroy Hastings' Indian following; had not Khwaja Petrus, head of the Armenian signatories, been a notorious adherent of Mir Kasim? While Kamal-ud-Din was still being prosecuted, to quote Impey again, with 'unremitting vengeance'.

Their own appointments were equally pointed. They could not do much for Joseph Fowke after the verdict against him for conspiracy against Barwell, his brother-in-law Walsh advising him to retire 'to the more profitable diamond trade at Benares'. That being so, it was convenient that the Three had just sent his son Francis there as resident. Clavering suggested too that Bristow might get the old man a contract for clothing the Vizier's troops. Bristow, indeed, was a most valuable asset. He told Francis the Vizier's envoy at Calcutta would always consult him, 'you may, when necessary, dictate his letters and any of your friends translate them'. In October the arrival of a Directors' despatch, dated March the 3rd, gave them a still larger opening.

This document was highly typical of their honourable employers. It pronounced on Oudh and the Rohilla war, with a gingerly balance. They were 'exceedingly concerned', yet the Rohillas had drawn their fate on themselves; the treaty of Benares, though not 'unexceptionable', was generally approved. They then plunged timidly, yet wildly, into Bengal politics. They much commended Hastings' conduct of the prosecution of Mahomed Reza Khan, but since he was acquitted were ready to employ him again, yet not in 'any improper degree of power'. And as Nuncumar's share in this had been discreditable, they recommended that his son Guru Das should be displaced from the office of 'Roy Royan', which should be given to the ex-Naib. Their facts were hopelessly at sea; Guru Das was merely a household officer, while the Roy Royan was the capable Rajballabh, son of Clive's famous supporter, Rai Durlab. No matter. Without a moment's hesitation, the Three revived in Mahomed Reza Khan the office of Naib Suba, which Hastings had abolished with the Directors' subsequent approval, restored his old criminal jurisdiction, and thus revived the dual system of evil memory. They simultaneously dismissed Rajballabh, filling his place with Guru Das. So culminated Francis' campaign for the restoration of 'the country government'.

If Hastings' rejoinders were ever inwardly digested over these six months by the Directors, they should have set up some discomfort. The aims of the Three, he began, had been clear from the day they landed, to blast his character and force his resignation. The work of his first administration was destroyed. All business stood still, for 'the Board is occupied in collecting proofs of my demerit, and of the virtue of my adversaries'. 'The contagion of the capital' poisoned every Provincial Council. The *Sudder Diwanni*, or civil appeal court, had been abolished. And of all this he must sit 'a passive spectator', 'the butt of everlasting contumely'.

When they came to 'the enunciation of their own services', he could find only negation, or 'temporary adjustment in a heap of old ruins'. He defied them to produce a single case 'by which a rupee was gained to the Company, or a rupee saved'. Their 'refined system' would have established the Mahrattas in Oudh, while they had so robbed the Vizier that his debt to the Company would be irrecoverable. Their restoration of the Naib Suba was in disobedience of orders, while in proclaiming the Nabob's sovereignty their 'vein of fancy' reversed all the past twenty years. 'All the arts of policy cannot conceal the power by which these provinces are ruled . . . the Nabob is a mere pageant, without so much as the shadow of authority.' Yet to accuse his own administration of subverting Indian institutions would be false; his measures preserved 'the ancient constitution of Bengal, revived with such modifications, and such only, as were absolutely necessary to accommodate it to the genius and principles of our own'.

As to the revenue, he must maintain that the famine had been 'an epoch', enough to account for a decline, yet the Three rigidly refused to allow any remissions. He was aware the lands had been overrated, but that was being corrected, while sale by auction had at least prevented corrupt dealings by Company servants. He appealed from 'theoretical and abstract principles' to 'principles of common sense'; 'my government was not spent in ineffectual or logical discussions'. But, satisfied with 'pure declamation', the Three washed their hands of responsibility.

His private letters this year convey more of his inner satisfaction. He declared to Sulivan, with 'pride of heart', that he had never spoken with ill will of a colleague, 'even Lord Clive', or allowed his pen to say more than he had face to face. He was proud, too, that he contrived to keep current business flowing, even on his enemies' lines if his own were impossible, for inaction was 'the death of public affairs'. He let John Stewart see something of his philosophy; 'remember that, though I made a number of chops and changes, I never called myself a Reformer, nor lamented that all men were not as virtuous and disinterested as myself'. With that we may couple the angry contempt with which Francis set down the Governor's character; '"I detest general principles" is a common expression with him'. This self-confessed preference for expediency, this contentment to tack about so long as the vessel moved, this it was which made Francis the ideologue write Hastings off as 'a projecting intricate politician', 'it is not in his nature to walk straight'.

This texture of Hastings' mind came out very clearly in the urgent problems with which this distracted government now had to deal. Of these the role of the Supreme Court was the chief;

one so inevitable, that it must have developed had Nuncumar never been born; one from which his Council could not escape, or Hastings' life be separated.

The Regulating Act and the Court charter were mutually inconsistent, and shirked every decision. They imported British law, yet without asserting British sovereignty. They gave the Court jurisdiction over 'British subjects' and Company servants, yet left all powers used by the previous administration in the Governor-General in Council. And whether the Court was confined to Calcutta, or extended to the provinces, was left equally in doubt. What, then, was the legal position of a *zemindar*, or the juridical status of a Provincial Council? The Indian zest for litigation promptly played on these doubts. Months before the Nuncumar case, a host of appeals clamoured for remedy, in revenue disputes which had long been dormant.

Extreme claims on either side circled round the ignominious figure of Kamal-ud-Din. The Three advised Provincial Councils to ignore the Court's ruling in revenue questions, and when Hyde and Lemaistre argued that the Act had transferred all such powers to the Court, Provincial Councils, irrespective of party, unanimously resisted. Dacca, for example, protested against Indians being dragged away for trial 'three hundred miles from their friends and families, in a language and mode of process totally unknown to them'. Civilians as upright as Bogle and Shore argued that revenue officers could not possibly satisfy the English technicalities of evidence, or even accept appointment without fear of ruinous prosecutions.

Though Hastings stood by the judges in the first instance, he well realized the threat to the entire system of government. So when the Court demanded to inspect Council minutes, he was found in unusual alliance with Francis; on the other hand, he bore witness to Impey's moderation. The Court, he allowed, had some reason on its side. It had prevented some 'glaring oppressions'; while, if it could not take evidence from Indians, or if the definition of 'British subjects' were left in doubt, all justice would collapse. He concluded that the solution must be found in some sort of union of courts and, having converted Barwell, in January 1776 put up his 'plan for the better administration of justice'.

Parliament, he politely suggested, had doubtless meant the

present system as 'an introduction to one more perfect'. For this, the essentials must be to legalize the powers which government exercised in fact, to sweep away the distinction between the *Diwanni* and the *Nizamut*, and to make British sovereignty 'all in all'. He proposed therefore to fuse the Company jurisdiction with the Supreme Court. Thus the civil Court of Appeal would be formed of Councillors and judges sitting together, having below them the Provincial Councils and subordinate *diwanni* courts. In criminal cases, Governor-General and Chief Justice would similarly act together in confirming the sentences of the Nazim. Police should be improved by making the chiefs of Provincial Councils justices of the peace, and by appointing Indian magistrates for Calcutta with petty powers. In March Impey assisted to shape the scheme as a draft statute. 'I sat up till one in the morning', Hastings told Vansittart, 'talking law with the Judges, of which I know no more than an infant', adding he had never thought so highly before of Impey's ability.

But for the time being no more was heard of his plan. A long jeering minute from the Three denounced any system 'forcibly introduced from the other side of the globe', followed up by a letter to North which declared Bengal was not 'tenable' if Indians generally were submitted to a British court. It was, indeed, quite contradictory to all Francis' philosophy for India; which emerged even more violently in the prolonged dispute over the revenue.

Hastings and Barwell, as we have seen, brought forward new proposals in April 1775. They had before them reports from the most experienced provincial chiefs, such as Vansittart, Dacres, and Samuel Middleton, who all agreed on three substantial points. To wit: that the land was heavily overrated; that *zemindars* were much to be preferred as revenue agencies to farmers; and that the nearer a settlement approached to permanency, the better. Hastings and Barwell consequently proposed to rent the lands for life, or two lives, giving a priority to *zemindars*; to recognize a claim to continuance in *zemindars'* heirs; to allow a *zemindar's* police powers, 'agreeably to the old constitution of the Empire'; to repeal all taxes levied since we took over the *diwanni*, but to safeguard government by retaining the power to sell up a defaulter, and a limited right of increasing the revenue upon a vacancy.

In 1776 Francis brought forward his alternative. The matter, Hastings wrote, came from Ducarel, 'the rhetorical part is his own'. And while Barwell said its principles were fair enough, he criticized its 'easy flowery' argument for a permanent reduction of revenue, and for the wholesale enthronement of the *zemindars*, — to the peril of the *ryots* whom Hastings and he wished to protect. But, in fact, Francis' revenue scheme was only a wing of his general ideal for India, which was the pride of his heart; this plan, he tells North, 'will either be the source of happiness to future ages, or a perpetual Monument of Repentance'.

His mentality, steeped in Montesquieu and the fashionable doctrinaires, demanded 'grand and simple principles', 'too luminous to require illustration', which must 'hold good at all times and in all places'. Bengal must be viewed as a conquered people, English should be the single official language, the royal sovereignty must be declared. But while British paramountcy must 'hold the sword' and enforce, in concert with Delhi, a sort of Indian Peace of Westphalia, none of this forbade restoration of the 'country government'. No European should touch the revenues or local justice; all we should ask was a fixed tribute; for the investment, we should go into the market on equal terms. Mahomed Reza Khan's restoration had thus been a first step to bring things back to 'their ancient and natural channel', and by such reasoning Francis damned all Hastings' new courts and the removal of the *khalsa* to Calcutta.

The revenue, then, must be fixed in perpetuity, while he found in the *zemindars* 'the natural proprietors'. Provincial Councils should be abolished, and collectors temporarily re-appointed until his plan settled down in its grand simplicity, which he commended to all 'whose intellects are a little higher than the standard of a rupee'.

Much to his annoyance, even Clavering questioned the wisdom of thus freezing the land revenue for ever; his doctrinaire condemnation of the salt and opium monopolies equally shocked the revenue-minded Barwell. And nothing could be further from the outlook of Hastings. While Francis expressed a doubt whether Britain had been wise to enter India at all, and a conviction that our taking the *diwanni* had been disastrous, Hastings believed with all his heart that, by fusing British power and Indian custom, life could be given to a structure in transition, and the inevitable day of decline postponed. While Francis despised 'what they call local knowledge', Hastings would build on nothing else, and as a preliminary to the new settlement, which must be reached by 1777, suggested an exhaustive local enquiry, to get at the lands' true values. Francis, in fact, was the doctrinaire who becomes an iconoclast, even proposing to abolish the universal Hindu custom of adoption of heirs, which (Hastings commented) 'is legislating with a vengeance'. The Governor would find a solution in equilibrium. Though English corruption was diminished, — 'God be thanked there are few such in the service' as Goring and James Grant — past experience bade him not to expose young men to over-temptation, and to centralize revenue authority. Government, *zemindars, ryots,* each had their rights of title, longer settlements were the ideal, yet without despairing of an increased revenue, *zemindars* should have police powers as of old, without being autocrats — all had their claims, which must be reconciled.

Much more than the settlement made him anxious as the cold weather waned. Terrible evils were piling up in Oudh, Bombay, and Madras; 'ruin and infamy must attend me if I am put in charge of the government a twelve-month hence'. The Imperial government was silent on their appeals, and meantime the first shadows of the American war fell across India. Not that he could much attend to them. 'My patriotism extends but weakly beyond my own sphere of action, and is grievously hurt by the inattention seemingly paid to the East while the West is all in confusion.'

He had warned Francis already that, if he recovered power, he would use it to recall Bristow from Oudh. And the confederates had taken the alarm. Francis advised Bristow that the Board of Trade had a watchful eye on his saltpetre trade and his clothing contract; if trouble came, he must destroy their ciphers. Joseph Fowke at Benares was also told to burn Francis' letters, and that the Vizier's more popular brother, Saadut Ali, had powerful friends.

Indeed, the Vizier Asof-ud-Daulah was a poor creature, often 'drunk as a beast', with the favourites whom he had chosen as his ministers. But the Three had not given him a chance. They had refused to protect his father's conquests, with the result that Rohilkund was threatened by the Rohilla survivors and the

Sikhs, and the Doab by the Mahrattas. He was crushed under debts to British creditors, Bristow among them, and in heavy arrears with the additional subsidy the Three had imposed. His *zemindars* refused obedience, revenue could only be collected at the point of the sword, all was vitiated by the poisonous system of *tuncaws*, or land assignments, earmarked both for the favourites and the British brigade. He had lately asked for the loan of more British officers, to train another so-called 'temporary' brigade; and these officers too, with others in his private service like Hannay and Mordaunt, were battening on this unhappy country. The one source of wealth left open, the great treasure in the hands of his mother, was closed by the agreement that Bristow had negotiated.

How northern India would shape was thus uncertain. The one able man in the Empire, the soldier Nadjif Khan, was in touch with the Rohillas who, said Bristow, still had their old 'thirst of power', and with Oudh rebels in the Doab, while Saadut Ali had fled to him for refuge. To win the friendship of this man, conqueror of the Jats of Agra, and to stop a possible alliance between the Moguls and the Mahrattas, Hastings sent Major Hannay on a mission. He was to offer the arrears of the pension which Clive had given, but to ask Nadjif to dismiss his dangerous mercenary soldiers, Samroo the murderer of the English at Patna, and the Frenchman Madec.

There were parallel troubles at Benares. Though Hastings had protected Chait Sing against Oudh, he could not protect him against the Three. Their settlement of 1776 made him not an ally but a vassal *zemindar*, guaranteed indeed against further demands if his land revenue were punctually forthcoming, but it must be paid to a British resident and he was forbidden to make foreign alliances. As Hastings predicted, this half-status encouraged friction. The revenue was constantly in arrears, while Chait Sing complained that British officers and sepoys terrorized his customs officers, and made monstrous demands for elephants and transport.

Far away to the south, the weak Madras Presidency was reviving every trouble with which Du Pré and Hastings had wrestled before. The standing quarrel with the Nabob, distorted by his debts, was inflamed by rival sets of corrupt Europeans with an influence, both on the spot and in England, which was fated to darken the life of Hastings. The chief British power in the *durbar* was Paul Benfield, the head of the private-creditor group, who were concerned to resist the Nabob's second, and favourite, son. But Hastings' most voluble Madras correspondent was John Macpherson; 'there is no one who tells you his sentiments so freely as your friend Mac'. John Stewart, passing en route for home, was much impressed, telling the Governor that, thanks to Macpherson, Madras was 'a nest of Hastonians'. And it was following on a midnight interview of these two worthies with the Nabob that a newly arrived governor of Madras dismissed Macpherson from the service.

This was Lord Pigot, hero of the siege and Governor in 1759, and now reappointed by a small majority over Thomas Rumbold, to the indignation of the North ministry. The views of Macpherson and Stewart were naturally biased; 'he has been either asleep or intoxicated since he left this chair in '63'. But both his appointment and his downfall provided the most sinister illustration of the Company's incompetence, the peril of Madras, and the evil connection between its internal corruption and its external policy.

Wedged in between the Nizam, Hyder Ali, and the Mahrattas, and exposed to what was left of French hostility, Madras was always in danger. One instance occurred just after the arrival of the Three. Alarmed by the French soldiers in the pay of Basalut Jung, the Nizam's brother, Madras suggested a move of troops to his frontier, and the Three supported them. But on Hastings' protest, — 'I know not to what lengths, nor into what wars, such a resolution may lead us' — it was agreed to try first a representation to the Nizam. That most dangerous prince was in his element, profiting by the anarchy in the Mahratta State; simultaneously offering alliance to the English if they would induce their client Ragoba to yield him some territory, and asking Ragoba's rivals for assistance against Hyder. Hyder, meantime, was consolidating his conquests from the Mahrattas, and others in Malabar.

The Directors' reappointment of Pigot in 1776 marked an abrupt reversal of their Carnatic policy. Three years before they had allowed the Nabob to swallow the dependent Rajah of Tanjore, but now they ordered his restoration. It was carried through by Pigot in person, with abundance of artillery salutes, rose-water, and betel, a garrison was installed of British sepoys, and Benfield's agent was flogged and expelled. But Benfield alone held assignments on Tanjore revenue worth a quarter of a million, other creditors were involved, and they determined to resist. Aided by the Nabob's sons and by Macpherson, they had a majority in Council, and Pigot's insensate violence gave them their pretext. On an August evening two British officers held up the Governor's chaise with their pistols, and carried him off as a prisoner to the barracks at the Mount. 'He was caught like a canary bird', wrote Francis, 'and there he may whistle.' While Brahmins, paid by the Nabob, were performing incantations with cobras for Pigot's death, the majority under one George Stratton proclaimed themselves as the legal government.

Hastings' attitude to this scandal was not directed by the insidious letters of Macpherson. He was always chary of encroaching on Indian princes, and from the first much disliked this matter of Tanjore. 'To compel the Nabob to make restitution', he wrote to Vansittart, 'and keep it ourselves, is a strange perversion of justice; something like our censuring the Presidency of Bombay for taking Salsette from the Mahrattas, and then declaring war on the Mahrattas, if they would not let us keep possession.' And he looked on the Mahratta Rajah of Tanjore as a potential friend to the French. For his future fame his steps at this crisis merit close examination.

Even before it came to a head, he came down on the side of the Nabob, our 'first and foremost ally'. His Council unanimously rebuked Pigot's violence, and as unanimously recognized Stratton's new government. Mediation, Hastings explained to the puzzled Admiral Hughes, was impossible in such a sudden emergency, and above all for himself; he would be accused of making common cause with Pigot, in defiance of the Directors' late ruling against a Governor's right to dissolve his Council, and they must simply stand on majority rule. Moreover, 'I feel a great repugnance to join in personal severities against any men, while I suffer, and have long suffered, so much from the persecutions and indignities offered me by others'. But, in congratulating Stratton, he added that he did not like his Council's emphasis on the Tanjore assignments. Such transactions with princes lay open to 'dangerous abuses'; 'there was a time when you and I both set our hands to opinions not very distant from this'.

Even with the best Madras government, however, there could be no peace in the South while the Mahrattas were at civil war. Having taken Salsette, in March 1775 the Bombay government signed the treaty of Surat with Ragoba, who in return for military assistance promised to cede Salsette, Bassein, and a share of the Gaekwar's revenues in Broach. But in the summer, while British officers led his shaky troops up sandy roads, or from one tamarind grove to another, decisions taken at Calcutta wrecked his cause.

Though the Bombay government evaded, so long as they dared, their legal responsibility to Bengal, in this phase Hastings' line was perfectly consistent. The occupation of Salsette was justified by Company orders; moreover, he told Hughes, 'they were driven to it by an unavoidable necessity', the fear of a pre-occupation by the Portuguese. Very differently he judged their precipitate embracing of the cause of Ragoba, which he denounced in Council as 'impolitic, unjust, and unauthorized'. But when the Three ordered instant evacuation by our troops, he would have kept a freer hand; for when either victory or a compromise with the rulers of Poona were in sight, such a withdrawal and breaking engagements meant 'national dishonour'. The Three, of course, had their way, and sent Clavering's nominee, Colonel Upton, to negotiate a peace; yet with instructions to insist on our keeping Salsette and Bassein.

From a Mahratta point of view, nothing could be more wholesome than this split between two British Presidencies. Bombay sent a Councillor to protest at Calcutta, but their request for reinforcements was refused, and Madras also forbidden to supply them. The Governor's temper was rising. While Monson harked back to the Rohilla precedent, Hastings urged the maintenance of our forces; 'my object is peace, which is most likely to be obtained by being prepared for war'. Clavering, going beyond Francis, was ready to abandon Bassein, which, Hastings minuted, would 'degrade the Presidency of Bombay' in Indian eyes.

Even Upton, with no cards in his hand, resented the lofty tone taken at Poona, and it was only in March 1776, under a threat of force from Bengal, that he got them to sign the treaty of Purandhar. Though this left Salsette in our hands, it annulled the treaty of Surat, stipulated the disbandment of Ragoba's army, promised us a small indemnity and some revenues near Broach, all of which was sure to be disputed in detail. Hastings disapproved of terms which he called 'the meanest that ever disgraced the British name'. And his belief that the treaty would break down was soon justified.

The Bombay government, openly defiant, gave Ragoba a comfortable refuge on Malabar Hill; at midsummer they were overjoyed to get from the Directors, hitherto so critical of offensive war, a commendation of their enterprise, and orders to keep what Ragoba had promised. Not only so; confusion at Poona promised to give Ragoba a second chance. There were jealousies between the brilliant Nana Phadnavis and his rivals, who suspected his intimacy with the infant Peishwa's mother, and rival ambitions of the military chiefs, Scindia and Holkar. And a Perkin Warbeck had arisen in the Deccan, a Brahmin whom the English called Sudaba, posing as a famous warrior killed years ago at Panipat, whose widow refused to believe him dead. Like Warbeck, this pretender had his charm, won over adherents even in the dead man's family, mastered the west coast, and was now reported as marching on Poona. Hastings expected his victory. And though before the year ended he was a captive, taken through Poona on a camel's back to have iron spikes hammered into his skull, all this summer he too helped to destroy the peace of Purandhar.

While Clavering wanted to remove Ragoba from Bombay by force, Hastings agreed that this poor treaty must be honoured, if the Mahratta rulers, — whether Sudaba or others — loyally co-operated. Not that he believed Bombay would resist the 'strong temptation' put in front of them by the Directors' orders. He disbelieved also in Mahratta solidarity, having for some time past been discussing with an agent from the Berar Rajah the possibility of an alliance.

As the summer passed in such doubts, in June an English budget of news reached them. An exhortation to unity from the Company at least produced, Hastings said, their first 'loud and hearty laugh' for some time. The Directors condemned the Rohilla war, though friendly proprietors had contrived to tack on a clause acquitting him of corruption. But they also condemned the majority's abrupt withdrawal of our army from Rohilkund, and their interpretation of the treaty of Benares as expiring on the death of Shuja-ud-Daulah. And while an official letter from John Robinson told Hastings the public expected a fair trial for 'the system', another headed 'most private' assured him 'when you shall have rendered your country those essential services which are in your power, you will meet with the rewards due to her best citizens'.

If this were agreeable, the Directors' condemnation goaded Hastings to fury. He would not admit the justice of charges contradicting 'my own certain knowledge of the integrity of my conduct'. Although he begged Macleane to hasten a decision, indignation stiffened his purpose to hold on. 'Prompted equally by duty and gratitude,' he told the Directors, 'I have hitherto resolved to bear my part in this distracted scene, and if I live I will see the end of it.'

His armour was wearing thin. Margaret Fowke, just out from home, noted his fixed and rather hostile stare; it was 'habitual', her brother Francis told her, 'when his mind is intent upon something which peculiarly occupies it. Your resemblance to us probably brought some disagreeable idea to his recollection.' And though all his Hindu and Moslem friends, Hastings told Vansittart, were predicting his victory, 'consulting the stars, throwing dice, and opening Korans at a venture', he felt unsure whether he could outlive these disputes.

In August, however, glad news came from England. When the Directors, by a single vote, resolved to recall both him and Barwell, a proprietors' meeting had immediately reversed their decision by a triumphant majority of 107. This settled him; 'I will stay here', ran the next letter to Vansittart, 'dead or alive, till I am dismissed in form'.

To the Three this was the coup de grâce. Francis furiously declared it was a government 'juggle'; 'H. and B.' were safe now for at least a year, and 'we unfashionable men' had been betrayed. He writhed at the spectacle of Hastings, 'with an air that would become Cato the Censor', glorying in this independent vote; as if Macleane or Stewart were just moved by his integrity. Victory, 'at one time apparently certain', was lost, and he declined to sacrifice himself for Clavering; 'you might as well hang me at once as make him Governor'. By July both Clavering and Monson were absent, ill; 'here am I sitting in Council, with those paragons of virtue, H. and B.' In August Monson announced his resignation, and in September Clavering, 'on his back covered with boils', sent his to the Directors, though he hid it from his colleagues.

The axe fell on September the 25th, when Monson died, and rejoined his wife in South Park Street cemetery.

CHAPTER XIV

The Home Front: 1775-77

Now that the latest intelligence went overland to Marseilles or Genoa, so on to Suez and thence by sea, Great Britain and India were drawn much closer together. If the general election of 1774 had turned on America, India was to be the battle-ground of 1784. So every motive power in British politics, — the need of votes, patronage and party, and rival ambitions masked as reform — reached out to take in the Nabob of Arcot and his creditors, the Council table at Calcutta, or the lucrative residencies and army commands strung out along the rivers of Hindustan. In those currents Hastings was engulfed, as Clive had been before him, sometimes deep in the trough and then again on the high crest.

He had learned at last that a Governor without 'interest' at home was doomed. And his was weak, or outmoded. There was his oldest friend Sykes, of course; finding fault with his extravagance, blaming him for the breach with Mahomed Reza Khan, and apprehensive that Hastings had somehow been trapped in the dealings out of which his own fortune had been made; 'I hope you have been very careful no proofs appear; if they do, they will ruin you by prosecutions'. He could count also on General Caillaud, and his most sensible brother-in-law, Pechell, who carried weight at the India House. And on a few others besides, like his old chief Du Pré and still older Robert Palk, with whom as Henry Vansittart's brother-in-law he claimed a bond. And though Palk was cautious and in retirement, he could return two members of parliament for Ashburton, near his home at Haldon.

Till 1774 one of his pocket members was Laurence Sulivan. Though he had dropped some £35,000 over the crash of Sir George Colebrooke, he was ever hopeful, still championing Hastings as the saviour of the Company's profits, and bent on retrieving his own finances by sending his son Stephen to Madras, where he might squeeze something out of the Nabob. But though Hastings kept up with these old friends, of late his confidence was given to others, men with more recent Indian experience or nearer to the inner circle of British politics. Of these Lauchlin Macleane and John Graham reached England late in 1775, George Vansittart and John Stewart half-way through 1776, all four fully instructed as to his conditional offer to resign.

The centre of the curious events that followed was Macleane. Sulivan was enthusiastic about him : by his account, it was only Macleane's eloquence and enormous energy which brought about the triumphant meeting of proprietors, which acquitted Hastings of improper motives over the Rohilla war amid rounds of applause. Yet Sykes, and not from any petty jealousy, warned Hastings from the first against him ; 'I do not think in the end he will do you much good'. In truth, Macleane's record did not recommend him to solid men. His association with the ruined Sulivans and Burkes, his stock-jobbing for Shelburne, the Madras government's censure on his intrigues with the Nabob, made him suspect. The world could not know he had got £10,000 from Hastings' attorneys, and £4500 a year from the Nabob, but it shrewdly guessed. Even Miss Mary Barwell was cajoled into lending him £10,000, to her brother's mild surprise.

This likeable and plucky rascal, — half dead with his weak lungs — had a tongue that could wring money out of a stone, and nursed ambitious dreams. At one time, according to Dundas, he hoped to buy up the whole of the Company's stock ; 'used to boast that the day would come when he would be pointed at in the street "there walks the East India Company"'. It was a nice question how this sort of man would stand up to political pressures, or how he would reconcile his two agencies, for the Nabob of Arcot and Warren Hastings. 'Poor Mac', Sulivan wrote, 'may make his own terms, if he could forget that you are his friend.'

Till the New Year of 1776, all seemed going well. True, Macleane found the King was 'bigotted' to Clavering, but North on the other hand, with America on his back, wanted every vote and would dread a party fight about India. He had, in fact, told his master that, though in fault over the Rohilla war, Hastings was generally invaluable, especially in finance. The

Hastings group therefore spoke gently. The Governor, they intimated, must defend his character, but would never lend himself to faction and would 'cheerfully resign' if honourably treated. But in January the rival despatches arrived, with news of Nuncumar's accusations, which convinced most men that one or the other set of Councillors must be recalled. On April the 4th excitement reached its peak, when the purser of the *Northumberland* brought word, which 'flew like lightning through all the offices', that Nuncumar had been hanged.

On May the 9th the Directors resolved by eleven votes to ten to recall both Hastings and Barwell. The majority was led by Gregory, Nuncumar's English agent, including also the new chairman Roberts, Wheler ex-chairman, who had been promised a seat in Council at Calcutta, Wombwell, whose son having run through a fortune at home had gone to be one of Francis' inner ring, and six who had received government contracts. And as it was believed that Clavering was to implement a plan to strip the Company of its political powers, the cause of the Company and of Hastings had become one and the same.

On May the 18th, however, the proprietors' ballot ended in the triumph for Hastings we have seen. Lord Bute's interest was active on his side; Frederick Stuart had seen to that. Alexander Elliot was there, with his father Sir Gilbert, most eloquent and reputable of the King's friends. Lord Rockingham came to vote in person. The Duke of Richmond was another Opposition magnate who took a leading part. Yet it was treacherous ground. Some voted for Hastings who had party objects of their own, while the Clive group and the Vanes had been active enemies. And though Mansfield loaded Hastings with thanks for his code of Hindu laws, his following voted wrong in the ballot, while a young nominee of his, Edward Hay, was an intimate of Francis.

So Macleane remained uneasy, fearing, he wrote, 'the operation of loaves and fishes'. He reported that Cabinet circles threatened parliamentary action in the autumn, and that the Treasury press was attacking Hastings. His information was correct. Robinson was preparing for the King a memorandum on the most appropriate legal means of recalling Hastings and Barwell.

Early in August, however, young Elliot came to him with a government overture, to explore the compromise first suggested for a 'retreat with honour'. The intermediary was a new figure, the talented and intriguing William Eden, at present employed under North, a close friend of Wedderburn, and soon to marry Elliot's sister. The government motives, as outlined by Jenkinson to Clavering, were clear enough. Action in parliament would divide the Cabinet; 'all the Indians to a man' defended Hastings, so did the Bute group, the lawyers were all champions of Impey, and finally they had no time nor mind for anything except America.

After some natural suspicion and several meetings, the parties reached agreement on 'the most liberal ground'. Though an immediate honour for Hastings was waived, as it might look like a bribe, a time limit was set for action, before the next General Court. Macleane got the approval both of Sulivan and of Hastings' brother-in-law, and in September went off to Palk's Devonshire home, where he met Vansittart, Caillaud, and Pechell. The terms they asked for were the restoration of Hastings' followers — Middleton, Stewart, and Frederick Stuart — to 'adequate' office; some marks of favour for the Indians in the same plight, — Rajballabh, Gunga Govind Sing, and Kamal-ud-Din; the cessation of all retrospects, and an honourable reception for the Governor on his return. His friends understood that his actual resignation should be timed as he himself wished, certainly not to take effect before the next sailing season.

Later that month Macleane met John Robinson and the 'chairs', yet another intermediary appearing in James Macpherson, author of *Ossian*, whom his cousin John described as 'Lord North's best and most confidential literary friend'. Macleane accepted a statement for the Directors, drafted by Robinson, which said that in the interest of unanimity Hastings had empowered Macleane to signify 'his desire to resign'. He then displayed his powers under letters in Hastings' hand, and rehearsed his verbal instructions, which were confirmed in person by Stewart and Vansittart. By the middle of October all was concluded, Edward Wheler being named to the vacancy which would be caused by the Governor's resignation. Sulivan sent off a paean of joy; 'the battle is at last ended with the preservation of your honour and fame, your friends restored, and the Ministry and Company disposed to receive you with every mark of respect'. And Vansittart echoed him.

Everyone did not accept this cheerful view. Sykes, who had been kept out of the negotiation, was most downright. The bargain was on 'miserable conditions'; Graham and Vansittart, he suggested, were fearful of 'worse consequences, perhaps to themselves'. Pechell wrote it had been hurried through, owing to 'the Arcot interest'; even John Macpherson called it 'weak and unaccountable'. Moreover, Macleane's own letters admitted the pressures, or temptations, to which he had succumbed. He deplored the instability of the Hastings group, yet was complacent over Robinson's confidences regarding the future government of India, which he thought could be turned in Hastings' favour. He emphasized that the Arcot interest made part of Robinson's 'system', and that government were committed to support the Nabob as against Pigot, who was backed by the Whig Opposition.

Within a month, however, he was shocked by the issue of a gazette which announced not Wheler's nomination only, but the grant of a red ribbon to Clavering. This, he wrote to Hastings, violated the spirit of the agreement, and he must not resign. Yet in January 1777 he spoke blithely of a baronetcy for the Governor, and his explanation of the 'resignation' grew more and more curious. Elliot, he said, took it too literally, — more so, in fact, than North and Robinson themselves. For when news came of Monson's death, they saw to it that Wheler resigned his first commission and took out another to succeed Monson, with the result that the Governor had no legal successor. Let him hang on until he received an adequate honour; government were committed by the compromise, and delighted by his opposition to Pigot. But 'the faithful Elliot' would soon bring him the latest advices.

Such was the news posting off to India, and never forgiven by Hastings. How could his friends have misunderstood him, and overlooked his retractation of his first offer, his many letters vowing to 'see the end of it'? He wrote to Woodman he had suffered 'from those whom I thought my friends. I mean Macleane and Stewart, and I fear Mr. Vansittart.' There was the bitter sting, for George had been as his brother Jonathan. He was, in fact, writing to him before the fatal news arrived, that his son Frederick was staying with him at Belvedere; 'he is amazingly like you, George, which is a great pity'. Move some

years on, and what a biting frost! George, he says, 'gave
testimony against me'. He wrote coldly to end their correspondence; Pechell told him 'your words were too harsh'. But it was
only in 1783 that he made amends, declaring one of Vansittart's
letters had never reached him : 'I desire your forgiveness both for
the injustice of my suspicion, and for the pain which you must
have suffered from it'.

Whether a calm would succeed or not to this storm, the waters
went on eddying from and to the East. In March 1777 Macleane
resigned his Company service, and when government decided to
recall both Pigot and his opponents, he dashed off to India
again to stand by the Nabob. Having engaged the whole Dover
packet, he just beat by a short head another passenger, a bird of
evil omen to Hastings. This was William Burke, now so entirely
ruined that he jumped at the chance of taking out despatches to
Pigot; he came as a link between the Opposition and their
protégés, Pigot and Tanjore, and was heralded by a flaming
letter from his cousin Edmund to Francis, 'let Bengal protect a
spirit and rectitude which is no longer tolerated in England'.
Indeed, all manner of flesh and fowl were on the wing. One was
an old associate of Macleane's in his West Indies speculations, a
mulatto adventurer named Mackintosh, who quickly fell into the
Francis camp. Elliot was coming via Suez, bearer of authentic
news. In May the *Duke of Portland* got away with Wheler the new
Councillor, his present wife, and his wife to be. She was in
convoy with the *Sea Horse*, bringing Francis' American cousin
Tilighman, who hoped for money at the Bengal Bar, Colonel
Watson, chief engineer at Calcutta with large schemes in his
pocket for building docks, and a Mr. William Hickey who
proposed to practise as an attorney.

They crossed en route John Macpherson, who reached England
in July. His letters to Hastings had become increasingly affectionate, rich in promises of support from his influential friends and,
if written when sober, most misleading. He would go into
parliament to defend him and, when he heard of Macleane's
doings, swore he must not resign. The Governor's farewell letter
threw himself on Macpherson's superior knowledge, 'in which I
am most deficient, I mean the knowledge of the British World to
which all my designs ought, if they can be, to be squared'.

News of that world seemed very confused. His nephew Tommy

Woodman, now captain of Westminster School, was not, after all, to come out to India, which his father thought 'too uncertain'. While Sulivan wrote as if Hastings would be on his way home, in addressing the Three Robinson confined himself to a 'hope' that Hastings had resigned. There seemed doubts at both ends what was Wheler's commission, or to whom he was meant to succeed. Stewart wrote that Clavering's brother Sir Thomas was mustering friends at Court, but that if the General died and Hastings resigned, they would never 'leave B. and F. to play at picquet together at the Council Board'. So they wrote, ever six months behind, while the Indiamen plunged and passed one another, out of sight. Another slow ship, incidentally, was bringing Continental news, that in June 1776 the Duke of Saxony's courts had granted the prayer of Baron von Imhoff, as 'an abandoned conjugal mate', for the dissolution of his marriage.

CHAPTER XV

Years of Decision: 1776-78

BEFORE Wheler reached Bengal that December, Clavering was dead, and as his successor Eyre Coote did not take office till 1779, for nearly three years after Monson's death Hastings was supreme. Yet though his casting vote could prevail, he lived in monthly expectation of recall, uncertain of support either in the Cabinet or the Company, and confronted by greater dangers to British India than any since Plassey.

On Monson's death his line was taken, in concert with Impey and Barwell. With the necessary exception of the revenue settlement, it should be a 'passive rule', not to use his power to make himself impregnable, but power used 'with great caution, and for great purposes only'. But if he had the 'conscious sense' he had served his country well, his letters into the next spring were full of gloom. 'The affairs of the other two Presidencies', he told Macleane, 'are completely distracted as discord herself could wish them.' Bengal might subsist rather longer, 'like an entangled skein of thread drawn out to the utmost length that it will go . . . the Judges of the Supreme Court have caught the contagion'. Yet 'I often indulge myself with the imagination that I see you and Elliot sailing triumphantly down the Red Sea, with the emblems of conquest and peace hovering over your sails. God grant it!'

He took up his tale with Vansittart. If this procrastination suited the Cabinet, 'it is death to me. I am made neither of stone nor iron, and a constitution of adamant would fail under a much longer continuance of such a scene, and how I have endured it I know not, unless there be a truth in the doctrine of Guardian spirits, and mine has given me preternatural strength. There is, indeed, one happy temperature which I have brought my mind to, that I can set it to a certain degree, a little above summer heat, and keep it there.' Let George consider his fate : 'To love peace, to feel sentiments of kindness to all men, and to be involved in everlasting squabbles. To be branded with the reproach of rapacity, avarice, and every beggarly quality, with my fortune going, gone almost, to the dogs. To have given 26 years of my life to the search of a good name with *proba pauperie* for my covering, and on the verge of old age to meet with a faction, supported by high authority, and determined to devote me to infamy.' He had great things in mind, ran his farewell letter to Macpherson, 'but I want the spirit of enterprise, with my spirits sunk with a long contest to which I see no end'.

He could, of course, drive things through Council, but at what a price! The General was not long for this world, but in Council as exhausting as ever. The time alone he consumed was portentous, Barwell timing one of his dictated minutes as lasting just under two hours. There was his comparatively agreeable style, as in this remark on one of Hastings' favourites : 'Mr. Halhed, I believe, understands the Persian language very well, and they say he is a good poet: had these qualities been the requisite qualities for the duties of a commissary-general, I should with pleasure have concurred'. And there was the style bombastic-furioso. So he accused Hastings of raising the salary of Richard Sumner, to induce him to testify that *aumils* (the lower revenue officers) had powers of corporal punishment, or would declare that his defence of the Rohilla war would have been 'unworthy of Mrs. Rudd', a famous murderess of the day. 'He may continue to revile me', Hastings answered, 'with language yet grosser, if grosser can be invented.'

But Francis was the arch enemy. He had differed with Clavering over revenue, patronage, and the Mahratta war. He looked on the immediate battle with Hastings as lost, and would have no more of 'odious unprofitable contentions'. And what, he asked D'Oyley, 'has General Clavering done, what could he do, what can he do, without me'? He still hoped for the government of Bengal; 'my conduct has been high, splendid, and invulnerable'. But as he moved from lavish hospitality at Dutch Chinsura — 'dull as Rotterdam' — to the blazing river, or to Lady Impey's tea-table, where he inflamed her against Marian, we see his hatreds are becoming obsessions. He accused Hastings

N   181

of glorying in Burgoyne's surrender in America, of shipping remittances to Holland, and of preparing a retreat in Switzerland. He was driven to frenzy on hearing that he always acted on disinterested motives, but his laughter echoed in his great house, as he wrote that he had the power of exasperating the Governor 'to a degree of madness'.

The other camp watched him with foreboding. Impey found him increasingly loathsome, denouncing to Dunning his 'corrupt, malicious, intriguing dispositions'. 'This man of levity', Hastings said, was just manœuvring by the prevailing wind; this 'vilest fetcher and carrier of tales' was 'without one generous or manly principle'. He would promise to support a policy, and then retract in detail. He would withdraw some scurrilous minute, but publish it in England; against which the Governor took precautions, for publication of his own replies.

Each side looked towards the judges, whose feud with Council could not be tolerated much longer. Impey and Chambers had carried a rule admitting the Company's revenue powers, with the result that Hyde and Lemaistre were incited by Francis. And as Impey was thoroughly alarmed by his home letters, he was struggling to be made a member of Council. Chambers was after the same thing, still corresponding with Jenkinson, to whom he wrote that Hastings had 'a greater degree of cunning, with less political wisdom, and even less Indian knowledge than I formerly ascribed to him'. A strong view for this academic lawyer, after a bare three years in India.

While Barwell agreed in Hastings' own defence of his moderation, 'vindictive' and 'arbitrary' sounded from the other side, and one step led to another, till all was fury. It was urgent to settle the revenue, for which he judged a special enquiry necessary, and that meant turning off the Provincial Councils the men he distrusted. In the same way, he could not give Bristow *carte blanche* in Oudh, which led to his recall and the restoration of Middleton. We come across signs of a temper frayed beyond all bearing, perhaps of some influence which made him demand precise or blind obedience. Middleton had thus to defend himself against a reproach of employing too many of Bristow's dependants, while Edward Baber, most independent of revenue officers, linked together two things in writing to Vansittart, so lately the Governor's dearest friend. 'His Honour', he said, 'hath mounted a hobby horse (*i.e.* his revenue enquiry) which he is riding at a devil of a rate. The measure is a mystery to me, and His Honour a riddle I cannot read. I wish that a certain person at Alipur was in the heart of Germany.' Was that, then, the way his best friends thought of Marian and her influence?

Before 1776 ended, not only was Middleton restored, but young Fowke was replaced at Benares by Thomas Graham, assisted by Barwell's brother Daniel, best known hitherto for his unexampled skill in snuffing a candle with a bread pellet. Restoration began also in the Indian world. The *foudjar* of Hugli, who had refused to oblige Nuncumar, was put back again, so was the potent Gunga Govind Sing on the Revenue Committee. The venomous Rani of Burdwan once more submitted to a *diwan* of Hastings' choice. Larger changes were in the air, for the Governor had got hold of a suspicious letter to Clavering from Mahomed Reza Khan.

But his heart was set most, for the time being, on his hobby-horse, usually called the Amini commission. For land revenue was the open sesame, not merely to solvency and popular contentment, but to the distribution of power; power as between the State and the great *zemindars*, who had been adding holding to holding for a century past, and again as between the factions in Council. Whoever could fix the assessment, and assign tenancies or contracts, had the chance of making a fortune, if corrupt, and in any event the disposition of the Indian 'interests', without which neither Council nor Directors could govern. The long dragging debates on this matter are the clearest example of the polar difference between Hastings and Francis. The last was full of philosophic quotation, to prove the blessings of simplicity and *laisser-faire*. Estimate once for all the needs of government, and settle the assessment in permanence accordingly. 'Government can never descend to the ryots'; the bargain must be struck with the *zemindars*, the natural owners of the soil.

Hastings brushed this speculation aside, when he proposed a special commission under his immediate control. He agreed on the present over-assessment, and the need of getting a settlement as near as possible to permanence. But all past experience, and the best revenue officers, confessed their ignorance, and as they could not embark on a valuation by survey, he would get at the truth by inspection of local archives. No *zemindar* had voluntarily given equitable leases; therefore the peasant must remain in 'the immediate care of government'.

As Francis' ablest revenue expert, Ducarel, refused to serve, he chose a team entirely his own, headed by David Anderson. They met with much local obstruction, which he had to stop; turning out, for example, the Rani of Rajeshai's officials, though temporarily only during inspection of their accounts. The commission duly filled three roomsful of Bengali and Persian accounts, and put up an excellent constructive report. But nothing in their previous record could surpass the violent absurdities poured out by Clavering and Francis. The General would prosecute any Provincial Councillor who co-operated. A black inquisitor would torture the villagers. 'The naked wretch who tills the earth' would be ground down by tribute. Francis' letters to England vowed it would mean 'a defenceless territory, a ruined people, — the question is, Bengal or not Bengal?'

Meantime, they could not forget the other Presidencies. In the west neither party were carrying out the treaty. Upton had been detained at Poona, seemingly by force; a Bombay agent had just arrived there, deeply committed to Ragoba. Unhappy Sudaba was dead of his hammer strokes, so the Poona ministers felt strong enough to resist Hyder Ali's advance on their southern frontier. But their domestic broils were deepening, Nana Phadnavis' rivals were turning towards Ragoba. There were symptoms of a much greater danger. Frenchmen and French munitions had begun to creep in by the little harbour of Choule, and in May 1777 a French adventurer reached Poona. This was the same M. St. Lubin who had stirred up Madras to wage their hapless Mysore war of 1767, and who now, with trunks of fleurs-de-lis and facings for uniforms, professed to be an agent of Louis XVI. 'Drunk and sober, jointly and separately', wrote one of Hastings' agents, 'I have examined all the Frenchmen', to find that some declared St. Lubin an impostor. Another French officer appeared at Surat; in the far north Hannay was trying to discover whether Frenchmen were reaching Delhi.

As for Madras, Pigot died this May, in fact of a chill, though the jury found it murder. In August Company orders recalled both sets of rivals, announcing the early arrival of Thomas Rumbold as Governor. Robinson wrote to Clavering that

Rumbold had 'fixed principles to act with you', so too would General Carnac, who was to succeed Hornby at Bombay.

Their nearest trouble, of course, was in Oudh. 'That brute the Nabob', as Francis described their joint victim to Bristow, was proving hopeless. Middleton could only report 'His Excellency is perpetually intoxicated', he was insulting his mother and half-starving his wife. Yet our system gave him little chance. He was crippled by debts to Bristow, which that worthy adroitly transferred to a client of Barwell. He had been made to pay for 14,000 stand of arms for the British 'temporary' brigade. And all the British were equal offenders, Middleton himself thus angrily protesting that contracts for muskets had always been the resident's perquisite. Under any outside attack this rotten régime would crumble. Daniel Barwell described poverty and depopulation in Rohilkund; in the Doab, while collecting revenue, Goddard lost officers in skirmishes against rebels, armed with bows and arrows and crude hand-grenades.

In May Hastings carried by his casting vote a measure which he claimed was, with the Amini commission, the best service he had done since the Benares treaty. The temporary brigade in Oudh, though still to be maintained from the Vizier's funds, was transferred to our sepoy army for command, service, and pay, for though, as ever, he blamed the system more than the men, he hoped this unified command and proper accountancy would end the worst corruption. Since the whole revenues of Rohilkund and the Doab were assigned to meet the British expenses, and to be paid direct to Middleton by collectors of his choice, Francis had some reason for saying that the Vizier had sunk to the level of the Nabob of Bengal. Yet what alternative existed, save bankruptcy, rebellion, and probably invasion?

In such disputes summer was wearing away. On June the 14th Clavering had gone down the river for his health, whence he was hurriedly recalled by Francis. For news was circulating that Hastings had resigned. He had in fact received a budget of letters by William Mackintosh, who had come ahead of the Indiamen in a frigate, and these letters advised him not to resign. Clavering and Francis, who had received none, spent the next day, Sunday, discussing their programme: Hastings' attitude in Council on Monday delighted them, for he cancelled an appointment he had given to a friend of Barwell, on the ground of the coming change. The Directors' official letters came in on Wednesday and were read in Council next day.

Hastings called Barwell into consultation, lodging him over these days in Government House, and it seems they agreed the game was up. Writing to Lord North, he said he had never intended to resist the intentions of government, or 'so many instruments, all of such force and all combined against me'. The Governor meant to go, Barwell confirmed to his sister, 'as a conciliating and healing measure'. But then what he described as a 'mad project', 'a boorish insult' by Clavering, transformed the scene.

On Friday the 20th the General was early in the field, ordering Auriol, secretary in the general department, to be ready with the Europe despatches by eight in the morning. A little later Barwell, driving in to attend a routine revenue business, received a command from Clavering as Governor-General to meet in Council at eleven; while he was talking to Hastings, the General's Persian translator brought in a note addressed to 'Warren Hastings Esquire', bidding him surrender the keys of the Treasury and the Fort by noon. At twelve-thirty John D'Oyley was told to prepare translations of the General's proclamation as Governor; he refused to obey.

With Sumner of the Revenue secretariat, Bogle, and his military secretary Palmer, Hastings took decisive action. He sent word to the officers commanding the Fort and at Barrackpore to take no orders but his, and the army proved solid on his side. He then asked the judges to the Council House, and offered to abide by their decision. After some argument, Francis induced Clavering to agree, and the judges met that evening at Impey's house. They did not hand out their unanimous opinion until four next morning.

Even on the public papers before them, it could hardly be in doubt. 'That Mr. Hastings is not dead is a notorious fact'; he had not been removed; 'we are firmly of opinion that he hath not actually resigned'. The documents spoke only of a 'desire to resign', and of Wheler's appointment as only to take effect when the office 'should become vacant'. Had they known of it, the second commission for Wheler to succeed Monson was given on that very ground, that 'no notice hath yet been received of the said Warren Hastings having resigned'.

When day came on the 21st, the strains were tense. Some of the bazaars had closed, the extraordinary speed of Indian rumour flashed through the provinces, at Benares Chait Sing was preparing to send his *vakil* to ask advice from Joseph Fowke. Auriol asked Hastings whether he should summon Council for Monday, and was told 'no'; on Sunday Clavering heard that the Governor was giving up.

Far from it. On Monday Hastings and Barwell held a Council, to which they had not summoned their rivals, and resolved that Clavering's illegalities had vacated his membership of Council. However, on this provocative challenge he agreed to defer to the view of the judges, who decided against him and advised reference of the dispute to England. On the 25th they all reassembled in Council, where Francis spoke of the 'precipitation' which had hazarded their peace, — 'let me have the happiness of assuming the character of mediator'.

It was an unusual role for him, and the outgoing post to England was loaded with suspicion. While Barwell wrote that Hastings had not finally decided, Impey betrayed his nerves to Thurlow about Clavering's enmity; to whom, however, he would give all proper support, 'as I find that the administration have made their final option'. Francis, in writing to North, presumed that Hastings and Barwell would assuredly be condemned and then, 'in any event that removes General Clavering', he came next in seniority. He therefore declared outright that he should view supersession by any newcomer as equivalent to dismissal.

Hastings' letters by the same ship were burning with passion. Though still clinging to the argument that only Clavering's violence had prevented his resignation, the bulk of his words to North struck a different note. The Prime Minister, he felt sure, had intended 'an honourable retreat', not one that should 'drag me into the power of my most rancorous enemy'. As things were, he felt bound in duty to keep his post, but though he did not expect to be confirmed in it, 'suffer me not, my Lord, to be dragged from it like a felon'. He spoke more violently to Sulivan and Sykes, Dunning and Macpherson. His resignation had been left to his own option in point of time, he would not yield to a 'brutal outrage' which would make him 'the derision and detestation of all mankind'. He alluded to the judges with some resentment; Clavering gave up 'because he was unable to go on.

But was this a reason for me to desist? . . . No man who possesses but the spirit of a worm, which will turn on the foot which spurns it, will keep on terms of cordiality with General Clavering.' Perhaps another influence touched his pen with fire.

For the gates of the Fort were open again, and marriage bells ringing. One of his 'family' at the crisis was a certain George Francis Grand, who had fallen in love with Mlle Catherine Verlée, daughter of a French official at Chandernagore. She was only fifteen, exquisitely beautiful, with a mass of auburn hair and, as Philip Francis later remembered, the figure of a nymph. By Barwell's good offices, the young man now got a post that would enable him to marry. As he was; twice over indeed, on July the 10th, both by Catholic and Anglican rites. The day before, Calcutta learned that the divorce so long expected from Germany had taken place.

They had waited long, and would not wait longer. The Governor settled on his bride a lac of rupees, and on August the 8th they were married by the sporting husband of Begum Johnson, Impey giving Marian away. When she first received company on the 11th, in a 'lalock' gown trimmed with fine point, and 'her cap' (a woman eyewitness says) 'full of diamonds and pearls', Clavering and Francis were there, — the General only after asking Francis whether he should go or not, 'I think the first has it on this ground, that it proves our opposition not to be personal'.

Society was set in two camps, there were heated arguments on hot evenings, and some duels, one between Nuncumar's crony, James Grant, and dashing Bob Pott, William Hickey's friend, whom Thurlow had recommended to Hastings. Clavering repented now of having given way, and was writing all round the compass, to Admirals on the station and to Councillors at Bombay and Madras. A late-arrived letter from North's secretary Robinson was endorsed by Francis, 'we were betrayed by everyone'. As for Barwell, he was divided between his sporting instinct and his notion of what was common sense. If Hastings would never voluntarily resign, and if government would never forgive the way he had duped them, he might have a chance himself. Yet he ruminated that Francis 'steps on my heels', and was sometimes carried away by more generous feelings about Hastings. 'I cannot drive him from his hopes', he told his sister, 'while a possibility against a probability remains of their being answered. It is true I might unite and drive him from his station, but that would brand me with infamy.'

Against his advice, Hastings sent a defiant reply to the Directors. His instructions to Macleane, he said, could not be twisted to imply resignation, and were contradicted by his repeated declarations since; nor had he authorized Vansittart and Stewart to testify. Even his sufferings had not enabled him to bear the humiliation of surrendering his trust 'by an imputed act of my own', without even the bare verification which would be asked for 'a common note of exchange'.

But the fated month for his enemies had come round again, and a third fatal Saturday; as one had killed Nuncumar, and a second Monson. On August the 30th Clavering died, leaving instructions that Hastings should not be informed till he was buried. Francis walked in the procession that evening, but before doing so had time to write to General Carnac and Admiral Hughes; how the Empire was at stake, and how his two noble friends were a sacrifice. Lady Clavering caught from him the proper note, when she too wrote of 'that glorious cause, in which my best friend lost his life'. But they were all writing that hot afternoon, Impey telling at least two Cabinet ministers that now he hoped for a place in Council.

So the Claverings were packing up, and Hastings bought the General's copy of their Council consultations. He conceived it more than ever his duty, he wrote to North, to keep his station, till 'special provision' was made. But was there not something providential, he asked Macpherson, about his health and temper over the past three years? It was the close of warfare, no other man would have Clavering's rancour: 'may God forgive him all the injuries which he heaped upon me, and me as I forgive him'. Late in September he heard from Macleane, just leaving Madras, who wrote that he would see North before the despatches arrived. But he was never to do so. For he left the Cape in November in the sloop *Swallow*, which went down with all hands. The fearful Sykes soon wrote that his papers were bequeathed to the historian Orme, — 'I hope there is nothing that you need to be apprehensive therefrom'.

Rid of the General, Francis struck out hard for himself. He discovered with indignation Clavering's secret resignation a year

ago; 'what is there', his journal says, 'that I am not entitled to?'
To North he wrote that Clavering and Monson were victims to
the common cause, 'your own cause, my Lord'. Surely Hastings
and Barwell would be recalled? He himself was 'a tolerable
master of affairs', and no new man could rival his knowledge.
To his own intimates, Wedderburn and Ellis, however, he vowed
there had been 'foul play somewhere', perhaps by that 'treacherous scoundrel', Robinson. And finally to Edmund Burke, with
the sensibility which that quarter required; how some day they
would compare their honourable strife as they descended 'the
vale of life' together. But 'you have men to contend with . . .
these are devils'.

And now young Elliot arrived, fresh from the back-scenes of
the 'resignation'. On his information, Hastings made a step
backwards. He had never realized, he told Lord North, how far
Macleane had committed him: he pledged himself to hand over
to Barwell, if someone arrived who was expressly commissioned
to fill the vacancy made by his alleged resignation. Rumours,
that he really meant to go, once more roused some tepid hope in
Barwell. In fact they were all marking time, till they found out
from Wheler what were his powers, and with whom he would
side. Rival coaches and carriages dashed off to meet the new
Councillor; rival emissaries, Elliot and Livius, clambered on
board, entreating him to keep his hands free. He reached the
capital on December the 11th.

Edward Wheler, a former chairman of the Company, was a
rich and placid parvenu, well married to a Chichele Plowden
wife, whose dresses were the envy of society. Though he had
worked hard for Clavering and for Hastings' recall, and was also
a partisan of Pigot, he was impressed by the growing strength of
the Governor's party. His business talent was good, but his lack
of self-confidence abysmal, so that the duel which raged this
winter across his timid passive body was exasperatingly incon-
clusive. 'Ned Silent', or 'Ned Wheelabout', were his baptismal
names from the *Bengal Gazette*.

Hastings certainly played his opening hand most unskilfully.
He professed, indeed, that he only asked Wheler to be neutral,
but the terms he sent him through Elliot were unyielding.
Though he would allow Francis his fair share of patronage,
Mahomed Reza Khan was to be dismissed, Rajballabh restored

as Roy Royan, and the present revenue settlement prolonged till 1779. It was an odd idea of 'neutrality', — to obliterate the principal measures of the Three, and Francis' most cherished principles. Francis, on the other hand, played his timid fish like a master, bade him disregard Hastings' 'sophistries' and trust his own conscience, and called in Justice Chambers to land him safely. So that all Hastings could extract, in a personal interview, was that Wheler would decide on every case 'without regard to persons or parties'.

They all met on Christmas night at the Governor's dinner, 'a wretched shabby dinner' as Francis thought, which he put down to Marian's thrift. On Boxing Day Hastings declared his intentions to Wheler, who by this time had the opposition phalanx round him, of Ducarel, Livius, and Charles Grant. On the 30th war broke out in Council. Wheler voted against all Hastings' proposals, Hastings retorted his union with Francis was preconcerted. His letter to Sulivan next day was jubilant, but unworthy of him. He did not fear the new coalition; there was all the difference in the world between their pretensions and Clavering, 'supported by the King, destined to the chair'. Wheler was a fool; he might have shared in government and 'his friends in its emoluments', while now he would be reduced to writing minutes of dissent.

So the New Year of 1778 opened, with war declared. Barwell was sitting pretty; if he were recalled, he hoped for a seat in the Commons, 'under the countenance of the Minister', for which his sister might go so far as £4000. But Francis was taking no chances. Bristow went off to England, primed with information, and commended to Will Burke at Madras. Farrer also, Nuncumar's counsel, having cleared his £60,000 at the Bar, left in March, pledged to buttress the good cause. The Directors' letter entreating Clavering to stay was translated, and circulated by Francis to Indian courts. Messages went to Ministers that they must intervene at the India House; to his jovial friend Godfrey, Francis wrote outright 'I am now, I think, in the road to the government of Bengal'.

Each stage on their road of controversy, whether domestic or over the Mahratta war, was signposted by some fight for patronage. In Dacca the 'Franciscan' Boughton Rouse resigned, and the appointment of Shakespeare restored a Hastings-Barwell supremacy. There was bickering over a small grant to Halhed, whose private press was just making the first English-Bengali grammar; more bickering over an army contract for one of the Johnsons, Joshua Reynolds' nephews, for one brother was believed to have managed the Imhoff divorce. Hastings was also rebuilding his damaged Indian clientele. He was pensioning the distressed Kamal-ud-Din; the horrible Nobkissen, whose share in hanging Nuncumar had been considerable but who had since been frightened by the Three, showed signs of repentance.

All his major schemes were driven through Council by his casting vote. The revenue settlement was extended, Rajballabh was restored, and, above all, Mahomed Reza Khan was dismissed. Against him Hastings' wrath was boiling. Once he had saved this man from Nuncumar, and what black ingratitude! He had volunteered information to Clavering, now he was the instrument of Francis. Wielding alike the *durbar* and judicial powers, he defeated British sovereignty; his salary and perquisites and *jagir* made him much richer than the Governor. The Nabob asked to be rid of him, Munny Begum had suffered much, and 'on my account'. So when the Naib refused to accept a compromise, Hastings brought it to Council, divested him of all authority whatever, restored Munny Begum to the Household and Guru Das as *diwan*. The language used on either side was perfectly inconsistent with their respective arguments three years ago. It was now Francis' turn to dwell on British sovereignty; whereas Hastings, who once had called him 'a mere pageant', was emphatic on the Nabob's right to manage his household and the *nizamut* as he wished.

So in all directions, with or without consistency, Hastings' struggle went on to keep his power. To Sulivan he dwelt on the rising revenue, the Amini commission, and a record investment. He was paying freely for overland expresses from England, — £600 in one case; another £1000 went to honour a draft of John Stewart. He had cleared the Provincial Councils of the worst nominees of the Three, while his own band of disciples was strongly placed. And when he looked for higher support, if Barwell was rather shaky, Impey was staunch. This, perhaps, was the heyday of their alliance. For the Chief Justice had an obsessive terror of Francis, nor could he abide the rough tongue of Justice Hyde. He meant to live for his large family and this summer was nursing his health by the sea at Chittagong, whence his letters to Hastings reeked of patronage, though always on some plausible ground. An illegitimate brother of Lady Impey gave some trouble by his expectations, but the storm centre was his impecunious cousin, Archibald Fraser, who from being mate on an Indiaman was now 'sealer and examiner' in the Supreme Court. This year Fraser was assisted further, by a contract for the *pulbundi*, or upkeep of bridges and embankments, in Burdwan; reckoned worth £15,000 a year. Hence the ugly nickname of 'Pulbundi', freely bestowed on the Chief Justice.

All this time every word and act from England was hostile to Hastings. Robinson had written to Clavering, saying that 'further measures' would be devised if the Governor did not resign. The Directors ordered the restoration of Bristow, vetoed an appointment for Halhed, and censured the Amini commission as waste of money. Their last letter, Hastings told Impey, was 'studiously abusive' of him, with 'a few gentle taps' for Barwell: 'I should be sorry to say that I did not feel it. . . . I have acquired the habit of patience, but am not callous.'

There was much dining and supping this year, even between the rivals. The Harmonic Tavern was booming, while at the new Catch Club William Hickey had introduced a delightful innovation, of burnt champagne. But poor Mrs. Wheler failed fast, and died in July, by which time gaieties and patronage were being submerged under greater matters. The Mahratta war was swelling to terrible proportions. In June they heard that the previous autumn General Burgoyne and his whole army had surrendered to the Americans; on July the 7th, that Great Britain was at war with France.

Foes and friends both saw how all this would affect the Governor. He was in 'high triumph', according to Francis; while Sulivan congratulated him on his 'knack' of frustrating his enemies. 'When one attack is formed, you overturn it with an investment of 140 lacs of rupees'; another, 'by a million and a half sterling in your Treasury'; and now, a French war. 'Who in such a crisis will they dare to put in your place? Therefore, good Governor-General, from this business sweep away friends and enemies, for if you remain, you will owe it entirely to Warren Hastings.'

CHAPTER XVI

The Mahratta War: 1777-79

'THE Mahratta war', wrote Hastings, 'has been and is yet called mine. God knows why. I was forced into it.' Even so. Yet for its prolongation, and for the ends to which it was directed, his responsibility was direct and overriding.

While controversy lingered about Ragoba, or the repartition of territories under the treaty, the Bombay government was emphatic that for it the hour of destiny had struck. For the French were preparing to repeat in the West the great deeds of Dupleix and Bussy in the East. In November 1777 their hand was strengthened by the Directors' authorization to renew alliance with Ragoba, if the treaty terms were not punctually fulfilled. Finally, they were decided by messages, asking their help, from the rivals of Nana Phadnavis. Their acceptance, taken as a matter of urgency without waiting for assent from Bengal, was known in Calcutta in January 1778.

With an experience tested at Murshidabad, Madras, and Benares, 'no man in England or India', Hastings said of himself, 'has more studied the political state of India'. And his conclusions, roughly sketched for North some years ago, were elaborated in letters to Elliot. Our dominion had 'radical and incurable defects', above all, the conflict between the Company's needs and 'the interests of the people'. Even the best of governments could only postpone the loss of 'a temporary possession'. Yet, though the Bengal European army numbered only one to eleven as against its sepoys, its disciplined power could accomplish great things. The dominion he foresaw was not one of extended territory, but of influence; 'to extend the influence of the British nation to every part of India not too remote from their possessions'. And 'if peace is to be our object, I cannot devise a more likely way to ensure it, than to command all the means of war'.

He therefore proposed to enlist the neighbouring States, especially Berar and the Carnatic, in the system he had attempted for Oudh, but this time as allies of the Crown. This would prevent the vacillating counsels of which Oudh had complained, would curb 'the rapacity of individuals', fend off the connection of Indian States with European Powers, and by the subsidy payments for our troops increase our strength without an increase of expenses. If given the necessary powers, he felt 'a moral certainty' of succeeding. Years back he had suggested such an alliance to Berar, which its civil wars had buried, and had never lost touch with its agent, Benaram Pandit.

Many years later he confided to his favourite diplomat, David Anderson, that the Bombay policy was wrong, and many times over in 1778 made plain his view that Ragoba was only a means to an end, a tool who would probably break in our hand. But his duty, as he saw it, was to extricate Bombay, to ensure British prestige, and to get out of the toils of the Purandhar treaty, now two years old and never implemented. Before receiving the Bombay request for help, he had put to Council a scheme for paying off Ragoba honourably with a *jagir*. At the same time, on hearing that the titular Rajah of Satara was dead, he encouraged the ruler of Berar to claim that barren honour, of the headship of the line of Sivaji, to which he had some hereditary right.

In the fierce debates of this spring of 1778, only his casting vote overcame Francis and Wheler. Bombay, he argued, was justified by immediate emergency, nor could it be called a breach of treaty, when they were invited to intervene by most of the Mahratta signatories to that treaty. But he dwelt most on the peril from France; reminding them how he had always believed France would try to recover her Indian power. Bengal itself he thought in no danger, being impregnable against attack by sea; it would come by a French alliance with some inland Indian State. Even 500 disciplined French soldiers might wreck Hindustan. Could they doubt the meaning of St. Lubin's mission, of French ships off the Malabar coast, of the hints Elliot had picked up at Marseilles and Cairo? He told them of the French-American secret treaty, imparted to Elliot by our ambassador at Paris, his old schoolfellow Stormont, and of the contacts between St. Lubin and Chevalier, Governor of Chandernagore, the immediate neighbour of Calcutta. As to Francis' argument that action might bring on war, it was surely more likely to prevent it, by crushing a French-Mahratta alliance in the bud. If Francis and Wheler lived to see such an alliance, it would be a bad excuse to their country, and to themselves, to say 'we had no proofs that it would be so'. He thus carried resolutions to send Bombay military assistance, instructing them to get the cession of Bassein in any settlement, and the exclusion of other European Powers from Mahratta territory.

Yet his purpose, he repeated, was defensive; 'it is not declaration of war to ask free passage for our troops from one of our settlements to another'. His private letters to Hornby stress there must be no 'spirit of conquest'; 'you must adhere to the letter of the treaty, and you must defeat the designs of the French, two points incompatible if the ministers continue united'. But he proceeded, 'don't abandon me'; if the enemy broke the treaty, he was to act.

Though he claimed we were still uncommitted, and that the confidence given by our armaments would alone be a political gain, his mind was daily more excited by his purpose to march a British army right across India. He told Leslie, its commander-designate, that success 'may prove the crisis of all my future fortunes', receiving with joy his optimistic answer and Mostyn's report from Poona that the bare idea had demoralized the Mahrattas. When Leslie's force crossed the Jumna in May and met some desultory opposition, Francis moved for its recall; this, Hastings minuted, would mean the 'irreparable loss of the credit of this government'. He assured Impey 'the eyes of all Hindustan are turned upon this great enterprise'.

But in the first months all his stakes seemed to be lost. Bombay was entangled in a maze of Poona factions; their supposed partisans were tricked by Nana Phadnavis, who threw them into fortresses. A minority of Hornby's Council wished to draw back, and within one fortnight asked Leslie to halt and then begged him to advance. Leslie was crawling on, moving only 100 miles in five months. Francis spread rumours his sepoys were dying, 'mad with thirst'; Impey wrote of his 'caprice, avarice, and favouritism'.

The replies that went to Impey in the good air of Chittagong — 'I wish you could bottle up some of it for my use' — were near despair. What could be made of Bombay countermanding Leslie? 'Is this ingratitude, envy, stupidity, or pusillanimity, or all together?' He felt as he had often done playing chess, 'when my adversary, by giving his Tower the oblique movement of a Knight, has placed the game in a position for which I had made no provision'. He confessed to 'great fatigue of mind'; if war with France did not materialize, they would be called to a heavy account. Ragoba, he believed, would certainly fail; should we bank all on Berar, or get Hyder Ali's help for Ragoba? Each scheme could be defended, 'but how would they sound in Leadenhall Street?' But this very letter of July shows his mind swinging to his grand design, with the Berar alliance as its heart. 'Take a pair of compasses' and a map, and see the manifold advantages. 'What a fund of resources this government possesses, if it had fit instruments to work them!' Then came the news of war with France.

Rapidly the Indian economy was turned over to these new necessities. Chandernagore was occupied within a week, its governor Chevalier escaping southwards. Madras was ordered to press on the capture of Pondicherry, and empowered to discuss terms of alliance with Hyder. Chait Sing of Benares was requested to contribute a war subsidy. The Bengal infantry was increased by nine battalions, the river fortified and gunboats equipped, and every male European mustered for a militia. Elliot was chosen as special envoy to Berar, and this, Hastings hoped, might begin 'a new system in the British Empire in India'. Yet added, as it were under his breath, 'let me not be too sanguine'. That was the other side of his strong shield, as Barwell wrote to his sister, 'his only foible, if it is a foible, is excess of confidence, the happy enthusiasm of genius'.

Elliot was given minute orders, but almost unlimited discretion. The permanent objective was a standing defensive alliance. He was empowered also to make an offensive and immediate treaty for war against Poona: but only if satisfied the French-Mahratta understanding was in force, and that any engagement he made did not clash with some Bombay commitment to Ragoba. If he thought the chances good, he might also promise assistance to install the Berar Rajah as hereditary head of the Mahratta State.

Even his most ardent friends at home criticized this programme.

It might have its use — to some degree it did — in dividing Berar from its fellow-Mahrattas, but it depended on too perfect a timing, and lay open to other grave objections. Hastings' officers warned him of Moodaji's jealousy of Ragoba; besides, his notions of the importance of Berar in the Mahratta world were exaggerated. And, after all, any alliance estranges other potential friends. In that light, Hastings' readiness to encourage Berar to attack the Nizam, and to treat Hyderabad as pledged to the French, was surely ill considered. There was another highly dangerous ruler in question. Hyder Ali, sworn enemy of any solid Mahratta government, had been backing Ragoba, and both Madras and Bombay had urged Hastings to win his friendship. He smiled on the idea, but when Madras wished to make an offensive alliance, Bengal advised against it as embarrassing their relations with Berar. He clung obstinately to his vision; of the Mahratta State as 'a virtual dependency', of our Empire attaining a greatness 'more permanent than any foreign State ever yet acquired over remote provinces'.

His vision, however, beat at once against harsh facts and obstruction, which made his mood unyielding. Why had not Leslie reached the Nerbudda? He himself had endured as much from Indian heat in old days as this dawdling detachment. He upbraided Wheler and Francis with attempting to break down in detail the military operations Council had approved. Francis' minutes, dwelling with some justice on the vague and contradictory policies involved in Elliot's mission, were a pale reflection of his letters and journal. Hastings was 'bewildered': India was not safe under such a man; Calcutta was endangered by a French fleet. He arranged that his news should reach Lord North, and made a special drive to win over Rumbold, just arrived to govern Madras. Let him note that Elliot's orders were concealed from his Presidency, that the army was sent to 'ramble' through India, and let him tell the folk in England so, since 'every avenue from Bengal is shut, or in his possession'.

In October they recalled Leslie, who died in fact before the order reached him, replacing him by Goddard, a sticky man over promotions and status, but at least considered an aggressive soldier. The powers given to Bombay were revoked, and he was to take orders from Calcutta alone. News came that Pondicherry had fallen at last, though on such lenient terms that some corruption was suspected. So they reached November, and on the 23rd Francis gave a ball, at which Hastings was present; it was noticed that the host seemed much attracted by young Mrs. Grand. But as yet no clear tidings of Elliot. Through *nullahs* swollen by the rains he had reached Cuttack, 'scrambling through the deluged country', Hastings wrote, 'like Satan through chaos'. There he found the missing M. Chevalier, whom with great enterprise he arrested and packed off to Calcutta; then a long silence. For he died of his exertions, of fever caught in heat and passing rivers, on September 12th, though Hastings did not hear it for another ten weeks. 'An irreparable loss', he told Sulivan; Elliot, he said later, 'whom I loved as a child'. But the vision must not fail. Goddard was therefore given Elliot's powers, and reinforced on the political side by David Anderson. By December he was moving from Bhopal to the Nerbudda, sometimes through long beds of rocks, and sometimes through dense wood-lands, which the sepoys must hack away before the guns could move.

Hitherto Berar had been most friendly, and Hastings was confident he could at least get the hostile ministers at Poona overturned. As for Francis' proposal to recall Goddard, 'I would rather suffer death than yield to it'. But now came into play the ambitions of Bombay. They had been told to act on the defensive, till receipt of further instructions; Hastings, in fact, had wanted to bind their hands absolutely, but was dissuaded by Barwell, who pointed to the Directors' orders in favour of Ragoba. Bombay pressed on; urged by their 'experts', Mostyn and Carnac, they signed a new agreement with Ragoba, to install him as regent.

By Christmas their army was climbing up the Ghauts. Their nominal commander fell sick, Mostyn died, and the overriding powers descended in practice to Clive's old favourite Carnac, now a man of sixty-four and intent on snatching the laurels. With 19,000 bullocks straining and stumbling, they advanced by two miles a day, none of Ragoba's supposed champions came to life, while the enemy retired, burning villages as they went. They decided to negotiate, then to retreat; at midnight on January the 11th, throwing their guns into a tank, they turned back. On the 13th, surrounded by 50,000 Mahrattas, they could fight no more. By the convention of Wargaum, signed through the mediation of Scindia, they promised to surrender all British gains since 1773, to make Scindia a gift of territories in Broach, and to leave two Britons as hostages.

Even when the first news of this campaign reached Berar, the Rajah shed his first enthusiasm, and Wargaum finished him. Goddard had marched on, with a true instinct disregarding Carnac's contradictory messages, and late in February 1779 reached the Indian Ocean at Surat. But both he and Governor Hornby concluded that this Berar policy was hopeless. So Berar was gone, Ragoba was a prisoner in Scindia's hands, and the British were left nakedly fighting, as principals, the whole Mahratta confederacy.

In those hard days the authentic Hastings shone out, matured and invincible. His plan, 'and all the fine hopes I had built upon it', was blasted, but never would he admit it had been mistaken. At least a fraction of the Bengal army had saved Bombay, having marched without loss 'from the Jumna to Surat'; what a contrast between his government putting forth its strength and the failure of 'an inferior Presidency'! And as, before Wargaum, he would have none of Francis' 'abject submission' to Poona, so after it he would extract good from this evil. The convention they must repudiate, and 'efface the infamy', but they must give confidence to Bombay, not add to their depression. 'Harsh and unoperating reproaches' would be worse than useless. He bent his efforts, then, to weld Hornby's government and Goddard's staff into a working team: terms of peace should be offered on the basis of the Purandah treaty, with additional safeguards against French influence; the promises to Scindia must be honoured. If such terms were refused, they must ally with the Gaekwar as Hornby proposed, and by revenues thus won in Guzerat enable Bombay to continue the war.

While tragedy and decision proceeded, suddenly the very foundation of his government threatened to collapse overnight. Barwell was rather weary of playing second fiddle; his sister, who was probably instigated by North's underlings, pressed him to come home, and in November 1778 his young wife died. The next month he told Hastings he would go. The Governor was resolved to stick it out; had he suffered so long, only 'to abandon the field as soon as I was master of it'? When in January Barwell announced his intention in Council, Hastings entreated, and won, his retractation in a memorable minute. 'For the sake of our common masters', by ties of friendship cemented by 'labour and sufferings', he conjured him to stand fast. Their government would in any case expire under act of parliament in October, but his information indicated there would be no change as regards Barwell and himself.

That danger being surmounted, the next rolled in with the advent that month of the Commander-in-Chief, Eyre Coote. The new member, as the fierce critic of Henry Vansittart, was an old antagonist, whose rapid disappearance ten years ago Hastings had hailed with joy. But now he was told from home that Coote would certainly support him, and especially, George Vansittart wrote, if the Governor were 'complaisant' regarding the military department. Certainly complaisance could hardly go further than the arrangements he made; so much so that they made one charge at his later impeachment. The General should have the princely estate of Ghyretty, just vacated by the French governor of Chandernagore. On top of his salary, he was to receive when 'in the field', that is, the moment he crossed the Bengal frontier, additional allowances making about £18,000 a year. The Oudh residency should be remodelled as he wished, that being his probable military centre.

Though they commonly spoke of Coote as a veteran, actually he was only in his fifty-fourth year, still the same heroic, foul-tempered, and avaricious creature as of old. When war came with Mysore, he showed that he could keep the saddle thirty hours at a stretch, and stiffen his will, after a stroke of paralysis, until defeat was made impossible. Though he spoke no Hindustani, his presence was worth many battalions with the sepoys, his stilted army orders had the same obstinate courage as the obstinate letters of his royal master. Yet his military notions were fixedly orthodox, his utterances on Indians smacked of the old Clive school. 'Blacks' was his common word for them, and very soon he was telling the Governor, as against Colonel Pearse, that 'establishing a black artillery must prove the first step to our ruin'. His stay at Madras en route made a bad start. Naturally consumed to attack the French, he fired off to the Directors a severe criticism of the Mahratta war, while a joint letter from Francis and Wheler told him the supposed danger of Bombay was an 'artifice of party'. His first argument then in Bengal was that to send reinforcements to Goddard would be 'unmilitary in the highest degree'.

Francis was counting on him; a terrible Irish cousin of his own, Major Baggs, had met Coote at the Cape, and brought information that Francis was to be next Governor-General. He was quickly disappointed. Coote declared in Council for no retrospects, and on one testing question, whether young Fowke should be restored to Benares, he declined to vote. By the summer Francis' journal records that the General's faculties, 'if ever he had any', were gone, and that on the war 'Coote bitches it as I expected'.

But he was hardly in a judicial frame of mind, for the judges had lately struck him a blow that he never forgave. On the day after his ball in November, he jotted down jauntily 'omnia vincit amor', though the entry on December the 8th ran 'at night, the diable à quatre at the house of G. F. Grand Esq.' It was, indeed, a very odd night, under a clouded moon. Selecting his date in advance, when he knew that Grand would be dining jovially at a tavern with Barwell, having sent on a dark suit to Shee's house near by and asked him to provide a bamboo ladder, behold this Councillor slinking down the lane like a lurcher and scaling the wall of Grand's compound. Very soon the *ayah* found her mistress' door locked, roused the men-servants, and all confusion was let loose. Intercepted, and his proffered bribe refused, the great man whistled loudly, his unwilling accomplice Shee took the alarm, roused Ducarel and Shore from their slumbers, and now they were all scrambling over ditch and wall. In darkness and hurly-burly Francis got away, but Shee was held fast till the fat Grand, called from his dinner, came running on the scene, backed by William Palmer, sword in hand. Grand's challenge next day was declined, it was 'a complete mistake', and so it came to the Supreme Court, with a claim for £160,000 of damages. After long delay, judgement was given in March, with damages of £5000.

This business proceeded on the usual lines. Hastings and Barwell forwarded Grand's complaint to the Directors; Impey and Hyde gave the verdict, with Chambers dissenting. Instantly, to his intimates at home, Francis knitted up this 'barbarous persecution' with the public cause. 'It is the second edition of the history of Fowke and Nuncumar', 'the men who hanged

Nuncumar to save Mr. Hastings will stick at nothing'. He would live to be revenged on Impey. 'My skin is as tough as leather, my flesh is all nerve, and my nerves are ossified.' As to the public cause, Mrs. Grand was sent in tears to her family at Chanderna-gore: Francis followed and soon installed her at Hugli, protected by the formidable duellist, Major Baggs. He found it a hectic summer, writing to old Fowke, 'I do not think I can stand it much longer'. And then his wife Betsy wrote in her most exasperating style, from Tunbridge Wells or Brighton, 'you tell me your wish is to quit India, but why don't you do it?'

He was sharpening a weapon which might bring this Chief Justice down, or at least separate him from Hastings. While the clash over revenue cases must sooner or later be firmly handled, the Court's virtues equally infuriated the English community at Calcutta. Should not a gentleman be able to flog light-fingered Bengali workmen caught in the act? From this popular belief there flickered, and then flamed up, the long affair known as Touchet's petition. A powerful committee was formed to demand the Briton's inherited liberty of trial by jury; it included members of both factions, signatures were forthcoming even in the Governor's household. Committed to the trusty hands of William Hickey, who was longing to see the lights of London again, this petition might shake Hastings' strength in Bengal.

He had enough to think of, to end the Mahratta war with honour. Ragoba he gave up for lost; all must turn on Goddard's negotiation with Poona, which should delay further fighting till after the rains. New French forces had reached Mauritius, he expected an attack on Bombay. But he would not hear of Francis' remedy, to concentrate all our troops in Bengal: 'had the politics of Great Britain been confined within such narrow limits as Mr. Francis would prescribe . . . her power and opulence must have been unknown beyond the seas which surround her'. Yet he felt himself being carried away by the stream, towards a peace enforced on us. 'In my heart', he told Sulivan, 'I dread its accomplishment, knowing that nothing but war can retrieve the fatal effects of the late miscarriage.'

Distance and long silences, messengers stealing from village to village with ciphered letters, broke his control and confused decision. Bombay did not get Elliot's instructions till he was four months dead; Goddard complained he had not heard for 'many months'. Bombay sent an agent to Calcutta — 'a hot-headed man with a most tranquil exterior' — to dispute Goddard's powers. Madras cried aloud for money. In June the inexhaustible Ragoba, on his way to imprisonment in Scindia's precipitous fort at Jhansi, broke from his escort and fled back to British protection. Bengal, though endorsing Goddard's pledges for his safety, vetoed any more financial assistance. But the harm was done. For the Poona ministers, who had lately been speaking of joining the British against Mysore, on getting this news abruptly drew back, and sent an embassy to Hyder Ali. In September Goddard furnished authentic detail of a great coalition against us, of Hyder Ali, the Nizam, and all the Mahrattas.

If the ruin of the Bombay policy and Hastings' preference for Berar softened the soil for this disaster, the final crash came from the wild incompetence of Madras. Thomas Rumbold, once a rival candidate for the Governor-Generalship, led his Presidency in pompous style from one rash position to another. Inheriting a dispute with the Nizam's brother over the French troops in his employ, he proposed negotiation for their removal, and for transferring the Guntur Circar to British control, of which Bengal approved. But the negotiation was begun without reference to the Nizam, and the ensuing treaty not communicated to Bengal for a year. In June they angered the Nizam still more, by asking in stiff tones for remission of the tribute they owed him for the remaining Circars. In August they calmly marched troops through Hyder's country; in October they were crazy enough to rent out the Guntur Circar to the Nabob of the Carnatic, Hyder's most detested enemy. His rancour against them had been much inflamed this spring, when Madras forces, on Coote's advice, occupied the port of Mahé on the west coast, which would close his point of entry for French arms and weaken his hold on Malabar.

Very little, it would seem, can be said for the handling of the Mysore peril by any of the British authorities. Bengal having already objected to an offensive alliance, in February Madras suggested one merely defensive, and the withdrawal of Goddard's army from the West. In April they recommended, on the contrary, a joint attack on Mysore by all three Presidencies. In May they sent the famous missionary Swartz on a roving enquiry, to discover Hyder's intentions. In June Rumbold assured John

Hollond, his envoy at Hyderabad, that it was safe to press the Nizam over the tribute, there being no fear of Hyder attacking us. By this time Hastings realized the mishandling of Hyderabad and was determined to stop it but, misled by Goddard's reports, did not as yet believe that Hyder would patch up with his Mahratta enemies. All this time he was being harried by gloomy news from the North; from Hannay at Delhi, of Nadjif Khan's coldness, and from Middleton in Oudh, that the Vizier's indebtedness to the Company and British officers had swollen to 14,000,000 rupees.

How could he face these storms without power? stultified if Coote's wayward vote turned against him, and fast bound by the Regulating Act from crushing the insolence of Rumbold, or the jealousy of Bombay. He broke out to Baber and Sulivan that he would not go on, as 'the pageant I am'; 'I am not Governor'. This government 'contains the seeds of death in it'. 'I will not stay longer if I am left in the same impotent and distressed state, nor will I leave this country, if I have an option, to the mercy of Philip Francis. How I am to reconcile these dissimilar resolutions, I cannot yet tell.'

CHAPTER XVII

Marian and Macpherson

THE first Warren Hastings, boy husband of Mary Buchanan, and the young man Reynolds painted, has sunk below our visible horizon. A second has succeeded, long-enduring, embittered, heroic. We now enter the years that formed a third; if life is stretched out so far, there may be a fourth, more like unto the first.

The first generation of his Indian friends were dead or dispersed. Henry Vansittart and Scrafton, long drowned; Sykes in England, despondent; George Vansittart, alienated. Poor Dr. Hancock, hard driven by poverty and now dead; soon we find his widow Philadelphia reproaching Hastings for his silence of 'so many years'. Of his chosen disciples, Elliot had gone; Halhed was loyalty itself but cranky, no one could collect wisdom from John Belli, or the deaf and gouty Charles Croftes. He relied more now on his young 'politicals', such as the two Anderson brothers, Chapman, and William Palmer. These he employed, to supersede regular officers, exacting arduous labour but rewarding it with full trust, fighting for their career, and holding out a loan in times of need. He felt sorely in need of their loyalty, for he was solitary in Council. After Barwell had gone and when Coote was away at the war, he was left alone with Francis and Wheler, since Macpherson did not join Council till the autumn of 1781, while it was a year afterwards that Stables' arrival restored it to full strength. And all through 1779–80 his old friendship with Impey was destroyed.

No one in India had a doubt as to the supreme influence on his being, or the main road to his favour. It was Marian, the secretary to the Madras government reported, who had the 'fixed ascendancy over his mind'. Praise of her in some casual conversation, or some service rendered her by a young soldier, made titles to his gratitude; honours for her from Delhi, gifts of jewels and ivory furniture from princes, showed that Indians knew it too.

He loved her incomparably more than his own life, would do things for her in his later poverty in defiance of good sense, and almost of upright dealing, while perhaps a third of his diaries over thirty years record his watchfulness for her every mood and slightest ailment. When they were separated, his professions of love pursued her; 'my Queen', 'my heart's treasure', 'the Deity of my Religion': 'continue, my sweet Marian, to love me, for in that hope and belief alone I live'. He worshipped her bodily beauty; 'adieu, my beloved, I will be your nurse to-morrow night'; 'your delightful looks, your enchanting voice, even your touch (O God! once more make them substantially mine)'. But most he loved her spirit, his 'elegant, amiable, most deserving Marian'; the 'sprightliness' that lightened his own depression, her 'generous and unequalled sensibility', the staunchness of her courage. In her, as it were returning from what he had made her, he found the sanction of all he lived for: 'O God! grant me the blessing of a satisfied conscience, and my Marian to reward it'.

Bound in a brocade case, their ciphers on either side within wreaths, she kept the poem he made in September 1782, when she had come 400 miles in three days to nurse him in his worst illness, and he had always by him a painting of the rocks where her boat was nearly lost on that journey, in a cross-eddy.

> Thy beauty first and sweet attractive grace
> My captive heart inthralled, and still inthrall;
> Not formed of features, such as painters trace,
> Which please at sight, and on the fancy pall.
>
> . . . .
>
> But each expression shines with varied charms,
> By the quick impulse of each thought inclined;
> With sense compos'd, with mirth or passion warms,
> The strong bright emanations of thy mind.
>
> . . . .
>
> Thy fortitude in one example shown,
> Of innate pride and virtue's precepts born,
> Not by presumption's breath to rashness blown,
> Might form a hero, or a crown adorn.
>
> . . . .
>
> Foe to hypocrisy, if anger swell
> Thy breast, or just contempt thy spleen provoke,
> Thy words and looks are both too prompt to tell
> The truths, for social quiet best unspoke.
>
> . . . .

207

One subject yet remains, and must, unsung;
The last, the first, for neither pen of steel,
Nor lungs of brass, nor adamantine tongue,
Can tell how much I owe, nor what I feel.

She was just thirty when they married, and though he trembled at every hot ray or cold wind on her 'tender frame', she lived to be ninety, only dying three months before the accession of Queen Victoria. Her physique was tenacious, inherited from a strong eighteenth-century stock, the Germans descended from Huguenot *émigrés*. Her appetite for food was not delicate. She loved riding the Arabs that Warren gave her, and occasionally wielded a gun. In her fifties she was sea-bathing, in her sixties rode round the Daylesford farms before breakfast, in her last year of life she was tracking down defamatory letters against her husband of sixty years back. If we call her very much a man's woman, it is not just from what the Madras secretary called her 'feminine art', or for her good looks and welcoming gaiety. She had the mind of a strong man, the loyalty and outspokenness and capacity for a human hatred that men of action approve. Soldiers who were with her in emergency were loudest in her praise. They noted in England that she was almost happiest with the roughest of politicians, Thurlow, who liked a jovial enemy like Fox and hated moral claims in anybody.

Her money sense was much better than Warren's, who never thought about it except for her, for she had been poor enough to enjoy saving, and what it may bring. Her marriage settlement money was remitted home, to be invested on 'the very best security', — some to be spent on her two boys, who were now at Harrow. Warren deposed during his trial that her fortune then was some £40,000. When she was 'Governess', she spent lavishly; Calcutta ladies said she spoiled the market by overpaying her sempstress; their staff at Alipur included sixteen gardeners, and four keepers for the deer, sheep, and cows. An immense milliner's bill a year after their marriage takes in many-coloured yards of ribbons, satin stays, ostrich feathers, baize-lined jewel-boxes; all that 'liquefaction' which Warren, like Herrick, found bewitching, and put into verse, though not verse like his.

Gay gown and stomacher so fine,
And petticoat of clouds divine,
With other silken things and lac'd things;

Marian and Macpherson

Admiring swains with rapture eye
The Pageant as it moves, and die;
And people call you Mrs. Hastings.

And her chief interest in Bogle's exploration of Tibet was the chance of getting some black fox-skins to edge her cape.

She was often considered grasping, and in some ways was vulgar. If she rejected the offer of a lac from the Vizier, it was not so much the gift itself as its mercenary form, and we know how one of the Begum's eunuchs found her playing with kittens in a basin of pearls, wearing ear-rings which he thought were worth £10,000. The jewels she wore in London, which astonished the not easily astonished Mirabeau, and were a gift to Whig caricaturists, were equally notorious in India. She must be preparing, the horrible Francis wrote, for a flight to Germany, — 'I question whether the Queen of Great Britain appears with more jewels in her drawing-room'. A young Captain Macpherson noted that her 'undress' up-country, when British rule seemed shaking, involved a black satin jacket and petticoat, edged with pearls and with diamond buttons, with more diamonds in her hat, worth in all, he supposed, perhaps £25,000.

James Augustus Hicky, sometime a clerk on the Western circuit and later editor of the *Bengal Gazette*, declared the way to a good post was to 'pay your constant devoirs to Marian Alipur', or 'the German princess', as the Fowke circle called her. We may be permitted to doubt it. Some of Hastings' most crucial steps were taken without telling her; his most loving letters convey a hint about her incivility, or warn her against her 'foible' of accepting Oriental flattery at its face value. At any rate she was clever enough, large-minded and good enough too, to lead society with dignity and spirit. She would dress as she pleased, — overdress, as Fanny Burney thought later in England — and wear her auburn hair flowing, unpowdered. She seems to have won over the once critical Lady Impey; had also a maternal side that made her plan happiness for other women. Her closest friend was Mary Touchet, whom she was credited with marrying to Hastings' early acquaintance, the diamond merchant Thomas Motte: not that this ended very cheerfully, for Mary went off to England with Marian, leaving Thomas desolate and finally bankrupt. Then there was Henry Ramus, a stupid young man, 'the great Nimrod of Bengal', who once killed nine tigers near

Chinsura, according to Joseph Fowke, 'with the loss only of a part of his elephant's rump'. He and his sister, the beautiful wife of the Advocate-General, Sir John Day, were children of the King's page, so forming a link with Marian's patron Madame Schwellenburg and Windsor. His marriage, too, Marian brought off to Mlle Vernet, daughter of those kindly Dutch who had been good to Warren in the black year 1756.

She was more successful with men, with whom perhaps her broken English — which all her life she never learned to write correctly — added to the charm. She kept on friendly terms with difficult or hostile men, better than Warren could with his scars all about him; with Richard Johnson for instance, and even with Francis, who attended her parties in their new house in Hastings Street. For Government House was found too cramped for a married Governor-General and his staff.

He was fifteen years older than she was, not fifty yet but worn very fine by years of strain. He had taken to spectacles for reading, and the portraits of the '80's show him almost entirely bald. Though Marian was all he asked for, and much though he longed she should bring him a child, he never let fall his own kith and kin. He still paid the annuity to his aunt, and perpetual small doles for his most unsatisfactory Buchanan stepdaughter. All the flotsam and jetsam of his first life were at his purse. His aunt warned him against a young Warren, a grocer, 'who has come out as a beau', and fancied life in India. Then he discovered that his uncle Howard, who had brought him up, had left a natural daughter; £600 of his went on her marriage, and more to set her up in a nursery school at Chelsea. To his brother-in-law he wrote, 'I have always considered you and my sister as entitled to share with me in whatever successes fortune had in store', and paid £10,000 into their account, adding 'I shall quarrel with Tommy, if he does not write to me', his nephew now being an undergraduate, which is not a letter-writing class.

However dire, then, the next few years, he had his paradise and his repose. How often he would escape from business for a few minutes and run up to Marian's room! There were Solyman and Beauty to ride, and all the beasts and trees and flowers to enjoy at Alipur. In the State *felcheera*, with its tiger-head bow and rowers in colour of rose, or Marian's pinnace the *Mary*, they were often on the river, which took them up to the Mottes at

Hugli, or Croftes at Sooksagur. He gave an annual dinner for fellow old-Westminsters, when friend and foe came together, young Markham the Archbishop of York's son sitting cheek by jowl with William Burke. There they sat till sunrise, though the Governor slipped away at midnight, reminiscing over Dr. Vincent's hatred of a false quantity, or subscribing to an annuity for 'Poll Puff', who had sold them jam tartlets at the school gate. Dinners too were interchanged with Councillors and judges, though with the subordinate ranks the Governor did not dine. Best of all, a game of chess with her at night, or a book from his full library, where Racine and Machiavelli were ranged with Lucretius and Colman's *Terence*, travel books galore, or Mason's *English Gardiner*. There he came as near as India allowed to his expressed ideal, 'a hard frost and my own fireside'. But when, and by what stroke of fortune, he would achieve that home, was being determined in London and Westminster.

The Government line was still strongly anti-Hastings. They were infuriated by the 'resignation' fiasco, the King more than once pressed that Hastings and Barwell be recalled. North was recommending high employment for Joseph Fowke. His patronage secretary Robinson was working hand in glove with the present chairman, Sir George Wombwell. All this, and much more, was retailed to Hastings in letters from Sykes, gloomy and reproachful. The party 'that stuck by you like glue' was broken, and by his own doing. He had made enemies of the Pigot group, slighted patronage recommendations (even for young Wombwell), and defied the Directors by refusing to restore Francis Fowke and dismissing Mahomed Reza Khan. His blind confidence in Macleane had shocked his old friends; George Vansittart's silence was most damaging. Altogether, he predicted his speedy downfall.

On the other hand, in 1778 Sulivan came in again as a director, defeating a government candidate, which was claimed by John Macpherson as the first-fruits of his return to England. Having got himself cleared from the Madras government's censure and restored to the service, Macpherson turned his unscrupulous energy to the restoration of Hastings to the Cabinet's favour. For a Hastings revival would serve his own ends; the sequence of which was to be a seat in parliament, then a seat in the Bengal Council, and finally the seat now filled by Hastings. As a beginning, he preached to the Governor some worldly wisdom. After asking his patronage for two Macphersons, a Mackenzie, and a Mackintyre he pointed the moral. 'There is another gentleman whom I must be very free in recommending . . . no less person than my friend Mr. Warren Hastings. Should you come home with that indifference about money, and that neglect of yourself which I always apprehend, you have neither wisdom nor good fellowship in you.' He kept up this stream of suggestion and self-praise. He had faced Robinson in a stormy conversation, and was steering North at least to neutrality. The King, he boldly added, was now on his side, which counted for much more than 'that unreasonable woman', Mary Barwell. His cousin James Macpherson, or 'Ossian', was helping with his pen. And, despite his 'vast fortune', Francis was losing ground.

He underlined one particular conclusion. What had enabled him to save Hastings from immediate condemnation was his own pull with the Arcot interest, which ministers valued: 'I have but one object, — it is to make your support inseparable from the cause of the Nabob'. Incidentally, that ungrateful Nabob had never paid his salary, 'this has obliged me to draw upon you for 30,000 sicca rupees at a month's sight'.

In 1780 the Macphersons seemed to be winning all along the line. John came in as member for Cricklade, his colleague there being Paul Benfield himself. Though there were still enemies in the Direction like Gregory, Sulivan became deputy chairman; for this, and a Cabinet decision to extend Hastings and his Council for yet another year, Macpherson took credit to himself. Cousin James added his testimony, 'I was present at the treaty and, in some sense, its guarantee'. As the year ended, John was chosen to succeed Barwell, the defeated candidate being Vansittart who, Sulivan wrote, 'feels for himself alone'. As 1781 dawned, however, cousin James indicated a price that might have to be paid; Paul Benfield, 'of whom you must have heard much', was anxious to be his friend. Government would support him, for he had 'a great political line . . . formed of men whose principles we approve, and on whose conduct we can depend'. But let us glance into the enemy camp.

England was full of Francis' adherents. Farrer was back, who had lately tried to do a deal with Barwell, and who soon filled the parliamentary seat at Wareham, once ear-marked for Francis.

Goring was there, busy publishing a Francis version of the Mahratta war. Bristow, the ejected from Oudh, was there till half-way through 1779, and particularly informing. When he first got home, he found Francis' position was bad, — much injured by Clavering's letters, and by that too notorious gambling party when he had bled Barwell. However, he contrived to arrange some interviews with Hastings' champion, Pechell, the basis of which was the Governor-Generalship for Francis within a reasonable time. Hastings had made a mistake in coming out so hotly against Pigot, while something might also be made out of the struggle between the Nabob of the Carnatic's sons; for while Macpherson backed the second, the elder corresponded with North and had William Burke as his agent. They would try 'bullying the Minister', with threats of how ugly Francis would turn if he were kept out. And anyhow, over a dinner in Downing Street, they got Macpherson's promise to work for Bristow's own career.

The good Pechell gave Hastings another version of these conversations. The enemy, he said, seemed strangely confident that Barwell would raise no difficulty; nor did he like to hear James Macpherson speaking as if he were in Hastings' confidence. For all that, he advised him to meet Francis half-way, since the Directors were ruled by Robinson and Sandwich. Then he was admitted to two long colloquies with North. The Prime Minister complained that Hastings had broken his undertaking to resign, had failed to stem corruption, and disobeyed the Directors; which was disappointing, for 'I had a great opinion of Mr. Hastings'. Still, he grasped the point when Pechell observed that Clavering was dead, that Hastings could be trusted as a man of honour, and that a majority of the proprietors were his friends.

With Sulivan, thus resurrected, the Governor's old links had never been broken. As his debts were so heavy — Macleane had died owing him £14,000 — he had sent out his son Stephen to Madras, whence Hastings quickly transferred him to Bengal as his personal assistant. Meantime he told his attorneys to lend the father anything he asked, up to £10,000. And after becoming deputy chairman, Sulivan's letters were much more cheerful. Macpherson, he predicted, 'will be to you a second Barwell'; North was cordial in support. 'But my dear friend, you must not again attempt to break through positive orders of the Company.'

That for the time being Hastings would not be removed, was confirmed by the shrewd Baber, who submitted to North in person Hastings' reform memorandum of 1766, and sounded his praises. 'To all this he gave a nod (for *entre nous* he hardly does anything else).'

All the English mail reaching Calcutta bore this impression of the concordat between government and Sulivan, which indeed was so official that the powerful Jenkinson wrote to warn Justice Chambers to watch his step. And Jenkinson agreed with Sulivan's intelligence on another head; that government meant to find time for a complete overhaul of the Company's administration.

Heat, rains, and fevers, and in their periodic succession these slow-dropping letters from home; falling on weary heads sometimes like splinters of ice, and then as sparks of fire. For a whole year they fell thus, while the Mahratta war was renewed, while Council and judges were in open collision, and while Hyder hung above the Carnatic like a dark cloud. Both in Hastings and Francis there were signs that they could not bear this tension much longer.

One persistent rumour drove Francis to a frenzy, that government would send out some disinterested servant of the Crown as governor. Surely North would not put a new man over him? 'If he does, he might as well at once fling Bengal into the sea.' His letters to North mixed resentment and prophecies of woe. He had not heard for two years, which was 'unmerited neglect'. 'The Indian bubble is going to burst. The two other Presidencies are ruined, and Bengal has nothing to spare.' To his oldest friends he was much more violent. The Cabinet had betrayed him, 'as they did Sir John Clavering and Colonel Monson from first to last'. The Directors were 'a mere instrument' in Robinson's hand. His shrillest epithets were kept for Coote, 'a character to which your English ideas of dirt and meanness do not reach': 'I despise him from the bottom of my spirit, and the moment it is in my power I shall treat the wretch as he deserves'. Early in 1780 he prepared to send home the fearsome Major Baggs, 'well instructed'. He was to menace Robinson with publication of secret documents, and to get in touch with the Burkes. All these months Francis was much at Hugli, keeping sorrow at arm's length in the company of Mrs. Grand. 'O Phillida', his Horatian journal put down, 'give me back my heart.'

The Governor-General was always revived by sheer emergency. But now he passed through one of those bouts of languid depression to which passivity, deadlock, and unseen enemies would reduce him. He poured out his gratitude for Macpherson's gay assurances, with all 'the warmth which glows in my heart'. And when Barwell turned moody, and Impey seemed an enemy, his letters to the incalculable Coote ring as an appeal to a fellow human being. He wrote, he said, in 'anguish of mind', 'I daily feel the weight and perplexities of my station accumulate beyond my strength to bear them'. The Company's last orders brought 'something more than the portion of disgrace which I have been taught to expect by every packet'. Every English letter, every haggle in Council, even his private finances, revealed the net in which he was caught. 'The curse of patronage', against which he exclaimed to young John Shore, pursued him from the lowest Anglo-Indian rungs up to the Cabinet. His payments ranged from the thousands lent to Sulivan, down to three guineas for Christmas-boxes at the India House. Cousin James Macpherson had hungry fellow-Scots to satisfy. Mary Barwell urgently asked favours for two nephews of the powerful government contractor, Richard Atkinson, much enriched by the American war. He minuted later that there were some 250 Company servants in Bengal, 'many of them the sons of the first families in the kingdom', and every one expecting a fortune. Yet, to defeat this accursed system, he must practise it himself; how otherwise could he get loyal service?

He turned to his honourable masters. Bitterly he contrasted his position with Clive's. 'I have never called the members of another Presidency to govern this; my name has received no addition of titles, my fortune of *jagirs*'; no passage money, no surgeon or chaplain, 'neither my constitution nor religious principles have been a charge to the Company'. Every soul he had personally promoted had been penalized, — Bogle, Belli, or Halhed; they had even ordered the refund (with interest) of the allowances made to Elliot, who had died in their service. To Sulivan he broke out against their 'duplicity', their 'malevolent acts'. The same men had first approved the Rohilla war and then condemned it; they had applauded Bombay's alliance with Ragoba, but doubtless they would soon blame him for the Mahratta war. He charged them with 'harsh and unexampled treatment'. They had rebuked him, their Governor-General, for dissolving a Council that encouraged charges laid against him by 'the most abandoned of mankind'; now they reproved him for supporting the Madras Council against Pigot, who had arbitrarily suspended a whole majority. But 'what were Lord Pigot's merits that I should submit to the humiliating measure of allowing him privileges denied to me?'

As to their last sweeping orders, he would communicate to the Nabob that for the restoration of Mahomed Reza Khan: but 'there it rests, and will rest, until Mr. Francis shall acquire a majority in the Council'. But to those for replacing Bristow in Oudh and young Fowke at Benares, he wrote to Baber, he would apply what he was pleased to call 'a more liberal principle'; in short, a blank defiance. Such orders, proclaiming his impotence to every Indian court, destroyed his office, and 'forfeit their title to my obedience'.

In this state of feeling Calcutta stood as 1779 was running out, when on the evening of Christmas Day Ducarel on behalf of Francis, and a Major Scott representing Hastings, held a note-worthy conversation, the gist of which was nothing less than this, that their two principals should bury the hatchet and come to terms.

CHAPTER XVIII

Francis' Last Year: 1779-80

AGED 47

THEY were fiddling while war and rumours of war were burning. Where the river reached tidal water, the buoys were repainted, a survey was ordered of the Andamans, Coote had gone up-country to inspect garrisons. For the first time for many years some King's troops were sent to India, the 73rd Highlanders. Since the Mahrattas declined to make peace unless we surrendered Ragoba as a prisoner and abandoned Salsette, Goddard was preparing the campaign which was to begin the New Year with the conquest of Guzerat. The reports, which his *munshi* read to Hastings for hours together, told that the North was shaky. Sikh bands were raiding the Doab; Chait Sing was disputing his liability to a war contribution; the Vizier asked the recall of all British troops except the one permanent brigade; each of them calculating, or so Hastings felt, on his loss of power. And the South was black with danger. John Hollond, the Madras envoy to Hyderabad, was convinced the Nizam would take the field against us after the rains. To stop this Madras bungling entangling us in a second war, Bengal decided to reassure the Nizam, appointing Hollond as their own agent. Vehemently calling for instant peace with the Mahrattas, Madras declared that Hyder was only biding his time to break.

For Ragoba, saving his personal safety, Hastings cared nothing, only asking from the Mahrattas the terms of the Purandah treaty and an explicit disavowal of any French alliance. By the spring of 1780 he told Goddard that 'for the first time' he leaned to peace, but it must be peace with honour; 'to you, my valued friend, I will own what I should not venture to proclaim to a Court of India Proprietors, that I regard this redemption of our national character as cheaply obtained'; yes, he added to William Palmer, though it meant 'deeds of uncommon enterprise, and even of blood'. But what weapons had he with which to redeem the English name?

Money he thought little of, though his honourable masters thought much, but the Mahratta war was costing lacs, and if Madras also got into war, that too would fall on Bengal. And without friends in Council, or even neutrals, he could not govern at all. At this moment events in Bengal revealed not merely that he had lost the indispensable co-operation of the judges, but that something next to an English civil war was wrecking his government. For two years now a case from Patna had been dragging on, which involved the whole legality of Provincial Councils and the right of the Supreme Court to protect Indians, while this November another arose which challenged the powers of Council itself. The Court issued a writ against the *zemindar* of Cossijurah, who was a collector of the revenue. Advised by their Advocate-General, John Day, Council bade him refuse to admit the jurisdiction. His servants resisted the sheriff, who thereupon marched in a scratch force of sailors and peons, the *zemindar's* house was forcibly entered, and his household idols distrained upon with his other goods. Council then sent sepoys to arrest the sheriff's army. Then the Court served writs on the British officer commanding the sepoys, on Hastings and all his Council, and on Mahomed Reza Khan's successor, head of all native judicature. Meanwhile, justice almost ceased. Impey complained that, outside Calcutta, his Court suffered an absolute boycott. The Company courts dared not act for fear of prosecution and fine. Hastings actually suggested a move of the government elsewhere, to escape 'the devil of the law'.

Here was a scandalous, dangerous, and unnatural business. He felt acutely being forced into alliance against Impey with Francis, 'his enemy and mine', and hated the loss of his best friend of school days, to whom (thinking of Clavering and 1777) 'I was at one time indebted for the safety of my honour, fortune, and reputation'. While Francis instigated him to an open clash, time after time the Governor kept the peace. Sometimes he bailed defendants at his own expense, sometimes privately begged a plaintiff to withdraw. Impey's demeanour we can guess from the tone of his private letters, in which he complained heavily of Hastings' ingratitude, blamed his secrecy, and explained the Council's action by a corrupt bargain with the *zemindars*. Indeed, his letter-bag was all gloom and fury, except when he commissioned some officer serving with Goddard to bring back pearls for Lady Impey.

But Hastings was clear he had no choice. The Court was going beyond its charter, against persons not 'British subjects', while their levy of armed forces was a flagrant offence. His government would never allow 'the descendants of men who once held the rights of sovereignty' to be arrested like felons, 'on the affidavit of a Calcutta banyan'. The worst Moguls had never so outraged the personal rights of the people, 'which their natural affections, their peculiar sense of shame, and notions of honour, and their ideas of religious purity, render most dear and sacred to them'.

If he had time to breathe, he could dispose of this, but there was the war, and more, a world war, for their letters spoke of French and Spanish fleets in the Channel, and invasion of England. How could he save his corner of Empire against Francis and Wheler? He despaired of Coote, yet 'I am lost if he abandons me'. Petulant letters, promotion of officers notoriously hostile to the Governor, these perhaps he might stomach. But now Coote was angrily resisting a project on which Hastings' heart was set; an alliance with the petty Rajah of Gohud, as a first step to help Goddard by a diversion against the Mahratta rear. The Commander-in-Chief suggested that Hastings' political agent Palmer was set on him as a spy, and trafficking in corruption. Francis, hearing of Coote's 'ravings', could only exult in the thought that 'this poor devil Hastings must buy him over again'.

Until December everything marched on the well-worn track of party. Whatever positive was done went through on the Governor's casting vote, or in Francis' absence at Hugli. Ugly contests were proceeding in Oudh for power and profits, between Coote's nominee Purling, the adroit Hosea, and Nat Middleton. And there was a dangerous group of ambitious 'Franciscans' in Clive's friend Ducarel, Sheridan's friend Peter Moore, and young Wombwell, against whom only the corpulent vote of Barwell served as a protecting wall. But Barwell was wilting. He had no hopes left of the succession, the Directors had accused him of revenue frauds, and sister Mary was nagging him to retire. If he could get away on tolerable terms, he meant to be off.

But if that were so, and if, as seemed certain, Coote reinforced

Francis and Wheler when he came back to the capital, Hastings must get some sort of truce, at least till a new act of parliament confirmed him in office. So he prepared for retreat. When he supped with Francis on Boxing Day, their agents had already met, a fact probably not mentioned to Impey, another guest at supper. What Francis would ask, and how faithfully he would keep any pact, was the question.

From the chameleon colours and windings of his journal and letters his motive can, within probable limits, be collected. He would hang on a little longer in case this weak-kneed Cabinet changed its mind, and made him Governor-General after all. At the same time he told Lady Clavering he was seeking an 'honourable retreat', and made some enquiries about a parliamentary seat. Meanwhile he laid on the colours thick for the good folk at home. 'The British Empire in India is tottering'; this 'dreadful aspect' was the ground for this 'temporary pacification', made 'on public ground and no other', — such was the tone for Godfrey and Barrington. He told Lord North that Barwell had 'taken fright', Hastings 'means to run away', and that he only joined him 'to prevent more mischief' and enforce a peace. To Ellis he added there was not a glimmer of truth in the supposed French-Mahratta contacts.

He was filled with the excitement of victory. 'I detest some few, I despise many more, and I fear no man.' Coote sends grovelling messages : 'at last I have got the scoundrel at my feet'. Hastings and Barwell ask for interviews, 'both at my feet after all their insolence'. Far and wide he insisted he was true to principle. There was no union with Hastings, this man of 'microscopic sagacity', far less any surrender, but 'an armed truce'.

The final intermediary was John Day who, though a nominee of Francis, was acquiring a steady admiration for Hastings. The principals met twice in the second half of January. On February the 4th, Marian gave what Francis called 'a pacific dinner', and on the 7th the terms were agreed. Though they were put in writing by Hastings, no formal documents were interchanged, for he counted on his rival's good faith. The first clause held what was to him the heart of the matter : 'Mr. Francis will not oppose any measures which the Governor-General shall recommend for the prosecution of the war . . . or for the general support of the present political system'.

To win this he made very great concessions. Orders issued for the return of Francis Fowke to Benares, while the Nabob's consent was won for the replacement in office of Mahomed Reza Khan. Even old Joey Fowke was provided for; a little dully, perhaps, for a man of his tastes, for he was put on to catalogue the Directors' proceedings, which should keep anybody quiet. The one thing on which Hastings stood out was over the reappointment of Bristow to Oudh, which he told Macpherson he could not accept without 'ruin to my own influence and spreading a distrust . . . throughout all Hindustan'. But a great deal was done for the Francis gang. Lucrative jobs for his house-mate Collings, for the Burkes' kinsman Shee, and for the rancorous Peter Moore, who had never forgiven his removal from the Calcutta Provincial Council.

Plainly the final proof of Hastings' sincerity was the departure homewards of Barwell, who would never have gone had he thought the truce precarious. Yet it does not seem necessary to think that Francis always meant to deceive, or used Barwell's departure as a trap. Coote's furious remark, that he was the victim of an unnatural coalition, is some evidence of that. It was, after all, only to last till October, when the existing government would legally expire, and made by both sides with eyes very much open to that event. 'If I am confirmed,' Hastings wrote, 'I will have my own agents . . . at the head of every capital department. If Mr. F. is to displace me (which God forbid), he will do the same, and has declared it.'

And if we allow to each of them some sense of public duty, what need was there not for the decencies of union! with Great Britain fighting three Powers at once, and a French fleet daily expected in the Indian Ocean. Emergency measures must be taken, if the great coalition rumoured of Indian States was not to descend on all three Presidencies. Goddard was an excellent soldier, but politically slow-minded, sticking out for Ragoba's lost cause far beyond the line Hastings' Council approved, and even now he entirely disbelieved that Hyder would ever join the Mahrattas. Indeed, Hastings himself minuted that, if ever made, so unnatural a combination could not last; Madras was officially told that its fears were exaggerated. But that was not the view of the Nizam, whose proper wrath against Madras the Bengal Council was doing its very utmost to mitigate. In February they repudiated the Madras treaty touching the Guntur Circar, and continued Hollond as their representative at Hyderabad. He was warned by the Nizam that Hyder would soon attack the Carnatic, and asked to consider an offensive alliance against him.

This intervention led to a fantastic paper war between Madras and Bengal, in which Rumbold surpassed himself. Rejecting their 'dictatorial reprehension' as unauthorized by their legal powers, he declared the Mahratta war every bit as 'unjust and ruinous' as the Rohilla war had been, and audaciously drew a parallel between his own repudiation of tribute to Hyderabad for the Circars, and Hastings' refusal of tribute for Bengal to the Mogul. The Bengal papers coldly noted the vagaries of this 'subordinate Presidency', Hastings moving that 'these extraordinary performances' be brought to the Directors' notice. It may be unjust to conclude with him that, when Rumbold sailed home in April, he was running away from the peril he had partly made; for he had declared six months before that his doctors would not give him another hot weather. Enough that he was gone; in due course a parliamentary committee reported he had remitted £150,000 in two years, — much of which, he protested, came from moneys he had long ago left in Bengal on investment. But Stephen Sulivan reported that 'black Jack' Whitehill, his successor, was taking the same disloyal and offensive line.

If to detach the Nizam would make one breach in the enemy coalition, Berar might make another, and revive the grand design of two years back. Yet it would call for most careful handling, for on this head the Nizam was intensely jealous. The Berar minister was inviting Hastings to meet him in conference at Benares, which might afford an opportunity of clearing up the quagmire in Oudh. But when he suggested this to Francis in April, it was agreed to wait, till news came of his government being confirmed.

So far the truce seemed operating, at least without open or serious friction. Hastings had large reforms in hand, notably an improvement of the *diwanni* courts and the system of salt revenue. And both in remonstrance to the Directors against the judges, and to Coote against his military promotions, he employed the acidulated pen of Francis. Some strains there were, of course, quite inevitable in a government built on patronage. Though

Hastings had spoken amiably to Bristow, he found he came 'hard bitten from the land of party'; was soon writing, in fact, in a style that even Francis described as insolent. Francis also was under fire from his allies, old Fowke and Livius, who wanted more done for them. And Wheler was manœuvring in this chase after patronage too.

Even the physical conditions conduced to these heats, for it was the hottest summer on record, and one of the most unhealthy. Francis was ailing, Hastings caught the ruling influenza, and for the first time in his life missed Council meetings for a week. Newly arrived young women were trying out new *cotillons* at the Harmonic Tavern. Lieutenant Norford made his name in theatricals for unrivalled success in female parts, but Councillors and actors alike were taking to the river, or seeking sea-bathing at Birkul, though crabs were a nuisance there, not to mention rumours of sharks. This was the birth-year of the Indian Press. In the spring James Hicky launched his *Bengal Gazette*, which with justice he claimed should be an 'anti-bilious specific'. It was agreeable to read in its pages of Impey as 'Pulbundi', or of the many suitors courting Amelia Wrangham, 'the Chinsura Belle'. It was noted that, on Francis and his doings, the editor maintained an unwonted silence.

But, well or ill, for good or evil, Hastings had made his sacrifices for one purpose only, to fight and end the Mahratta war. Goddard's winter campaign made an admirable beginning. He had taken the rich twelve-gated city of Ahmedabad, his storming-party led by the brave Hartley, the one hero of the defeat at Wargaum. Guzerat was effectually in his control; he had driven Scindia and Holkar back and, now the rains had begun, was well posted for a new advance. The Governor's letters commemorate the heroism of long-forgotten subalterns, 'the incomparable behaviour' of Lieutenant Welsh, for example, who gaily mopped up one fort after another. But he was meditating a more decisive concentration of force. Mediation by means of Berar might come in due course, the instant need was to go on striking till the Mahrattas gave way. He held up to Goddard the picture of a junction with the Rajput States, making 'a continued chain from the Jumna to Guzerat'. To this end he detached Palmer, to make contact with Udaipur, Jodhpur, and the rest of these illustrious martial dynasties, whose lands stretched south and west of Delhi, with their lakes and marble palaces. Hitherto the Rajputs were silent, waiting on the result of the British advance to Gohud.

He had to fight every inch in order to get that expedition launched; of little over 2000 men, originally raised as drafts for Goddard, and commanded by Captain William Popham, whom Hastings was soon to call 'a noble fellow'. In spite of every possible obstruction from Coote, who starved him of artillery, in April Popham mined and then stormed the fortress of Lahar. Our sepoys, wrote Palmer, 'would have done credit to the best troops in Europe', but both British leaders of the forlorn hope were killed, one of them being Hastings' cousin, Cornet William Gardiner. He wrote proudly to his brother-in-law how their kinsman had fought 'with great gallantry', how by his will he had left the Governor as guardian of his little son William by an Indian wife, and 'I have accepted of him'. In the autumn the boy was sent home, to be brought up at the Governor's expense, and in time 'I beg you will send him to Westminster'. The tireless Popham went on, laying his plans for the storming of the mighty fort at Gwalior, where Coote predicted failure, — as he had at Lahar.

In May Council considered a letter from Goddard, asking for 'a powerful diversion' in Scindia's rear. Hastings' first proposal was to send Popham to join Goddard, and to replace him in central India by a more powerful force under Major Camac. Early in June, however, having news of a Berar army threatening Cuttack and of Hyder Ali's mobilizing on the Carnatic frontier, he urged that Popham's force should be joined to Camac's command for the invasion of Scindia's country. He almost went on his knees to his rivals. Twice this month his minutes have the unusual opening 'I entreat'. He pleaded in person with Francis. It was of no use. Francis exclaimed in his journal against 'insidious proposals', and 'this wicked man'; his joint minute with Wheler, of June the 15th, stated the impossibility of continuing war 'on any terms', without reducing expenses.

While these debates continued, Hastings received an offer of two lacs from Chait Sing of Benares, a peace-offering after his many attempts to evade payment of his war subsidy. This sum he paid into the Treasury and, on the 26th, offered it to defray Camac's expenses. His minute declared the sole objective of this diversion was peace, but 'feeble measures', changes of plan 'by desultory votes', would merely postpone peace and discourage our friends. They had given him the responsibility for the war, and if so 'it is hard they should bind my hands'. Finally he turned to Francis. Let him take the lead, if he thought he could end the war better, or that 'he can in honour deprive me of the right which I claim'.

Two replies on that day, and a third later, widened his colleagues' objection far beyond the ground of expense. These distant expeditions would lay Bengal open to invasion. After two years the war was 'as far from a conclusion as ever'; so much for 'vigorous measures, in the sense in which vigour has been hitherto understood'. As for our friends, 'we wish that the names of these friends had been mentioned': 'in fact, we see the principal powers of India either armed, or ready to arm, against us'. After such an experience, they would not join in new measures. They would co-operate in the making of peace, yet 'to accomplish a peace ourselves, against his inclination, we know to be impossible'. Francis appended a few words of reply to Hastings' appeal to their engagement, — 'as I understand it, there is no point of honour in question'.

In a later statement during this long controversy, Francis said very truly there was no final test 'but the public opinion of our respective characters'. For each swore solemnly, both in public debate and private correspondence, to the sense in which he had understood their compact. Hastings argued that Francis' promise was unconditional; not just to support the campaign in western India, but all measures touching the Mahratta war. Pointing out that months before their engagement the Gohud treaty provided for operations against Scindia, and of that treaty Camac's expedition was 'the necessary consequence', he may have used the very words that Francis quotes, 'Sir, this *is* supporting the war on the Malabar Coast'. But his main ground, now and hereafter, was always the same, 'my security was in his honour'; that Barwell's departure was dependent on the agreement, as he himself had told Francis by Barwell's advice.

His decision was fixed now, unknown to any save his two secretaries, Belli and Markham; for the next month his every step was measured and inflexible. After a week spent, his memorandum says, 'in continual debate with myself concerning the

225

manner of noticing and defeating Mr. F.'s opposition', he determined to kill him. Morally, he hoped, in any event, by exposing his dishonour; physically, it might be, if his words led, as he thought probable, to a challenge. Or perchance to be killed by him? Very well, much would be gained. A Governor situated as he was, 'a mere name', would make room for a sober government by Wheler, or someone else, with the powers which he had been denied. For of one thing he was assured: that Francis would never be appointed to succeed a Governor-General who had died at his hands. On Sunday July the 2nd he finished the minute which should perform these things; when Markham, to whom he was dictating, ventured to point out the consequence, the Governor grimly praised his discernment.

The morrow would be a Council day, but meantime John Day asked Hastings to hold his hand and went to Francis whose suggestion, to suspend Camac's march till they received the English despatches, Hastings immediately refused. For one thing, it would imply that the engagement was null and void. On the 3rd, however, Day found Francis prostrate with fever, ready to acquiesce that, while he was absent, Hastings should do as he pleased; that evening, in fact, orders issued to Camac, to march. But Hastings wanted more: the offending minutes must be withdrawn. On the 7th Day brought word that Francis agreed; Hastings carried his resolution in Council, and that evening left to join Marian in a yacht near Chandernagore.

While she and Mrs. Motte sailed to Hugli, or to stay with the Dutch at Chinsura, he came back often for meetings of Council (none of which Francis attended). There were countless people to see, — he noted sixteen in one morning — important letters to Palmer in central India, new guns to inspect at Ghyretty. On the 17th he heard that Francis, who had gone to recuperate up the river, repudiated Day's message, refusing to withdraw his minutes if Camac entered Scindia's territory. That night Hastings supped with Impey who, perhaps, could not resist an 'I told you so'. Day went off to try to overtake Francis, hoping to bring him round.

Hastings' diary over these weeks, and short notes to Marian, were tranquil and commonplace. He advises her against buying a chariot advertised as 'most elegant', condemning it as 'old and vamped'. He buys her two rings. He reports on his influenza, describes how he went to the riding school to cure his stiffness. On July the 28th, when at anchor off Chinsura, he received information, which hardened his mood, that Francis was approaching Coote for reconciliation, and had gone further up-stream to meet him. This came, it seems, from Richard Johnson, who was judged an intriguer; which emerges from an important letter to Hastings from Day, who had failed to find Francis. He disbelieved, he wrote, some of this information, as coming from 'a beardless Machiavel, who has played upon you all in turn'. He had learned to look up to his character 'as standing upon an eminence and alone', and would grieve to see it 'mixed with those who now obtrude themselves upon you'. There were others than Johnson, who were glad to prime the Governor with such information. Captain John Scott, once his aide de camp, volunteered his conviction that Francis' certainty of being Governor-General was broadcast in Oudh.

On August the 14th, leaving Marian at Chinsura, he returned to Calcutta, on hearing that Francis was back there; his short letter to her that night did not mention that he had just sent his minute to Francis, not wishing to spring it on him in Council. It had been standing ready these six weeks past.

'I did hope that the intimation conveyed in my last minute would have awakened in Mr. Francis' breast, if it were susceptible of such sensations, a consciousness of the faithless part which he was acting towards me. I have been disappointed, and must now assume a plainer style and a louder tone. . . . I had a right to his implicit acquiescence. . . . I do not trust to his promise of candour, convinced that he is incapable of it. . . . Every disappointment and misfortune have been aggravated by him, and every fabricated tale of armies devoted to famine, or to massacre, have found their first and ready way to his office. . . . I judge of his public conduct by my experience of his private, which I have found to be void of truth and honour.'

When next day they finished at the Revenue Board, Francis took him aside and read his challenge. Hastings replied that he had expected it, and they agreed to meet at Alipur two days later. The rest of this day and Wednesday, Hastings passed in writing a new will and a memorandum for Markham, together with a last letter to Marian, to be given her if he did not survive.

My beloved Marian,

My heart bleeds to think what your sufferings and feelings must be, if ever this letter shall be delivered into your hands. You will too soon learn the occasion of it. On my part it has been unavoidable. I shall leave nothing which I regret to lose but you, nor in my last moments shall I feel any other affliction. Let it be a consolation to you to know that at this moment I have the most grateful sense of all your past kindness, and of the unremitted proofs which you have daily and hourly afforded me of your affection. For these may God reward you! I know not how. How much I have loved you, how much beyond all that Life can yield, I still love you, He only knows. Do not, my Marian, forget me; but cherish my remembrance to the latest hour of your life, as I should yours were it my lot, and my misery, to survive you. I cannot write all that I feel and that my heart is full of.

Adieu, my best wife, and most beloved of women. May the God of Heaven bless you and support you. My last thoughts will be employed on you. Remember and love me. Once more farewell.

Your

Warren Hastings.

On the 16th Colonel Pearse, whom he had asked to be his second, breakfasted with him, and hour and place were settled, — 5.30 next morning, near Belvedere. The fire-eater Colonel Watson was to act for Francis, who was burning papers that day, — 'dull work'; he wrote also to Wheler, 'defend my memory . . . farewell for ever'.

Thursday morning broke fine and windless; soon after four, Pearse called for Hastings, who complained he was too early, and lay down again another half-hour. When they drove off, they met his bodyguard, surprised to see him about, whom he dismissed; they found Francis and Watson walking up and down on the Alipur road. It was getting near the time for people to take their morning ride, and they looked for a suitable place, Hastings objecting to one avenue of trees as too dark. Finally they chose an empty lane, just outside his old property at Belvedere. As they watched their seconds' preparations, Francis said he had never fired a pistol in his life, while Hastings could only remember doing so once or twice. On Watson recommending a distance of fourteen paces, Hastings commented 'it was a great distance for pistols'; when the paces were measured, he asked if they were to stand on the line, or behind it. 'I had resolved', his diary says, 'to defer my fire, that I might not be embarrassed with his'; the only thing troubling him was an old coolie woman looking on, who was calling others from the village to see what the sahibs were about. Once Francis' pistol missed fire, twice he went to the present and came down again. A third time, and they fired almost together; Francis narrowly missed, while Hastings' bullet struck his right side, was turned by a rib, and lodged under the left shoulder. He fell, crying 'I am dead'; Hastings ran across, saying 'Good God! I hope not'; 'shocked, I own,' he entered in his diary, 'and I can safely say without any immediate sensation of joy from my own success'. After much searching for palanquins and missing their way, Francis was taken into Belvedere, while Hastings drove home full-tilt, to send out the surgeon-general and his own doctor, Clement Francis. That done, he sent word to Impey that, if the wound proved fatal, he would instantly surrender himself, 'that the law might take its course'. It was still only seven o'clock as he sat down to write, firmly and legibly, to Day, telling him to break the news to Marian, and enclosing a line to her saying he could not leave while Francis was in danger: 'My Marian, you have occupied all my thoughts for these two days past and unremittedly'. By the evening he was able to write that Francis' recovery was assured, and to advise her in his usual vein, — 'do not presume upon your good appetite, and be abstemious at night'.

Within a month Francis was sitting in Council, though even years later he still felt the wound, a month full of big news and decisions. Five days had not passed since the duel, when Impey wrote that 'Hyder Ali has entered the Carnatic, laying all waste with fire and sword'; a bare week, when Popham reported that he had captured Gwalior, mounting a sixteen-foot escarpment and then a forty-foot wall with rope ladders. It was 'the key of Hindustan', the Governor rejoiced, a triumph as great as Plassey. Meanwhile Coote returned from his long absence, eager for action and cordial to Hastings, for which Richard Johnson claimed some credit. But on September the 20th Stephen Sulivan arrived from Madras, bringing dire news, that Hyder had annihilated the Presidency army. So every engine must be put in reverse. The Mahratta war, which seemed at last near a good ending, must take second place. Bengal must rescue Madras from destruction, as Clive from Madras had formerly saved Bengal.

But in one, and to him maybe the chief, respect Hastings' work was done. Francis would have no place in the scroll unrolling. By early October his resignation had gone to the Directors with a reproachful letter; let them look back to the days when 'Sir J. Clavering's efforts and mine' kept peace in India, and then consider how they had retained in office the man who had systematically disobeyed them. He took pains elsewhere to paint himself as a beacon of light in this dark picture. Lady Clavering was reminded how narrowly he had escaped 'following my colleagues to their grave'. His friends must press home that he had risked his life on a public cause, 'Mahratta war, or not'. 'The British Empire in India is tottering to its foundation', 'in spite of everything I could do to save it', this was to reach Burke. And as the public danger grew, so that Wheler and Coote supported Hastings, he could only presume corrupt motives. Wheler was being bought by patronage, while Coote's appointment to command the Carnatic army was merely to get him out of the way in Bengal.

If there was some magnanimity in Hastings to his enemy, of which we shall find traces again, there was a certain *naïveté* too. He offered to call on the convalescent, only to get a message which he calls 'unexpected', that Francis must decline to meet him except in Council. And in those last meetings the old Francis bared his teeth. His vote was cast against sending money and reinforcements to Madras; peace must be made with the Mahrattas on any terms, whether they joined us against Hyder or not. He severely denounced Hastings' proposed compromise with the Supreme Court, which was to make Impey head of the *diwanni* appeal court also. He carried Bristow's restoration to Oudh, Coote voting for him on the single ground of obeying the Directors. Once more Hastings fired up at this 'degradation of the first executive member of this government'. But as Coote was leaving soon, the best he could manage was a compromise, to send back 'the wretch' as resident, but leave Middleton in charge of the Vizier's tangled accounts with the Company.

He woke suddenly to the danger of letting Francis reach the British public, uncontradicted. So he hurried off Barwell's friend, Shakespeare of Dacca, to get home before him. Major Scott, chosen as his formal agent, who followed in January, in a last message recited Hastings' final instruction: 'I shall particularly attend to what you observed to me this morning, that I am to look upon any anonymous attack upon your measures as coming from the pen of Mr. Francis'.

At least we owe to this same egregious Scott the first suggestion of the motto Hastings should take, when he received (as surely he must) his peerage, — 'Mens aequa in arduis'. And as the Governor stood four-square this autumn when all seemed lost, with Hyder at the gates of Madras and a French fleet approaching, Goddard driven down to the west coast again, and Berar cavalry nearing Bengal, surely he drew a long breath on December the 3rd as Francis sailed away for ever. The congratulations he received did not blind him to the prospect of 'an exhausted treasury . . . the curse of patronage . . . a war either actual or depending in every quarter'. And all the fruit of this long discord, 'which has been permitted, how unaccountably'. Yet he hoped that Francis' going meant the end of the worst. No one now to encourage faction, 'to write circular letters', 'to teach foreign States to counteract me'. 'In a word, I have power, and I will employ it.' He had beaten his enemy and he would leave it at that. When Macpherson asked him a couple of years later if he had not proofs of Francis' corruption, his answer was 'no, and if I had, I should scorn to make use of them'.

So, though for the most part Marian was away till the New Year, he wrote in good spirits. The lion in the compound of Government House roared 'like the scraping of fifty great kettles', and had driven him to sleep in Hastings Street. He attended Wheler's second marriage, 'how it agreed with them I know not, but it has given me a cold and sore throat'. And then to do the honours on New Year's Day, in a waistcoat embroidered by Mrs. Motte. For did not this season spell, as he was writing to Sulivan, the end of the dark epoch of his life, 'and the beginning of a new one'?

CHAPTER XIX

The Last Five Years of Power

AGED 48-52

'BUT who', he borrowed from a letter of Marian's after the duel, 'who can look into the Seeds of Time?' It was in the years after Francis had gone that the Hastings of the impeachment appeared, as well as the Hastings canonized by later history. Now came the deeds that made the gravest charges against him, but now also the substantial measures of government, peace with the Mahrattas, Tippu Sahib beaten to draw breath, and an Empire saved. And now it was that his name became the standard of battle between British parties, the touchstone by which the British people variously judged what in public life should be condemned, and what approved. Before we reach any one such crisis, it is well to consider these years as a whole, what sort of man he had become, and what vision he held for British India.

Outwardly, or it would be truer to say, in his inward heart, he was the same simple, benevolent, and normally English being as the young man whom Batson had struck, and whom Clive had reproved for too much deference to Indians. The artist William Hodges, who went with him to Benares, noticed his plain attire, amid pomp and circumstance, and how he stepped in to stop his servants treating the common people roughly. His purse was as open as ever to almost any appeal, his Indian accounts were heavily charged with loans to young officers, and when we read them for the last time, as revised by Larkins after the governorship ended, they bring to life the man whom Indians admired. His last pension list thus included the widow of his first body servant at Kasimbazaar, the widow of a coolie killed by a fall from the roof of Hastings House at Alipur, a man of ninety-three — 'his age', said Larkins, 'seems to have been the motive that induced you to grant this pension', — the seven-year-old son of one of his *bhistis*, killed in the Benares rebellion, and a blind man who had sung, time out of mind, in Calcutta streets. This was the man whom his familiar subordinates worshipped, Palmers or Chapmans or D'Oyleys, who for generations christened their sons Warren and their daughters Marian; a chief so affectionate, cheerful, and sympathetic; to whom soldiers were grateful, since he liked them so much more than 'clever fellows', and missed no opportunity of publicly thanking those who won the laurel in heat and dust. But this was not the whole man.

For a clear year after Francis left, Coote being away at the war, he acted alone with the placid Wheler, and it was a year of immense emergency. There followed a second, when Macpherson joined them; then the last two, after Stables was added, when the full-dress attack began in parliament, and once more he felt himself alone, with all three colleagues listening for the verdict at home. Never was he more tranquil in danger, more fertile, more predictive. And yet, even in the first stages, it is borne in on us that his mind is becoming frozen. 'He would have no other rule', said Clive's surviving friend Walsh, 'but with me or against me'; while foolish Mrs. Fay, whose rascally barrister husband joined the opposition camp, tells us the Governor was reputed never to desert a friend, or forgive an enemy.

His choice of subordinates was sometimes excellent. Thus his successor Cornwallis warmly praised the complete integrity of Larkins, and wished to bring David Anderson on to his Council. And his, after all, was the selection of many admirable soldiers, Goddard and Popham and Achmuty, so far as patronage and seniority left him free to choose. But some of his chosen were dim, like Thompson his secretary, and some downright foolish, like Major Scott, the truth being he could no longer stand what he once taxed Richard Johnson with, 'a half attachment'. He was warned there were traitors among those he appointed, such as Macleane's friend Mackintosh, and giddy Bob Pott. And the services were full of those he called 'the lees of Mr. Francis', such as Bristow and Shee, and the opium magnate Mackenzie. There were a few good men associated with them. Such were John Shore, who styled him 'Don Quixote' for his war policy, or young Jonathan Duncan, or Ducarel, 'whom I have laboured to make my friend'. Indeed, he was the prisoner of a system which he never ceased to denounce, whether in talking to Shore, or in the solemn 'Review' which he composed on his homeward voyage; a system 'no man dares avow, yet many combine to maintain'. He was Governor in a Council whose continuance depended on satisfying the claims of patronage; where 'each member stands in need of support from home, and owes returns for the support which he receives', and the more so as power passed from the Directors to the Cabinet and the Commons.

That being so, and remembering what he had endured and what a weight rested on his shoulders alone, is it surprising that his temper was soured? 'The wonder was', said Macpherson, 'that he had any left.' He claimed for himself 'a natural benevolence' which, taking the most severe test, he proved in the case of Francis' adherents, for he promoted his client Hay to be secretary of Council, and one of his first acts in England was to recommend his kinsman, Tilighman, as the fittest person to follow Day as Advocate-General. But the horrible miasma of the India House had filled Calcutta, and he grew more and more incapable of bearing 'reproach, hard epithets, and indignities' from the Directors, or of distinguishing honest doubt from faction.

So often betrayed, and so often the one man willing to take all responsibility, he became in temper and in status alike something of an autocrat, 'the great Mogul' satirized in Hicky's *Gazette*. The powers he entrusted to William Palmer, his personal agent, angered persons of routine like Middleton. He left men carrying a heavy burden much in the dark, Goddard complaining of an 'unfriendly silence' for a year on end. Disclaiming any self-importance, he yet welcomed 'the awful distance' preserved towards his person as a token of British power. And his characteristic criticism of Wheler was 'his strange policy of hearing whatever any man has to say', even a friend of Francis; not for him such a flabby neutral world. To Macpherson, as his probable successor, he recommended a habit of mind of a dangerous magnificence. 'Resolve with decision, and not by halves. But when your resolution is once formed, and in execution, never admit even a thought of withdrawing it, but persist in it, even though in itself it should be wrong, if not ruinously wrong.'

Certainly he was growing away from any understanding of England, and filled with some contempt for the British treatment of India. The tarnished Rumbold had fled home, but 'I do not think there is sufficient virtue left in England to effect his punishment'. His tone to the powerful Robinson was cynical, in substance excusing himself for sheltering guilty men against a persecution shared in common. Something dated, a whiff perhaps of his uncle Howard, in his view of British society. He could enthuse over the dignity and independence 'which constitute the idea which I ever entertained of a true descendant of the ancient nobility', while the ebullience of the British Radical movement in 1780 made him indignant. 'At the spectacle of the kingdom full of associations, concerting plans for defeating the actual administration . . . and the government against which they declare open war permitting them.'

He grew away from England, as others did after him, because he was absorbed in the India with which he had grown up, and had helped to make. A people so submissive and adaptable, a land so defensible in 'its mountains and hilly borders, its bay, its innumerable intersections of rivers', asking nothing for greatness (and oh! that he had been given the power!) but 'attention, protection, and forbearance'. How furiously, just as thirty years ago in Bengal, he exclaimed against the exploitation of Oudh! Lucknow was 'the sink of iniquity', ruled by as many sovereigns 'as there are Englishmen in it'. 'Every power in India dreads a connection with us.' The subjection of Bengal, though an 'inevitable necessity', and our usurpation on the Nabob of the Carnatic, were 'terrible precedents against us'. In beginning the Mahratta war, Bombay had not 'the shadow of a plea' except Directors' orders. This indignation sprang from the sympathy he felt for Indians since he had lived among them, even as a refugee from Siraj-ud-Daulah; there were individuals, Benaram Pandit, for instance, from Berar, for whom he felt at least as much affection as for any Briton. For, unlike the Victorians, he was not race, or religious, or colour conscious.

His large outlook and intellectual curiosity deepened his interest in the history of those he was called upon to rule. He was still buying Persian, Arabic, and Sanskrit manuscripts, — offered for sale to the Company when he was old and poor. He was collecting the vivid miniatures of the Mogul artists. William Hodges painted for him the scenes where his life had been at its most intense, from Fort William to Benares. He alone made possible the life-work of Charles Wilkins, pioneer of the great

Orientalists in the Company's service. Against Francis' vote he had already carried a project for a government printing press, with Bengali and Persian founts; he championed in Council Wilkins' rendering of the Mahabharata as a work that 'may open a new and most extensive range for the human mind, beyond the present limited and beaten field of its operations'. He wrote the introduction to his version of the Bhagaved-Gita, noting privately it was 'part of a system which I long since laid down and supported, for reconciling the people of England to the natives of Hindustan'. He rejoiced that 'the liberal and beneficial purposes', for which we had used the Hindu code compiled by Halhed, had overcome the Brahmins' objection to throwing open their lore. And in his last year, in asking reimbursement for expenses he could no more afford from his private purse, he showed he had done as much for the Moslems. Their scholars were paid to translate their legal classics from Arabic and Persian. He founded the Mahomedan college, or Madrasa, at Calcutta, buying the site himself: it would 'soften the prejudices', he said, 'excited by the rapid growth of the British dominions'. Before he left, the Naib was asked to choose his Indian magistrates from its students. In 1784 the great Oriental scholar, Sir William Jones, arrived as a judge of the Supreme Court and, with Hastings, founded the Bengal Asiatic Society; many were their literary conversations, by which, Sir William wrote, '(without compliment) I am always the gainer'.

To conciliate, to elevate 'the British name', by fair and magnanimous dealing, this was the Roman theme, first acquired maybe at Westminster, and never out of sight. The pains he took at Benares to protect its pilgrims were designed, he wrote, for 'conciliating a great People to a Dominion which they see with envy and bear with reluctance'. His earlier project for provision against India's recurrent famines, 'a chain of granaries on the banks of the two great rivers', was part-fulfilled at Patna and Bhagalpur, to remain, he hoped, as 'a monument of the good policy and humanity of our nation, to ages remote beyond every other remembrance of it'. This high objective it was which made him applaud and champion Augustus Clevland, the young collector of Rajmahal who, unarmed and by the plain ways of goodness, first civilized the marauders of the jungle Terai, and died of his work at twenty-nine, for whose monument in those hills he composed this epitaph: 'employing only the means of conciliation, confidence, and benevolence . . . attached them to the British Government by a conquest over their minds, the most permanent as the most rational of dominion'.

Though we may judge that his policy could be diverted by a gust of passion, or lie open to a charge of inconsistencies, — the 'wild projects' which Grenville denounced to Dundas — something of the prophetic mind was added with the years. Soaring above the petty scale of the Company's Bengal, he thought for all India. There was the route by Suez to be developed, and soundings to be taken in the Red Sea. Chapman must be sent to explore Cochin China. His cousin Samuel Turner's mission to Tibet, his interview with the reincarnate but infant prodigy, the Teshoo Lama, must be followed up, not end with the Governor's gifts of pearls and coral. Let a caravan be organized to push India trade, of coloured cloths and cheap watches, coral 'real and false', cloves and amber. What were the investment and land revenue now but things of 'trivial moment in the great scale of the Company's concerns'? His last State papers dwelt on the downfall of the Moguls, and pointed to the Sikhs as the threat of the near future. 'In these papers', he wrote to a director, 'you will view the seeds of future systems, which require but a small portion of fostering care to give them present vegitation, and they will mature themselves into such a State as shall yield the fruits of permanency and prosperity to the British Dominion in India.'

If charity seeketh not her own and endureth all things, he was a good man, striving to further all good causes. Not that he was moved at this, or perhaps at any stage of his life, by any deeply-felt Christian belief. The thanks of the Greek church in Calcutta reached him, as 'its founder and protector', and he took his due share, owing something here perhaps to Marian's German piety, in building the new St. John's church which at last replaced the ramshackle chapel in the old Fort. But what we note, rather, is a personal faith or code, a mystic confidence, more Oriental than Christian, that his life was borne along as part of a long beneficial process. See his pen travelling in the great cabin of the *Berrington*, on his last voyage home, to vindicate the Company rule. 'I am not its author. The seed of this wonderful production was sown by the hand of calamity. It was nourished by fortune, and cultivated and shaped (if I may venture to change the figure) by necessity. . . . It is impossible to retrace the perilous and wonderful paths by which they attained their present elevation.'

How often this 'delegated and fettered power' had nearly perished, and where would it have been but for his 'exploring the wilds of peril and reproach'? His life, he told Marian, had been 'ever regulated by an influence overruling and defeating my determinations, making these the instruments of its own decrees'. Yes, though he began as 'an unconnected and un-patronized individual', he had been raised by 'the invariable train of success' attending his measures, exciting a 'superstitious belief' among Indians that he would triumph till the end. 'I myself avow the same belief, so long as my actions shall be directed by the sole impulse of duty, unbiased and unmixed with regards of personal interest, and even of personal reputation.'

So his sanction lay within. If he disobeyed the Directors, he asked his friends not to deem him ungrateful, — 'I shall yet have a resource in the testimony of my own mind, which will bear me superior even to worse than that'. With rapture he received Marian's letter, 'that you on all occasions have acted as a man of virtue and honour ought to do, whatever consequences may ensue'. For this exactly echoed maxims he had quoted to her from the Gita as 'the invariable rule of my latter life'. Twice he repeats them. 'Let the Motive be in the Deed, and not in the Event. Be not one whose motive for Action is the Hope of Reward. Perform thy Duty. Abandon all thought of the consequence.'

Thus satisfied of his own integrity, he accommodated himself to a system he despised, often using devious and reckless ways of raising money for the Company. The bribe from Chait Sing, diverted to finance Camac's contingent; loans, through the medium of Cantoo, from the base Nobkissen, to bribe the Berar army not to attack; gifts from revenue farmers in Bengal and Bihar, — rumours of such transactions worried his friends, so that David Anderson taxed him with these reports; only to be told he saw nothing against taking such contributions in times of public distress, and that they had all been accounted for to the Company. As, indeed, they were, but piecemeal, casually, and after a warning from Larkins, accountant-general, that an exact record would be expected. The Berar business was never brought before Council; of the Benares bribe he wrote 'I believe I shall communicate this fact to the Court of Directors', and in fact reported both before the end of 1780. But it was only in 1782 that he gave them dates, Larkins' affidavit, and full detail, and then with a protest that he would have 'disdained' to do so if they had given him their confidence, 'never withheld from the meanest of my predecessors'. Almost wearily he refused to enter into his reasons for concealment, perhaps to avoid public curiosity, or no 'studied design' he could remember. After thirty-two years' service, they should know his integrity. These sums would never have been given direct to the Company; 'I could have concealed them, had I a wrong motive, from yours and the public eye for ever'. Ending on his now recurrent note: 'the applause of my own breast is my surest reward'.

As for his cash transactions with individuals, part of them may be described as deeds of charity, and some also explained by the conditions of India at war; the sheer difficulty of realizing any salary at all, when French cruisers might capture shipments of specie, when the Directors refused to honour bills, and the rupee exchange was ruinously low. Hence Joseph Fowke pressed on him diamonds for remittance, promising favourable prices 'if you are not flush of cash'. 'Flush' was the last word ever applicable to Hastings. He lent Laurence Sulivan and his son £7000 in 1783, on which interest was much in arrears fifteen years later; lent money to the respected but now bankrupt Richard Becher, who had returned to India as a free merchant. On the other side, he drew a bill on Barwell in 1782 for £10,000, and another for the same on Impey, the second being apparently designed as a parliamentary fund to buy seats for Impey and himself. All this, part and parcel of his temperament and that older lax Bengal, could hardly put him in an independent position in regard to the Chief Justice or the Sulivan interest.

So too, while his world wagged as it did, he must grease the wheels of his government by fair shares in patronage. Take the case of Wheler, for over a year his single colleague. Instead of forcing issues by his casting vote, which would rally every disgruntled civilian, Indian *vakils*, and *zemindars*, to Wheler's banner, 'I have made it a rule to give him a first option in most vacant appointments', and hence 'I cannot desire an easier associate'.

Sir Robert Chambers likewise was conciliated, with a paid judgeship at Chinsura when we took over the Dutch settlements. Under parliamentary attack, he now and then struck a less pleasant note; he would not reduce establishments till he knew his own future: 'I will not create enemies in order to ease the burthens of my successors'.

In actual fact, this did less than justice to the efforts of his latter years to cleanse corruption and enforce economies. He had warned Madras (but that is a longer story) against yielding to the Benfield creditor gang. Against his protest, the provision of the annual investment in Bengal had been given to contractors instead of agency through *gomastahs*, and administered since 1774 by the Board of Trade. The result had been hideous. Contracts were taken up by Company servants, members of the Board themselves had their rake-off. Profits were being made, he said, 'unknown to the service till lately'; profits, he candidly added, never made in his time at Kasimbazaar, when his income came not from the investment but from private trade. In 1780, with both the other Presidencies swallowing millions of rupees for the war, and no revenue to spare for the investment, the money was found for cargoes by public loans, to be repaid by bills on the Company. If the Directors violently objected to acting as intermediaries for the sale of their servants' goods, Hastings' difficulty was to convince his subordinates that they must put up with a lower profit. He told Macpherson 'I am killed with solicitations'. He estimated the Board of Trade's earlier rate of profit at 50 per cent, which he aspired to reduce to 20, while he made Cantoo withdraw his tenders; 'it will be said that I have some rascally interest in it'. It is not surprising that his successor Cornwallis prosecuted, and broke, several senior civil servants.

In two other directions, he laid the foundation of revenues more assured than these relics of the dying investment system. Far up-country at Patna, vessels holding poppy juice simmered in the sun, to be moulded into cakes of opium, an article of exchange quite indispensable for what was fast becoming the Company's richest market, the China trade, and which by long custom had been the perquisite of their servants in Bihar. He took it over in 1773 as a government monopoly, to be manufactured under contract; first Francis' ally Mackenzie held it, and then his own servant Stephen Sulivan, on the same terms. That the margin of profit was very wide was proved by Sulivan's speedy sale of these lucrative rights, to Joseph Fowke's son-in-law John Benn, who again resold it for an enhanced profit. Of these secondary transfers Hastings knew nothing. As things had been, every other Company servant had a finger in opium, and he could easily have taken the lion's share for himself instead of creating a system which at least gave the Company a rising income of over £50,000.

On the salt revenue he had a better case. The monopoly he had arranged in 1772, working through the revenue farmers and Board of Trade, had broken down; in 1780, against solid opposition in Council, he turned it into an agency, young Henry Vansittart being his choice as the first controller. From a mere revenue aspect he was amply justified, the annual yield rising to nearly half a million sterling. But he prided himself on higher grounds than that. Here was no conquest of territory, 'purchased with the blood of thousands' and rewarded by parliamentary thanks and bonfires, but 'a bloodless access of public income, gained by the silent operation of official arrangements . . . ministering subsistence to a whole people'. Unhappily, it seems to have been subsistence at a high price.

In short, scandalous though the abuses in British India long continued to be, and obsolete or easy-going his view of them, there remains a good deal to vindicate his statement of his intention 'to eradicate every temptation for perquisites, embezzlements, and corruption . . . and to unite the interests of individuals with that of the public'. His rule in every department, which Cornwallis followed, was to substitute fixed commissions on net receipts for concealed profits. By new checks on paymasters and commanding officers, he began to clean up the boundless corruption of the army. He set up also a committee of audit, and separated the public and secret departments of Council, appointing a secretariat for each.

There was another set of transactions which came to their climax in these years, and formed a group of charges at his impeachment. These were the military contracts: one for supply of transport bullocks, given to Croftes; a second, for victualling Fort William, to Belli; and a third, for shipping rice to the other Presidencies, to Auriol. All transactions of war are costly, and so were these. Belli's commission was at the rate of 30 per cent. Auriol was allowed 15 per cent, not on his purchases only, but on other costs, such as freight and demurrage, and apparently cleared about £34,000 on the deal. Croftes' contract stipulated for more bullocks than Coote had asked for, and at a higher figure. War transactions, again, and the more so the more primitive the conditions, are direct and personal, and here all three assignees were near dependants of the Governor. To supplement their absurdly low salaries by such patronage was the universal practice, both in India and at home; so the old majority had given Francis' friend Livius 15 per cent commission as military storekeeper. When Clavering attacked Belli's original agency, wildly insinuating he would go shares with Hastings' 'black inquisitors', the Governor replied 'he is the only person in the world who could have formed such a suggestion', but insisted that, the Fort being his special responsibility, he must commit its maintenance to a man he could trust. All these contracts made part of his political fortification. When in 1779 he converted Belli's agency into a new five-year contract and did the same for Croftes, he openly avowed he meant to save his faithful friends from 'future oppression'.

For the rest, he could defend himself with the hard facts. Except for one short crisis, the Madras Presidency was in sober truth saved from starvation. Had the French laid siege to Calcutta, as not he but Francis predicted, the Fort garrison of 15,000 men could have held out three months. Again, all Goddard's experience, and Coote's, proved that the 6700 bullocks he contracted for were not too many, but many too few. As for his lavishness, he could say that Croftes' sub-contractor put his gain at only 15 per cent, and that Auriol's commission on incidental costs was scaled down to 5 per cent. And as regards the Directors' rigid rule for annual contracts and assignment to the lowest bidder, even the Francis majority had condemned it as applied to opium, and when it came to supply in time of war, punctual performance through personal agency, even on what he allowed were liberal terms, was his best defence. But what the eighteenth century was wont to attack was not the job, but the man who held it.

If economy did not come naturally to this middle-aged Company servant, a hundred evidences show him faithful to his rooted belief, that young Britons could not safely be exposed to the temptations of sole power in the districts. He had obeyed with reluctance in 1773 the Directors' orders for constituting the Provincial Councils, only accepting them, in deference to his Council, as a transition to a permanent plan. Their violence and misconduct during the struggle with the Supreme Court, their division into Hastings and anti-Hastings cliques, impelled him to root and branch reform immediately Francis' departure gave him a chance. In 1780 he restricted the Provincial Councils to revenue business only, setting up six civil courts of *Diwanni Awdalut* under covenanted servants. The next year he enforced the permanent plan, as sketched eight years before. The Provincial Councils were dissolved; the entire charge of the land revenue and its collection was committed to a Committee of Revenue at Calcutta, — its members being Anderson, Shore, Charters, and Croftes, with Gunga Govind Sing as their *diwan*. Within a year or two half the collections were being paid direct to Calcutta, in time he hoped all would be, so eliminating intermediate profits. Temporarily and on grounds of humanity, some of the displaced Councillors were left as district collectors, others filling places as judges of the new courts, which were now increased from six to eighteen. This intense centralization, however, was never final, for some collectors continued and were ordered to tour their districts; it came under heavy criticism later, notably from the upright Shore, as throwing an impossible burden on the Committee of Revenue, and leaving far too much power in the hands of their *diwan*. There were others already, who for a century were to reign supreme, prepared to dispute the very essence of Hastings' view, that land revenue and local government were best left in the hands of Indians. Yet it must be said that, in condemning the oppressiveness of British collectors, Cornwallis wholly endorsed Hastings.

His revenue changes meant all manner of friction. Withdrawal of Europeans implied reinstatement of the *kanungoes*, the Indian clerkly class to whom many evils had been due. Absorption of the *khalsa* by the new Committee of Revenue involved the displacement of Ducarel, Francis' friend, and his relegation to the obscurity of Burdwan. But in the mechanism of revenue Hastings clung to his flexible doctrines of 1775. Settlements were made annually, as the Directors had required, and based on the highest figure of the last decade. The Committee, however, gave a distinct preference to the *zemindars*, recommended fixed settlements for lives, and under Shore's leadership used much administrative experiment.

Much more was needed if elementary justice was to prevail in Bengal, where criminal law was the province of the Nabob and was applied by ill-paid Indian judges. Prisoners might be lingering years without trial. By Moslem law, much murder was venial. On the highways one perpetually met ex-prisoners, lacking hand or foot, hacked off by the axe. Though Mahomed Reza Khan had legally the last word, Hastings did something to amend this barbarism. Thus he appointed a remembrancer, to assist him personally in supervising the Naib's rough and ready justice, and transferred the Indian magistrates' police powers to his judges of the new *diwanni* courts. But, once again, only Cornwallis was enabled to do what Hastings had once done, and then been compelled to undo ; that is, to deprive Mahomed Reza Khan of all judicial powers, and restore the final criminal court to Calcutta, under British control.

His most resounding change in 1780 was his accommodation with Impey, for which Impey was two years later recalled to England. Though Council had forcibly stopped the Court extending its jurisdiction over all Bengal, and its interference in revenue cases, the vagueness of the Regulating Act or even the hot temper of Justice Hyde might any day revive the controversy. Neither did Hastings' new *diwanni* courts, nor his re-establishment of the *Sudder Diwanni* which the Three had abolished, remove the danger. He and his Council had neither time nor competence to make the *Sudder* an adequate appeal court ; his new judges were young and untrained, one of them being sourly described by Impey as 'totally illiterate'. Hastings' solution was to amalgamate the two systems of courts, by making the Chief Justice — 'not as such, but as the person assuredly the best qualified' — also head of the *Sudder Diwanni*, which was in fact the solution effected by the legislation of 1861. No question, his immediate purposes were achieved. Legal peace reigned in Bengal. Council was relieved of work it could not do, clashes were avoided by professional supervision and a proper scheme of appeals, a code compiled by Impey taught the new courts some grasp of principle, and he was relieved from this hateful state of hostility with Impey, — 'I have always loved him in my heart'.

Yet it was only carried by his own casting vote and a reluctant Coote, as against Wheler and a last fiery vote from Francis; it was doubtfully legal, at least the extra salary attached, and unpopular with all who disliked Impey and the Supreme Court. As for Impey's position, it is true that he referred acceptance of the salary to the Lord Chancellor and publicly declared, after his recall, he had made no compromise. But his large family made him welcome the money, he still hoped for a seat in Council, and the appointment certainly undermined the independent role which he was meant to hold, by making him a man of two capacities and two paymasters. The public issue was settled, as a result of Touchet's petition, in the Amending Act of 1781, which forbade the Supreme Court to hear revenue cases, freed *zemindars* expressly from its jurisdiction, and empowered the Governor-General in Council to regulate the Company courts.

'Let the motive be in the Deed, not in the Event'; even this bargain with Impey was true enough to that. To some such shape of character the Governor-General had grown in these latter years, raised on a pinnacle above friends and foes, obeying his monitor within, and struggling towards what he knew were righteous ends by all available earthly means. Into his office at Calcutta, and pursuing him to Alipur or on the river, flowed all the intelligences and pressures of India; letters from Madras Councillors, from political agents in Mahratta and Rajput States, from soldiers begging for instructions, and Company servants pleading for patronage. There were summaries from Bombay of the last London news, come overland, a report from Clevland on the possibilities of Kolgong as a capital city in lieu of Calcutta, and the usual suggestions from Impey that someone was terribly hard up and must be found a job. Through it all he persisted, as these few illustrations may show, in the reform of law, justice, and revenue, still clinging to the fundamentals he had reached fifteen years before, though now with an enlarged conception of what British India might be.

Not that reform was his first duty in these years; on the contrary, it was to save British India from extinction.

CHAPTER XX

The Great War: 1780-82

AGED 48-50

IF such a word could ever appropriately be used of Bengal, these were years of austerity. War broke up the cantonments, scattering British officers to every point of the sub-continent. The investment was suspended, profits vanished, and perquisites were reduced. Impey was ailing. A dark cloud overshadowed the happy Chambers family, whose eldest son was lost in the tragic wreck of the *Grosvenor* on the African coast, in which the Hoseas also perished. Justice Hyde contrived to maintain his hospitality, processing with his guests to the new Court House opened in 1782, as he had to the old. But when the learned William Jones arrived to reinforce the Court, he proved a semi-invalid who declined all supper parties, so that old Joey Fowke, now reduced to one evening of cards a fortnight, wrote irritably 'the society of Bengal appears to me to be growing worse and worse . . . our plays are gone, our music is gone, our fellowship is gone'. The Governor's pleasures, in his own phrase, were 'quiet and domestic'. Year in, year out, he never but once was beyond fifty miles from Calcutta; rising early and early to bed, riding hard and taking little to drink, he carried all he was asked to without flinching, flourishing all the more, it seemed, as the tests grew sterner.

How intense they were can be baldly stated, but more severe, one may think, for British India than any before or since. For the Mahratta and Mysore wars coincided for three years with the American War of Independence, and with an attack on Great Britain by France, Spain, and Holland. The Indiamen had therefore to sail past enemy bases at the Cape, Mauritius, and Ceylon, and midway through 1780 how dark was the military prospect! When the rains halted operations, Goddard was standing on the defensive between Guzerat and the Ghauts, while Hartley was darting from point to point in the coastal region, to stop enemy penetration south of Bombay. In July Hyder Ali, leading 80,000 men trained by French officers, burst into the Carnatic, where every fort on the frontier fell, save some few held by British subalterns. A desert of burning villages isolated Madras; as Auriol sailed down the coast, he saw 'the horizon in flames every night'; the unhappy peasants who clung to their homes were tortured or mutilated. By August Hyder's cavalry reached the sea, south of Pondicherry, and he laid siege to Arcot. On September the 10th Colonel Baillie's force, marching south from Guntur to join the rendezvous with the main army, was annihilated; of 86 British officers, 36 were killed, and 600 European ranks and 4000 sepoys were dead or prisoners. Within sound of the firing, at two miles' distance, Sir Hector Munro, no longer the hero of Buxar, hesitated and did nothing; finally retreating on Madras, with a total loss of his guns and stores.

Now was seen the stark truth of what Hastings wrote in the following spring, that 'in no part of the world is the principle of supporting a rising interest, and depressing a falling one, more prevalent than in India'. From Hyderabad John Hollond wrote that, since this disaster, the Nizam was swollen-headed, demanding that we make a clean break with his enemy Ragoba, and accepting without grace the restitution of Guntur, which Bengal had forced on the Madras government. From Moodaji of Berar whom Hastings asked to mediate at Poona, he received a refusal. Goddard took Bassein this winter, but his march eastwards early in 1781 was heavily checked, and he was driven down from the Ghauts. And Camac's diversionary campaign from the north had been disappointing. William Palmer accused him of 'despondency, ignorance, and misconduct'; our ally of Gohud was weak and sulky, his subsidies fell into arrears. The effects were lamentable in Rajputana, where Jodhpur refused to see Palmer and Bhopal felt too insecure to move. Meanwhile, with every month wasted, demoralization spread to the North. Mogul Delhi lay in ruins, Mahratta occupation and Rohilla troopers had ripped out the palace silver ceilings, its fair waterways were dry, and its woodwork burned as fuel. Hastings' agents reported the river line shielding Oudh was unsafe; some called for alliance with the Emperor, or renewed subsidies to his minister, Nadjif Khan. Chait Sing of Benares refused his war contribution. Hyder's envoys were negotiating at Delhi. If the French fleet, which appeared on the Coromandel coast in January, had known its business, Madras must have fallen. But it sailed away.

It was still touch and go eighteen months later, even though Mahratta fighting was dying down, when the French reappeared, this time under the brilliant seaman Suffrein, whose twelve ships of the line outnumbered Hughes' squadron. After the five dogged naval battles of 1782, the situation was that Hughes was forced to Bombay to refit; that the French had taken his Ceylon base at Trincomalee; that they cut off the Bengal grain which was keeping Madras alive; and that the once illustrious Bussy was ashore with 3000 Frenchmen, to fight alongside Mysore. Only the signature of the Peace of Versailles in 1783 rescued British India from the supreme dangers into which the home government had plunged her.

Long before war ended, John Shore predicted bankruptcy. Government had to offer 8 per cent interest in Bengal, its bonds were at 18 per cent discount; in Bombay the rate was 50 per cent, and no interest was paid for four years. The Company's Indian debt was hard on £10,000,000, and even more at home. In four years, Bengal shipped 265 lacs of rupees to the ruined Madras Presidency. All salaries, all army pay, were in suspense; a Madras servant writes 'I have seen the native troops perishing in the streets, selling their children for a rupee'.

This long war, demanding concentrated and united effort, was fought till 1782 without help from home, except for one royal regiment and Hughes' few ships, foul with long service. It was fought by a government doubtful of its legal tenure, merely prolonged from year to year, and armed with only the loosest control over Madras or Bombay. For three crucial years Hastings was dependent on a commander-in-chief whose commission was from the Crown, who despaired of the cause, and criticized the Governor behind his back. The Mahratta war, Coote told Goddard, was 'a most ruinous policy', while to the Directors he condemned the Governor's 'extraordinary excursion' to Benares. And by what hands, and through what infamous corruption must Hastings wage war! Honest Colonel Pearse, marching overland towards Madras, told him the Company servants 'to get a rupee would sell an army', while for the Nabob of Arcot's creditors this war was 'too lucrative a job to be ever ended'.

In this disgrace and gloom the masterful spirit of Hastings stood firm; so sure of himself and his cause that he could see no good in any alternative, so sanguine that he took many wrong turnings, so decisive that he was sometimes unscrupulous. But he never doubted, never was passive, never despaired. Hear his criticism of Madras, where 'little minds vibrate with every successive touch of adversity and prosperity'; the rule he sent them, 'resolve that the war shall be transferred to the dominions of your enemies'; his defence of the bold decision to march Pearse's detachment through Berar, 'self-distrust will never fail to create a distrust in others'; his marginal replies to Pearse's many hypothetical questions, 'no, march on'; his severe sentence on Camac's retreat, 'every peril becomes multiplied by a confession of inferiority'. When all was over, describing how 'murmurs, suspicion, and despair' had travelled from India to England, he preached the doctrine of all great spirits. How blind and foolish the attitude of mind which believes that the strain of war 'operates on one side only, without producing a similar effect on the strength of our enemies'. 'Our adversaries have also their difficulties to surmount.' This retrospect ended with a challenge: 'I have never yet planned or authorized any military operation . . . which has not been attended with complete success . . . I have never in any period of my life engaged in a negotiation which I did not see terminate as I wished and expected'.

We return to the week-end of September the 23rd, 1780, when young Sulivan brought the news of Baillie's tragedy, and the rout of Munro. Asking Coote and Francis not to hurry back to Calcutta so as to avoid panic, Hastings laid an embargo on shipping and ordered fifteen lacs from the Treasury to be packed in readiness; on the 25th he met Council with his policy complete. 'This is not a time', he began, 'either for long deliberation . . . or the formal and tedious process of negotiation', but for 'the most instant, powerful and even hazardous exertions'. Money, European infantry, and guns must be instantly sent to Madras. Our Madras forces, 'so long formed to the habits of conquest', would never recover under 'unsuccessful commanders'; he therefore made it his personal request that Coote should at once leave for the Coast. 'I mean not to compliment. It is military experience . . . the high estimation in which his name is held by the world, and especially by that part of it where it was principally acquired, which mark him out as the only possible instrument to retrieve our past disgraces.' Terms of peace must be immediately offered to the Mahrattas through the medium of Berar. All this being resolved by his casting vote, Coote and the troops sailed at the end of October. He took with him orders to suspend Whitehill, the acting governor of Madras, for his criminal tardiness in obeying the order to hand over Guntur to the Nizam. 'The creature', Hastings scornfully wrote, 'made some show of resistance'; not much, however; he was suspected of going shares in a French privateer.

All the autumn and winter the engines were put into reverse. Goddard was ordered, if Poona responded, to make an armistice. Through Berar terms were put to the enemy. We should keep Bassein, if in our hands: our allies, the Gaekwar and Gohud, should respectively have Ahmedabad and Gwalior, but all else must be surrendered. Ragoba must be found an asylum, but not near Bombay; the Mahrattas were invited to enter into an alliance against Hyder and the French. Three lacs were paid to Berar on Hastings' own responsibility, with expectation of more to come. The home investment was stopped, — 'a desperate measure', he said, 'from which I apprehend the worst personal consequences'. Traditions of past bad treatment at sea, sometimes, he wrote, 'brutal in the extreme', inhibited many sepoys from volunteering; all the more need, then, to hurry on the force Pearse was to march by way of Cuttack.

Nothing was more remarkable than his realization that all must be changed; to peace with the Mahrattas and, if possible, union with them against Hyder, 'whom I will never quit, if I have the power, till the war is ended with his extirpation'. He was deaf to soldiers who argued that Hyder might be reconciled, more than deaf to Madras' futile assurance to Hyder of their 'friendly disposition'. Sometimes he despaired of Coote's manner of war, 'what he calls offering battle'; to march his exhausted army hither and thither, devoid of cavalry and carrying every ounce of supply in a gigantic bullock train, to attack an enemy whose horse cut every road, and swept up every grain of rice. He despaired much more at his black pessimism; his formal declaration within three months of reaching the theatre of war that 'we are altogether unequal' to the enemy, his seeming readiness to buy Hyder off by ceding a fortress so important as Trichinopoly. How much more welcome the gallant Popham, who already advocated in essentials the strategy which was later to prevail, — to land with Hughes' marines at Tellicherry on the west coast, and take Seringapatam by a *coup de main.*

In what a spirit he would himself fight, he put most clearly to Macpherson who, to his dismay, arrived from England inclined towards the war-mongering charges of Francis. 'I call God to witness my truth that I seek for nothing but Peace.' But 'if you would employ effectual means for obtaining peace, you must seek them in the terrors of a continued war'. 'I must use for this end the weapons which I can trust, which I can manage, and which I have hitherto practised. I will throw away the sword before those who appear unarmed before us; I will keep it sheathed in the presence of those who are yet undecided; and I will hold it with the alternative of peace or destruction to those who are armed against us.' He would hold it so, even 'if my superiors, and the whole people of England in a body, join in proscribing this system of policy, and in exclaiming peace, peace, peace'. But he was alone. Against Coote, against the Madras government, against the Directors, against a group in Calcutta itself of Ducarel and the remnants of Francis' school, who played on the nerves of Wheler and Impey.

Not a doubt, either, shook his mind that he was guiltless of either war; not a qualm whether, as every man in Madras swore, the Mahratta and the Mysore wars were not as cause and effect. No! 'the war with Hyder was exclusively Rumbold's act, and he knew that it was so when he abandoned his post'. 'The Mahratta war was the war of the presidency of Bombay and the Court of Directors'; 'begun without my knowledge, and with a design adverse to my government'. And never a doubt as to his duty. Wargaum was 'no concern of mine. I could have suffered the Carnatic to fall an easy prey to Hyder, when Francis opposed the measures which I suggested for its preservation.' But if he had clung to this 'prescribed and beaten path', he could not have made the boast for which he asked Shelburne's pardon, 'I have been the instrument of rescuing one presidency from infamy, and both from annihilation'.

He moved thus unshaken through a half-war with the

Mahrattas to a half-peace, and to the grievous dangers and ignominies of the war with Mysore. That was a scene of barbarity, unknown to Britons since their fathers had fought the Spaniards. From the first massacre at Baillie's surrender, when English heads were piled at Hyder's feet, to Braithwaite's surrender in Tanjore in February 1782 and Mathews' at Bednore a year later, or the shameful day when Suffrein handed over to Hyder the prisoners he had taken at sea, our countrymen endured every savagery. They were chained together and marched to windowless dungeons, where Baillie and hundreds more died in irons. Young High-landers were drugged and forcibly circumcized, silver rings in their ears marked their slavery, they were offered life if they would drill Hyder's recruits; midshipmen were degraded as dancing boys. Those who refused, or those who survived, passed years scrounging for a plate of rice, without change of clothes or linen, listlessly turning over a volume of Smollett or a fragment of Johnson's Dictionary they found in the bazaar, listening for news or distant gun-fire. One of these strong survivors was David Baird, who lived to storm Seringapatam in 1799, and later out-lived the retreat to Corunna.

While Baillie's men turned over in fetters, and while Pearse's expedition, hard hit by cholera, pushed on to Cuttack, the Governor tightened his controls. Bristow had gone back to Lucknow as a result of Francis' last gesture, but he was now recalled. 'His abilities are contemptible,' Hastings said, 'his political principles mean, and centred in himself', so Middleton was put in charge again. Francis Fowke was dismissed from Benares, and on the same ground, that the residency was 'a representative station', the Governor-General's 'instrument of control'. But it was done more genially, the young man being provided with a comfortable agency to organize river craft and even old Joseph receiving a small pension. The successor at Benares was young William Markham, a protégé of Wheler and son to Hastings' loyal supporter, the Archbishop of York. More and more we find power exercised by the Governor and his personal agents, especially Palmer and Anderson. But even his chosen subordinates complained of his long silences, — as Pearse, for instance, that he had heard nothing for a year.

With infinite subtlety, advances and part-retreats, he moved towards one end: to win time that would save Madras, to split the enemy combination, to isolate Hyder. As Coote and Madras both called desperately for more European troops, he proposed to get them from the Dutch, in return for the cession of Tinnivelly and the pearl fisheries; indeed, as he thought it vital to have the alliance of Hyderabad, he even suggested surrendering all the Northern Circars to the Nizam. Madras, rightly we may think, rejected both notions, nor was he sorry for the fact, but irritated by their 'levity' of mood between elation and despair. Nevertheless he pressed forward for the Nizam's alliance, and hoped still more, as of old, from Berar. But here he used his sheathed sword. Since their refusal to mediate showed they considered we were falling, Pearse was ordered to march across their territory, using force if resisted; soon his vast letters describe through what wild country he moved, 'made up of the shreds and fragments of a world . . . sad and craggy rocks, brackish water, and pestiferous winds'. At the same time Anderson, sent as political agent, reported that money would do it. Under the agreement of April 1781 the thirteen lacs outstanding of those promised were paid over, some Berar cavalry would join Pearse, and a formal treaty should follow. So he transferred 'the most formidable member of the confederacy' to our side; 'I have achieved what no other in my place would have achieved, or perhaps attempted'. By what means exactly he could bring about his larger objective of turning all the Mahrattas against Hyder, on this his mind was as yet perfectly fluid. Perhaps by encouraging Berar to supplant the Peishwa, or maybe by exciting them both against Scindia. But the events of the spring and summer suggested another alternative.

Scindia's kindness to British hostages and captives had been remarkable; he spoke obscurely of one day fighting on our side, while his feud was notorious with the Brahmin group led by Nana Phadnavis. Could he be induced to join us? Oddly enough, the first lever came from Major Camac, whose heart hitherto had failed him. In March, stimulated by Captain Bruce, one of the heroes of Gwalior, he turned in his disorderly retreat and totally routed Scindia's army. A much more determined soldier, Colonel Muir, then superseded him and was now camped in Scindia's territory during the rains. Behind him a new command was set up, reaching from the Jumna, near Agra, to the Nerbudda; characteristically, it was given under the Directors' orders to a

Sir John Cumming, a client of the powerful politician Wedderburn who, Hastings was told, might thus be weaned from supporting Francis.

Here was another motive for doing what had been in his mind for a year past, to visit northern India himself and tie together many wavering strands. He was equally ready either to leave Mogul Delhi open to Scindia's attack if he respected our allies, or to stir up Delhi against Scindia if he turned recalcitrant. Then there was Oudh, supposedly bankrupt, and Benares, where Chait Sing was evading requests for money or men. Above all, he was set on a meeting to which he was being pressed by the venerable minister of Berar, which might make 'a new political system, and decide the future fortune of the British interest in India'. There was some information already how much that friendship was exasperating Poona.

However flexible he might be in the choice of means, proofs abound of his sympathy with Indian States as against British encroachment, and his insistence on keeping faith. We were pledged by treaty to hand over Gwalior, our most splendid prize, to the Rajah of Gohud, and he was resolved to keep our word. Coote protested, there was a general clamour that the Rajah was false. But 'what title had we to his attachment?' Hastings asked: 'we have conquered for ourselves. We treat him with contempt.' And what effect would a breach of faith here have on our credit with Berar? It was our encroaching spirit, he held, 'the protected licentiousness of individuals', which had wrecked that and other alliances before; 'every power in India dreads a connection with us'. In April he issued orders for the surrender of Gwalior.

The same month, on the invitation of the Nabob himself, he planned an assignment for the period of the war of all Carnatic revenues to the Company, yet safeguarding the Nabob's sovereignty, and carrying credits forward, both to the Nabob and his creditors, for the moneys so derived. R. J. Sulivan, a Madras servant, was appointed to act for Bengal in carrying this transaction through. One of his motives is not in doubt, stated alike in private and official letters; 'I saw, or believed I saw, an influence prevailing in that government which I could not approve', the vested influence of the creditors, who intercepted the funds needed for war.

This was to be a long bitter story, charged with recrimination.

'I have, for aught I know, given equal offence to the Company, the government of Madras, and the creditors.' His long-declared view, that the Nabob had a right to require assistance from his vassal in Tanjore, the paymaster of William Burke, would echo in Edmund Burke's library at Beaconsfield. His intervention in the internal economy of another Presidency, however vital for the war, could be represented as illegal usurpation.

Apart from the harsh facts, that every rupee, every reinforcement, every gun and ton of supply, came from Bengal, he had surely a weight of authority on his side. Madras had confessed their inability to make the Nabob contribute, and in such an event the Directors had authorized his immediate interference, with all means 'short of compulsion'. Early in 1781 they went further, telling both Presidencies that, in negotiation and joint operations, Madras must obey Bengal. Nothing, too, could be more fallacious than to read in Hastings a lust for power as such. His first use of his extended authority, and his expression of it, were gentle: 'we venture to offer some considerations', or 'we do not command, we only recommend'. In June he was cheered by the arrival of a new governor at Madras, Lord Macartney, making a new departure from the disreputable line of Madras servants, and Hastings' best friends at home vouched for his co-operation. Nothing could be more conciliatory than the Governor-General's first gestures. He put his proposal about ceding the Circars to Macartney privately, rather than 'suffer it to be pressed upon you in official form'. He said that, if 'a man of your Lordship's character' had been in office, he would have left this assignment business to him. But as it was now in action and solemnly guaranteed, he begged him to maintain it.

If there is one outstanding instance of his large mind and magnanimity, we should point to his attitude to Coote, whose double-dealing and clash with Macartney brought many misfortunes. Well he knew the General from of old; he had endured his obstruction, and pandered to his easily injured dignity and greed. But when he saw he was the one man to save the Carnatic, and sent him there armed with the powers which Madras in like case had given to Clive, he would not let him down. No, not if he offended against the civilian supremacy which no man more than he honoured. And not in the teeth of violent suppression of his own orders; as when Coote instantly incorporated Pearse's force with his own, and Pearse wrote 'he flew into such a rage that I thought he would have beaten the table to pieces, and have knocked my brains out with the shivers'. For he loved a brave man, and thought less of protocol than of winning the war.

He therefore dilated to Shelburne, the Prime Minister, on Coote's 'infinite merit', 'and he cannot have a better testimony than mine, for he has never been over partial to me'. When Coote heaped reproaches on him, how magnificent his answer! 'Perhaps you are the only man now on earth from whom I could sustain personal grievances, and not only forgive them, but allow him to extort from me my applause and even my esteem for his public virtues.' When both sides appealed to him, he mediated with generous justice. To Madras he wrote that the drain on Bengal 'obliges us to consider the war in the Carnatic as our own', and hence the advice he begged them to take in good part. On the matter of bullock transport, which immobilized Coote's army, 'if you cannot obtain such means without violence, violence must be used'. On the larger aspect, operations of war called for 'uniformity of system and authority', and this must embrace the negotiations to end the war. 'Who is charged with the conduct of the war, especially if he has shown himself deserving of that confidence in an eminent degree, ought, we conceive, to be trusted with an implicit discretion.' He might avail himself of the powers permitted by the Directors, but preferred not to; 'as co-partners in a common cause, we mean only to contribute our councils'. Then he turned to the old General. 'You cannot possess the confidence of this government in a greater degree than that which it is already disposed to give you . . . if I myself stood alone in the charge of the government of Fort St. George, I would give you an unbounded liberty of action.' As it was, he must depend on others, who 'have a right to judge for themselves'. 'My opinion, which cannot operate as authority', must therefore be confined to influence and conciliation.

If Coote's faults were glaring, his sufferings and difficulties were unparalleled. In 1782 he had a first stroke of apoplexy, but went on campaigning from his palanquin. When the old hero, after a spell of convalescence in Bengal, returned to the Coast in the following spring, Hastings wrote home he might survive this one campaign: 'may God grant him life to enjoy at home the reputation, rewards, and honours that are due to his virtues', and this though 'he will quarrel with me the moment we are separated'. With rare sympathy he pleaded with a member of Macartney's Council, whom he thought he could trust. He had read 'with infinite concern' the sharp words they had used to the General. Let them remember his infirmities, and what he must endure again; 'he merits at least the return of personal attention and tenderness', and not 'official letters written in the spirit of reproach and hostility'. And when at last he turned on the Madras Council, he burned in indelible words their public crime. 'No artifice of reasonings . . . no stings covered with compliments, no mechanism of the arts of colouring or sophistry, can strip Vice-Admiral Sir Edward Hughes or Lieutenant-General Sir Eyre Coote of having, in repeated and well-fought days, defeated the powerful invaders of the Carnatic on the ocean and in the field.'

His mind, grasping large diplomatic combination and the springs that move the action of governments, had also the minute and tactical gifts that rest upon knowledge. Popham came out of one conference saying 'he should have been a general'; the unmapped miles, over which Goddard had safely gone, were not blind spaces to him. And he knocked down a scheme to send horses from Oudh to Madras, as if he had been a blend of a sailor and a veterinary surgeon. Rising far higher in the scale of the qualities that win wars, and compel human beings to hope, was his undying confidence. Hyder's resources were dwindling, even if 'we lose men by every victory'; a drawn naval battle with the French, stretched so hard and so far from their base, was equivalent to victory.

Sometimes in this summer of 1781 he looked ahead to returning home, discussing with Impey how they might both enter parliament. For as war proceeded, one conclusion at least grew upon him, that 'the season of contention is past'. If he were refused full confidence, he would go.

In May the arrangements were decided for his journey to the North. The rains would suspend military decision; he was hopeful that he had detached the Nizam and Berar from the enemy league; the new revenue system was adjusted. Best of all, he minuted, was 'the mutual confidence which, after a period of so many years, is at length happily restored' in Council; confidence in fact, between himself and Wheler, who readily gave him full diplomatic powers and command over all troops in the North. He had every confidence of being back by the end of October. On July the 7th he left Calcutta with a large staff, reflecting the mixed business in front of him; Hay, secretary to government, Sumner the revenue secretary, Stephen Sulivan his own secretary, his favourite agents Anderson and Palmer and Chapman, Richard Johnson from Lucknow, and the injured Mr. Grand. His escort was small, just two companies from Popham's command, and how peaceful this excursion was expected to be was shown by William Hodges coming along to paint the river; even more by the presence of Mrs. Hastings, Mrs. Motte, and Mrs. Sulivan. There was a pleasing prospect that the Impeys — for the Chief Justice meant to inspect some country courts — might join them at Benares or Patna.

There were a few loose ends to be tied before he went, or proceeded far. In case of his death bringing any claim on the Company, he handed to Larkins, the accountant-general, the bonds he had taken for the various presents he had received. News of the outbreak of war with Holland meant that he must seize Chinsura from his very good friend Johannes Ross, whom he treated with immense consideration, and in due course shipped safely to Europe. Another item was an interview with the young Nabob at Murshidabad, an injunction to economy and reproof for a bad choice of friends. But, he told Wheler, 'his disposition is gentle', he would defer to D'Oyley our resident, 'our national credit is concerned' in his character. At Bhagalpur they spent a restful week with Augustus Clevland, on the island from which he ruled his rude hill tribes like a young patriarch, and where Markham came from Benares to meet him. There after breakfast, on the flat roof of Clevland's house, he told Markham he meant to fine Chait Sing fifty lacs, or half a million sterling, though granting, when Markham exclaimed at the amount, they could talk about it at Benares. At their next halt, the healthy upstanding Fort of Monghyr, he decided to leave Marian and her friends, pressing on himself to Patna, where great crowds collected to see him, and finally to Buxar on the Company's frontier. Here, on August the 12th, he met Chait Sing whose boats, filled with some two thousand soldiers, crowded the river.

CHAPTER XXI

A Black Half Year: Chait Sing and the Begums of Oudh: 1781-82

CHAIT SING owed his very existence as a ruler to Hastings, who had saved him from absorption by Oudh; his exact status, on the contrary, was due to the majority of 1775, who ranked him as one of the Company's *zemindars*. If he were allowed some unusual privileges, in regard to coinage and police, his *sanads* or title-deeds left his tenure dependent on his punctual payment of revenue, and forbade him to ally with other States.

It is not easy to reconcile Hastings' various explanations of this agreement, or what he understood by it. How unjust, he exclaimed when facing impeachment, to blame him who had proposed to make Chait Sing 'an independent prince', but must necessarily deal with him as what the majority had made him, 'a tributary landholder'. Three years earlier he told Major Scott that he had supported fixing Chait Sing's tribute once for all, so that 'he might not be made the tool of private rapacity, or in other words, as Mr. Barwell will well remember, of Philip Francis'; yet declared this was only an 'optional indulgence', conferring no right. He appealed finally to the terms of the *sanad* as his justification. But that very *sanad* was amended in 1776 at Chait Sing's request, in order to prolong the validity of an earlier *sanad* from the Vizier that fixed an invariable tribute. Notwithstanding which Hastings, at his trial, argued this earlier *sanad* had lapsed when the British took over.

Whatever the rights, they first came to a practical test on the outbreak of war with France, when Hastings asked for five lacs to equip three infantry battalions. He agreed it should be asked only for the period of war, but declined to allow Francis to discuss the principle, 'deeming it a right in every government to impose such assessments as it deems expedient' for the common protection. 'Extraordinary emergencies' outweighed any limitation of tribute. In 1779 the same demand was renewed and carried against the vote of Francis and Wheler, Hastings declaring their argument would give Chait Sing 'the independency of a tributary prince'. In June 1780, when a third demand was pending, the Rajah sent two lacs to Hastings as a bribe to avert it, having earlier tried to bribe Coote, and we have seen how it was applied to the urgent need of Camac's contingent. This did not prevent Hastings asking for the same war subsidy, payment of which was so long delayed that Camac's sepoys began to desert. In September it was followed up, as part of Coote's recommendations before he left for Madras, by orders for cavalry, and this Francis did not oppose; maintenance of such a force had been recommended at the time of passing his *sanad*, though not incorporated in it. There ensued many protests of impossibility, an offer of matchlock men instead, a scaling down of our demand from 2000 to 500, but no horsemen materalized.

Chait Sing, then, on the face of things, had been a *difficile* subject, but there was more to it than that. Though in manner he was gentle, would play chess with British officers, and was painted by an English artist, he had the fears and jealous pride of a parvenu, being illegitimate by birth, and suspended unhappily between British power and the revengeful dynasty of Oudh. He allowed much influence to those whom our resident politely called 'minions', resented being treated as a British subject, while his spies surrounded the *diwan* we had chosen for him; whom he once expelled, but to whom Hastings forced him to grant a *jagir*. Now this *diwan*, said much rumour, had been his mother's lover and was possibly his father. Meantime, Chait Sing was extremely debauched, and had lately taken to heavy drinking. Markham reported on his State as a den of 'murder, robbery, and rapine'. His predecessors, Graham and Fowke, agreed on his growing armaments, he had munitions of French make in his forts, all of which was borne out by Coote's report while on tour, that he kept up 30,000 troops and could well afford to pay more. Hastings' reply to this was noteworthy. Only 'the incapacity of the Nabob of Oudh, and the turpitude of his character', prevented him restoring Benares to 'its ancient constitutional sovereign'; early in 1781 he declared 'either that ought to be done, or the Rajah reduced to the condition of a *zemindar*'.

Something else, doubtless, weighed with the Governor. Chait Sing's patron, he told Coote, was Francis and, like other Indians before him, he would probably try to stir up trouble in England. Indeed, the story harked back to Hastings' most bitter memories. From the very first the Rajah had links with the opposition. Clavering had sent him assurances through the elder Fowke, from whose *munshi* he continued to receive messages how Hastings was to be recalled. The Governor was aware, too, that at the crisis of 1777, when the General tried to seize his government, Chait Sing had sent him an emissary who chanced to be a kinsman of Nuncumar. Hastings overlooked this, indeed Graham spoke of his 'partial regard' for the Rajah, but Chait Sing was incorrigible. He delayed payment of the war subsidy, counting on better terms from Hastings' successor, his evasive letters reproduced the very arguments Francis used in Council. Unless we dismiss wholesale all testimony from men of British birth, at the turn of the year 1780–81 he was becoming dangerous. The officer commanding at Buxar complained that our boats were constantly stopped and subalterns joining their regiments were assaulted, one for instance being stunned by brickbats when his servants asked villagers for milk. Francis Fowke agreed Council would have to punish 'these enormities'. He openly rejoiced at Hyder's defeat of Baillie, and impressed the English crimes on his people. Finally, in March 1781 Markham submitted that, 'if any serious accidents happen to our arms, he has told his minions he will declare independence'.

Two months earlier, on giving Markham his instructions, the Governor warned him that Graham had been too harsh, and enjoined on him 'moderation and mildness'. At what date, then, did he determine on an exemplary fine, and from what admixture of motives? In principle, plainly, some time between Markham's report in March and his own departure in July. He told Wheler it should be forty or fifty lacs, late in June he told Palmer that Chait Sing had offered twenty, but he was resolved to get fifty. He viewed him as wantonly ungrateful both to the Company and himself, while if punishment were called for, what crying need had he not of money? Famine was raging at Madras, which in fact was bankrupt. Goddard and Bombay were drawing heavily on Bengal. Briscoe, commanding in Rohilkund, appealed desperately for funds. Council had taken loans and could borrow no more; the French fleet was daily expected to return. His own narrative says he meant to tap Chait Sing's 'overgrown power', to save the Company from sinking. Not that this was the first object of his journey, which was to get a Mahratta peace, nor was this fine his single demand on the North. It was combined with a requisition on the surviving Rohilla chieftain, Fyzullah Khan, to produce the cavalry he was pledged to supply to the Vizier in emergency; moreover, he meant to recover whatever he could of the million and a half sterling in which Oudh stood in arrears to the Company.

Once at Buxar, and again en voyage to Benares on his pinnace, he received Chait Sing who, laying his turban in Hastings' lap, was all verbal humility: expressing his fears that the *diwan*, who was now in Hastings' train, and his own family might poison the Governor's mind. Hastings refused any discussion till they reached Benares, looking on the Rajah's show of force as a serious insult. But he was unperturbed, writing cheerfully to Impey that he hoped he would get as far as Benares and sketching an awning that should keep him cool on the river. If he said to Richard Johnson 'this trip will cost me my government', it was not in apprehension of trouble at Benares, but rather of the jealousies he would excite by a wholesale purge in Oudh. He had other things to think of. Both on his way up, and at Benares, he was writing at length to Lord Macartney, and supervising the truce for which Colonel Muir was treating with Scindia.

On the morning of August the 14th the little squadron reached Benares, its palaces and temples sloping down to the sacred river, its tortuous streets and alleys shimmering in extreme heat, and crowded with armed men, pilgrims, jewellers, and priests, besides the Mahratta merchants who traded from Delhi and the Deccan in silks, nutmeg, and cinnamon. He was lodged in the suburbs, a mile and a half from the garden-house to which Chait Sing proceeded: on the south bank opposite was the town, and vast palace-fortress, of Ramnagur, filled with the Rajah's troops. He acted promptly. Forbidding the Prince to visit him that evening, next morning he sent Markham, requiring an immediate explanation of his 'disaffection and infidelity'. That night he got an answer which, in contradiction to Markham's view, he interpreted as a defiance: certainly it was made up of half-truths, and repudiated responsibility for delay in his payments. Presumably he was prepared for this, for his action was instant. Having decided that to confiscate the *Zemindary* would discredit the Company, at ten o'clock he ordered Markham to put Chait Sing under arrest; in which Markham concurred, fearing that otherwise the Prince would escape to his forts.

Early on the 16th this was done, though Chait Sing's hand strayed to his dagger as Markham spoke. Two companies of sepoys held him a prisoner in his own apartments, whence he sent several notes of abject apology. Hastings' intention was to levy a fine, to insist on surrender of the fortresses, and the dismissal of evil counsellors, terms which Markham was to take immediately. But as James Anderson, the Persian interpreter needed, could not be found, the Governor said he was not going to dine alone; Markham could go after dinner. A message was sent that Markham would follow at three-thirty, with a note from Hastings telling the Rajah not to be unduly alarmed. But that sort of afternoon never came.

Just before noon Markham got a pencilled note from Stalker, one of the three subalterns with the Rajah's guard, saying that boat-loads of armed men were crossing the river, and (incredible to say) that their sepoys had been sent without ammunition. That was not the only fatal mistake this day, for many more of his followers had been admitted to Chait Sing's rooms than Markham had prescribed. A third company of sepoys, sent with the missing ammunition, was held up 200 yards from the palace by the Prince's soldiers. Hastings sent a message to Chait Sing by one of Markham's orderlies, unhappily one of Graham's hated servants, who was killed on the spot, just as firing began outside. Then it spread to the inner courts, a fusillade from the *zenana* terrace killing the defenceless sepoys: 'two hundred of the best sepoys in our service,' Hastings wrote after, 'the same veterans who had stormed the Fort at Gwalior'. They were wiped out almost to a man, and their British officers killed and mutilated. Chait Sing, lowered by a rope of turbans to a boat, escaped to Ramnagur, and thence to a fortress some ten miles distant.

The Governor's account to Wheler that day and the next was unmoved. He had acted, he said, with 'delicacy and prudence'. He had now deposed Chait Sing, but was in touch with the royal family, meantime appointing the dismissed *diwan* as acting Naib. As he had a bare four hundred men left, he was ordering up more troops from Chunar, fifteen miles to the west, and other stations within reach. He did not expect to be detained much over a week.

He wrote on the 17th to Marian. By the same sort of telepathy between them as that he obeyed when he left her at Monghyr, she had come nearer to him, to the British factory outside Patna. Uneasy rumours filled the bazaar there, the daily posts had ceased to arrive. On the morning of the 20th, when she received this letter, the worst stroke had fallen at Benares.

The battalion coming from Chunar was to link up with a strong force detailed from Mirzapore, and Popham to command their combined attack on Ramnagur. Before he could take over, the artillery officer commanding pressed, in disregard of orders, into the narrow lanes of the town, and was destroyed with half his men, the survivors falling back on Chunar. From that morning until mid-September all was chaos, and all things possible. The severed heads of British officers were paraded through the villages; north of the river all eastern Oudh, dominated by the Vizier's mother at Fyzabad, was spurting out in flame. The Begum was said to be offering 1000 rupees for an English head, and one for a sepoy's, mobs armed with clubs and mattocks blocked the roads. Of all this not so much alarmist letters to Hastings, as those from one Briton to another, give the best evidence. 'Look to yourself, Nat', one wrote to Middleton at Lucknow, doubting whether the Vizier himself would not go over. Hannay, who commanded some of his army in eastern Oudh, certainly feared it, and despaired of being able to cut his way through to Lucknow. Writing from Cawnpore, Cumming said western Oudh would follow, if it were stripped of troops. Another reported that Chait Sing's letters, bidding them kill Europeans, were reaching the *zemindars* of Bihar, while as the weeks passed, the agitation even echoed in distant Sylhet, where Moslem mullahs proclaimed 'the reign of the English is at an end'. Plainly the supreme need was to get Hastings' orders through to neighbouring garrisons. Written, almost etched, in his smallest hand, on tiny five-inch scraps, rolled in quills and hidden in the messenger's ear or turban, some got past, but many did not. Even by August the 29th not a line had reached Colonel Morgan at Cawnpore who, with a true instinct, marched on his own initiative.

The rest of the day of the Ramnagur massacre passed quietly. But great activity was seen across the river, the house he was in stood in a huddle of buildings amid trees shutting out the view, he had no money, and food only for one day. So dawned August the 21st. To retreat would be equivalent to another defeat, nor could he abandon his wounded sepoys, though these he contrived to save by commending them to the Vizier's brother Saadut Ali, who was in Benares. On consulting Popham and all field officers separately, he found they advised evacuation; at twilight, just before seven, David Anderson got word through his servants that the attack was coming that very night. By eight o'clock the flight to Chunar had begun. Struggling through a tumult of panic-stricken servants and baggage, with nothing but the clothes he stood in, Hastings marched on foot through the narrow streets and gained the open country safely. The night was very hot, and when they made a halt he found, much exhausted, the corpulent Benaram Pandit of Berar, and his brother, who both refused to leave him. Then they met the Chunar battalion coming to his relief, who turned back with him, and by five in the morning reached the shore opposite the grey citadel.

He had left behind his *banyan* Cantoo, too fat or too late to get away, who was holding conversations with an agent of Chait Sing. But Hastings would not hear of them, judging them just manœuvring to gain time, and hardening his heart never to treat with 'a vassal and a murderer'. He could bear all things but one, — danger to Marian. Day after day his minute rolls in quills trudged down over the hundred miles of enemy country : 'all is well, and will be better', but 'return to Calcutta', so they went on till August ended, and not till September had half gone was he reconciled to her staying at Bhagalpur. For she too had gone through a panic at Patna, where not twenty years back Samroo had murdered the English, and the factory was on the eve of a flight down-stream, which might have sent up Bihar in open rebellion. This Marian's presence, and her courage, did most to stop. He never forgot it. On his death-bed, entreating the Company to make provision for his wife, he reminded them that once 'her own independent fortitude' had saved them a province.

No such letters ever came out of a ragged messenger's ear. 'Be confident, my Marian. I will return to you triumphant. . . .

I never loved you as I love you in the midst of my greatest troubles, and have suffered more in my fears for you than, I hope, I ever shall for myself. . . . I never was better than I am. . . . I was ever happy in my Marian. I am now proud of her. . . . I love you more than I ever did, nor are you ever from my thoughts. . . . Adieu my beloved, my most amiable, my best Marian.'

But the first fortnight at Chunar was a black time. He found a distant Worcestershire cousin there, who rigged him out in her husband's clothes, for their boats had been sunk and everything looted, though Hodges managed to clutch some of his drawings. How long their sepoys would endure was dubious, without pay and short of rations; Colonel Blair read a scrawl on the fortress wall, 'Chait Sing will pay us our arrears'. The Vizier might be personally loyal, he believed he was, but his family was either actively or passively assisting the enemy. A first skirmish on September the 3rd showed they must wait for reinforcements, the Rajah's artillery was surprisingly good, and our casualties were heavy. And if Chunar fell, it almost certainly meant the fall, for a time at least, of British India. Had his mistakes put his country in such peril? He knew there was much to explain, and used these waiting days to write the opening sentences of his apology, dated September the 1st. 'In whatever manner the scene may close in which I am now engaged, the calamities with which it opened' must leave their impression. He would write 'less to efface that impression than seek to divest my mind of all partial bias. . . . And may the God of Truth so judge me, as my own conscience shall condemn or acquit me of intentional deception.' So he made appeal again to his own tribunal, the monitor within. When after long intervals he had time to finish this 'Narrative', his self-sufficiency was fully assuaged. He was racked with anxiety, not more 'for the issue of the impending contest than for its consequences on my own reputation'. 'I will suppose for a moment that I have erred', treated Chait Sing with injustice; so be it, but let them consider his motive, 'an excess of zeal' over-balancing his judgement. Not that he admitted it; 'much stronger is the presumption, that acts prompted by an unmixed attention to the public interest are founded on just principles than that they are the result of a misguided judgement'. His friends, he wrote to Laurence Sulivan, 'will see nothing done which ought not to have been done, nor anything left undone which ought to have been done'. If this were self-deception or self-righteousness, it had its magnificent side.

He would depend on none but himself, and his own prestige. He asked no help from Calcutta. He refused large assistance from the Vizier, and bade him go back to Lucknow. As if he were sitting in the garden at Alipur, he laid down for Muir the terms on which peace could be made with Scindia; Gwalior must be kept for Gohud, there must be stipulations for non-aggression against Oudh or the Gaekwar. With a few lines he commended soldiers who, like Morgan, had dared to act on their own, 'you have acted nobly, and with a decision that does you honour'.

On September the 11th he wrote to Wheler, 'all will terminate happily'. That day the Vizier came in person with a small guard, reinforcements had come in from Cawnpore, more were on their way. Benaram Pandit spontaneously offered him a lac of rupees. They could think of the offensive. In concert with Popham he changed the first scheme, to retake Ramnagur, 'scene of our first disgrace', deciding instead to march in two detachments simultaneously against both the strong forts where Chait Sing held out with some 30,000 men; Patita in sight of Chunar, with its four towers and deep moat, and Latifpur, six miles further on, sunk in bamboo forest and only to be reached by rocky tracks. On the 21st he stood in conquered Patita, listening to the signal gun which told that Latifpur was ours also. 'Our credit and influence are restored', he told Marian, and the unity of British India was now his theme. Writing to greet Macpherson on his reaching Madras, he spoke of soldiers and landowners who had 'assembled uncalled' to help him: 'the behaviour of my countrymen reflect more honour on our nation than any instance of modern history'.

Now the tide had turned, it ran strongly. He had signed a treaty with the Vizier at Chunar from which he hoped great things, and received from him a gift of ten lacs, which went to pay the army. Moodaji of Berar asked for an envoy, to discuss mediation at Poona. Chait Sing seemed to have lost heart. Leaving his mother in his last stronghold, on the eight-hundred-foot hill of Bijaigarh, he took what treasure his camels could carry and fled south into Bundelkund. On September the 28th Hastings returned to Benares and enthroned the boy Rajah, a grandson of Bulwant Sing through another wife than Chait Sing's mother. He appointed the boy's father as Naib, but made over care of police and justice to the Moslem he had long admired, Ali Ibrahim Khan, once servant to Mir Kasim. Henceforward the Rajah was to be nothing more than a *zemindar*, a lower status which was also marked by an increased land revenue. But he took special pains to protect the well-being of the sacred city, by abolishing the tax on pilgrims and cutting down the oppressive tolls on trade by land and river.

He was not a man to war with the defenceless, as his orders to Popham show, to treat Chait Sing's family with the 'respect and decorum due to their rank, and still more to their misfortunes'. And it is a pity his accusers could not read his letter to Impey, hoping that Popham would not be forced to use his shells, 'for the sake of the poor women'. But he was doubly disappointed when Bijaigarh fell at last in early November. For our sepoys plundered the Rani's following as they came out, while Popham, taking advantage of some casual phrase of Hastings, divided the whole treasure without more ado between his officers and men. When the officers sent the Governor a fine sword, and jewelled boxes for Marian, they were returned. All he asked for was Chait Sing's manuscripts, and he sent his family, under safe escort, to join him in exile.

Such was the end of Chait Sing, though he lived another thirty years, a shabby wanderer in central India. The fine proposed was therefore never levied, and had he submitted in humility, might have been remitted or relaxed. As it was, he was driven, or carried away, by his soldiers into revolt, when a British resident arrested him in his own palace.

On October the 25th Hastings went to meet Marian and the Impeys, who returned with him to peaceful Benares, where many things of weight kept him until January. He must wait for some practical results in Oudh, while he hoped for an interview with Scindia, with whom Muir had just settled some preliminaries of peace. But he was torn in two. His treaty with the Vizier was made without consulting Wheler, it would affront many Englishmen, and when Macpherson reached Calcutta he invited him up to Benares. Though he put it in a flattering form, his fears were hardly disguised; 'some decisive and effective assurance should be given to the world, that in the addition which has been made to the body of our government the power and influence which I possessed before have been improved, instead of being impaired'. Parts of the Council minute might well make him anxious. He did not like their hypothetical questions, even if they were dismissed; 'if the Governor-General had been even harsh and unjust', or if any Rajah had been 'too severely punished'. While even this tempered approval was damped down, by allusion to questions which 'rigid investigation' by 'judges at a distance' might ask. Nor did Macpherson leave Calcutta, and if Hastings had seen his letters to Macartney he would have been more uneasy still. 'W. H.', he said, had done well at Benares, 'but further we go not in our approbation without the most decided lights'. And, weeks before, these two worthies had joined Coote and Admiral Hughes in a perfectly unauthorized message to Poona, assuring the Mahratta ministers that the British thirsted for peace; coolly telling Hastings they were confident they had anticipated his wishes. Yet this message would destroy his new understanding with Scindia, hopelessly embarrass Goddard, and cheapen us in every Indian court.

Two months passed thus in Benares, part engaged in nursing Marian back to health, for her strength had ebbed as the crisis passed, besides smoothing away friction between her and Mrs. Sulivan, who complained of 'cruel slights'. Rather more important, he must wait to see how Oudh behaved, send Anderson to settle final terms with Scindia, who had an agent of Chait Sing in his camp, and commission Chapman to Nagpur to keep amiable the wavering ruler of Berar, now much eclipsed by Scindia, with some hope of making the peace 'an object of competition' between them. But most of all was he occupied in completing the 'Narrative', which was to be his justification. For his 'build-up' of the crisis was near completion, not by any means the defence of a man who felt himself guilty, but the product of a temperament which was developing a superstitious faith in a happy influence protecting him, and of a mind which, convinced of its own integrity, identified its convictions with the just ends of British government, and collected reasons for triumph out of calamity.

He wrote thus to all and sundry of the spontaneous rush of officers and men to save him, the loyalty of Indians and the tributes from Indian rulers, reflecting that all this would not have been done for a Rumbold. When he finished his 'Narrative' in December, sent it off to Scott for publication at home, and expounded his case to Laurence Sulivan, his picture was gilded, varnished, satisfied. Chait Sing's outbreak was 'a mine sprung before its time', the prologue of a conspiracy to extirpate the British name, in which the Begums of Oudh were deeply engaged. The person of Warren Hastings might be mean but, by accident or Providence, it was 'the talisman', 'the essence of the State itself'. 'I lost the *Zemindary* with a revenue of twenty-two lacs. I recovered it with a revenue of forty. . . . I did not despair of the safety of the State, but supported its dignity, when I lay at the mercy of the rebel. . . . I conducted a successful negotiation of peace with Madaji Scindia, in the most desperate period of my distresses.' He had been the instrument of evoking 'the inherent virtue of my countrymen', and of making known once for all the resources of our government, which would contribute more to 'the permanency of the British influence . . . than the most splendid victories'.

His first minute, on resuming his seat at Calcutta, sounded the now habitual mystic and defiant note, that the Governor-General, indifferent to censure from 'avowed enemies', was assured of 'the applause of his superiors, from the internal conviction of his own mind that he has laboured to the utmost of his abilities to merit it'. So sure was he that he had deserved well of the State, that he reported to the Directors, though not to Anderson or Middleton, the Vizier's gift of ten lacs, asking them to repay it to him as token of their approbation. It would have argued 'poorness of mind', he told Scott, to conceal it, or his hopes about it. But this begins another story. While locked up in Chunar, what he had feared most was for Oudh which, he told Wheler, 'has caught the contagion', and might be lost.

This unhappy country had gone steadily from bad to worse, since the death of Hastings' friend, Shuja-ud-Daulah. The Clavering majority had robbed it of rich Benares, yet imposed a larger subsidy and the so-called 'temporary' brigade which, like the permanent one, Oudh had to pay for. Another host of British officers commanded the Vizier's bodyguard, and the dangerous rabble styled his army. Asof-ud-Daulah was an amiable vicious weakling, a collector of clocks and watches, governed by court minions whom he rewarded with *jagirs*. His *zemindars* were in chronic rebellion: his greater vassals, such as the Pathan Rajah of Furruckabad, or Fyzullah Khan the Rohilla, entirely defied him. But his worst trouble came from his own family.

His brother Saadut Ali was restless and ambitious. His grandmother, the Burra Begum, who lived on good English testimony 'in a religious blaze', so heartily hated him that she had any chair broken to pieces on which he sat during their conversations. His mother, the Bahu Begum, to whom he owed the succession, and who had once saved him from his father's sword, had a tigerish temper and royal pride, and had brothers whom the people much respected. With the whole family she had protested against the loss of Benares, she was indignant at her son's vile incompetent ministers. She had angrily resented the settlement forced on her by Bristow in 1775, with the part-surrender of the vast treasures left by her husband. But she held the remainder under a British guarantee, together with the wide stretching *jagirs* which, like the Burra Begum, she possessed in eastern Oudh. In the bickerings between mother and son no language was sterner than Hastings', that our faith and credit must prevent 'even the appearance of oppression on a person of the Begum's rank, character, and sex'. Francis, on the contrary, argued that the donation long promised for the Rohilla war could properly be extracted from her, as having inherited the treasures in violation of Moslem custom, and that she might justly be asked to meet her husband's debts.

What stands out most prominently in his 'Narrative', and in the affidavits attached, is the fear that all Oudh might fall away. The British officers' letters involve Saadut Ali at least as much as the Begums, indeed some involved the Vizier himself; so did one to Hastings from an English Jewish diamond merchant, written while a prisoner of Chait Sing. But the mass of this evidence came from Colonel Hannay and other officers commanding the Vizier's most hated troops, while the affidavits were partly organized by Hannay and taken in his tent.

A second impression from this evidence is that there were two distinct periods of disturbance. The first was at its height in early September, a phase of what reads like a spontaneous combustion; part-aimed at the weak Vizier and his officials, largely rising out of hatred of Hannay and his revenue-collecting troops, but in any case a demonstration of sympathy with Chait Sing and his revolt against the foreigner. All eastern Oudh was in sheer anarchy. Hannay's Indian subordinates are found disguising themselves as fakirs, or hiding in tombs; even in October Major Naylor, who was marked by his humanity to the Begums later, spoke of all the Gogra country as in revolt. That the Begums allowed Chait Sing to draw recruits from their *jagirs* cannot be doubted; Wheler certainly believed it, while Popham could testify that he saw such men in Chait Sing's garrisons, in the blue and yellow Oudh uniform, and a priest from Fyzabad was found to be inciting our native officers. The second phase, however, of January and February 1782, which was directly connected with the Begums, seems only to have come after a three months' lull. On October the 1st Hastings told Impey he saw no future possibility of danger; on the 17th, Middleton at Lucknow spoke of an almost restoration to 'their usual tranquillity'; in November Impey travelled there with a few servants and a *munshi*, and John Belli was happily married there to a widow he adored. A regular battalion had dispersed the rebels threatening Hannay which, together with the Vizier's return, 'restored the quiet of the country'. So said the Governor's 'Narrative', finished in December.

When therefore he signed the treaty of Chunar on September the 19th, the Begums were far from being in the forefront of his mind. His first purpose was to re-win the Vizier by large concessions, to stabilize a shaky dynasty, and to make revenue arrangements which would bring a steady stream to his empty treasury. The treaty provided that the costly 'temporary' brigade should be withdrawn; that the Vizier should no longer pay for Hannay and his forces; that George Shee, the British agent, should be withdrawn from the court of the Vizier's vassal at Furruckabad; that the Vizier be allowed to resume the *jagir* of the Rohilla Fyzullah Khan, and pay him a cash allowance instead; that he also be permitted to take any other *jagirs* he thought fit, on condition — and this would cover the Begums — that he paid an equivalent income to such as held them under British guarantee. Such were the arrangements for which Hastings claimed credit, as making him many enemies among the profiteers so discarded; 'the Nabob demanded it, and with what face could I refuse it?' the alternative was 'public ruin and infamy'.

Four days later, however, his instructions to Middleton put a different complexion on the surface clauses. The prime object being the speediest payment of the Vizier's debt, his personal expenses must be rigidly limited, and his troops reduced; payments to troops and officials must be managed by the ministers, 'with your concurrence', nor must such payments interfere with the lands assigned to the Company; the surplus that should arise from resuming the *jagirs* must be earmarked for the debt. His military officers must not be 'of known disaffection to our government'; revenue collectors must be chosen 'with your concurrence', so must the judges of the courts, which he must be urged to set up.

The Vizier made some objections, but Middleton was equal to the occasion. He told him, so he reported later to Hastings, 'conceiving it to be your desire', that 'it was necessary to have something to show on your side', but that, once the debts were cleared, the agreement would not be 'fully and literally enforced'; 'I believe upon the faith of this assurance principally was his Excellency's acquiescence obtained'. From the start, then, there was a good deal of haziness. Was the resumption of *jagirs*, for instance, to be universal, as Hastings urged, which would apply not only to the Begums but to the Vizier's wretched favourites? And from whom did the initiative proceed for this proposal? On this point his explanations, on his impeachment, were confused and contradictory. In even darker obscurity is wrapped the violent step of confiscating the Begums' treasures. Unhappily, such beams of light as we can discover leave a murky air, like coarse tallow in a tomb.

It was one thesis in the Bengal despatches, and in his later defence, that this confiscation was determined only when the Begums took up arms to resist the loss of their *jagirs*; it was also represented, both this autumn and over later years, that seizing the treasure was proposed by the Vizier, unsolicited and uncompelled. Neither statement seems to be true. Late in October Sir Elijah Impey, rosy-gilled and now enjoying his holiday, reached Benares with his wife and Marian. He found his host preparing his 'Narrative' which, in view of British opinion, he advised him to reinforce by affidavits, offering to go on to Allahabad himself to give the swearing of them greater weight. But Hastings was also digesting Middleton's *rechauffé* of Hannay's reports, and told Impey the Begums were in rebellion, at which the Chief Justice suggested that, in that case, their treasures could properly be taken away. Middleton's temper, Hastings added, was so mild that he feared he would not drive on the execution of the Chunar treaty, which was life and death to the Company and his own good name; why should not the Chief Justice go right up to Lucknow, where he could not only see to the affidavits, but explain the scheme about the treasures to Middleton? Impey therefore went off, taking a message to the Vizier, via Middleton, that 'the proposition coming from him' would receive concurrence. He was offended by the Vizier's meagre reception, but Middleton put that right by arranging 'a masquerade'. After six full days at Lucknow, by December the 1st he was back at Benares, able to tell Middleton that Hastings 'highly approves . . . I need not mention the necessity of taking care that the money be applied to the Company's use'. Middleton saw at once that the treasure notion was much easier than a long squabble over the *jagirs*; he duly put up the proposal to Hastings as a suggestion from the Vizier, and on December the 6th wrote 'the measure heretofore proposed will soon follow the resumption of the *jagirs*'.

Late that week Impey had some difficulty in persuading Hastings not to go up to Lucknow himself, when Middleton reported signs of the Vizier's resistance. He was making 'puerile excuses', and when under repeated pressure he issued the orders required, protested it was 'the act of compulsion'. Middleton, indeed, confided to Impey that he thought the *jagirs* matter might mean 'some active service'. In short, the treaty was breaking down. The Vizier felt humiliated at being induced to attack his family. We had removed our resident from Furruckabad, but he was displeased by Hastings' criticism of his misgovernment there. Then there was the sorry business of Fyzullah Khan, equally discreditable to both parties. By the 1774 settlement the Rohilla chieftain was bound to provide what military assistance he could, when required by the Vizier. The feud of the two dynasties still smouldered, but an enquiry by Daniel Barwell cleared Fyzullah Khan of the Vizier's accusations, and he received the Company's guarantee. To them he proved a loyal ally, spontaneously giving help when war began with France. In 1780 Hastings instigated the Vizier to demand of him 5000 horse, which was entirely unwarranted by treaty; his protests were ignored, and hence the clause at Chunar allowing the Vizier to resume the *jagir*. But now Hastings drew back. Oudh was incapable of action: let the Vizier first get his own territories under control.

He was in despair, his letters to Middleton over Christmas were violent and menacing. The expenses of the 'temporary' brigade were thrown on to the Company, the eviction of the Vizier's British pensioners and their losses 'make me odious to my own countrymen'; nothing to our benefit in the treaty was realized, 'my reputation and influence will suffer a mortal wound'. 'Your total inattention to my instructions' has prevented any reduction in the Vizier's troops. Both the *jagirs* and the treasures must be taken, and promptly; he must be present in person to prevent abuses, but allow no 'forbearance', and 'prosecute both services until the Begums are at the entire mercy of the Nabob'. He would tolerate no more 'fruitless inaction', and if Middleton felt he could not do it, would come to Lucknow himself. If the contrary, he would go down to Calcutta but would 'leave you a dreadful responsibility if you disappoint me'.

Middleton's letters were all readiness to oblige. Though he answered officially 'in the form you seemed to expect', he wrote privately he was willing to shoulder the blame for the treaty not being literally fulfilled; he had conceived that discharge of debt was all the Governor really wanted. But he piled up a good many warnings. He had ordered a regiment to move from Cawnpore, and if the Governor persisted in his intention of sending still more forces and making the Vizier pay for them, he would be glad to know, so that he might send his family away to safety. The Vizier believed 'the annihilation of every shadow of his power is meant'; 'a settled melancholy has seized him'. Everything marked out the British as the real movers; too great violence, another straw added, would mean an open breach. His assistant Johnson added it could only be done 'by a campaign'.

Desperately Hastings drove on. When at the New Year the Vizier marched on Fyzabad, he was met by a grateful letter, yet one intimating that more British troops were available, and ending 'I have determined to set out immediately by dawk to Lucknow'. When Middleton proudly described how he had contrived to take the palace at Fyzabad without loss of life, how the Begums' men were dispersed and the eunuchs surrendered, but how he had since allowed some 'temporary forbearance', in order to discover the whereabouts of the treasure, Hastings stormed back that negotiation encouraged resistance, and that if the measures failed, 'I shall hold you accountable'. He had left Benares on January the 7th, and all the way down the river he goaded and doubted. But on the 25th Middleton wrote gaily to Impey that, though it had needed 'considerable address' to get hold of the eunuchs, now it was done, and 'by using some few severities with them, we at length came at the secret hoards of the old lady'. So when Hastings rejoined Council in February, he could tell them that Middleton had already taken fifty-five lacs, while another twenty-six seemed to be owing. The resident apologized for his temporizing, 'where force could be employed it was not spared', but after all no man but the Vizier and his uncle could enter the *zenana*. The Begums' lands were grasped, their troops dispersed, their eunuchs in irons. 'And in this situation they . . . are to continue (excepting only a remission of the irons) until the final liquidation of the payment.'

For many more months this squalid affair continued. The eunuchs' irons were reimposed; they were kept short of food; they were moved to Lucknow, where Richard Johnson gave access to the Vizier's officers who were detailed to inflict corporal punishment. And if the irons weighed two pounds only, and flogging was probably never used, it was all bad work for the British Raj. Johnson, again, through Impey asked the Governor's compassion for other indirect victims, the hordes of Shuja-ud-Daulah's concubines and children, now plunged into misery and hunger through these confiscations: of whom several British officers kept sad memories, of screams and breaking out of the *zenana*, and forcible drivings back by sepoys. As for the two eunuchs, they were not finally set free till the spring of 1783.

Some good, some money, might in time come out of his northern journey. But not as yet. 'I return to an empty treasury which I left empty', and he realized there was no hope of clearing the debt that year. His pen and his hand fell heavily on Middleton, who groaned to Impey that, though assured of the Governor's affection, 'people about him' tried to destroy it. He was disgusted at this weakling. Even his affidavit to Impey had been 'meaningless', while it was plain the Vizier repented of his engagements, was even proposing to 'comfort the lady mother' by restoring her *jagirs*. Hyder Beg, the minister he had chosen and whom Indians viewed as a British tool, must be inspiring his master to argue in this 'unbecoming' tone. The 'temporary' brigade looked like becoming permanent again, for only force could extract revenue; desultory and greedy Britons still lingered in Oudh. By this time, too, he distrusted Middleton's black picture of Fyzullah Khan, and decided to enforce a compromise with the Vizier. This futility would never do, and in May he deputed his favourite Palmer to clear up the mess. More money would be welcomed. A second gift of ten lacs was accepted for the Company, though declined when the full extent of debt was realized; the ministers were invited to subscribe to the Company's loans.

But this game would not further go. Middleton, who endeavoured to resign, was sternly told he would be held accountable till the debts were paid; 'all means, gentle or harsh', he told Major Gilpin at Fyzabad, must be used on the eunuchs. Johnson, aspiring to succeed Middleton, freely employed troops to mop up taxes, and was suspect of corruption. 'Weary of the reproach of being the instrument of a nation's ruin', at one moment Hastings thought of removing altogether both our troops and our residency, but as the debt continued mountainous as ever, in September he recalled both Middleton and Johnson to face heavy charges. They were not convincing. On Palmer's word he accused them of conspiracy against Hyder Beg, whose evidence they feared; yet Middleton's letters to Impey are full of the minister's praise. He held Johnson guilty of advising the Vizier against paying over the ten lacs to the Company, as a bad precedent. Not that this indignation lasted very long. It did not prevent him giving Johnson the Hyderabad residency, or from borrowing largely of Middleton during his impeachment.

He replaced them by Bristow, the friend of Francis and now the friend of Macpherson, whom the Directors had long ago ordered him to reinstate. But as his full failure became apparent, his frayed nerves showed themselves in despotic tone and command. There could be no medium, he told Bristow; either the resident would be like Middleton, 'the faithful echo' of the Vizier's ministers, or the minister must be at the resident's 'absolute devotion'. Letters 'in the spirit of opposition' were an insult to our government; to make the treaty operative we must have assignments of land in perpetuity. The Vizier must be advised to punish guilty *zemindars* by death. And the same word issued to Markham at Benares, where the Naib whom Hastings had chosen turned out tyrannical and incapable. Unless he liquidated the revenue owing, 'his life shall answer for the default'.

He had failed so badly that friends and enemies alike thought he would stay on in India till the failure was redeemed. Even the professional mockers shot their tongues out against him. He had jailed Hicky of the *Bengal Gazette* for contempt, but the tireless ruffian this spring got out a skit on the 'congress at Sooksagur'. In this he was audaciously parodied as 'Sir Francis Wronghead', and set down for a song, 'How I am weather-beaten and shattered'; here, too, was Impey as 'old Poolbundy, taking affidavits gratis', and Macpherson as 'the Thane', whispering 'keep all secret, mon, and I'll help thee oot'. This was the end; Hicky's types were confiscated, and his *Gazette* expired.

British opinion was a stronger thing than James Augustus Hicky. The Governor had sent home his Benares 'Narrative', written so that 'every intelligent old woman in England' might grasp it. But this did not seem to embrace the legislature. In October news came to Bengal that the House of Commons had passed resolutions demanding the recall both of himself and Impey; news which would soon run like wildfire through every *durbar*.

CHAPTER XXII

The House of Commons: 1780-83

WHEN Hastings set out to the North, and when Macpherson with the last English information reached Calcutta, they congratulated themselves that the home glass was set fair. Within a year, however, it fell to storm. If the causes for this outside India could be isolated, three were pre-eminent: the fall of the North government, the return of Francis to England, and the furious driving of Edmund Burke.

In the parliament elected in 1780, Hastings' only personal allies were old Palk and Francis Sykes, as against a considerable bloc of the Clive-Francis group, including Strachey, Farrer, and D'Oyley. In a by-election the next year another enemy joined them in Rumbold, though he could be paired with Barwell, who contrived to buy a Cornish borough. He and his sister had been bidding some time, — 'you'd think', Pechell told Hastings, 'they were at market like oxen'. Though the Nabob had also bought Lord Halifax's vast house outside Chichester, others reported him as nostalgic for Bengal. Occasionally, he wrote a bilious letter to Hastings. Four-fifths of the Commons, he said, did not care a rap about India, 'being habituated to forego the fatigue of thinking on great national subjects'. With an expert eye he contended that 'India is innocence, the purest innocence, compared with Europe'.

However, with both ministers and Directors, Hastings seemed tolerably secure. Thurlow and Stormont were his special champions in the Cabinet, while outside it the latter's veteran uncle Mansfield was a strong supporter, together with the vigorous Archbishop of York, Markham, father of the young resident, whose letters from Benares praising his patron went the circle of friends. The selection first of Macpherson, and later of Stables, as Councillors was taken as decisive proof that North was well disposed, for Stables was a kinsman of the all-powerful patronage secretary Robinson, and had backed Hastings against Clavering. For the first time, in truth, Robinson wrote a full cordial letter to the Governor. He was going to 'forget the past', when Hastings had seemed to him to be shielding others' bad conduct. Union was all-important; he was enthusiastic about India as 'the glory of this country'. Cynics believed that India was at least meant to be the glory of the ministry, outweighing the fatal news of Cornwallis' surrender to the Americans at Yorktown. For three years North had been fighting a war in which he did not believe; for two, he had vainly urged a coalition Cabinet on the King. Some of his strongest ministers had resigned, leaving him with figures dear to the King but odious to the nation, Sandwich and Jenkinson and Lord George Germaine. But now Robinson pointed to a dawn of salvation in the East.

And nothing in the legislation of 1781 looked ominous for Hastings. One statute disposed of the controversy with the Supreme Court, which it deprived of revenue jurisdiction. A second did, indeed, arrange a partition of the Company's profits somewhat more favourable to the Exchequer, and gave government more hold over the Directors' despatches, but at least its charter and privileges were extended, till 1794 at the earliest. Sulivan, once again chairman, was all confidence, telling Hastings 'you have conquered', and promising to remove the difficult Coote if a fair chance offered; the King had been pleased to see pictures of Gwalior. Furthermore, he was strong enough to get his son Stephen named as provisional successor to any vacancy in Council. Up to the New Year of 1782 the peering eye of James Macpherson vouched for the 'perfect confidence' between the chairman and Robinson, while the sour old Clivite Walsh wrote to his nephew, Francis Fowke, that 'Mr. Robinson, Mr. Sulivan, and Mr. Hastings appear to me three in one'. But in fact all was undermined.

In the biology of parliamentary politics there is a law of dissolution. Once a ministry has reached an advanced degree of weakness and shown signs of decomposition, the death struggle begins; not as a rule over causes part-eliminated, but on one potential and unexhausted, capable from its nature of masking the contest for power as a crusade: death coming thus, not so much from the original ailment as from a new contagion on a reduced resistance. As North's government had reached this stage, India provided the contagion, the mask, and the operating theatre.

Quite apart from party rivalry, for some years everyone had realized that our Indian government cried out for reform. The India House was choked with alternative schemes for revenue or justice. Hastings himself had never ceased asking for larger powers. One session after another Robinson declared India must be taken next, only to have it postponed to the calamities of America. He was telling his ally Jenkinson now that they must get rid of the 'fetters' of the charter; he also had a meeting with Burke, where there was talk of giving the Governor a veto, but of binding him by royal instructions in dealing with Indian States. Hastings' good friend Baber likewise saw Burke, whom he tried to persuade that the swiftest remedy for abuses was to enlarge the Governor's authority. While such conversations proceeded, evil tidings flocked in from India, and the vultures flew nearer to the carcase of the Company.

It began with the return of jovial William Hickey, bearer of Touchet's petition against the Supreme Court. What with his amours and his dinners, and having his Indian servant baptized, he was tolerably busy, but he saw much of the Burkes and in November 1780 listened to an Indian debate, dining well afterwards at the British Coffee-House. The January following, the petition passed to a Select Committee, whose rambling reference might cover almost anything, not merely the 'administration of justice' but 'the happiness of the native inhabitants'. Its chairman was the most vulgar of Nabobs, General Richard Smith, once chairman of the Carnatic creditors and lately sentenced for corruption in a pocket borough, yet powerful by his riches and now busy repainting his portrait as a reformer. But its ruling voice was Burke, and next to him Sir Gilbert Elliot, brother of Hastings' beloved disciple.

In this spring of 1781 the Indian disasters of the year before first came home to the British public, hard strained and embittered already by the American tragedy, loss of command of the sea, unemployment, and Radicalism. Rumbold arrived and bought his way into parliament, followed up by heavy charges of corruption and of causing the Carnatic war. The Directors were thunderstruck at the loss of their investment, and angered by Hastings' proposal for counteracting the loss by loans from their own servants. Even before the worst news came of Hyder Ali's triumph, they were deploring the cost of the Mahratta war; that this war and his wild diplomacy made Hastings responsible both for the Indian confederacy and the loss of the Carnatic, such was the version publicized by Francis' agents.

The first and most serious result was the appointment in April of a second, and Secret, Committee on the Carnatic war, the composition of which reflected government's determination to get the credit by keeping this matter in their own hands. Its chairman was Henry Dundas, the Lord Advocate; his colleagues included the King's confidant Jenkinson, Orde, a very able follower of Shelburne, the director Gregory, so long Sulivan's enemy, and an intelligent Adam Ferguson, who owed his seat to Dundas and believed the Company should be brought to an end.

Hastings' friends took the alarm. Sykes wrote that a better defence would be called for than good Pechell's 'long and tedious' pamphlet. In August Sulivan said 'the plot seems deep, and the Mahratta war, I conjecture, is to be the engine to crush us'. James Macpherson enlarged on a conspiracy in very powerful quarters. A loyal and most eccentric friend, Captain 'Joe' Price, was wielding a rough pen for Hastings — 'I think I have not gone out of my depth' — yet even he begged him to get a quick Mahratta peace, and drop 'Hornby's hobby-horsical love for the useless harbour of Bassein'. All over London the wires thrummed and crossed, all sounding of India, from Baber in Brook Street to Barwell in Great Ormond Street; from Robinson in St. James's Square to Burke in Charles Street.

From midsummer onwards figures of more recent significance joined the fray. The disreputable mulatto Mackintosh was home and lobbying North. Then came John Shakespeare of Dacca, much accused by Francis and now hurried off by Hastings to reach home before him. He had only done so by taking a Dutch ship from St. Helena, where he left Francis gnashing his teeth, and as that Dutchman was captured by a British fleet, arrived sooner than he bargained for. In October Francis landed, and in December Hastings' official agent, Major Scott.

Though Hastings wrote that Francis' return made it 'indispensable' to have his own representative, the men who knew the scene, incomparably better than he did, agreed it was a great mistake. Not only did it invite attack, but it lost the advantage

THE GOVERNOR-GENERAL AND MRS. HASTINGS, 1783–84, BY ZOFFANY

of the slow six months' pause by reference to India. However this might be, Scott was an unmitigated disaster. His merits were a blind devotion and incessant activity. But Windham compared his zeal with that of a grasshopper, whose chirruping interruptions to Prime Ministers and other busy men were meant to be downright, but in fact were impertinent. Without humour, easily deceived, without standing in English life and without political knowledge, he swamped Hastings under his mistaken judgements. For three years, by every ship, they posted off, in duplicate, quadruplicate, and on occasion extended to six copies, nay, rising to ten. So he wrote of Burke, 'I cannot write of the fellow with common patience . . . a miserable speaker with a vile Irish brogue'. If Francis counted on the Rockingham Whigs, he said in 1781, he was doomed; 'I have completely done for that fellow' followed next year. His choice pearls of 1783 were a verdict that the Fox-North Coalition made Hastings secure, and an advice to reward the services of Paul Benfield, whose circle had given substantial help in parliament and the City. These selections are perhaps enough to bear out Francis' grim remark that 'ce garçon' was by no means a second Macleane.

Incidentally, the Major was an expensive luxury. After a bare year at home, he had spent on Hastings' account £3843, of which some £1200 had gone on special messengers. His bill for 1783 rose to £5664. He explained how he must dine with ministers, keep a carriage, and take a furnished house in Holles Street; there were also appearances to think of; 'I sit under a confounded barber's hands in great pain, one hour at least every day'. In a later stage he was provided with the eligible parliamentary seat of West Looe, at a cost (to Hastings) of apparently some £4000.

No doubt as he rolled out of Holles Street he sometimes caught a glimpse of his Harley Street neighbour, Philip Francis. Faithful Major Toone reported seeing him, 'pale yellow, and a look of diabolical purpose'. He had come home, after seven years, to his sore-tried Betsy and the delicate children to whom he was all sweetness, but on Indian subjects one malign incarnation of hatred. His first act was to sell out all his India stock at a loss of £2000, convinced it could never rise again. He had killed some time in the Indian Ocean and at St. Helena, which he christened the Isle of Ennui, in writing a memorial to the

Directors : that old, old song, that all was lost, Berar a dangerous enemy, and Oudh ruined. Within a week of landing he was received at a levee in a way he thought distinguished, not knowing North had advised the King that he might do 'considerable mischief', — and gratified Lady North with Indian muslins. But the Directors were silent. At last he forced an interview on Sulivan, and very unpleasant it was ; then they formally received him and his memorial. Finding the majority so hostile, he turned to the parliamentary Opposition. Burke produced him to testify to the Select Committee on Hastings' defiance of orders, Goddard's aggressive march, Coote's huge perquisites, and the corrupt contracts. Their first report condemned the Directors' attitude to him as 'a silence strongly expressive of guilt'.

Startling news from India redoubled their ardour ; of Impey taking the salaried post as head of the *Sudder* Court, and then of all the happenings at Benares. The Committee became Francis' arena. There friendly witnesses, Goring or Boughton Rouse, were displayed, coached in advance by Francis and Burke ; there Shakespeare was turned inside out, and there Scott complained how 'Burke turned and twisted me for about two hours'. And there Sulivan's tail was hard twisted too, as regards Macpherson's restoration to the service, and a supposed attempt to screen Impey. In February 1782 they reported against Sir Elijah ; in March presented the famous 9th report, in which Burke had reworded a whole volume of Francis' minutes, and which depicted the whole Indian government as 'perverted from every good purpose'. Nor was the Secret Committee neglected, Dundas receiving from Francis' pen a long anti-Hastings questionnaire.

While Baber and Halhed hastily compiled pamphlets of refutation, Francis wrote in highest spirits to his Indian friends, Ducarel and Hay, Wheler and Livius. Hastings 'totters', his own evidence had made out Impey 'black as the devil', nor would prosecution stop at him. 'Nuncumar is returned and, like Caesar's ghost, with Ate by his side, is now raging for revenge.' All England held the Mahratta war in execration, and rightly ; 'Hastings' projects always gave me the idea of a lottery, with an infinity of blanks to a possible prize'. So deep burned the hate and the purpose, and now they found out their way, for in March the moribund North government resigned. Instantly word went to Hastings, James Macpherson sending a special messenger overland; 'your and our enemies are in the plenitude of power . . . the removal of you all will be the least of their vengeance'.

Thus it happened exactly as the shrewd Pechell had predicted, that if North supported Hastings, the Whig Opposition who had been for him in 1776 would swing over. Yet that Opposition had two wings, led respectively by Rockingham and Shelburne, whose rivalry might make one of them relent. So late as March 1781 Burke, severely though he denounced the Rohilla and Mahratta wars, spoke of Hastings soberly: 'I was always an admirer of his talents, and the farthest in the world from being engaged in a faction against him'. As for Shelburne, he was profusely flattering to the Governor, 'the more power is lodg'd in your hands, the better for the Empire'.

It would be mistaken to attribute the vehement change in opinion simply to Francis' rancour and propaganda. On a war-worn political class, report and rumour poured in of disobedience, avarice, and disaster; of a Mahratta war six years old, of all India banded against us, of Madras nearly lost. On the misdeeds of the Court and his own bargain, Impey found hardly a single defender except his friend Dunning. Rumbold came home with his half-million, and while Radical England was up in arms against a war in America waged by German mercenaries and Red Indians, the first accounts arrived of Chait Sing and the Begums' wrongs. Old Horace Walpole noted, as Major Scott would never have noted, the first success in attacking Indian abuses of Henry Bankes, close friend of the younger Pitt, and later best known as Wilberforce's lieutenant in the group of 'the Saints'.

Francis or no Francis, this feeling must have found a vent. North himself just before his fall told Dundas that Indian measures must come foremost. And measures depend on men. Now Dundas had served a long apprenticeship, had won many Scottish seats for North, and felt himself ill-used; he had turned against the American war, while his speeches showed that he already saw in the younger Pitt the hope of a wider political future. In this mood he took the chairmanship of the Secret Committee, as one means of keeping himself to the forefront. Many Scots, including Macpherson, were among his Indian correspondents. And, a fortnight before the North Cabinet collapsed, he sketched for Robinson a stronger one in which he figured himself as 'Secretary for India and Plantations'.

Burke, the energizer of the other Committee, had long been the Company's champion. But no public cause weighed in the balance, unless it could be made to coincide with the fortunes of the Burke clan. William Burke had come back as agent of the Rajah of Tanjore, the vassal of the Carnatic Nabob whom Lord Pigot had restored. But Hastings had declared for the Nabob and supported against Pigot the majority Councillors, whom the Directors of 1780 proposed to restore to the service. Wildly Edmund wrote to Ministers of 'the only yet remaining native government', or of 'millions of innocent people' sacrificed, and bargained with Robinson for Tanjore against the Arcot interest. Every week in the Select Committee some fresh document from Francis heaped fuel on his private indignation.

And now, at last, the Burkes were in power under Rockingham. Edmund was Paymaster-General, his bankrupt brother Richard was secretary to the Treasury, for the equally bankrupt cousin William a perfectly unnecessary job was created, as deputy-paymaster in India. Their private fortunes, however, must be anchored to a public crusade. In April Edmund wrote to William in Tanjore, 'your cruel and unprovoked persecutors are on the ground. . . . I think the reign of Sulivan is over, the reign of Hastings is over.' And the holy cause had another use. He warned Rockingham that Shelburne and Dundas would try to shield the 'Indian delinquents', and it was understood that the new Cabinet would fall to pieces if he were not allowed to pursue the attack on Hastings. The same month, the Directors installed in the 'chairs' Fletcher and Gregory, both notoriously anti-Hastings, and his loyal friend Pechell died.

Before May ended the campaign was launched. Dundas depicted Hastings as Francis had drawn him. The Commons addressed the Crown for the recall of Impey. A bill of pains and penalties was drafted against Rumbold. And finally, armed with a hasty report on Oudh and Benares, Dundas carried resolutions that it was the Directors' duty to recall both Hastings and Hornby of Bombay, for actions 'repugnant to the honour and policy of the nation'. In June the proprietors declined to adopt such 'suggestions' from one branch of the legislature. Furiously the Burke section asked whether reports and resolutions of the faithful Commons were to be treated as waste paper, Fox threatening legislation in the next session. But on July the 1st Lord Rockingham died. Fox, Portland, Sheridan, and the Cavendishes refused to serve under Shelburne, and most of all, Burke; 'sunk', wrote the foolish Scott, 'never I hope to rise again'.

Shelburne, the new Prime Minister, lived up to his common reputation. Scott called him 'slippery', Sulivan grumbled he was kept 'at a princely distance'. Actually, of course, he was in a parliamentary situation that could not possibly last. If Fox and the North group combined, his minority could not carry anything, not the vital American peace treaty, let alone an India Bill. And he was miserably weak in the Commons, dependent wholly on the younger Pitt and on the hardihood of Dundas, who was committed to recall Hastings. Indian patronage would thus be a mighty lever for the capture of votes, nor were all the Indian 'interests', either in the City or the Commons, on Hastings' side. The merchant and shipping interests usually followed the government of the day, while the Arcot interest were separately marshalled by James Macpherson. For these reasons, and because Fox was accusing him of sheltering criminals and clearly meant to make India his trump card, Shelburne must occupy some ground by way of compromise, before parliament met in the autumn.

While, then, he issued orders for Impey's recall, and blarneyed Scott with talk of recalling Hastings with all honour, he sounded the India House with a suggestion for recall of the whole Council in Bengal. The new Governor-General should not be Francis, but someone outside faction, in the person of Lord Cornwallis, although conceivably, it was hinted, he might begin as second to Hastings. The Directors' majority took up a line which Dundas must have approved. Once more they ordered Hastings to replace Bristow and young Fowke; his arrest of Chait Sing had been 'unwarrantable and highly impolitic', his application to keep the Vizier's gift was rejected. But a substantial minority protested against his recall, and at the special meeting of proprietors called in October, Hastings' friends carried all before them, voting in his favour by 428 to 75. Duly a bill for £65 16s. 5d. went down in Woodman's office, spent on beer, brandy, wax candles, and waiters, to entertain 'the friends of Mr. Hastings' at the 'George and Vulture'.

In this deadlock parliament reassembled in December. Sykes advised Hastings to get out while the going was good; Sulivan warned him that North's party was concerned to defend Macpherson and Stables rather than him. And as Scott was expressly forbidden by Hastings to breathe the word resignation, he and Caillaud were inclined to think that to get Cornwallis named as second and successor was perhaps the best way out. Barwell was unusually positive; 'be prepared to quit your seat and the country at a moment's warning'. For if the tone of the different parties varied, it was only in degree. Moving his resolutions again, Dundas promised action after Christmas; not on any criminal charge, but for sufficient political reasons, Hastings must be recalled. Shelburne opined that he had been duped by Scindia, and that no peace was in sight. Burke and Fox attacked him as a great delinquent. March the 2nd was fixed for Dundas' bill, demanding non-intervention between Indian States and arranging the appointment of Cornwallis. But on February the 18th, 1783, the Shelburne government was defeated on the American peace and, after a month of dour resistance by the King, was succeeded by the Fox-North coalition.

While Hastings dealt with Oudh and Madras, and waited anxiously for Scindia's signature to the Peace of Salbai, this chronicle of parliament became known in India. Impey took the alarm, resigning the *Sudder* Court, and on getting his letters of recall, left India late in 1783 when the Bay of Bengal was free of French cruisers. The Governor was more resilient. He had hardly returned from the North when he began assembling the necessary documents to clear his alleged authorship of the Carnatic war; 'I am not afraid of the Committee of Secrecy', he told Macpherson, whose reports were 'black as hell with the turpitude of Rumbold'. He counted on soon closing the Mahratta war, while if he looked back he found nothing to be ashamed of. To the Directors, his letters sounded a most scornful challenge. Thrice this year of 1782 he went into the ten lacs given him by the Vizier, and the other sums 'occasionally converted to the Company's property through my means'. The account he drew up in May, and sealed in the presence of Larkins, did not, however, leave India till December. To guard himself from 'the meanest imputation', that he disclosed these gifts only after hearing of the parliamentary enquiries, he added Larkins' affidavit; 'I feel most sensibly the mortification of being reduced to the necessity of using such precautions'.

Wearily the summer wore away, enlivened only by the marriage of Bristow to Amelia Wrangham, 'the Chinsura belle'. The Governor's private letters from home were full of other people's worries. Marian's gifts to her sister-in-law had all gone astray, pearls sunk in a wreck on the Dutch coast, and shawls confiscated by the customs at Holyhead. John Stewart's widow wrote distressfully she had 'not a morsel of bread'. The Reverend George Austen deplored the marriage of his niece Elizabeth Hancock to a Frenchman and a Catholic. Of his inner circle Bogle was dead, Halhed had gone home, Motte was a bankrupt. His public burden was enormous. The guns of Fort William, firing salutes for victories, seemed to bring peace no nearer; Coote was coming back to Bengal in the bare hope of saving his life. Oudh was shocking, and in the distrusted hand of Bristow; he sorely missed David Anderson, who was entangled in the humiliating procrastination of Mahratta politics. While the Madras government, he complained, continued to blame him for their own collapse; Macartney 'does not disdain to tread in the dirty footsteps of Sir Thomas Rumbold'.

Such frustrations left him, perhaps, all the easier victim to the first serious illness of his life in August, a long bout of fever and dysentery lasting till October, and leaving him a wreck. Everyone was ill this unhealthy summer, and he minuted a proposal to move the seat of government. Marian had not been well, and was far up the river; on September the 4th he drew up a will, leaving her all. But she had got word of his illness. Escorted by Captain Mordaunt, she left Bhagalpur on the 5th, and raced down 375 miles by boat, reaching him at dawn on the 8th, having nearly been wrecked where a tributary *nullah* poured on the rocks of Colgong. Her presence healed him, and he never forgot her courage, nor her escape; 'Blessed be that Being', he wrote two years on, 'whose Providence has been extended . . . to the best object of its guardian care'. Though he found even talking a strain, he sat up to give Bristow three hours of verbal instruction; then went up to Nuddea to convalesce.

While there he heard, and felt as 'an electrical shock', the news of North's downfall; very soon followed up by the Commons' resolutions for his recall, and the proprietors' stand for him.

'Not all the Rockinghams and Richmonds that live' should jeopardize Marian's health, by hastening their return to Calcutta. And when he did get back in December he told Anderson, far off in Mahratta country, to open any letters coming for him via Bombay; 'if they contain good news, publish and make the most of it; if bad, keep it to yourself'. But 'I am not so easy to move'. Rockingham's death left him even more confident, as meaning the resignation of Burke, who — 'I know not why' — was so set against him. And Shelburne, the best-informed politician in England about India, had always written to him in flattering terms; 'if no new charges not foreseen intervene, I am sure of remaining as I am'.

He sent the new Prime Minister his reasoned defence. He did not wish, he said, to keep his place beyond the duration of the war; if circumstances made it desirable that he should be 'honourably relieved', he could well conceive it and accept it cheerfully. But suffer not 'my character to be blackened by criminal accusations . . . nor my peace of mind wounded, and my influence blasted with official reproaches'. Let him think of the effect of British and foreign newsprints circulating the Commons' resolutions to Indian courts, at the very crisis of a negotiation with the leading Mahratta State.

His minute for the Directors' eyes spoke more bitterly. The least evil that could happen would be delay in the peace with Scindia; the worst might be a break off, and the loss of the Carnatic. What Indian State would trust governments whose policies were so lightly reversed, or link itself to an expiring interest? Between the denunciation of his government and the appointment of another there must intervene some 'stagnation of power', 'a general scramble at home', and in India temptations to war and rebellion. For these evils he must disavow responsibility. Yet he would keep his post and do his duty; 'let my past conduct be the pledge'. For eleven years now he had held 'the first nominal place', yet 'I have received nothing but reproach, hard epithets, and indignities instead of rewards and encouragements'.

There was one light in the storm. Stables had just arrived; he judged him a man of honour, who years back had served bravely as an ensign under his old friend Caillaud; he told Shelburne what happiness he had in his colleagues, above all in

Macpherson. To that 'dearest' friend he enlarged on it with emotion; 'what a pity that such a group should be broken! For I do not think that a knot of more rational, or better tempered men . . . could be selected from all England.'

Peace and goodwill, then, on this eleventh Christmas of his governorship. Yet within three months he wrote to Scott, 'I am deprived and abandoned', and sent in his resignation to the Directors. And this, even before he could have heard that Shelburne also had fallen, and that Burke and Fox were again in power.

CHAPTER XXIII

Lord Macartney and the New Deal: 1781-83

ONE month later again his angry friend Pearse wrote from Madras, 'many are called, but Macs are chosen'. It was, indeed, the combination of Lord Macartney and Macpherson which drove the iron into Hastings' soul. This inter-connected opposition in London, Madras, and at his own Council board cut the web of his policies, made peace precarious, branded him with his countrymen, and imperilled his standing with Indians. So that when, in the drear year 1783, he at last made amends to George Vansittart for five years' silence, he harked back to another opposition they both remembered: 'my situation is not much better than that of your brother's, when similar acts of violence provoked the vengeance of Mir Kasim on our nation'.

To close the Mahratta war, and then to mass every effort against Mysore, such was the vista for which he began to cut the roads, while half a prisoner at Chunar in 1781. By that time Pearse's force from Bengal had joined hands with Coote, Berar was lavish in promises, the Nizam was passively watching, but the first positive step was Muir's treaty of October with Scindia. That great prince's ambitions lay in the North; he would not be driven southwards and sacrificed to Nana Phadnavis, his subtle rival, and he therefore promised his neutrality and to negotiate peace between Poona and the British. Six months followed of tension and suspence. The prestige to be won by mediation wakened the jealousies between Indian States. Scindia was indignant at a separate mission sent by Goddard to Poona. From Hyderabad, Hollond reported the Nizam as insistent on our totally dropping Ragoba, and yet as anxious that we should not yield too much to the Mahrattas. From Berar, Chapman noted a tendency to make a peace with Hyder part of the general peace conditions. It proved necessary to centralize all the treaty-making in the hands of Anderson.

Hastings would have no ignominy, no talk of indemnity, no Mahratta claim on the Doab, and no breach of faith with our allies. But he had long seen, had so instructed Goddard even before Benares, that our concessions must be large, even of the prized Bassein. 'It is not peace with conditions of advantage that we want', he told Anderson, 'but a speedy peace.' Bassein must go : as Gohud had proved a false ally, let Gwalior go too ; Ahmedabad also, if the Gaekwar received an equivalent. 'We want nothing from the Mahrattas, but their alliance against Hyder.' In April 1782 an event occurred in the North which might have wrecked an understanding with Scindia, but which Hastings finally used to improve it. This was the death of the one strong man at Delhi, the regent Nadjif Khan. For a moment he hesitated, whether not to press his unwilling Council to save the Emperor 'from the thraldom of his ministers'. But Scindia was being approached by Hyder, and tempted by one Delhi faction to invade Bengal ; that being so, he let the dream go, leaving the Empire open to Scindia and future chances.

Anderson was therefore enabled to sign the treaty of Salbai in May 1782, Scindia acting in the dual part of guarantor and also plenipotentiary for Poona. We agreed to relinquish every conquest since 1775 ; the Gaekwar was restored to his *status ante bellum* ; Scindia received the territories assigned in Broach. On the other hand, Ragoba was to be decently pensioned off, and French factories were to be excluded from Mahratta possessions. Above all, the Peishwa was to oblige Hyder to restore all he had taken from the British, and from the Carnatic.

Yet for almost another year the treaty hung fire. Hastings and Anderson both believed in Scindia's loyalty, but his rival Holkar was obstructive, while Nana Phadnavis had a more crafty game. For by encouraging Hyder he might compel the British to yield their solitary gain of Salsette, while by the threat of a British alliance he might force Hyder to surrender his gains on Mahratta soil. For months Anderson was detained in Scindia's camp, watching the ebb and flow of Hyder's agents. Ugly rumours of the Nizam's intentions came via Berar. Chait Sing was said to be in contact with Oudh rebels, our Cawnpore garrison was on the *qui vive*. But on December the 7th Hyder Ali died, and the Peishwa ratified the treaty, which was formally exchanged by Nana Phadnavis in February 1783.

One war, in fact, as is the habit of wars, had prolonged the other, and the Mahrattas had dallied till the balance in the Carnatic was more pronounced. Coote's year and a half of campaigning ended, for the time, with his return to Bengal in September 1782, a broken invalid. Even Macpherson and Macartney saluted his dauntless courage, the alacrity with which he sought out the enemy, like 'a subaltern thirsting for glory'. But courage alone could not win this war. Now marching north to meet Pearse, sometimes hurrying south to keep the enemy out of Tanjore, in general he was beating up and down an ambit within a hundred miles north and west of Madras. In a waste land, marked by dead men's bones and blackened ashes of villages, without cavalry, dependent for supply on sea transport from Bengal, or what he dug up from buried hoards, he could never pursue or fight to a finish. In clouds of dust Hyder's horsemen drove off herds of cattle. His own spies were in the enemy service. His sepoys must desert if they would have food for their families. His sad despatches dwell without end on his lack of transport, or bullocks so weak that they could not move the officers' tents, sodden with the rains. After a year of this, Hastings had written 'no decisive advantages have been gained, and we lose men by every victory'.

This military position became critical during 1782. Hyder made clear to Coote's agents that, without some gains of territory, he would fight on 'till never a lamp was left to burn there'. In February Admiral Suffrein fought a drawn battle off Madras, while in April some 3000 French troops were landed at Cuddalore, just south of Pondicherry. After three more sea fights, Suffrein took Hughes' alternative base in Ceylon; in October, against the bitter protest of the Madras government, Hughes sailed for Bombay to refit. By the time he was back again in April 1783, the renowned Bussy had brought more French troops to Cuddalore, while Suffrein's cruisers were capturing food ships even in the entrance to the Hugli. That month Coote died, struck down at sea by paralysis, while returning to his command. After all their storms, his last letter to Hastings from sea was affectionate, 'I wish to God I may have strength to weather this business through'. Nothing had been done during his absence to take advantage of Hyder's death, nothing but internecine quarrels between Macartney and the acting commander, that same intriguing General Stuart who had once arrested Macartney's predecessor, Pigot. When Suffrein once more beat off Hughes' fleet, nothing prevented a crushing defeat of our army but the news in June that peace had been signed between Great Britain and France.

It was not, it seems, till late in 1782 that Coote was converted to a more hopeful strategy, advocated by Hastings. That is, to stand on the defensive in face of the Mahrattas and to advance from the west coast, aided by whatever reinforcements came from England. This would divert Hyder from the Carnatic, threaten his much-prized conquest in Malabar, and finally his own dominions. A first step was taken when Hastings sent Colonel Morgan to supersede Goddard, whose scale of expenditure terrified Council. This was, indeed, the move which finally did most to end the war. But it began in sporadic efforts and in disasters, which proved the total inability as yet of our Indian government to make war for India as a whole. Decisions taken by officers on the spot, disjointed relations between Madras and Bombay, a clash of royal and Company officers, orders issued by John Sulivan, Macartney's agent in Tanjore, but disregarded by army commanders, such causes led to General Mathews' wild march to Bednore early in 1783, and his surrender to Tippu with all his force, whose fate awaited them in the tragic prisons of Seringapatam. Nor was it till much the same time, and too late, that adequate use was made of a southern force striking upwards from Tanjore. But if the non-existence of an Indian government was the fundamental reason, a good deal was due to human beings and not least to Lord Macartney.

George Macartney, a good-looking voluble Northern Irishman, had a political experience which no servant of the Company could acquire, and the entrée to official circles which they could not share. A mission to Catherine the Great of Russia, chief secretary in Ireland, a member successively of the Irish and the British Houses of Commons, governor of the Caribbee Islands, all these were over by his early forties. A protégé of Holland House, he had acted as tutor to Charles James Fox, and brought with him to India a natural son of the first Lord Holland, yet having married a daughter of Lord Bute he had an easy footing in the rival camp. Inevitably, he came to Madras with some un-Indian prepossessions. He was convinced of the corruption of British India, laying immense stress in his homeward letters on his own integrity; no one but Clavering, he concluded, had such a spotless record. He found their policy both iniquitous and parochial. We must have peace, at any price, with the Indian States, concentrating all our force against our European enemies with stakes in India, France and Holland. After six months he wrote back to Jenkinson that no one ought to be sent out as governor or councillor who had already served in India.

He inherited, of course, the fixed Madras view, that Hastings' Mahratta war had brought about the tragedy of the Carnatic, as well as Hastings' feud with Rumbold over the direction of peace and war. His first measures showed his ideas, and the conception he held of his powers. Within a month of arrival he combined with Coote and Hughes in suggesting peace to Hyder; within three months, the same group joined with Macpherson in addressing a plea to the Peishwa. These things passed while Hastings was far off at Benares. But Macartney went much further. So desperate had been the Carnatic that Hastings had been ready to purchase Dutch European soldiers by ceding Tinnevelly; Macartney, on the contrary, brought orders to seize all Dutch possessions. Hastings, again, was so anxious to win the Nizam's alliance that he proposed to restore the Northern Circars to him; Macartney distrusted the Nizam, and refused to hear of giving up this potentially rich and strategic territory 'without special authority from home'. The Governor-General had invited a candid expression of opinion, but he was not used to candour like this. Their difference, however, found most to feed on in the most thorny of all subjects, Coote's supreme powers, as given him by Bengal, and the role of the Nabob of the Carnatic.

Though Macartney flattered himself on 'good humour and good breeding' in his relations with Coote, his contempt for him passed all bounds. His own success in attacking, against Coote's advice, the Dutch port of Negapatam increased his complacency, and he accused the General of excessive prudence. He soon acquired the habit of sneering at the salutes ordered for his hard-fought battles — 'these victories almost ruin us in gunpowder'. He hoped against hope that the old man would resign, breaking out to Laurence Sulivan 'in God's name how could you send such a man as old Coote here?' even 'persons of his own silly trade' had lost faith in him. Then he diverged from personalities to the searching ground of power.

His official response to Hastings' courteous letters was sardonic: 'if in some instances we cannot consider them as commands, we shall be thankful for them as most respectable advice'. But his first long private letter, after twelve weeks in the country, though in his usual blarney, was a most impertinent lecture. In the old bad days, he said blandly, Hastings' arrangements for Carnatic revenues would have met with 'derision', nor could he accept the position of his Madras agent, R. J. Sulivan, despite his 'engaging manners'. His intervention had thrown the Presidency government into 'imbecility', and if pushed too far might be challenged in law. His lordship, Hastings noted, 'reasons like a lawyer'.

But his lordship had made one useful discovery, that the root of his troubles lay in the creditor gang, headed by Benfield, whom Macpherson and his London friends so warmly commended. He told Hastings that they solely controlled the Nabob and his second son Amir-ul-umara, and sent word home that Benfield was 'very dangerous', a man whom 'the Company ought never to employ on any pretext whatsoever'.

He discovered this when he tried to tie down in black and white the general agreement which Hastings had made in April 1781, for the assignment to the Company of Carnatic revenues. Warning Hastings that he believed the Nabob had simply made that agreement so as to bind their hands, in December he carried through a new one, assigning all revenues to Macartney in person, who should make contracts with renters for five years and appoint collectors, though subject to the Nabob's confirmation. One-sixth of the receipts should go to the Nabob's privy purse. By the spring of 1782 this paper scheme was breaking down. Macartney was assured that revenues were intercepted, sticking to the hands of the royal father and son, or their British creditors. He saw nothing for it but a revenue assignment in time of peace as well as in war, and extension of it to Tanjore revenues also. So when the Nabob refused to confirm the renters, Macartney issued the necessary documents under his own seal: a Bengal letter encouraged him to assume 'the whole sovereignty' in case of necessity. But by the autumn the strains between the two Presidencies had passed into violent hostility.

Macpherson, 'Johnny MacShuffle' as they called him on the Coast, has often been made the villain of the piece. It seems a little hard, for if he had some crooked ways, he liked things to run smoothly, and people to behave in a civilized way. Many times over he pleaded with Macartney to forgive Benfield and make use of his talents with the *durbar*, so able a man and capable of good service both 'here and at home'. And if we said that he meant to 'frame' Hastings, it was not, to begin with at least, in any sense of an evil conspiracy. 'He has pledged himself to follow my ideas', he told Robinson, and though Ducarel prophesied to Francis that Macpherson would find the Governor 'untamable', his letters to Macartney do not breathe disloyalty about Hastings, only the possessive picture of a man whom he feels he can manage. While in England, he declared Hastings 'the most capable, the best-hearted, and the most liberally uncorrupt servant ever employed by the Company'. When he saw Macartney at Madras on his way out, he left him with assurances of bringing about economy and peace. Hastings, he continued from Calcutta, 'thirsts for peace as much as your lordship or I can', and painted him as a necessary and a praiseworthy figure. An 'experienced hand to guide the reins', this was his moral late in 1782, and how much had been done already! Mainly, he implied, at his own instigation. We had peace with Scindia, Goddard's vast expenditure had been cut down, they were shipping home an investment of a million and bought 30 per cent cheaper than before, for which he must give Hastings 'the sole executive merit'. And then in Oudh, on discovering his own men's misconduct, he had behaved 'nobly' in restoring Bristow. It was pleasant thus to bandy civilities with Macartney over their joint and several integrity: to declare he had never accepted a gift except oranges, or how content he was with a lowly lot like his forebears, who had been quiet Highland clergymen. But, on the substance of the quarrel between the two Governors, he was openly on Hastings' side.

Moreover, Macartney's extreme interpretation of a revenue assignment, which in principle Bengal had approved, does not account for the scale of the quarrel. His notions of diplomacy were abject. He seemed bent on making an enemy of the Nizam, whom Bengal was straining to make a friend. He objected to any notion of granting him some fraction of a defeated Mysore, as against the Company's policy. When the Nizam's brother Basalut Jung died, he prepared to seize the Guntur Circar for ourselves, even contemplating alliance with one of the Nizam's rebel feudatories. While Anderson was using every argument to range all the Mahrattas behind Scindia, Macartney, as Hastings bitterly noted, begged him 'for mercy's sake' to sign the peace at any price. And no sooner was Salbai signed than he asked authority to approach Hyder; to which Bengal replied, 'till Hyder is compelled to solicit for peace . . . every advance to a negotiation with him is but an encouragement to him to persist in the war'.

All this time the vagueness of the Regulating Act, and the Directors' despatches, offered plenty of scope for a conflict of powers. Hastings had only just returned from Benares when the rival claims were brought to him in person; Coote's, by his Persian interpreter, whom Macartney suspected of a deal with Benfield, and Macartney's by his secretary, Staunton. The latter's rather servile letters told his chief that people at Calcutta looked to him as 'the only resource'; that Hastings seemed to have 'little solid judgement', and much resented the tone of Macartney's lectures. And when in March 1782 Bengal tried to adjudicate, the fat was in the fire.

Sulkily brushing aside the conciliatory language of Bengal, Madras fastened on the single fact that they were advised, except in imminent necessity, to leave all military and diplomatic initiative to Coote. 'The ancient constitutional system of this government subsists no more'; they 'did not venture' now to make suggestions, and washed their hands loudly and pompously. In July Bengal, drily suggesting that their advice had not been designed 'as an obligation to inaction', asked them to regard it not as orders, but as 'inevitable conclusions drawn from principles of truth'. A Madras rejoinder of twenty-nine folios, declaring the powers given to Coote to be illegal, called the Bengal doctrine of joint responsibility 'so extraordinary and inadmissible that we can scarcely give credit to those senses which inform us that it proceeds from your Board'; hinting further that Coote was only retained in command in order to keep him away from Calcutta. This last was too strong, as Macpherson wrote, even for 'the cool and gentle Wheler'; this 'paltry fellow' Macartney made Hastings despair. In fact, the matter of Coote's powers was hopelessly bedevilled by the assignment. Wriggling to get out of it for an easier bargain, the Nabob offered the whole of his government to Coote, and sent off his *diwan* to Calcutta to underline his grievances against Macartney. The Governor had usurped his royal seal; his son's coach had been seized for debt, his servants were dismissed, he had to mortgage his jewels. Bengal did, indeed, instantly forbid Coote to accept the offer, but when in October he rejoined them in Council, their tone changed.

Well before this, Macartney complained to Macpherson that he was 'frozen' by Hastings' neglect, and their relations suffered from more than a clash of temperaments. Macartney's language was, of course, highly exasperating; as of a most superior person, come from a planet better informed. His everlasting protestations of righteousness — 'an incorruptible governor of Madras is not the person for their purpose' — the repetition that, 'after the stations I have held', he looked no higher for himself, yet with hints of the might of British public opinion behind him; his dismissal of the Nabob's case as just 'oriental vanity and rage'; this flabby pressure, just like Francis', for peace at any price, — all these sickened Hastings. But he had another suspicion. He heard that Sulivan, as indeed was the truth, was putting forward Macartney as his successor, and he never liked to see his winding-sheet before his eyes, least of all such a one as this. His instinct was not at fault. Though Macartney vociferously disclaimed any such intention, to Burke and Robinson and Cabinet ministers his song was one and the same; 'an honest man', 'a good English-man', a candle in a naughty world, a void to be filled. He had not come out just to work as 'a bullock agent' for this demented Coote. In due course he was to write how Hastings 'is not what he was', 'much impaired', and of ungovernable temper, and to bracket him with Rumbold and Sykes as a despoiler.

On Coote's arrival, then, Bengal took up the Nabob's stream of complaint, coming as it did on top of the growing insolence of Macartney's letters, his bungling negotiations, and his total failure to make any use of Hyder's death. Hastings, we remember, ever since his Madras service, had felt that a satisfactory treaty with the Nabob was a prime necessity, and always shown what importance he attached to the dignity of Indian princes. The

Mahratta war might be taken as closed; surely Carnatic revenues might be secured without this naked usurpation of a sovereign's rights, which both he and Macpherson were certain other Indian States would take as a breach of faith, and as proof of the supreme government's lack of power. The Nabob declared the conditions of the assignment had been violated, and that assignment derived from a treaty to which Bengal was pledged. On these grounds, and from 'the faith and honour of a gentleman', Hastings would stop this pedantic intriguer treating the Company's oldest ally with such 'unparalleled indignities'.

Historians have discovered another conceivable motive, in the usefulness of the Benfield-Arcot vote in the proprietors and the House of Commons. Such, indeed, had long been the advice of John Macpherson, reinforced in past years by his cousin James' letters to Hastings, and rather later by Major Scott. But more proof would be necessary to make this a determinant with Hastings. He had never been a creditor of the Nabob, like Macpherson. His warnings to the Madras government on Pigot's downfall, his comments on first taking over the assignment, and his letter to Macartney from Benares, were all of a piece, — on the scandal of the creditor gang. Moreover, his trust in Macpherson had evaporated, and he was warning Scott to watch the machinations of 'James'. He had ample ground, without this ulterior motive, against Macartney and Madras, and if he went wrong it was through a temper worn to shreds, not through corruption.

So in October he took up his terrible pen, to end the paper war which Madras had begun, a war so exhaustively prolonged that we heartily endorse Macartney's account of his working day, 'the only hour of comfort in the four and twenty is when I am undressing to go to bed'. They understood, this Bengal series began, that hundreds were dying of famine at Madras, that their treasury was empty, and Hughes leaving for Bombay. 'We look to the arrival of every post from Madras, — we open our letter and peruse its contents we may say, indeed, with astonishment.' They hoped the future might yield 'more solid proofs of your political merits', and would themselves strive to keep 'a moderation that you shall neither surprise nor provoke'. In January 1783 they unanimously ordered the cancelling of the assignment, and the return of R. J. Sulivan to make a new agreement with the Nabob, who engaged to provide revenues greater by a third than those raised by Macartney, and promised a right of re-entry if he failed. Macartney's action, they minuted, was a breach of treaty; his claim that Bengal had approved his actions was 'criminating' their government with charges that would, 'if believed, have a dangerous effect upon our present negotiations for peace and alliance'. Hastings was determined that Coote must go back to save the Coast, carrying powers to suspend Macartney if he proved defiant.

But the Carnatic assignment, like Schleswig-Holstein and others, is one of the historic questions that will not bear exhumation. A rambling intervention from the Directors set up another flow of recrimination, charged with almost theological rancour. It left Macartney pleading Directors' orders, and Hastings in the curious role of appealing from those orders to the powers given him by statute. But the basic facts remained unchanged.

Further minutes of March and April lashed the culprit. Till Coote arrived, he was forbidden to negotiate. He had thrown away the golden chance on Hyder's death; 'laborious altercation, stinging invective' were no compensation 'for a neglect that may cost millions'. He now asked powers to seek peace through a Tanjore agent, offering Tippu some frontier concession. How 'humiliating' and 'inauspicious' to beg Tippu's 'commiseration'! and all in direct violation of our treaty with the Mahrattas. As for his 'collected map of complaints and invectives' against the Nabob, Bengal, Coote, and Hughes, if only they had thrown in Bombay as well 'your description of the universal misconduct of the managers of public affairs in India (the President and Select Committee of Fort St. George excepted) would have been complete'. Their audacity as 'censors of the State' was astonishing; 'you act criminally towards your country'. Turning to the peace, 'nothing could be more fortunate than that you were not possessed of those powers for negotiation'. 'It was not to submit to terms thus dictated' that Bengal had surrendered its Mahratta conquests, and supplied Bombay and Madras with three million sterling in a year and a half.

But when Coote left for the Coast late in March, he was without the powers to suspend Macartney which Hastings pressed on his colleagues, who voted to wait and see. In February he heard of the Directors' resolution condemning his treatment of

Chait Sing; when their general letter followed, it also contained a severe criticism of his views regarding Tanjore, which he had unguardedly given Macartney permission to quote. Whatever the precise right and wrong in this instance, Macartney had a nasty trick of using private letters, of which Macpherson also complained.

Like a blast of despair, the impression swept over Hastings that once more he was alone and betrayed. 'Are these men aware', he exclaimed to Scott and Sulivan, 'they are sowing seeds of new war and rebellions?' declaring in favour of 'the murderer' Chait Sing at the very moment of completing the Mahratta peace. And would they pursue this reprimand, with orders for his restoration? That at least he would never do, he told Governor Johnstone, 'though the whole race of mankind should join to execrate me for the refusal'. This apart, though he wished to stay till Tippu was driven out of the Carnatic, he would not keep his place at the risk of 'public ruin and private ignominy'. Ever since this despatch, 'my colleagues have wholly withdrawn their support', objecting to the most trivial proposition as if 'afraid of being suspected of anything like a leaning towards me'. Bristow was back in Oudh, on Macpherson's pressure, and Fowke restored to Benares. He had proposed Richard Sulivan as resident at Hyderabad, for '(David Anderson only excepted) I do not know his equal', but they vetoed his nomination. Yet 'if there is any department of government which is exclusively mine, it is the appointment of my own representatives in foreign courts'.

And so it was everywhere. 'Sour looks' greeted every suggestion. They objected to a prolongation of the grant to Clevland, 'that he might complete the civilization of those districts in which he has made a most wonderful progress'. Save for Belli and one other, every dependant of his own was 'in absolute indigence'. He still believed in Wheler's affection, but Wheler had no confidence in himself. Stables he judged 'an honourable and well-meaning man', though disposed to jobs for his friends, but 'his mind has been tainted'. He sat 'sulky and silent' in Council, disclaiming personal offence when Hastings remonstrated, but talking of the Company's stress on economy.

Reviewing them all, he had no doubt who moved these 'puppets'. It was Macpherson, to whom all this year he continued to sign 'affectionately yours'. Even in these first letters, he wrote 'the language of false friendship is dangerous and imposing', hinting that Macpherson would not touch the Carnatic problem because of his own guilty past. Before the year ended, he looked back at a ghost of friendship. He had all too lightly dismissed his 'ray of inspiration', which once had flickered on 'the naked character of Macpherson, with his borrowed robes lying by him'. 'All sweetness', with 'an elegant and unceasing flow of words', this false giant blew Stables 'into a continual tumour', while both together intimidated Wheler. 'He loves the crooked better than the straight path'; let Scott watch for his 'strokes' in his homeward letters.

After six weeks of hesitation he made his decision, when he failed to carry Council with him over suspending Macartney. In the Clavering and Francis days, he told Scott, he had neither power nor responsibility, but 'I am now without power — and am alone responsible': 'the veriest stock with a human form — will perform more service to the Company, with proper powers and confidence reposed in him, than I can do with neither'. On March the 20th, he addressed his honourable masters. After refuting their version of Chait Sing, he asked them to reflect on what must follow from 'your proclaimed indisposition against the first executive member of your first government', as proved once more by the reappointment of Bristow and Fowke. To think also on what might have happened, if their declaration in favour of Chait Sing, 'the murderer of your servants and soldiers, and the rebel of your authority', had arrived two months earlier, before the Mahratta peace. Of that peace he must claim to be 'the sole instrument', having opposed 'firmness and defiance' to a hundred obstacles. 'Pardon me, honourable Sirs, this digressive exultation.' 'That pride is the source of my zeal so frequently exerted in your support, and never more happily than in those instances in which I have departed from the prescribed and beaten path of action and assumed a responsibility which has too frequently drawn on me the most pointed effects of your displeasure.'

Then he looked back to the eleven years he had held 'the first nominal charge'. 'You, honourable Sirs, can attest the patience and temper with which I have submitted to all the indignities which have been heaped upon me.' He had persevered, 'conscious that I possessed in my integrity and in the advantage of local knowledge, those means of discharging the functions of it with credit to myself and with advantage to my employers, which might be wanting in more splendid talents'; hoping, too, that either his 'long sufferance' or the 'rotation of time' might bring a remedy. But now the case was different. While his government was resisting the greatest powers of Europe and India, 'you annihilated the influence of its executive member. . . . You virtually called on his associates to withdraw their support from him, and they have withdrawn it; but you have substituted no other instrument of rule in his stead.' So 'the season for contention is past': but for the effects on Scindia and the probable resignation of Coote, he would have asked to be relieved at once. He asked them, therefore, to obtain the early nomination of his successor; though if orders passed for restoring Chait Sing, he would resign immediately. Alternatively, if 'the acts of which I complain' were revoked and their confidence demonstrated, he would continue till India was at peace, or till they allowed him to resign. Simultaneously he began the necessary private arrangements. He would leave India, he told Woodman, the following January, while his attorneys were to call in some of his moneys in England, now out on mortgage.

Life at Calcutta pursued the familiar tenor of its way. They rose at gun-fire for their ride, and at evening drove gigs and high phaetons round the Course, or out to Alipur. They had their music, Mr. Playdell's fine voice was much in request for 'Let me approach my sleeping love', and while the harpsichord thrummed there were senior corners for whist. Richardson's novels and Sterne were all the vogue. The Governor seemed unmoved, so Shore wrote, by the dangers surrounding him, but their home letters told them that the House of Commons was on the warpath, and that the day of high profits was nearing dusk. Young Fowke at Benares heard from an old uncle, 'put some thousands pounds of diamonds in your pockets, and come away'. The learned and amiable Sir William Jones came to reinforce the Supreme Court. Zoffany too appeared, and was painting Marian, with her hair more than ever flowing. A ghost of Clive's day, old General Carnac, lately so bad a councillor at Bombay, came to stay with Stables, once his aide de camp. But public life was *triste* and bitter.

For though the Mahratta peace was finished and the Nizam

quiet, two tragedies in April reminded them how very much alive was the Carnatic war. Coote reached Madras, but only to die as he was brought ashore. On the other coast, the impulsive General Mathews was taken by Tippu in a net at Bednore. But the Lord Macartney was in his glory. Confident that Hastings could not survive the Commons' vote, he was hugging news from his wife that the Duke of Portland thought he was the man to succeed. He was in touch with both Edmund and William Burke. And he was good enough to assure Stables that he would be retained in the new dispensation, though Hastings and Wheler would be recalled.

Publicly he was all arrogant defiance. Coote's eyes were sealed in death before he could read a last insulting message. They prolonged the quarrel with his successor, General Stuart, whose claim to be present at the Select Committee was supported by Bengal, but who was arrested by Macartney and sent home. As for their conduct of war, it went from bad to worse. Fighting ceased with the French in June; Tippu's forces were locked up the whole summer besieging Mangalore, where a gallant Colonel Campbell was holding out with a few hundred Highlanders and three battalions of sepoys. John Sulivan, resident in Tanjore and a man of spirit, had high hopes that a force formed under Fullarton in Coimbatore would soon drive into Tippu's home territories. But Macartney intervened. Tying himself to the literal terms of the Peace of Versailles, without consent of Bengal he arranged a cessation of arms, vetoed Fullarton's advance, and sent off peace commissioners. Meanwhile, evading the armistice, Tippu contrived to starve out Mangalore by January 1784. This, said Bengal, was 'unwarrantable and disgraceful management'. Tippu had 'dictated the terms of a treaty', in a separate negotiation which infringed our agreement with the Mahrattas. Their hand was so far forced that they must authorize Madras to treat for an armistice, but they expressly forbade them to sign a separate peace.

Since Coote's death, Richard Sulivan reported, the Nabob was cowed, and Macartney entirely refused to hear of cancelling the assignment. His reply of May, in 250 pages, dwelt with 'fatiguing repetition', said Hastings, on the Directors' orders, and proudly welcomed the threat of suspension. Wearily Hastings again urged his colleagues not to temporize, not liking, 'in the words of my old and wise friend Dupré, to show my teeth without the power of biting'. When their second order for restoration was disregarded, he definitely moved for suspension, but they would not follow him, referring the whole controversy home. In short, as he told Scott, 'seeing a standing committee of the House of Commons on the watch for matter of crimination against us all, — a powerful party covetous of our places, a weak administration courting support from all quarters, — they do not choose to add to the number of their enemies the connections of Lord Macartney'.

If Macartney's defiance thus disintegrated Hastings' Council, at the same time his own violent doings in the North were coming home to roost. He had already thrown into prison the Naib whom he had installed at Benares. Chait Sing was reported as in touch with Oudh *zemindars*, and as working for restoration through Francis Fowke. And Oudh was more distressful than ever. The air of Calcutta was hot with the charges laid against Middleton and Johnson, and their recriminations in defence. At Macpherson's instigation the Governor had restored Bristow, counting on his gratitude, but Bristow was writing resentfully to Francis that he was counteracted and spied upon by the Governor's personal agent, Palmer, and how Wheler was deceived by 'the sophistry of the great man'. As regards the Begums, he said that force could do no more, and released the eunuchs; then he acted on the razor-edged path of Hastings' instructions, which bade him treat the Vizier with due respect but to reduce his minister, Hyder Beg, to obedience and to secure severe punishment, even of death, for the rebel *zemindars*. Lands must be taken over to maintain the punctual payment of our brigade, courts of justice, competent revenue officials, control of accounts by the resident, all must be organized.

All the later history of our subsidy treaties was to show the vanity of Hastings' picture, of a puppet ruler who was somehow to retain the dignity of an allied sovereign. Least of all was it possible with a creature like Asof-ud-Daulah, who kept fifty barbers and 4000 gardeners, whose palace purlieus housed 1200 elephants and cagefuls of pigeons, fighting cocks, and snakes, but whose troops and servants must scramble for their pay. To reconcile the hard swearing between Bristow and Hyder Beg is beyond possibility, or that between Bristow and Palmer. Of Rohilkund, for instance, Bristow said it was a desolation, while

Palmer praised its rich cultivated fields, at least in Fyzullah Khan's Rampur. What is certain is that Bristow had not been back at Lucknow five months before complaints streamed in from the Vizier and his minister, and that Palmer painted the whole province as in 'universal dread', and fleeced to make fortunes 'for Bristow and his friends'. All of which was in some degree borne out by Colonel Martin, the remarkable Frenchman in the Vizier's service.

It was in these months that Hastings wrote to Scott that his last year's illness had left its mark, 'I have not now that collected firmness of mind which I once possessed'. We feel it in these dealings with Oudh. His impulses were violent, moved by his latest information, or by evidence telling in the direction he desired. In July he asked for Bristow's instant recall, without hearing his defence, suggesting further the withdrawal of the residency entirely; though 'if ever there were a period', as Wheler justly noted, when this step meant 'peculiar hazard', it was now. In this his Board was solid against him. In truth, he was swallowing wholesale stories that Bristow was predicting the fall of his government, which he connected with 'the wounds which have been inflicted on my official influence'.

For even while the Bristow controversy flared up, his treatment of the Begums was called in question. They trusted, the Directors said, 'for the honour of the British nation', that the resumption of their *jagirs* was justified in Indian eyes. They thought it probable that their resistance arose 'entirely from motives of self-defence': they hinted, rather than ordered, a further enquiry. Wheler and Stables voted for more reports from Middleton and Bristow, but Macpherson's vote helped Hastings to defeat the motion. The Governor was insistent that it would only revive the feud between mother and son; let them appeal if they would, 'they will not need to be prompted'. Ending with words which he was often to hear reverberating round Westminster Hall, 'the majesty of justice ought to be approached with solicitation, not descend to provoke, — much less to debase itself by the suggestion of wrongs'. The Directors' letter, he wrote, was 'insolent'; 'are these men the rulers of India?' Bitterly he recommended a restoration of Munny Begum's pension, 'the Directors are in the habit of taking the part of oppressed Begums, and she might come in for her share'.

He was suffocating in this air of distrust and impotence, nor was his suspicion baseless. Francis' letters came to Wheler, to Hay, secretary to government, and of course to Bristow. If Wheler were amenable, he too had his limits; nothing, for example, could induce him to send Markham back to Benares. Stables, who laid bets on Hastings' recall over his wine, supplied Bristow with the records of Council and, if his word can be trusted, Macpherson was advising Governor Johnstone to get the dismissal put through. Hastings still had hopes of recognition from Shelburne, even suggesting to Impey that he might be allowed to have a *jagir*, though on lines more modest than Clive's. And sometimes he attempted to fortify his defences, thus proposing to Shelburne the choice of David Anderson as next governor of Bombay, as a guarantee for Mahratta goodwill. But Macpherson was inexorable, overflowing with patronage requests for various Macphersons, Cummings, and Macleods.

In October he suddenly reached his resolution. 'I have held a court of conscience in my own breast', he would not stay with these men any longer. Yet Macpherson would drive the Vizier to desperation. 'I would meet poverty, death, or even popular infamy', he wrote to Palmer, 'rather than give my sanction to the acts in which Mr. Bristow is abetted by others.' If only he could succeed in Oudh, 'I shall close my service with glory, and leave a lasting good name behind me', despite 'the inventive malice of my countrymen'. Then there was the wretched Carnatic Nabob, who looked to him as his last refuge. 'In honour', in duty, he would stay until the Directors answered his letter, or till his successor was appointed. But not, on any consideration, beyond the sailing season of 1784–85.

But Marian must go. Her constitution 'visibly declines'. She felt it herself, had said of another woman 'she stayed a year too long', and the doctors agreed. He would have to endure alone, the double expense would cripple him, and as everyone knew he could not live without her long, that would weaken his influence. But though his heart protested, his head yielded to his friends' opinion and Marian's depression. So he asked John Woodman to find her a good furnished house; 'she prefers Portman Square'.

CHAPTER XXIV

The End in India: 1784-85

AGED 52

CAPTAIN COWPER of the *Atlas* Indiaman, a fine seaman, held the view that a sailor must live. After some argument he accepted £5000 to give Mrs. Hastings both the state cabin and the round-house; her faithful Mary Motte was to have the chief officer's cabin, for which the Governor gave another £1000, her hapless husband being bankrupt. An aide de camp was to go as far as St. Helena; Markham would be on board, besides Augustus Clevland, whose life could only be saved by a sea voyage. Though the thrifty Marian left some jewels to be sold in India, the ship's hold bulged with her treasures; ivory furniture, a silver-plated bedstead, thirteen gallons of rose water, ninety squirrel-skins, a tortoise-shell dressing-case, and golden cloth trousers, over all of which His Majesty's Customs later on held serious debate.

They had their last evening together, his diary notes, 'at home', and on January the 2nd went down the river in their budgerow, transferring fifty miles down to a Company pinnace where tidal water began at Kalpi. On the evening of the 6th they boarded the *Atlas* at Kedgeree, and here on the early morning of the 10th they parted; Warren 'gazing back', as he told her later, 'with fondness and with despair on all the wealth that my soul ever sought to amass'. By the night of the 12th he was back in Calcutta, from which he escaped whenever he could to Alipur, where kind Lady D'Oyley and her children relieved his loneliness. Perpetual headache and heavy colds plagued him. Only at the end of the month do we find him at the theatre, and giving many sittings to Zoffany.

While he waited for the return of the pilot-boat with the last news, and arranged for messages to overtake Marian at St.

Helena, he began to clear his decks. He advertised for sale both his Alipur property and his land up-stream at Rishera, near Danish Serampur, and sold all his mares except those with colts at foot. Work kept him from despair, he gave up his midday siesta to make sure of sleep at night, but though he told Scott he did not repent, in fact he repented most bitterly. His first letters to Marian are demoralized, 'peevish, desponding, and unmanly', by his own account. Looking from his bed at Zoffany's portrait of her, he groaned at his folly; she could easily have gone up-country, and kept her health till they could sail together, without these estranging leagues of sea.

'I come home to a solitude, — no Marian to infuse into my heart the fullness of content'; no more 'the look of benevolence unspeakable, the sweet music of her tongue'. Fear for her 'tender frame' harried him, deepened by the pilot-boat's return with poor Clevland's dead body, and reports of heavy weather. His soul fought like a madman's to keep her presence, and found it 'torment'. 'As I lay upon my bed, — I felt a sensation like the fingers of your hand gently moving over my face and neck', stretched out his arms, and held a void. When each day's work was done, 'I have found out a method to see and converse with you whenever I sleep'. But the vision did not always look on him kindly. 'You had returned to me from sea, and looked pale and dejected', 'you constantly appear to turn from me with indifference'. He racked himself with memories of any trivial petulance he had shown, and much more with a fixed obsession, the fear lest his sickly health in the past year had injured 'the delicacy of your affection'. Pitifully he begged her to think of his constant attention, how his 'caresses' had helped her in illness, or how often he had run up to her room between business. But how could she love a husband so 'healthless and pennyless', with a mind 'soured perhaps with long, long, and unabated vexation'? 'How hard . . . the real happiness of my past life appears as a dream. . . . Adieu, my beloved. When shall I hear from you, and how do I know but that every day that passes till then will be but so many saved from a life of irretrievable misery?'

So the letters proceed, from his budgerow, from Alipur, sweltering days on the march, or the palaces of Lucknow, and all breathing the same adoration. 'I never cease to think of you, nor my soul to bless you . . . I love you to the extremity of passion, and live only in the hope of regaining the possession of my adored Marian. . . . O ever love me, for no man ever merited by love a larger return of it than I do.'

Resolved to live to rejoin her, he watched minutely any feverish symptom, kept early hours, and gave up wine. But work and a vision of fame sustained him, a hope, like Ulysses before he saw his Penelope again, that

> something ere the end,
> Some work of noble note may yet be done,
> Not unbecoming men that strove with Gods.

Before Marian left he volunteered to go up to Lucknow, and though his Council rejected it, returned to the attack. He would take Anderson with him, whose overdue sick leave must wait, and could count on Palmer, to whom he wrote 'I wish to close my public life with one act that shall sweeten the moments of all my natural life to come, by saving a sovereign from oppression, a country from ruin, and the English faith and honour from infamy'. It would take him out of the malignant air of Calcutta, where they had no mercy on his weariness, and give him a chance of mending our relations with Delhi and the North. Once more he would see the ancient cities and sacred places, where he had served in youth and made his fame, — Murshidabad, Allahabad, and Benares — sailing the great rivers, *'fluminaque antiquos subterlabentia muros'*.

No doubt the last home news contributed. He knew by this time that Shelburne had fallen, giving place to the Fox-North coalition. Burke had proposed sending out a commission of enquiry, suggesting as its members the hated names of Macartney, William Burke, and Francis; Fox promised early legislation. Angrily Hastings repudiated North's bleatings of his esteem. 'I want not such friendship, nor shall I thank him for it. I thank only those who support me because they think me fit for my office.'

But he knew that his fair name was deeply involved in Oudh. He was 'personally aggrieved', he told Council, by Bristow's audacious appeal to his instructions. He himself had always treated the Vizier with the 'studied respect' and 'plain dealing' he had used with more formidable princes; not least with 'the acute apprehensions and quiet susceptibility of Mir Kasim'. No resident should go beyond 'advice and persuasion', and had we kept faith with Indian States, as we had not with Oudh, the Nizam, and the Carnatic, 'the British dominion might have by this time acquired the means of its extension, through a virtual submission to its authority, to every region of Hindustan and Deccan'. But 'they all dread the connection'.

Twice he put to Council the logical alternatives. Either let them frame new instructions for Bristow, allowing him to use openly the sovereign powers he had usurped, or else let them remove the residency, as the Vizier asked. At present all was chaotic, our troops half-starving, and our revenues despaired of, especially from the dreaded results of the famine which, after three years of drought, was killing many thousands all the way from Lahore to Bihar. Inch by inch he wore his colleagues down. In a joint minute they pointedly commended Bristow's conduct, yet agreed to withdraw the residency, though premising that, if it were restored, Bristow's rights must be preserved. It was agreed that the Governor-General must be 'specially answerable' for a measure that controverted their joint opinion.

Macpherson's absence through illness simplified the next stage, during January and February. Though Stables objected, Hastings told Impey, 'in his usual coarse and surly style', that the Governor should never leave the Presidency, Wheler was gradually weaned over. Hastings was thus given leave, with full powers, civil and military, in Oudh and Benares. Bristow was on his way down, leaving Lucknow without submitting his accounts, and even carrying off, so Palmer said, the carpets assigned to the residency. His last despatch sounded a Cassandra note, of the wound given to 'the cause of humanity', and made lengthy quotations from Hastings' earlier description of Hyder Beg, on Bristow's reading the villain of the piece.

Before he set sail on February the 17th, or at the first halting-place, there were several matters to dispose of. He signed that day a new codicil to his will, naming Larkins and Croftes and Thompson his executors in India. He wrote his fine epitaph to be carved on Clevland's monument at Bhagalpur, where he posted his protégé Chapman as successor. Richard Johnson, his Oudh offences forgiven, was sent to Hyderabad. He was pestered by

Wheler to let old Fowke visit his children at Benares, while Francis' friend Colonel Watson even pleaded for 'the infatuated and ill-advised Chait Sing'. But this last, Hastings answered, he would oppose 'even to death', and for the same reason would not have old Joseph near Benares. Whereupon Joseph told his son, rather needlessly, 'I shall not keep my temper much longer', predicting after Fox's India Bill that Hastings would be driven out of England, 'there will be no rest for the sole of his foot'. Perhaps it annoyed him to find his daughter Margaret sending this scoundrelly governor some Hindustani music, and his son Francis ordering a print of the Zoffany portrait.

There was another very awkward letter to be written, to the Directors. It was to say he was charging their *durbar* account with the sums he had spent in the interest of Brahmin and Moslem learning; a moving, but not a very wise letter. He admitted that his request was an afterthought. 'Improvident for myself, zealous for the honour of my country — I seldom permitted my prospects of futurity to enter into the views of my private concerns.' But now he was becoming infirm, and tired in mind. He made his claim to their justice, 'you have forbidden me to appeal to your generosity'. Better such small expenses by their Governor than 'a single example of a life spent in the accumulation of crores for your benefit, and doomed in its close to suffer the extremity of private want'.

As to his method of financing this claim, the Directors made no objection, but he was to hear much of it in after days. In the previous year, when the Company treasury was empty, his salary was heavily in arrears, so that he apparently received only one month's instalment in cash. He consequently borrowed three lacs from Nobkissen, for which he executed bonds, but as the money-lender asked him to take them as a gift, he kept the bonds in his own hands, pending decision. It was this money which he was now treating as a gift to the Company, asking the Directors to set it off against his expenditure on these good causes.

For the last time, what was left of the kindergarten gathered round him. Gouty Charles Croftes hurried to meet him at their old Sooksagur plantation. Anderson was political assistant, Palmer was to meet him, Halhed was back from England and would wait for him in Oudh. He took also Toone of his body-guard, Stephen Sulivan, and Scott's brother Jonathan, a learned

Orientalist and a much wiser person than John. Zoffany went too, for Indian princes were good patrons, and Dr. Balfour, surgeon at Chunar, to watch the Governor's health. On February the 19th his pinnace reached Sooksagur; then, after two days' rest, his budgerow was towed against the stream to Nuddea; on the same day, on by carriage, towards Bhagalpur, where he inspected Clevland's corps of hillmen; on the 28th a night journey by water to Patna, where his cousin Turner presented furs, useful on these cold nights, gifts from the Lama of Tibet: on March the 3rd he got to the Soan, and left Bengal next day. Reaching Benares on the 12th, by palanquin and elephant he went on into Oudh, and on the 27th settled at Lucknow.

Except for a political journal of 1773 at Benares, he never hitherto seems to have kept a diary. But now he began the series that only end with his death, beginning perhaps in the intensity of loneliness. This summer's has the stamp of fatigue, and perhaps of a too fast-coming old age. One page may have Wilkins' recipe for indelible ink, another the Vizier's for rare Indian dishes, a third some gloomy and undistinguished verses. He noted his headaches and his moods, 'fatigued, hot, and out of humour'. But the eye of the old Hastings, who loved India on the march, lighted up as he mounted his Arab in the morning, or jotted down 'a full moon', 'a fine country and well cultivated'.

For though he had crawled ashore hardly able to reach Croftes' bungalow, each day of colder air and each cooler night invigorated him, till he found himself stronger than for three years past. Often he set off at four in the morning, riding the first fifteen or twenty miles, bathed in the Ganges at Lucknow, hunted and killed an antelope on his way down. There was the joyful feeling of a welcome on Indian ground, that Councillors and parliaments could not take away. Welcome from Munny Begum and Mahomed Reza Khan, and great crowds, at Murshidabad; Ali Ibrahim Khan and Benaram Pandit to greet him at Buxar, whom 'I reckon among my first friends'; the Vizier's presents of horses and armour. The Emperor himself had lately styled him as 'Pillar of the Empire, Fortunate in War', while Marian's titles were engraved on a ruby seal, 'Imperial Governess, Elegance of the Age', with due allusion to the Queen of Sheba. He gloried in the fact that, for a week on end, his camp and the Vizier's were pitched next each other, or that his bodyguard was

315

quartered now in the royal palace, without trouble or disharmony.

Yet he had predicted it would be a desperate service, as he put even more emphatically to Marian. 'From a divided and hostile Council — to a country wasted by famine, — to a government loosened by a twelve months' distraction, — my superiors at home labouring to thwart and, if they can, determined to remove me; and all this as well known to the Indian world as our own.' The Fox ministry, he felt sure, would rouse an 'impolitic and mean clamour against war'. He lay sleepless in his palanquin one night over a Bombay packet of news, that Macartney was to succeed, with Francis and General Richard Smith in Council; 'a fine encouragement' with which to start on an 800-miles journey. He would not buy even Marian's presence at the price of 'such a mortification as to be thrust out of my seat by such fellows'.

Wheler wrote despairingly that Macpherson was returning to duty, and what with that and Stables' temper he could not answer for the consequences. But Hastings replied briskly, 'pay no regard to Select Committee reports. They are grown into universal reproach.' While to Bodham, the new governor of Bombay, he declared his confidence that Fox's India Bill would be rejected (as it had been), to be remembered only for 'impudence and profligacy unparalleled'. When he learned later his prophecy was right, he wrote of his fortune as being at its zenith. Why did his friends make suggestions equating him with those 'to whom I do not allow an equality'? He would refuse an annuity, 'or any title given me that shall place me on a level with his Lordship of Madras'. Such was his summer mood in this sea of glory.

So far as paper arrangements met the case, the specific work he had come for was done. He stayed at Lucknow five whole months. And though he found the Vizier weak as water, and 'in vile hands', he liked him; 'I do not know a better tempered or a better humoured man'. He was with him perpetually, even at one of Colonel Mordaunt's famous cock-fights. He would never threaten him or treat him as a vassal, but hope for the best. Hopes of the revenues hung on the rains; if they failed a third year running, nothing could save the country. As he came up, he crossed deep river-beds that now merely threw up clouds of dust. Lucknow was a 'dreary picture of drought and infertility', its streets full of dying skeletons; 'it pains me to go abroad, to hear the cries, and see such spectacles of human misery'. But in July the rains began, not to cease for nineteen days, and giving hope of the best harvest for years.

This made the whole odds. Bristow's misappropriations were referred to the Board. Some temporary payments of the troops' arrears were forthcoming; he was able to reduce the rate of exchange on Lucknow bills, from Bristow's 16 to 5½ per cent. Settlements for five years were made with responsible collectors, who, however, stipulated they would resign if the English returned. His presence seemed to evoke some real goodwill. At the Vizier's request he agreed to return their *jagirs* to the Begums, who made a contribution to the revenue; so did the injured Rohilla, Fyzullah Khan; a large loan came from the much-accused, and most powerful *zemindar*, Almas Ali Khan. He believed, in fact, he had secured a total liquidation of debt by the end of the year and, if things were left intact, solvency for the future.

Benares city was prospering under Ali Ibrahim Khan, in whose praise all united. But the country outside was devastated, the inhabitants in flight at the appearance of soldiers. He turned out the second Naib he had appointed, then thrust his predecessor once more into prison, and chose a third from the reigning family, recommending that the young Rajah's name be made prominent in business. He concluded with an unusual tribute, for him, to a Fowke, commending the resident's 'gentleness of manners' as a good omen for his collaboration with Ali Ibrahim Khan.

So all that personal prestige could do, and oaths and assurances, were accomplished. And little they came to. Within three years Cornwallis was reporting in the darkest colours on 'the Augean stables of Benares and Lucknow'.

Even so, he had to struggle with much tardy correspondence from Calcutta, and many 'flat and ungracious refusals'. Stables tried to block the new Benares regulations, in Fowke's interest. Hastings again, protesting against 'perpetuating or multiplying commands', proposed to withdraw Cumming's brigade from western Oudh; this also was voted down. A much sharper difference arose from May onwards on a graver issue, the final exploits in peace-making of Lord Macartney.

Hastings had made the treaty of Salbai his instrument to drive Tippu to peace, by the threat of combined British-Mahratta operations; as part also, he hoped, of a lasting diplomatic security, since the Mahrattas and the Nizam were planning to attack Mysore. But this ground was cut from under his feet by Directors' orders, received late in 1783, enjoining an immediate peace, seizing on which Macartney had hurried off his commissioners. Bengal assented to the negotiation : to stop half-way would defy the Directors, and let the world see their differences. But they warned him to respect the Mahratta treaty, and strongly objected to one clause he proposed, — that neither party should aid enemies of the other. Which might mean, for example, that if the Nizam were attacked by Tippu, the Company must remain neutral.

Very different were the terms of the treaty of Mangalore, as signed in March 1784. It was to be ratified by the other Presidencies within three months. The Nabob of the Carnatic was unmentioned. So, too, was the Mahratta peace. There was nothing repudiating an old Mysore claim on Trichinopoly. And the offending neutrality clause was incorporated. Too late, on hearing reports of the humiliating treatment of our commissioners, Hastings wrote recommending their recall; he was now confronted at distant Lucknow with a treaty which his colleagues, though with reluctance, had signed and returned to Madras. Loudly he deplored this exposure of 'the nakedness of our political system'. At his fierce protest against Madras disobedience and this violation of 'the faith of the nation', his Council added a declaratory clause, to safeguard the Nabob of the Carnatic. He wrote urgently to Scindia to reconcile him to terms which left the Mahrattas exposed to Tippu's resentment, and to acknowledge our obligation to the treaty of Salbai. But so the Carnatic peace was made, on terms affronting our allies, and in a grovelling attitude on the British side which two heavy wars of after-years had to bury in oblivion. His colleagues ignored his repeated advice to suspend Macartney, who cheerfully disregarded the Bengal orders on the declaratory clause.

He collided with them again in a much more dramatic and characteristic episode. Oudh was a vassal and neighbour of the Empire which, since Nadjif Khan's death in 1782, had fallen into sheer anarchy. Sikhs crowded in on Delhi, Rajput rebels on the west, Scindia's cavalry on the south. The weak impulsive Shah Allum was dragged hither and thither, between a Mogul, a

Persian, and a Mahratta faction, his soldiers fought for pay in the streets of the capital, assassination removed one claimant for power after another. Hastings had therefore commissioned Major James Browne who, after many obstructions, reached Delhi early this year of 1784; his mission was to be mainly one of explory, with an eye on agents from Mysore, though the Governor's instructions certainly smiled on the idea of sending up a British contingent. In fact, however, Browne, who seems to have been jealous of Anderson, sent back reports that the arch-danger was Scindia, who might master Delhi and thereafter menace Oudh. He threw himself into the anti-Mahratta group round the Emperor, cried for more British troops in the Doab, and even for military alliance with the Sikhs. Influenced, perhaps, by Wheler's entreaty that he should not dissipate the Oudh money in new adventures, Hastings' first reaction to Browne's reports was adverse. He admitted he had been in favour of action in 1782, but since then there had been several palace revolutions, and to embrace one faction might antagonize everyone else. Nor did he think that the Sikhs were an immediate danger. Most of all it would be lamentable to alienate Scindia, whose help for the Carnatic peace was vital, and whose own interests were linked to our alliance. But his letter had hardly gone when news came that Prince Jehandar Shah, heir-apparent to the Empire, was nearing Lucknow as a refugee.

Now for a last time shone, in the full northern sunlight, the ingredient of truth in Francis' comment that it was 'not in his nature to be quiet'. All one May day he followed the procession of welcome, riding behind the elephant that carried Prince and Vizier, watched his host present the peshcush of jewels and a silver palanquin. When first he met the Prince, penniless and abandoned, his pity was stirred; his sense of grandeur was moved, 'fallen as the House of Timur is, it is yet the relic of the most illustrious line of the Eastern world', he told his Council. As he listened to his story, of his dropping by a rope from the sixty-foot wall of Delhi Fort, his lying hidden in river-beds and cottages till dark, he thought him gentle, intelligent, and courageous. He took Zoffany to paint him, and after seeing him every day for months, the charm grew. Meantime, letters came from Delhi to say the Emperor desired his son's return, and with British assistance. What, then, must be done?

If the Prince was not to linger on at Lucknow as a pensioner, which would infallibly mean a breach with the Vizier, Hastings at first thought it best for the Company to offer him refuge. But Council jibbed at that, asking that he be sent back to Delhi 'with safety and credit', and forbade the Governor to commit the Company. Their letter crossed one of his own to Wheler, a prophetic letter, yet full of special pleading. 'I most ardently wish to close my service with some act that will reflect a credit on my nation.' Though he would not engage in new wars after their 'fatigues and bruises', he asked for 'power to dictate'. If the Mogul Empire fell, it might mean the rise of some new adventurer more dangerous to our safety, 'which subsists but loosely on the weakness of our neighbours, and on the illusion of popular opinion'. 'We shall be applauded at home if we take the generous side.' Very daringly he used his own act in depriving the Emperor of the Bengal tribute as an argument for helping him now; even more boldly, argued they had commissioned Major Browne 'for the express purpose of tendering our assistance'. To Admiral Hughes he wrote that, if he were given the tools, ways to help the Prince were 'easy and immediate'.

Perhaps only to Marian he showed all he felt about this last vision. Here was 'an opportunity of closing my government with an act that would have reflected a lasting honour on my reputation in India', and how could he abandon this 'illustrious youth' who at such hazard had come to ask his help? 'Your pride will feel for what mine must suffer in the impotence enforced on me.' But since he could not do what he wished, — to march on Delhi and 'set them at defiance', — he fell back on employing the friendship of Scindia. The Mahratta promised safe escort and security for getting the Prince a *jagir*, while some of Hastings' bodyguard and five Oudh battalions would go with him as far as the frontier.

On August the 27th, in intense heat, the Governor left Lucknow, making his way to Benares over swollen rivers and flooded roads, in which some of his following were drowned and his budgerow wrecked. The Prince came with him, 'a painful incumbrance', for he wanted to come on to Calcutta, which would never do. But he lavished attention on him, even to provision of his favourite tea, while he still tried to conjure up means of helping him. In November the reigning villain at Delhi, Afrasiab Khan, perished in his turn by assassination, which made Scindia hesitate to install this able heir-apparent. Hastings' resilience was equal to this. Since his Council would not remove Cumming's Cawnpore detachment, let money be saved by lending it to the Prince for service against the Sikhs, whom he now described, in contradiction to his view in April, as a potential threat to British India. In prophetic language he foresaw how 'one man of superior capacity and enterprise, aided by the spirit of religious enthusiam', might found a new dominion on the ruins of the Empire. They could deride this as 'effusions of a wild imagination'. 'But I trust to time, and that not distant, for verifying my prediction, if this people is permitted to grow into maturity without interruption.'

Far off, on the evening she reached London this July, Marian read the letter written as he set off on this northern journey, 'I live only in my love for you, and in my hopes of being reunited to you, never to part again'. But for him what a silence over the ocean! In the palace at Lucknow he felt 'another season would end me'. Each night 'images of terror', 'dreams of death' mingled with Marian, and it was through this racked mind that he abruptly projected, or withdrew, his political decisions. It was only on September the 30th, at Benares, that he received her first letter from St. Helena, mentioning her perfect health. At once he wrote 'the fixed gloom' was gone, he felt sure he was 'once more destined to happiness'. There was a still greater joy to come. On October the 7th Captain Phipps arrived, with a packet to be delivered only into his own hand. It held much more than Marian's wishes for curtains for her ivory bed, and for six peacocks; news that made him 'the happiest man living', and drove forward the decision he had pondered for months, whether to go or to stay.

It was that Marian was going to bear him a child. Perhaps after seven years' marriage he had given up hope, and he could not contain his happiness. Marian begged him not to set his heart on it; 'indeed, but I do, and so peremptorily that it will be almost broken if I am disappointed'. He refused to believe he had been raised 'above the heights of mortality, to be dashed to the ground with a severer fall'. As he went down-stream with the 'world of friends' who met him at Bhagalpur, Chapmans and Touchets, Powneys and Blairs, he shared his joy. Lady Jones writes to Margaret Fowke, 'he seemed so delighted with the idea of an heir'. With his doctor Clement Francis he conned over every promising symptom and auspicious date, for this 'pledge of my Marian's dear love'; 'let me but follow, and be once more in possession of my heart's treasure'.

While Prince and Vizier badgered him, and his heart was far away with Marian, he wrote at Benares the introduction which Wilkins asked, of 'his preceptor and patron', to his translation of the Sanskrit philosophical masterpiece, the Bhagavad-Gita. In this Hastings once more depicted the India in which he gloried; its character as shown in writings that would live, 'when the British dominion in India has long ceased to exist, and when the sources which it once yielded of wealth and power are lost to remembrance'.

On October the 20th his stay at Benares was cut short by the news of Wheler's death, which he felt sincerely, and which furthermore left him at the mercy of a hostile majority. He finished in two days what he had planned for ten, and took farewell of the Prince, on whom he found only one blot, his attachment to 'an ugly old cat of a woman' he had got entangled with at Lucknow. Then he drove off with Halhed, who was going home as the Vizier's agent. So on by river to Buxar and Bhagalpur; at midnight on the 27th, under a full moon, he looked on 'the memorable rocks of Colgong', scene of Marian's danger two years back, and reached Calcutta on November the 4th, after eight and a half months away. He went back to Marian's house in Hastings Street, and found all his bad symptoms returning, fever, dejection, and swollen ankles. Schemes for economies, the problems of the North, and Lord Macartney, tied him tightly to Council, yet he got relief with his week-ends at Alipur. His diary records that he saw *Hamlet* and *King Lear* at the theatre before Christmas, even went to Mrs. Hyde's ball, though he escaped before supper. For his head ached with thinking, and re-thinking, over one question.

They went on in Council 'pretty cordially', he told Scott, though Macpherson tried to shield Bristow, but he had never meant to stay with such men or such puny powers. His line to the Directors had been quite explicit, his pledge to Marian equally so, that he would follow within the year. Certainly nothing from the Directors indicated a change of heart. Their last letter called his account of the presents he had taken, and carried to their credit, 'unintelligible', and asked explanation of his secrecy and ways of payment: which he did not mean to answer hurriedly. He had gone north vowing to Marian his decision was 'fixed and unalterable'. But by August we detect a change: 'my whole life has been a sacrifice of my private ease and interests to my public duty'; a call might come with 'the force of an obligation'. For one thing, having given his word to the Vizier, he must swear his colleagues to abide by his Oudh settlement, and if they refused 'I must stay, though Death should await me'.

As the last news from home came in, he brooded, balanced, and wondered. By his side Halhed echoed what Scott was writing, that all England entreated him to stay; he heard that Pitt had won a triumphant election, and that his India Bill would give the powers he desired. But when Scott wrote, 'Lords Temple and Thurlow say I *must* come into Parliament', he thought this nonsense, and much more so the idea he should succeed to Scott's seat, 'a condition unsuited to my talents'. He feared Scott was a dupe. The proprietors, of course, had voted him their thanks for restoring peace, but they had thanked Macpherson and Stables too, 'now my greatest enemies'. And if they wished him to stay, 'why am I not told so by authority?' If they took him as just 'a wedge to keep the old frame together till they can make a new one, I do not choose to be a wedge'. Nor could he collect any satisfaction from Pitt's speeches. He had defended the Company ably enough, but with 'a profound silence' as to Fox's onslaught on the Governor. It was easy enough for the authorities to act. All the Directors had to do was to order Council 'to yield me the lead, with the responsibility, in all points in which I shall think it of importance sufficient to assume both'. Let them issue this order, and 'require me, in virtue of it, to remain . . . I shall deem myself bound'. In any event this 'state of suspension', after thirteen years, must end. He might be home in time to assist in framing a plan for our Indian possessions, 'which may render them more profitable and lasting, or in preventing some plan that may accelerate their ruin'. As he closed this letter in September he received the blissful news of Marian's hopes: his postscript said he would hasten to Calcutta, and leave, if he could, by the end of the year.

When he got there he ordered the *Berrington* Indiaman to be held up for him, but soon added that his last postscript had been written 'when I was incapable of thinking like a reasonable being'. He would await the Directors' next packet for a final decision. On December the 5th he wrote to Marian of the supreme happiness which must have come by now; 'I will believe that I am now a blessed being, and most fervently pray that I may die, though instantly, in that belief if the reverse of this has actually come to pass'. Surely her arrival in England would save him from being used as 'the instrument of their own political jobs'. And perhaps Providence had parted them so as to confirm his resolution, 'which required a strong attraction to overcome that which I did feel to my present station'. But on the 11th he swung back again. Taking advice from (of all people) the old jobbing sea-captain, Joseph Price, he sent Scott a six-page letter to be handed to Pitt.

He opened on his grandest note. 'It is long since I have presumed to address the Minister of the British Empire. I have not often seen its measures conducted on the unmixed principles of National Policy.' Having paid that tribute, he defended the character of his government, and looked back at the evil days that were passed : the harm done by patronage, by fluctuating majorities in Council, and the Directors' 'fatal error', — to degrade the head of their government, 'while its success always, and its existence sometimes, has hung by a slender thread on his exertions'. But 'it has been one maxim of my conduct (pardon the apparent boast, but necessary allusion) to do what I knew was requisite to the public safety, though I shall doom my own life to legal forfeiture, or my name to infamy'. His covering note to Scott said he believed Pitt was 'both a man of virtue and of business . . . would to God that I were in England ! I would give to such a man my labour with pleasure, without office or reward, or desire for either.'

India still poured in on him its dangers, doubts, and desires. Palmer's letters showed the cracks already wrecking his Oudh settlement. Admiral Hughes ('Ned Durbar' as coarse Hicky had called him) wrote commending the Carnatic Nabob, 'I pity the good old man's situation'. From Hyderabad, Richard Johnson told how Tippu was already attacking the Nizam's southern border, and held out a dream that the Nizam might take over the Carnatic and pay off the Nabob's debts. Colonel Pearse, as usual, begged him to protect his fortune from 'the long list of Macs ready to devour it'. And he was able to reassure Francis Fowke that the Board would remit some duty on his opium cargoes. Only his old military secretary, Ironside, hinted that, though Hastings' friends had assisted Pitt into power, he would prefer to wait and see whether, 'after getting safely on board, they do not kick away the accommodation ladder'. But late on December the 20th, on getting home from the theatre and *King Lear*, he found letters from Marian and Scott, of August the 3rd, and the latest English newspapers.

He tore open Marian's letter. His hopes of an heir were gone. 'I could not go to bed but sat reading it till past two . . . I fear my disappointment on the one subject equalled my joy for your safety. . . . I have since thought only on the good, and I thank God for it.' They should keep him no longer, there were 'incontestable proofs' of Pitt's hostility. Unless he got countervailing orders by January the 31st, he would embark; once Macpherson agreed to uphold the new status in Oudh, 'it is determined absolutely, absolutely'. Another year would mean he would come back 'like Ulysses an old man, and a beggar, to my Penelope'. And 'yet, my Marian, forgive me. I do not feel the joy which I ought, I am too much attached to my public character and its relations, and dread the ruin which I see impending over them.' As for Scott, he added in his next letter, he was astonished he could support Pitt's measure; 'an Act more injurious to his fellow-servants, to my character and authority, to the Company . . . and to the national honour, could not have been devised, though fifty Burkes, Foxes, and Francises had clubbed to invent one'.

He cancelled a fierce draft to the culprit himself; 'its substance is mortality, — how could you, my friend, give your support to it ? — I would not, for any honours that the King could bestow, stay to be the instrument of the vengeance that hangs over the service'. In the letter he let go he traced, paragraph by paragraph, the condemnation of the Company in Pitt's speech, breaking out 'what devil has Mr. Pitt dressed for his exemplar, and clothed with such damnable attributes of ambition, spirit of conquest, thirst of blood, — and am I this character?' How heartily he repented now of his letter, which Pitt would doubtless read as Francis would, 'it will be sneeringly called a fine poetical fiction'; he would trust no mind 'capable of using such insidious means to taint an innocent character with such a mass of infamy'.

He would wait, then, till the end of January, but every step showed he felt the end had come. Having ordered the lading of the *Berrington* to be hastened, on New Year's Day he wrote, and rewrote, a last letter to the Directors. Perhaps he kept back his first version as revealing his heart too openly; had he kept his health, it said, this parting would have been 'the stroke of death upon my feelings'. Or it may be he felt he laid himself too open to his critics. For it also argued that a Council of equals called for 'a disinterested virtue, which is not the common lot of humanity'; as it was, he had received both 'unmerited censure and unmerited commendation'. What he actually despatched was more prosaic. Authentic advice from home, and the impossibility of his receiving further orders till the next sailing season, had determined him. At least his departure would end an inefficient government, 'disgraceful to the national character'. But his conclusion was worthy of him. 'I do not part from it with indifference. I owe to my ever honoured employers the service of my life. . . . Such professions are indeed easily made, and I know not how mine can ever be put to the test. But my conscience both avows them and prompts me to declare, that no man ever served them with a zeal superior to my own, or perhaps equal to it.'

On January the 13th his Council gave a solemn pledge to leave his five-year plan with the Vizier 'unchanged and unmolested'; which he asked them to ratify, even if they did not approve, as 'the last test which I shall exact from the Board of that spirit and mutual conciliation which no difference of opinion has yet been able wholly to extinguish'. His last ceremonial was on the 25th, a review of the survivors of Pearse's force, just home at last from the Carnatic, to whom he distributed medals and standards, dining afterwards with 107 officers.

He did his best to make sure that his own supporters should not suffer by his going. He counted on Palmer being left at Lucknow. In the Revenue department he left a challenging minute in favour of Gunga Govind Sing; he asked Fowke at Benares to allow his friend, Biseram Pandit, to fly a flag at the headquarters of his *jagir*. Larkins would attend to the charities going back so many years; the pensions to Madame Vernet and to humbler people, the widow of John his coachman, and Peggy, his first wife's *ayah*. There were less pleasant people to deal with. A loan must be repaid to Gopal Das, banker of Lucknow. Nobkissen was asking return of the bonds for £30,000 which Hastings had lately accounted for to the Directors as a gift, and for which Thompson was vainly searching in the confusion of his papers. And there was a letter from Macartney, declining to recede from his views on 'these unpleasant subjects' of the assignment and the Peace, but hoping they could distinguish public from private differences. These might wait a little longer.

On February the 1st he held his last Council at which, not trusting his voice to read, he minuted a last tribute to the service. Having been able to share in the executive duties of every department, he said he felt entitled to judge its character; 'which I pronounce to be eminently marked with a liberality of sentiment, — a disdain of sordid emolument, with a spirit of assiduity, and the consequent expertness in business exceeding, I dare venture to affirm, the habits of any community under the British Empire'.

That done, he handed over the keys of the treasury and the Fort, and then, having listened to an address from the European inhabitants, went aboard his budgerow. On the 3rd, Hay and some fifty other friends and subordinates gave him a farewell dinner at the Powder Mills, eight miles down the river; he left them at four-thirty 'with benevolent heart', Wilkins wrote, 'too big for utterances, — there never was a man in private life so universally beloved'. Of the faithful, David Anderson, Popham, Toone, Dr. Francis, were to be fellow-passengers; so was John Shore, of whom he had made something like a convert. His young cousin Samuel Turner, Thompson, and Larkins, came down to Saugor Island to see him off. There he boarded the *Berrington*, which sailed on the 7th, losing sight of Bengal early that afternoon. His diary has little more that day, except 'Mrs. Hastings' birthday'.

He was far out at sea when Thompson noted, with fury, that his furniture had been bundled off to the old Court House, and that Government House was swarming with Macpherson's young men 'as if they had been born there'. Joseph Fowke wrote complacently that Macpherson's 'Prime Minister' was Peter Moore, client of Francis and friend of Sheridan, while plenty of other folk were abandoning the ship that had lost its captain.

CHAPTER XXV

From One Exile to Another: 1785-86

AGED 52-53

THE *Berrington*, a fast sailer, left the Hugli on February the 7th, stopped six days at St. Helena, and anchored at Plymouth on June the 13th. Four months, during which the three dimensions within which this life had moved, — England, India, and the sea — touch and blend and drift apart.

Behind him at Calcutta, the Hastings epoch was fast dissolving. The auction that ends every Anglo-Indian home dispersed his plate and glass, china-cupboards and card-tables, and the books he had no room or taste for now; Radical Mrs. Macaulay's *History of England*, Lord Lyttelton on Henry II, Robertson's *America*, Bolingbroke's tracts, Johnson's *Lives of the Poets*, *Elements of Heraldry*, Wharton's *English Poetry*, a Lucretius and a Demosthenes, charts and voyages of Australia and the Mississippi. Zoffany's picture of Marian was being packed for shipment; a copy of his portrait of the Governor was sent to Indian friends at Benares. The Alipur estate was sold in lots, Turner and Thompson jointly buying the new house on which he had lavished such costly detail. Meantime Macpherson was brandishing measures of retrenchment, though the axe seemed to fall first on Hastings' nominees; Johnson being promptly recalled from Hyderabad, and Browne from Delhi. Thompson and Palmer wrote angrily of traitors and apostates, even of Cantoo as an 'old avaricious hypocrite'. The rascals Nobkissen and Sudder-ud-Din were trying to ruin Gunga Govind Sing by law suits. And in June Lord Macartney visited Calcutta. Since his assignment had been cancelled by the Directors, he would not, at least till he had been home, accept the Governor-Generalship they offered him. But he spent some hours examining the Bengal records.

Far ahead, whither the ship was pointing, lay the life of Marian and England, of which many details, passing like birds in the night, were still travelling outward, too late to catch him. He knew that his sister Anne had met Marian at Portsmouth, all the church bells ringing a welcome, and of the comfortable house awaiting her in South Street, looking over Hyde Park, complete with servants and a coach with the Hastings arms. Had he received a last batch of news on the wing, he would have heard from Impey that he had never seen Marian in higher spirits. She had twice been to Court and most graciously received, conveying their gifts of a state bed to the Queen, and Arab horses for the King. The Directors handsomely paid up her customs duties. She drew out £2000 in her first four months at home, was seen at Brighton and Bath, and at Tunbridge Wells, where old Lord Mansfield squired her about, and escorted her to Penshurst. Mrs. Motte chaffed him on the conquest she had made of Thurlow, the surly Chancellor. In December she had rented Lord Vere's house in St. James' Place, where she soon gave a dance for Warren's friends. In fact Marian, with her diamonds and thick unpowdered hair and gorgeous dresses, had become a public figure, for whom the great Tory ladies, Bathurst and Weymouth, opened their houses. There was some debate at Windsor if the Queen had not made a mistake in receiving this *divorcée*, but her old patron Madame Schwellenburg spoke up for her, and so did the little lady-in-waiting, Fanny Burney — though she found Marian rather noisy — who explained that in Germany incompatibility was proper ground for divorce. But the *Morning Herald* and *Daily Advertiser* had got their knife into her. They were publishing the satires, later collected in the *Rolliad*, which made terrible fun of Major Scott and the Bengal squad.

> For sniff! rich odours scent the sphere:
> 'Tis Mrs. Hastings' self brings up the rear.
> Gods! how her diamonds flock
> On each unpowdered lock.
>
> Illustrious dame, on either ear
> The Munny Begum's spoils appear.

Family and Cotswold news was on the water too. Rough uncle Thomas Warren was dead at last, and Woodman had gone to inspect the little holding he had left to his nephew. He was keeping his eyes open still for the house of Warren's dreams. And as it chanced, a few acres at Daylesford came into the market, which were immediately snapped up by Marian's order.

As to the last public news, Pitt's Act was now law, with Dundas in real command of the new Board of Control; its secretary being Francis' former follower Boughton Rouse, who, the idiotic Scott wrote, 'is a good boy again, compared with what he was'. 'That reptile' Burke, he added, was silent; 'in truth he is a contemptible enemy, even with the assistance of Francis'. George Vansittart had been mentioned as a possible Governor-General, but that, after being declined by Cornwallis, was offered to Macartney. What the ministry would do for Hastings was unknown. Thurlow and Gower spoke warmly, saying he was the maker of the Cabinet; he must have a peerage, though it might be an Irish one, and 'Lord Daylesford' sounded the right style. Scott gathered that Dundas, though still critical of the Mahratta war, brought no charge against Hastings' integrity. In November Thurlow approached the Prime Minister, who thought the Commons' resolutions of 1782 a serious obstacle; Hastings had to be cleared of disobedience, profligate expenditure, and antagonizing the princes of India. Even Thurlow blamed his carelessness in accepting presents and allowing excessive salaries. But if that were all, he said, — mildly for him — 'why the devil don't they order them to be lessened?'

All this, to the latest he received, was cheering; and cheering, too, the *Berrington's* speed, — 'a clean and tight ship' — in sunny weather. When he wished, he had 'a society I loved'; if he went astern he looked at his own Arab, with the cows and goats he meant to acclimatize at home. Daily he noted any change of weather or sea-colouring, or the catching of a shark. He had goods in the hold, insured for £20,000: his only trouble was not finding aboard his bureau, holding many secret papers.

Though he felt languid and had some fever, he was often writing in the round-house. With some effort he concocted a civil answer to Lord Macartney. Had he continued in office, he said, he would have tried for a better understanding; as it was, in some circumstances advice, 'even with the most candid motives, is liable to the imputation of covert reproach'. What a relief, after that, to turn to the Gita and give a final polish to the foreword he had promised to Wilkins! And even better, to read his Horace, looking over a blue sunlit sea.

So he took the 16th ode of Book II, which sings of the rest that men pray for and so rarely achieve, turning it into an Anglo-Indian paraphrase, which he presented to Shore. Here 'the starved Mahratta' and 'hardier Sikh' did duty for Horace's Greeks and Medians, and Clive, robbed of 'his valour's well-earned meed', for the great Achilles. He dwelt on Elliot, cut off in his prime.

> An early death was Elliot's doom,
> I saw his op'ning virtues bloom,
> And manly sense unfold
> Too soon to fade! I bade the stone
> Record his name mid hordes unknown,
> Unknowing what it told.

And, last, on what he asked for himself:

> A state above the fear of want,
> Domestic love, Heaven's choicest grant,
> Health, leisure, peace, and ease.

But Horace's deepest line,

> Patriae quis exsul se quoque fugit?

warned him that change of sea and land promised no escape from himself and his destiny.

Most of his writing hours, however, were spent on his retrospect, the *Review of the State of Bengal*, which turned into a justification of the past thirteen years. He defended his resignation on hearing of Pitt's India Act, which was a death-blow to his hope that, given full powers, he might be the means of 'raising the British name'. He warned his countrymen not to suppose that, by his removal, they could 'retrace the perilous and wonderful paths', or 'redescend to the humble and undreaded character of trading adventurers'. Once more he threw back the charge that he was 'a man of ambition, — misled by projects of conquest'. He had inherited an India requiring years of peace: 'a tempest, or an earthquake, could not be more fatal to a builder whose walls were uncovered, and his unfinished columns trembling in the breeze, than the ravages or terrors of war would have been to me and to all my hopes'. Once more he dilated on the curse of patronage, and on the bloodless triumphs of Clevland and the salt revenue. Once more he avowed that 'if the British power in India yet holds a reprieve from ruin, it derives its preservation from causes which are independent of its constitution'. As 'the devoted victim of a party', he did not expect to convince them. Enough that he warned them that only a governor with full powers could ward off a catastrophe: 'assured, if successful, of my reward in the conscious applause of my own mind brightening the decline of my existence'.

On April the 15th he went ashore at St. Helena, ceremoniously received by the Governor. Here he met a good many Indian officers, among them that kindly Major Gilpin who had been in charge of the Begums and their eunuchs during the troubles. He spent his Sunday riding round the island, another day visited Longwood, and on the 21st the *Berrington* sailed on again. He landed at Plymouth on June the 13th, and spent his first night at Exeter. After two more nights on the road, in blazing hot weather, on the 16th he drove into London, to find that Marian was at Cheltenham. That day he passed in seeing his sister, announcing his arrival to the chairman, and calling on Thurlow and Mansfield in their courts at Westminster. Marian wrote, and he sent back her servant to say he would set out the next afternoon. On the 17th he had to see Pitt at three o'clock, called on Shelburne (now Lord Lansdowne), but managed to get off by seven; that night his carriage drew up alongside Marian's on Maidenhead Bridge. They came back to London the next day, and on Sunday the 19th he dined at Caen Wood with Mansfield, to meet Thurlow and Archbishop Markham. On the 20th, Burke rose in the Commons to give notice that he would move resolutions regarding 'a gentleman just returned from India'.

Ten days went in ceremony, welcome, and reunions. On June the 21st he dined with Barré, where he met Impey; next day, introduced by Sydney, the Home Secretary, to the King, who was graciousness itself; then, with Marian and Madame Schwellenburg, to see the Queen. Calls on the Directors, dinner with Sir Elijah at Parson's Green, calls on his old aunt and Lady Coote. On the 28th he attended the Directors to receive their formal thanks, which the chairman emphasized were unanimous, and to dine with them at the London Tavern, whence 'returned late, much inflamed'. Dundas called on him, asking him to

DAYLESFORD HOUSE

return to London if required. The Company consulted him on their military establishments, which gave him an opening to insist that Bombay and Madras must be made self-supporting, the paramount need being to increase their European troops in Bengal as 'the vital strength of your constitution'. He hoped that some of his fair fame would always remain, but his first letter to India said he felt a voice within, 'all this will expire in less than three months'. Even now he could ill bear the press attacks, especially when they dragged in Marian; 'a vile science', he thought, of men who 'get their bread by detraction'.

He was not well, pestered by rheumatism for which he tried electrical treatment without much profit; nor was Marian. So at the first moment they could they went to lodgings at Cheltenham, which made their base till September. Here they drank the waters, feeling rather the worse for it, which the doctors said was a capital sign. And here some of the loyal periodically joined them — Baber, Scott, Toone, Impey — and the musical Alderseys of still older days. Visits to the Woodmans at Ewell, Sykes at Basildon, or Caillaud at Aston, spaced out the dying summer.

But Cheltenham was a base for something better; for Daylesford, to acquire which he opened his campaign within a fortnight of landing. Three grandsons were alive of the John Knight who seventy-five years ago had bought it from Warren's great-grandfather. One at least was insane, two were unmarried; the third was seventy-eight years of age, with two daughters. The house was empty; indeed, its rebuilding had never been finished. Hastings approached the one hale and sane brother, twice refused to take his 'no' for an answer. He could hardly tear himself away; 'paced the great meadow' by the river. In August he stayed with Mr. Leigh, parson of Adelstrop, the next parish, and 'rode over all the grounds of Daylesford before breakfast'. Bills from his agent, Mr. Walford of Red Lion Square, crept up to £400. But before long the scheme broke down, Woodman being despatched to inspect other suitable Oxfordshire houses.

He did not neglect his humbler kinsfolk. At Stub Hill, Twyning, the little property left him by Uncle Thomas, he met his mother's sister, Mrs. Turner, mother of his faithful Samuel Turner of Tibet, and of William, a tallow chandler at Gloucester. Master William Gardiner, the half-Indian son of the cornet killed at Lehar, was being schooled at Croydon, whence bills duly reached Hastings for an Eton grammar, dancing lessons, and 'two panes of glass'. But this small exile died in 1789. A £30 bill went for a surgeon attending Mary Gardiner at Stub Hill and, needless to say, another £38 to evacuate his stepdaughter, Mrs. Findlay, from London to Dublin. She was a hardy perennial, turning up again a year or two later in a cellar-dwelling at Liverpool.

As his first assault on Daylesford had failed, their present home was the furnished house in St. James' Place; presumably he sub-let the other first taken for Marian in South Street, for which he paid £312 a year. Not that they spent much time in London this wet cold summer. When they were there, he would call on Mrs. Wheler, or talk with his venerable aunt at Kensington. He exercised his horses at Angelo's *manège*, and kept up his play-going, much admiring Mrs. Siddons as Desdemona. Once a group of King's officers back from India gave him 'an elegant entertainment' at the 'Star and Garter' in Pall Mall. But he needed more peace, though whether he got it at the spas where society and Anglo-Indians forgathered, may be doubted. Thus, in September they spent three weeks at Tunbridge Wells, where 'a bad landlady' gets a bad mark; his diary, in fact, seems a trifle fussy, for at the White Hart, Salisbury, he complains of being kept awake by 'tea-drinkers'. That was on their way to Bath, where they stayed over Christmas.

All these movements and furnished houses, and horses to ride in Lord Bathurst's Cirencester woods, ran away with money. He wound up his account with those who, all his time in India, had been his trustees, Sykes and Woodman, who put his fortune at roughly £74,000. But much of this was out on mortgage, while Larkins' estimate of what might come from India was most depressing; sometimes he felt he might have to begin the world again, or live abroad. Marian, indeed, had her own money, about £40,000. Still, her two boys were growing up, for whom she had great ambitions, Charles being destined for the army, and Julius for India.

He admitted to feeling a 'great void', as he rode with the author of *The Bath Guide*, or had a mild dinner with old Lord Mansfield. And what he heard from Sulivan and Thurlow disturbed him. He had, in fact, come back to a political world quite revolutionized since he left England sixteen years before; one of which he was as ignorant as a child in arms, and with which he was perfectly unfitted to cope. India had become a furious public question, a touchstone of party, and the ladder to power. Fired by Burke, the Whigs were committed to an attack on the Company; on the other side, Dundas was pledged to drastic legislation. The proprietors had defied the Whigs and, in alliance with the King's friends, Pitt, and Dundas, had over-thrown the Coalition. But, since Pitt's triumphant election of 1784, that alliance had disintegrated.

In this new parliament there were some thirty-two members of the 'Indian interest', men who themselves, or whose relatives, had served there; fourteen of them being reckoned as the Arcot group, interested first and foremost in the Carnatic debts. There were another twenty-eight or so, connected with the Company through the City or shipping. Of the whole, Pitt had now a comfortable majority, Fox's Indian members being mostly either associated with an older India, like the Clives or Strachey, or set partisans such as Francis. Hastings' personal friends made a very short list: the two veterans, Sykes and Palk, George Vansittart, Barwell, and the egregious Scott; R. J. Sulivan and a young Sumner joined them on by-elections later.

Control at the India House had disappeared. The leaders of the various Indian interests, Sulivan for the Hastings party, the deaf but able Francis Baring for the City, and James Macpherson and Atkinson for the Arcot gang, only agreed in resisting Fox, often opposing each other over directors' elections. Moreover, their clashes with the Cabinet were increasingly serious. The India Act, ostensibly framed in collaboration with the Company, gave large vague powers to the Board of Control, which in effect could govern all policy and, by a right of recall, undo the highest appointments. Before Hastings came home, the central liaison man, Atkinson, died of consumption, and on a series of large questions Pitt and Dundas resisted the Indian interest, and Hastings' friends in particular. They rejected Sulivan's candi-dature as chairman, kept out Scott as a director, and finally plumped for Macartney as Governor-General. True, they agreed to cancel his assignment of Carnatic revenues, but against the protest of the Sulivan-Hastings group capitulated to the Arcot gang, arranging to pay off even the most questionable items of the Nabob's debts.

This was public evidence enough. Privately, Dundas was

meditating an extension of royal sovereignty over British India and ending the Company's trade monopoly. Besides, he made it clear as daylight he would have no truck with Hastings. He wrote of the Company as 'over-stocked with unnecessary servants', living on plunder; so long as this faction in the India House backed Hastings, he told Grenville, the act would never get fair play. If there was no talk now of punishing Hastings, equally there was none of giving him honours. Pitt held to his earlier ground that it would be time to speak of honours when Burke's motion had been disposed of, and the Commons' resolutions of 1782 made void.

Their hostility was not surprising. Every activity of Hastings since his return seemed designed to offend them. If there was one colleague they specially distrusted, it was Thurlow, while if they had one fundamental, it was their purpose to use the new act to its furthest extent. But here was Hastings in frequent conference with the iron Chancellor, trying to repeal the act, or at least working for its wholesale amendment. He had not forgiven Pitt's speeches, libelling the service he loved; which he vindicated to Thurlow, as 'men by whose zeal, wisdom, valour, and blood, the first and most perilous trust under the British Empire' was acquired. And though in fact he did his best to damp down the violent petitions signed in Bengal, it could not please Dundas to hear that, but for Hastings, British India might have broken away. Over and above this, ministers were making a commercial treaty with the French East India Company, which he thought 'weak or wicked'. Dundas, again, had another scheme much at heart, for transferring the Indian debt to England, which Hastings criticized as fatuous, as indeed it proved. Finally, in the face of his recommendation, Dundas forced through a sharp reduction in the Company's army.

By this time, when they came back from Bath in January 1786, they were much in the public eye, subjects of much speculation and considerable malice. Horace Walpole had a snigger over Hastings' pride of his ancestry; William Eden set up rumours of his 'gallantry'. Fanny Burney, on the other hand, was charmed with his 'plainness and simplicity', and the courteous candour of his conversation. And Marian had made another conquest, of old John Wilkes, whose interest in womanhood had always been catholic, and who gave them what must have been a queer dinner-party, with the Chevalier D'Éon as the show-piece. But Hastings clung to old friends and old loyalties. He exerted himself to get Shore appointed to Council in Bengal, — 'the best thing done for India for these many years' — and was delighted when Cornwallis at last accepted the Governor-Generalship. He promptly sent him a lengthy list of his chosen, whom he begged him to employ or advance; Larkins, Palmer, and Turner in the foremost. Nor did he forget Gunga Govind Sing, nor, above all, Benaram Pandit of Berar and his brother, 'faithful companions of my flight to Benares and my inseparable attendants during the last ten years of my government'. His guests at dinner, his daily company this winter, — Mrs. Wheler, Anderson, or even Bob Pott — kept him living in that past.

He was meticulous in going to Court, but the public men he saw most of, like Lansdowne, were not those agreeable to Pitt. He was sketching for Thurlow the heads of a remodelled government in which a Governor-General without a Council would be supreme, with sole power over civilian appointments. With the India House he was losing touch. The Directors had repeated their request for more detail about the presents, which he did his best to meet by writing to Larkins for full accounts. His oldest link there was severed when, one night at the Opera in February, he heard of Sulivan's death; 'afflicting news', he wrote in his diary, attending the funeral next day in heavy snow. Though he knew nothing of Burke's intentions, he disliked feeling this axe suspended, and was sore at the delay in any honour or reward; even 'the wretch' Macartney had got a Company pension of £1500 a year. He felt still more the anonymous calumnies which embraced Marian and her diamonds. Shop windows were full of caricatures. A conjurer in Cockspur Street was much in vogue, who professed to eat stones, and a picture of the King, as 'the greatest stone eater', swallowing Hastings' diamonds, amused the town. He would stop this campaign and fight in the open. At his request, therefore, on the first day after the recess, Scott asked Burke in the House when he would move the motion of which he had given notice in June.

The Burke clan were in low water, and being in Opposition threatened to bankrupt them. Their chief creditor, Lord Verney, was himself a refugee at Boulogne and might launch legal proceedings. Poor William was writing despairing letters from

Tanjore. But Edmund saw that the road back to everything good, both at Westminster and Beaconsfield, passed through India. His fame was bound up with Fox's bill, of which he was chief author, he would avenge its loss on 'the grand delinquent'. Amid the jeers of Pitt's back-benchers he cried 'I swear by this book that the wrongs done to humanity in the Eastern world shall be avenged on those who inflicted them'. Reports of his obsession grieved his old friend Sir William Jones; threats, in fact, that Jones should be recalled if he sided with Hastings. He needed no challenge from this foolish Scott; his moves were planned the previous autumn, while Hastings was enjoying Bath. Moreover, he could not live his life without a crusade.

Yet a crusader needs a spiritual director, and for his he had taken Philip Francis. They had been working together now since the Select Committee of 1782, for which they had schooled the witnesses, and whose most important reports they jointly compiled. Many times Burke paid public tribute to Francis, this upright man, unrewarded except by his 'inward sunshine of the soul'. Now Francis sat by him in the House, multiplied pamphlets to answer the efforts of Scott or Halhed, and invited anti-Hastings letters from Chambers and Stables at Calcutta.

By the autumn of 1785, then, their armaments were nearly ready. Burke spent part of the summer at Minto with Gilbert Elliot, whom he had converted, and took a new disciple with him in William Windham, who had been Chambers' pupil at Oxford. Just before Christmas he was deep in discussion, either at Beaconsfield or Francis' house at East Sheen. They agreed it was imperative to win the support of Fox, but Burke was clear it must not be fought as a measure of party. To get Hastings convicted in this 'bribed tribunal' of Pitt's Parliament, he believed impossible; nor would it be wise indiscriminately to denounce all his acts, some of which, over a long administration, public opinion would condone, and judge in the light of his professed intentions. No! let Francis and himself go forward alone, not thinking of party majorities; pile Pelion on Ossa, omit nothing in the catalogue of offences, and prove not so much legal crime as 'a corrupt habitual evil intention'. This would at least justify them to posterity; nay, the Whigs would hear things 'which in debate they must support, or disgrace themselves for ever'.

From One Exile to Another: 1785–86

A party meeting at Portland's house just before the session vainly tried to make Burke retreat. In February he had the resolutions of 1782 solemnly rehearsed, and called for the relevant papers. In some cases ministers refused them, as confidential; indeed, they went further. Dundas, though upholding his earlier views on mistaken policy, said he saw no ground for criminal prosecution. Pitt almost went out of his way to declare that the Mahratta peace did Hastings 'immortal honour'; he would not abet impeachment, save on more definite charges, nor hear witnesses for the prosecution without hearing the case for the defence. The twin accusers were ready. During April Francis drew up a portentous volume of twenty-two charges, which Burke brought to the House. They were delighted, and surprised, to have made such progress. Burke saw truly enough that Pitt and Dundas were not ready to surrender to the right wing of their own party, like Thurlow and Jenkinson, with whom they had other quarrels, and who opposed any Indian enquiry at all; and were equally unready to present the Whig party with the cry that the Cabinet were shielding delinquents. Francis boasted the perseverance of two men against the whole kingdom had made it certain that the charges would reach the Lords; adding 'Mr. Hastings, I am well informed, is sunk into the lowest state of misery'.

He was singularly ill informed. Hastings was all confidence. His friends were saying that, when the documents showed Mr. Hastings 'as he really is', even his enemies would be ashamed. To Fanny Burney, one of his conquests, — incidentally, his Indian doctor Francis had just married her sister — he spoke of his 'certainty of victory'. He would handle this in his own way. 'I have not visited any of the ministers since the prosecution began. . . . I have not desired the attendance of a single member. . . . I have disdained every species of management.' Taking up Pitt's hint, he petitioned to be heard in person by the Commons. Though everyone but Thurlow thought this a dire mistake, Hastings was sure that the truth had only to be heard for it to prevail.

For five days he and his friends were hard driven, composing this 'defence'. He himself wrote sections on the Mogul tribute and the Rohilla war; Halhed did Benares, Shore the revenue, Anderson and Baber also contributed. On May the 1st he began reading it at the bar; when he wearied, young Markham and Hatsell the clerk took up the story, which lasted from 3.45 till 10.30 at night; he finished it the next evening. It was a curious, uneven, and most characteristic performance.

On some specified charges he made some massive points. The Mogul Emperor was under obligations to us, and not we to him. The Directors had expressly allowed our withholding tribute, if he 'flings himself into the hands of the Mahrattas'. The Rohilla war was just, and justified by the Directors' latitude on security and by the revenue obtained. The 'hard and odious task' of using Nuncumar to convict Mahomed Reza Khan had been imposed on him by the Directors; once again, he had no concern, 'directly or indirectly', with his arrest and execution. As for Chait Sing, he was but a *zemindar*, accused only on public grounds; 'implacability to my inferiors is no part of my character'. He was accused of 'rudely and insolently' declining the Rajah's visit, but 'is it rude to be peremptory, or is resolution insolence?' Replying on the head of corrupt expenditure, such as Croftes' bullock contract, he raised it to a higher plane; 'the very existence of the Empire in Bengal depends upon our army being in a situation to move, if required, at the shortest notice'.

But the sting of this defence lay in its general positions. He had endured these 'criminations' five years, and always from the same quarter. They had damaged the public interest, yet invective had not shaken his conduct; he had not resigned until 'I had fulfilled every duty which required my continuance'. He had received grateful addresses from Europeans, army officers, and Indian princes, and the Directors' unanimous thanks in formal audience. With such testimonies, 'and with the internal applause of my own mind superseding all evidence', he was astonished at this 'load of slander'. Boldly he implied that 'no power on earth' weighed in the balance against the gratitude of his own employers. The charges were spurious 'histories and comments'; 'even my imputed thoughts, as at the final day of judgement, are wrested into accusation against me'. And this 'state of perfection' was asked of a man who had left England 'while yet a schoolboy'.

On each burning question he staked a challenge. All Asian history went to prove 'the invariable exercise of arbitrary power'. The Mahratta peace was 'honourable and advantageous', though he had to contend with difficulties greater than those confronting 'any minister, at any period of time, in any nation'. He protested that his character stood as high in Europe 'as any man of my own rank and pretensions', and exclaimed against being 'punished before conviction' by invective. And if acquitted, if it were shown that he had saved British India, he asked, 'what atonement will this honourable House in its justice ordain for the injury I sustain by having been branded on its records — with the vile and abhorred character of a Verres, an oppressor, a defrauder?'

Yes, he felt sure this appearance in person had been 'a blessed inspiration'. Evidence given on the following days did not seem to damage him. Veterans of the Rohilla war were dragged in, among them a broken Colonel Champion with failing memory. A rather dubious Major Marsac (a natural son, it seems, of Frederick Prince of Wales) testified to the wrong-doings of Colonel Hannay, but as he had himself been dismissed from Oudh service and had tried blackmail on Hastings, he did not bring credit to the prosecution. Nathaniel Middleton made a bad disingenuous witness, — they soon nicknamed him 'memory Middleton' — and endured a harsh five days of gruelling from Burke. On the other hand, several officers (though called for the prosecution) gave evidence on the constant rebelliousness of Oudh, and the prosperity of Rohilkund. Not least Major Gilpin, whose correspondence with Richard Johnson proved a decent humanity to the Begums in British officials, and who testified he had often heard complaints that Hastings paid more attention to Indians than to his own countrymen.

Yes, he felt a growing confidence, even in ministers. Dundas, who had accepted his Benares narrative, was on friendly terms with Anderson and Shore. And in this mood of optimism, in May, he paid £12,000 for Beaumont Lodge, Old Windsor, with ninety acres included. Here he hung Hodges' paintings of the scenes nearly connected with his fame, and here settled to enjoy the hay-making, while the Caillauds or Toones came to stay. He would drive to dine with George Vansittart at Bisham, or to listen to music in the Abbey, as he had when a schoolboy. He wrote off to India for lichi and cinnamon seeds, and an Arab for Marian to ride. What a poet Horace was! He could not find better words than his to express what he promised himself at Beaumont

Lodge; peace and honour, a garden, and rest at nights.

His defence was not thought over-modest, but some competent members found his case better than they had expected; anyhow, the papers were so voluminous that it was hard to make a full House. And some experienced and cynical persons, Horace Walpole for instance, and Gibbon's most unlikeable friend .Lord Sheffield, thought that this particular House of Commons would never drive this prosecution through. They seemed to be justified when, on June the 3rd, after two days of hot debate, the Rohilla charge was rejected by 119 votes to 67. Pitt was silent, though voting with the majority; Dundas' chief argument was that, be the rights or wrongs as they might be, since that date Hastings had thrice been confirmed as Governor-General. This at least silenced Lord North, and might be extended far.

So this 'scene of iniquity', the accused believed, should soon be over, nor did he despair of further employment in the service of the State. Later that week, at Pitt's request, he sent him a note on the meaning of a '*zemindar*'; for the charge touching Chait Sing of Benares stood next on the list.

CHAPTER XXVI

Nine Years' Persecution: 1786-95

THE first heavy blow fell five days later, on June the 13th, when the Commons voted, by 119 to 79, that the Benares charge gave ground for impeachment. Intrinsically, that vote was carried by the voice of Pitt.

His speech dumbfounded his party, and most of his colleagues, some of his nearest friends, William Grenville among them, voting against him. And the reason he gave was almost ridiculous. Fully accepting Hastings' view that Chait Sing was nothing more than a *zemindar*, and as such liable to demands in emergency, and that he had been properly punished for his contumacy, he fastened solely on the 'exorbitancy' of the fine, — mentioned by Hastings to Wheler and Markham, but never in fact levied. Here, he argued, was a cruel and criminal intention.

Here it is well to get rid of some legends. Pitt was certainly reading the Benares papers against time, yet we need not believe that his 'conversion' only came that very morning, after conference at breakfast with Dundas, as Hastings declared thirty years later. If conversion came into it, it would proceed more naturally from his close friends among the 'Saints', Wilberforce and Bankes, who we are told 'besieged' him on the subject. It is more material, that this vote did not yet commit him to impeachment at all.

That was the view both of his brother Chatham, and of Shelburne's very able correspondent, Thomas Orde. And Pitt's language could not have been more guarded, explicitly limiting his censure to the single point of 'exorbitancy'. In this debate, as throughout, he severely attacked Francis; depicting him as sitting through the Council decisions on Benares 'with a secret satisfaction, contemplating the errors of Mr. Hastings as laying the foundation of future persecutions against him'. There is another consideration. His time was enormously occupied this year with the French commercial treaty, his new Sinking Fund, and a state of things in the Netherlands which might land the country in war. Then, again, his majority was split into factions, and had several times refused to follow him; Lansdowne's nine members, for example, could not be depended on. His Cabinet itself was composite. To one side were Thurlow, who perpetually undermined him and growled that in this Benares debate he spoke 'like a girl', and Jenkinson, *bête noire* of all reformers; over against them were pronounced Whigs like old Camden and Richmond. If the majority were not to get out of hand, or the reforming group not alienated, he and Dundas must move with extreme caution.

For all that, the Benares vote was a disaster for Hastings, as he well knew. Though he professed to think his credit unaffected, he recognized that what he called Pitt's 'caprice' had put new heart in the prosecution. Political voting on a judicial question shocked him; press attacks infuriated him. And paragraphs about Marian reached even the tea-tables at Windsor, at least providing Fanny Burney and Madame Schwellenburg with one subject on which they could agree. The day after the vote, a coincidence redoubled the fracas, when the King was presented with a large diamond, a gift of the Nizam and transmitted through Hastings. And poor dear Major Scott explained at such length, but quite in vain, how sheerly accidental was this timing.

The man who hated Hastings most was in an ecstasy. Francis was always jumping up in debate to blacken the picture, coaching Windham in his facts, and briefing young James Erskine, Wedderburn's lumpish nephew. He wrote out to India for more information, to Chambers and Hay and Shee. Hastings, he rejoiced to say, 'has had a pleasant summer of it', and Impey would be prosecuted too; whatever the outcome, the trial would 'gibbet their characters to all eternity'.

A sorry summer, and in July one who had loved him longest died, so escaping the wrath to come. 'Visited my aunt,' says a Sunday note, 'who scarce knew me', and she died that night. What with settling into Beaumont Lodge and preparing his defence, he did not get far afield this autumn. His rheumatism was so troublesome that he felt, when he could, he must try a drier climate.

If he could have realized it, his defence at the bar had not only bored the House to extinction, but done him positive harm. It had been thought arrogant, seemed also to convict him of holding Oriental despotic notions of government. But he could not see it. For his accusers he had extreme contempt; 'they would not dare' to push impeachment into fact. To David Anderson's offer of assistance he sent a long reply, outlining the points he wished brought to the forefront; in some ways the best defence of his whole career, but in others most revealing and disturbing. Justly he described the marble structure he had built out of ramshackle brick. All departments of government, all courts of justice, salt and opium revenue, the end of double government, all were of his making. Justly he pointed to the Directors' gross contradictions, the hostility of the Three, the second opposition of Macpherson and Stables, and justly argued how the Directors and Bombay between them had brought about the Mahratta war. Of Benares and the Begums he did not speak; but the Rohilla war was made 'on just grounds surely, unless any other process than that of the sword can be devised for recovering the rights of nations'.

He described his triumphs in words ringing with pride and defiance. Against treacherous colleagues, directors, parliament, 'half the people of England', and patronage used 'in the seduction of my fellow-servants', he had no arm but 'the superior weight of my own character, and the consciousness of superior desert'. 'I suffered in patience, — no meanness of submission ever afforded my assailants the triumph, even of a moment, over me. . . . My antagonists sickened, died, and fled. I maintained my ground unchanged, neither the health of my body nor the vigour of my mind for a moment deserted me.' In the darkness of war, 'my confidence and pretensions rose in proportion to the despondency of my rulers at home and my colleagues of the other presidencies. . . . If I might be allowed to point out the best features of my character in office, I should place these in the catalogue; integrity and zeal; affection for my fellow-servants, and regard for the country which I governed . . . sincerity and unreserve in my dealings with the Chiefs in connection with our government . . . patience, long suffering, confidence, and decision.' True, he ended, 'let no man see this, I am ashamed of my own praises'. Yet his 'hints' came from his monitor within. A few weeks later

345

he confided to Anderson that he still thought some office was possible, and if so he would ask his advice 'in the crisis that may precede it'. What folly of Major Scott, or wild words from Thurlow, lay behind this day-dreaming? A wiser counsellor, Archbishop Markham, gave him very different advice. Even his friends, he said, thought parts of his defence required better proof. In any case, his attitude of 'confident innocence' would never do; 'be persuaded to recollect what sort of world you live in'.

In these same autumn months, and into the new year of 1787, the battle royal between Dundas and the Company was at its peak. He saw to it that every vacancy in the directorate was filled by a Pittite or a Scot. He ignored them in negotiating with the French; in settling the Arcot debts he flatly opposed them. The proprietors finally accused him of devising 'a secret system', and called for an enquiry into the working of the India Act. If news reached Hastings through Jenkinson (now Lord Hawkesbury) that Pitt wanted to get rid of the enquiry, he was also told 'my friends take too high a tone'.

February was the deciding month. In its first week Middleton and Impey were examined, damaging each other and the accused. Dundas was markedly hostile; Impey was 'worse than Hastings', he said to Elliot, who, despite Impey's affection for his lost brother Alexander, gave notice he would move for impeachment. On the 7th the Begums' charge went against Hastings, by the much more decisive figure of 175 to 86. It was moved by Sheridan in the most famous of parliamentary speeches: coached by Richard Smith, that past master in Oudh scandals, the author of the *School for Scandal* had warmed, as Burke said, 'with a sort of love passion to our Begums', and made this a superb dramatic occasion. On one side, two princesses exposed to a cruel soldiery, and their faithful servants tortured; on the other, Hastings as both 'trickster and tyrant', 'a felon kite'; 'the Grotius of India', Impey, 'ferreting with affidavits'; 'memory' Middleton and 'trading' Colonel Hannay. Strangers in the gallery clapped their hands, young Whigs threw themselves on the orator's neck. In vain George Vansittart and the ex-chairman Nathaniel Smith resisted the current; in vain Scott repeated how only the Begums' funds had saved Coote's army. Pitt, though ready to condone the resumption of the *jagirs*, found the seizure of the treasures indefensible, and Hastings' acceptance of the Vizier's ten lacs as unaccountable except by corruption. His argument converted the sober Addington, who wrote that he voted so 'with pain'.

Impeachment was now taken as a certainty, even by Chatham and Lansdowne, who had never thought so before. A good Pittite, Daniel Pulteney, summed up the causes as he saw them, for Pitt's near friend, the Duke of Rutland. Hastings' defence was 'unguarded', the case had turned out worse than anyone imagined. He had relied on the King, and 'caballed' at the India House; many members wanted to 'frighten the East Indians', who were opposing Dundas. All this had forced the hand of Pitt, who felt that Hastings must be 'at least charged', however unpopular it might be with his party.

The stream turned to a torrent. Burke suggested in debate that Hastings' person should be secured to prevent his absconding. Francis told Sir Thomas Clavering his attendance was vital, 'your brother's honour is at stake as well as mine'. Hostile witnesses dwelt on what Wheler (conveniently long dead) had told them, of Hastings selling Bihar revenue farms; how he had offered this money to Wheler and, on his refusing, had said 'then it shall go to the Mahratta fund'. And though young Markham flatly contradicted Peter Moore's gossip, the mud stuck. In March, Pelham carried the much more dubious Furruckabad charge. The great Admiral Hood conjured the House not to weaken the hand of servants of the State, acting in emergency, but Pitt, speaking with marked effect, rejected both the doctrine and the parallel. Hastings himself, he added, would allow no defence based on his service as a whole, and had asked for a declaration of innocence on each particular charge. Indignantly Hastings noted that day, that hitherto Pitt's 'specious candour' had deceived the public, but now he was 'provoked by an animated speech of Lord Hood's to betray his hostile disposition'.

The scroll grew ever longer. Windham carried the charge of oppressing the Rohilla, Fyzullah Khan, with Pitt again in the majority. On the head of peculation he spoke, too, with great severity of the emoluments given to Coote. By April the only doubts were the choice of articles, and the date of the trial. Dundas' private letters to India said it was 'not pleasant to many of our friends', but Pitt and he had found much of the defence 'perfectly unsupported'. There was some talk of a commission to take Indian evidence and moves for delay, which were put down to Grenville, but in letters between Dundas and Burke the ministers' position was soon clarified. Impeachment must proceed. But they refused to be frightened by Burke's canard that the vindictive Hastings group hoped to make a rival Cabinet. They would take no active part in managing the impeachment which, however, they would support, so far as was consistent with 'national justice and the credit of the House of Commons'. Although the articles were framed after joint consultation, the list of managers was therefore a Whig party list. And from it, though Dundas voted for him, Francis was excluded, a large majority agreeing with Pitt's view of his inveterate malice.

In May the articles were approved; no one seconded Wilkes' observation that no accusation had come from India, or the argument of a Lansdowne member that the nation, which was impeaching Hastings, gladly swallowed the moneys he had taken. On the 10th Burke took the charges to the Lords; during the next week Hastings' diary shows he paid no less than eighty-three 'visits', presumably leaving his card on his judges. On the 21st he was taken into custody by the sergeant-at-arms, who passed him on to Black Rod, and appeared at the bar of the Lords. There he endured what he described as the single thing he felt in this 'base treatment', the ceremonial of kneeling, 'a punishment not only before conviction, but before the accusations'. But his appearance, the Archbishop of Canterbury thought, was 'proper, neither daunted nor insolent'. Anyhow, he spent two days of June at Ascot races.

His chief anxiety was still for Marian. 'She has suffered more than I have done, — and I only for her sufferings.' He seems to have decided that life must be lived as usual, or rather more so. So Beaumont Lodge was running full tilt, with seven men servants; they would tour and see friends, he sent off his Arab to be painted by George Stubbs. He even reopened his campaign for Daylesford. Though prepared for the worst, even now he was quite confident that all would be over in a year. Rather wistfully he hoped that friends in India were collecting testimonies in his favour, for no man 'ever laboured with so passionate a zeal for the welfare of a nation as I did'. He had written accordingly to Shore, now in Council, not so much for the purpose of the trial, which he explained must be over before such evidence came to hand, but to clear 'my future and lasting reputation'.

This done, in August they set off for two months' holiday in the north. Along the great road his diary paces it out; from the 'Swan' at Welwyn, 'a bad inn, low shabby chamber, dinner not clean'; better fare at the Kingston Arms, Newark, 'the best mutton I have eaten in England'; always noting good horseflesh and good water; by Wetherby, 'bad horses and a vile rider'. So on the 29th they reached Edinburgh, where Anderson awaited them; a dinner at the East India Club, and on to Stirling, Perth, and Glasgow. Not always happy. Marian had one 'hysterical fit', 'bad night, in which I, too, had my share'. On the way home they stopped in Bedale with Marriott, who had bought silks with him at Kasimbazaar long ago, and so in mid-October returned to St. James' Place. Here he must sit down to correct his defence with Scott, and meet the very able counsel retained for him: Plumer, who had made a name defending Rumbold, Law, whose brother had served in Bengal, and Dallas.

On November the 28th he kneeled once again before the Lords, delivering his reply to the Commons' articles. He guardedly reserved parts of his defence, to charges so rambling and tendentious; which put on him 'a responsibility, equally new in its kind and unlimited in its extent', for the sins of others, and those not of British councillors only but of Indian princes, or their ministers. Naturally he made much of the fact that many of the wrongs alleged were prior to his repeated re-nomination as Governor-General. Some he parried with a flat denial. On others his response was dangerously dogmatic; denying, for example, that he had ever concealed the receipt of gifts, and asserting that the initiative in taking the Begums' treasure had come from the Vizier. Once more, with his vulnerable ingenuousness, he dwelt on his separation from English conduct at a very early age, and the contrast between English and Oriental principles.

On February the 6th, 1788, his diary reads 'went to see the preparations at Westminster Hall', where within the week he must come 'as a criminal'. Workmen were putting the last touches to a vast improvised theatre. Red-covered seats for all but the Commons, whose seats were green; at the far end, the throne and royal boxes, with the Chancellor, judges, and heralds beneath them. To the left were the peers, to the right the Commons; over the heads of each, galleries for peeresses and all the ticket-holders favoured by peers, or the great officers of the Palace of Westminster. For himself a little box near the door, divided only by the witness - box from the Commons' managers.

Here on the 13th, at noon, having passed through horse and foot guards, he knelt; then sat, cynosure of the British political world. A solitary and almost emaciated figure, in a plain poppy-coloured suit; he measured himself this year, and he stood five foot six, but weighed only eight stone ten. Neither Pitt nor any of the commoners in the Cabinet were present. But the Queen and princesses were in the Duke of Newcastle's enclosure, Mrs. FitzHerbert in the royal box; the Prince, talking too loudly to Sheridan, in the managers', where Joshua Reynolds looked in too. And here was young Richard Burke, jumping on a bench to catch the eye of Fanny Burney, just above them. She, looking down on her friend Hastings, thought he seemed 'pale, ill and altered'. Elliot, uncomfortable at memories of his brother, wrote that he looked as if he could not live a week; Hawkins Browne, M.P., on the contrary, declared his expression was 'bold, determined, and indignant'. One manager at least saw what he must feel.

Fanny Burney's account of her conversation with Windham in that gallery gives us some real light, if we eliminate the archness she could not keep out of her dialogue. 'A prouder heart,' she makes him say, 'an ambition more profound, were never, I suppose, lodged in any mortal mould. With what a port he entered ! . . . An arrogance, a self-confidence unexampled.' 'O could those, the thousands, the millions, who have groaned and languished under the iron rod of his oppressions — see him there !' Yet 'enclosed now in that little space, — how he must feel it !' Impey, that 'very pitiful fellow', would pocket any indignity provided he got off. But 'Hastings has feeling'. Fine or imprisonment could not rack him further; 'the moment of his punishment — was the moment that brought him to that bar. . . . I must shake all this off, — forget that he is there.'

Windham, who could not act, could feel rightly. This wound to Hastings was mortal; most of all, to his pride in the fame and good name he had brought to Marian. 'She suffers her spirits to be affected', he wrote in his restrained way, 'more than they ought', while she told her son Charles in her half-English, that she found it 'biergatory' to be in London. But there he was to sit for 142 days, chilled in winter, but on hot days of June 'exceeding oppressive', in this Hall crowded with women trooping to see the last sensation. To see managers levelling opera-glasses at him, to hear Lord Derby move a three-days' adjournment over New-market races, to hear the clatter of knives and forks and glasses in the boxes. His trial, he wrote to India after two years of it, 'adds one to the public entertainments'. Here, says another fragment he drafted, he must sit, 'the common gazing stock of thousands of spectators, — to see their attention riveted to an orator bellowing the grossest invectives, to hear their bursts of laughter, and even their claps as of theatrical applause'. He must listen to young Charles Grey's sallies on 'that benignant divinity, Mrs. Hastings'. We do not wonder that he found 'aversion to general society' growing on him; 'if I could forget one attraction, I could pass the remainder of my days in the woods of Kentucky'.

Even so, with that enduringness which had worn down Clavering and Francis, he set himself to treat this as an evil that would pass. Indignation hardened this long-acquired control. Though the basest criminal was reckoned innocent by English law till he was proved guilty, here was he, defenceless, spattered with invective over years. Yet 'I hope I possess that within me which would support me with equal fortitude under bodily torture'. No! life should proceed as he had planned, and with the dignity to which he had grown. So, this first summer, he dined with Reynolds at Twickenham, and Gibbon with him, while in winter he dined regularly with the Bengal Club. He kept up his theatre-going, seeing *Macbeth* and *Twelfth Night* this season. He may be found at a ball at Tunbridge Wells, and bathing at Weymouth. In between those jaunts they took a furnished house at Malvern, where he rode Suliman again and went on writing verses, including a poor and lamentably un-fulfilled ode on the Prince of Wales' marriage. And there they took the decision which, more than any single thing, exhibits the frame of his mind, coming as he did from harsh weeks of abuse at the hands of Fox, Burke, and Sheridan. For, on August the 26th, he executed the deeds that made him owner of Daylesford. Blessed September days, when the Cotswolds begin their short Indian summer, during which he took his architect to survey the ruins and plan his plantations; an interlude of peace, when the ex-Governor-General's diary was content to say 'fished in the Evenlode for gudgeon'.

And so he continued through 1789 also. They made a summer visit to Margate; 'bathed, rode in a hot sun to Kingsate, — sailed out to sea a-fishing, and was very sea-sick'. In September, to stay with the D'Oyleys in the New Forest; 'dined in an open tent on the further bank of Beaulieu river; a delightful day'. From there, to a riding tour in the Isle of Wight; 'pleased with our excursion, which we rendered pleasant and effectual by not yielding to present difficulties, and by a proper exertion of perseverance, hope, and the spirit of adventure'. In October, riding back from his sister's home at Ewell; 'rode from Guildford to Farnham over the Mare's back, the most beautiful in prospect of any that I have seen'. Finally, in December, lodgings at Bath, in Rivers Street. Periodically he dashed off to Daylesford to hurry on the new building, too slow for his impatience; the winter of 1788–89 had been cruel, with 'the Thames frozen as far as I could see, above and below Kew Bridge'. And as Beaumont Lodge was inconvenient for his attendance at Westminster Hall, he sold it to another 'Nabob', — for a miracle, without loss — moving this November to a house at the top of Park Lane, which was his London home till he was a free man again.

The duration of his trial was spaced out as follows: in 1788, 35 days; 1789, 17; 1790, 14; 1791, 5; 1792, 22; 1793, 22; 1794, 28; while the proceedings of 1795, mostly in the House of Lords, lasted from January till April. The case for the prosecution was not closed till May 1791; that for the defence, in May 1793; another two years went in controversy between the managers and the court, efforts to reopen evidence, or conflict of Lords and Commons. About a third of the peerage died during the trial; the number who gave the verdict, by the honourable agreement that those only should do so who attended continuously, was only twenty-nine. His own witnesses often waited in vain to be called; Colonel Polier, for instance, went home to Switzerland after two years of it. There were better reasons, of course, for this drawn-out tragedy than any lassitude of eighteenth-century government. The King's madness and the Regency crisis, the election of 1790, with the consequent dispute whether the dissolution had not abated the impeachment, outbreak of war in 1793, all contributed. Even more, perhaps, the decision that the judges must be present, who were often away on circuit. It was not so much the time consumed, barbarous though it was in result for Hastings, which makes this trial a blot on our history; rather, the exposure of what injustice is done when political charges are strained through judicial forms.

The atmosphere was poisoned from the moment that Pitt disclaimed responsibility. Formally Burke and his nineteen fellow-managers spoke for 'the Commons of Great Britain', but in fact only represented the Fox party. Pitt, it is true, continued (in the accused's version) 'as he has ever been, my personal and inveterate enemy'. On some points, Coote's allowances for one, he showed that he would vote 'guilty'; he stood firm with Burke, against his own law officers, that the dissolution had not suspended impeachment. But though his followers, who were very far from being a united party, unwillingly followed his lead in general, many revolted against Dundas' tightening grip on the Company, while the strong legal element rebelled at the managers' alarming notion of what constituted evidence.

One early sign of these growing doubts was the acquittal of Impey. Not, indeed, by a convincing majority, for Sir Elijah was not universally esteemed, and average opinion was well represented by Lord Cornwallis, who wrote that he was sorry for Hastings, 'it is not fair to judge his conduct many years ago by the temper of the present times; he has certainly many great and amiable qualities'. But 'if you are in the hanging mood, you may tuck up Sir Elijah Impey, without giving anybody the smallest concern'. However, Sir Elijah declined to be tucked up, unless Chambers and the other judges swung with him. He made a masterly speech in the Commons, devastating Gilbert Elliot, whose peroration on 'the murdered Rajah' moved himself and some other Whigs to tears. So, while Fox called out for capital punishment, Pitt and his lawyers acquitted the Chief Justice of any corrupt motive, also declaring his disbelief in a conspiracy between him and Hastings.

The law of England, interpreted by the Lords with the judges advising, defeated every vital move in the managers' tactics. Their first effort was to press that each charge should be brought to an end, and judgement given on it, before proceeding to the next. Hastings' counsel argued, and the Lords acquiesced, that such isolation of one charge might anticipate their line of defence on another, and exclude evidence that ought to be taken into account. The managers' second ground was more fundamental. The high court of parliament, they held, 'should not be fettered by those rules of law which prevail in inferior courts'; its duty was to do 'substantial justice', regardless of common law and precedent. Doctrines of slander could not apply to 'the Commons of Great Britain'. They must be free to use circumstantial evidence, even if unproved, to bring home presumptive guilt on some connected charge. On all this arbitrary claim of sovereignty, they were overruled.

The matter of their speeches was mostly borrowed from the reports of Burke's Select Committee of 1782, first derived from Francis' information, and brought up to date by his later activity. He was, for example, still goading a most unwilling Bristow to supply more evidence from Oudh. The charges and speeches, thus manufactured, were full of distortion and misstatement. They alleged that Hastings' foreign policy was just devised to increase the investment; that he set out to 'extirpate' the Rohillas; that the revenue farmers of 1772 were 'almost all banyans'; that property in Bengal was inheritable in the *zemindars*, that 'ancient nobility'; that Chait Sing was a sovereign prince; that the Provincial Councils were a brilliant success; that Hastings was author of the Mahratta war. To blacken the chronicle in Oudh, they blended events of 1782 with those of 1784, blurred Hannay's contingent with the temporary brigade, and asserted that the Begums' eunuchs were scourged. They proclaimed that a Mogul-Mahratta alliance had no necessarily bad consequence for the British, and that Hastings' emphasis on the French danger had been a mask to cover aggression.

If this were mostly Francis' contribution, it was Burke who made the trial an infamy. True to his plan of making a 'habitual evil intention' do duty for evidence, he assumed guilt without affording proof, setting out so to darken Hastings' character that an innocent interpretation would be inconceivable. Not enough to show errors, or even political crimes; he must be painted as something low and sub-human, a Caliban wrapped up in a Tartuffe. So, echoing Lady Anne Monson's malicious gossip, he dwelt on Hastings' birth and upbringing as 'low' and 'vulgar'. He had begun his Indian career as 'a fraudulent bullock contractor'. Here was no heroic lion, but 'a rat', 'a weazel', 'a keeper of a pig-stye, wallowing in corruption'. A heart 'gangrened to the very core'; responsible for 'desolated provinces and ruined kingdoms', the destruction of religion, and the torture of women. 'This swindling Maecenas', this 'bad scribbler of absurd papers', was a compound of corruption and cruelty. 'He never corrupts without he is cruel. He never dines without creating a famine.' 'Like a wild beast he groans in corners over the dead and dying.' 'Every drop of blood that was spilt in consequence of his acts was murder.'

The raving vulgarity, that disgusted his hearers in the Regency debates, was poured over any and all associated with Hastings. So Wheler became 'his beaten, cowed and, I am afraid, bribed colleague'. That 'harlot', Munny Begum, 'kept the greatest gin shop in all Asia'. The best Company servants were Hastings' 'gang': Larkins, whose honesty Cornwallis praised so highly, was 'his agent in bribery'. 'Any witness in India' must be considered as coming from 'the enemy's camp', to be treated with insolent contempt as themselves guilty. He browbeat Larkins for the 'impudence' of his answers, and abused Auriol like a pickpocket, till Archbishop Markham burst out that the managers were as barbarous as Marat and Robespierre. He did more behind the scenes. Middleton deposed he had been bullied in private. Threats were conveyed to the Directors that, if Bristow were sued for unwarrantable profits, 'he should not suffer alone'. Most vile of all, perhaps, was his attitude on the choice of Shore in 1792 as Governor-General, whose recorded opinions tended to clear the accused; the managers, ran Burke's letter to the chairman, would resent this appointment. But nothing was more crooked than his general build-up and manipulation of evidence.

Trading on the enormous ignorance of his audience, his opening speeches deviated far outside the charges. Legends were revived of the Bengal of Hastings' youth; the fantastic story how his friend Caillaud had plotted to murder Shah Allum, or 'the providential flash of lightning' that, by killing Miran, put Mir Kasim in power. After two days of such stuff, Burke sprang on his audience the melodrama of Devi Singh, which months before he had pointed out to Francis as a winning card; 'has stuff in it that will, if anything, work upon the popular sense'. He addressed himself to the sensibility of the boxes; how this fiend, nominee of Hastings' evil servant Gunga Govind Singh, had tortured and harried; how his agents scourged their victims with poisonous thorns, beat fathers and sons bound together, tore women's breasts in cleft bamboos, raped others in dungeons. As he hushed his voice at the worst obscenity and buried his head in his hands, Mrs. Sheridan was taken out fainting, an oppression of horror fell on the Hall.

Devi Singh seems, indeed, to have been a low specimen of a low school, the Hindu revenue agents chosen by Mahomed Reza Khan. There had been complaints against him years before, though his then collector, Francis' friend Ducarel, had defended him stoutly. In 1782 Hastings had referred new charges to Shore, who, as acting head of the Revenue Board, was directly responsible; two years afterwards, when he was away in the North, the information used by Burke came to a head. A special commissioner, one Paterson, was sent to investigate, whom Hastings ordered to avoid contact with Goodlad, the collector, whose weakness or complicity was suspect. Before he left India, further enquiry was ordered and continued by Macpherson's government. Paterson, a new set of commissioners reported, had swallowed much garbled stuff; the worst alleged outrages had never happened at all. This is backed by a contemporary letter of the then young H. T. Colebrooke, later the Company's most famous Sanskrit scholar, and a man distinguished by his dislike of the 'harpies' whom, he said, Hastings' laxity had allowed to make fortunes. Moreover, Paterson himself wrote to Hastings' Indian agent that he was sorry to hear his report was being twisted against Hastings, whose conduct had been blameless. Worse still. When Burke was using these charges, or very soon after, he was well aware that Paterson took objection; his reply was to let Paterson know that, if 'the Commons of Great Britain' were thus discredited, he should be punished for giving false information or, conceivably, for corruption. He dared not frame a charge out of this material, but to the bitter end he flung in the name of Devi Singh whenever proofs failed him.

Nor was the death of Nuncumar a charge; it hardly could be, in the teeth of the Company law officers' advice, the sorry role of Francis and Chambers, and the recent vote clearing Impey. No matter. It should be dragged in to build up the circumstantials which, on their sort of law, constituted guilt. So, after many half-suggestions, we reach the climax of April 1789 in Burke's words, 'he murdered Nuncumar by the hands of Sir Elijah Impey'. That brought an immediate petition of Hastings, against this importation of crimes outside those which parliament had required him to answer; a debate in which Pitt took his side; an insolent letter from Burke, attacking 'this poor Indian stratagem', practised by Devi Singh and Hastings and 'other banyans black and white'; and a vote, of 135 to 66, that Burke's words 'ought not to have been spoken'. No matter. The managers continued to dwell on Nuncumar's 'murder' as their individual opinion. At the election next year Impey was unwise enough to stand against Sheridan at Stafford. He did not persist long, for a black man hanging on a gallows was carried about by the Sheridan crowd.

Less intrinsically evil, but shocking in waste of time and distortion, was the amount of sheer rant the managers exhibited. Elliot made the Commons weep about Impey, but Sheridan's speech to the court on the Begums was the show-piece. The rush for tickets sent up the price to fifty guineas. Peeresses were queueing in Palace Yard at eight in the morning. The sensitive Elliot could not remember ever crying 'so heartily and copiously on any public occasion'. Gibbon was there, to hear a compliment to his 'luminous page', and drops the curtain on this four days' spectacle; 'Sheridan, on the close of his speech, sunk into Burke's arms, but I called this morning, he is perfectly well. A good actor.' And when Sheridan let his sensibility go free, the effect was terrible. 'Filial love, the sacrament of nature'; hardly the truth about Asof-ud-Daulah. 'O Justice, Faith, Policy, fly from this spot.' 'At that fell glance peace, faith, joy, careless innocence, and feeble confidence receive their inexorable doom.' Too much of this. 'A few pages of the *Spectator*,' wrote the accused, 'a few extracts from Sterne's *Sentimental Journey*', or scraps from Buffon, would do as well as Sheridan.

Though he wrote few letters about his trial, some of his stray memoranda shed a little light. Burke, he said, accused him of more murders than one; 'speaking of Colonel Monson's death he paused, and repeating the word 'died', he added 'died of a broken heart, to say nothing else'. And after four years his diary has this judgement on his arch-accuser: 'he can better bear reproach than to hear others praised, and his hatred of others infinitely exceeds his love of himself'. Stressing the difference between deed and imputed intention, for which he was condemned in the matter of Chait Sing, the fire of 1781 breaks out again; 'there was a time also when I did intend to put him to death, which I certainly should have done if I had catched him, but I am not for that reason guilty of murder'. There exist also his instructions for a possible cross-examination of Francis:

    (i) What passed on the voyage between him and Monson and Clavering?

    (ii) Whether he did not himself receive presents?

He had some private troubles during 1790. Marian lost some considerable money, when her bankers failed and one partner shot himself; 'would to heaven', this stark German woman wrote, 'he had did it ten years ago'. Then his post-chaise upset him on the Woodstock road, breaking his collar-bone. In London he kept up some state in Park Lane. His butler was paid forty guineas a year; to have charge of wine and plate, 'sit at the head of the servants' table for order', and dress his master's hair, — this last, surely, not a heavy duty. Resolutely he concentrated on the building of Daylesford, where he went in all weathers. For part of the summer he took a house near Reading, where he rode with his old secretary Thompson; the visits he paid were all to such old friends, Sykes, Auriol, or the D'Oyleys. Messages from India sustained him. Colonel Pearse, fiery as ever, wrote of 'the beasts' of England, but 'let the fire glow, the gold cannot be hurt'. The Indian testimonials that Thompson had first organized were coming in, despite strict government neutrality. The Benares Brahmins and the Moslem royal family at Murshidabad were equally ardent. The two ever-loyal Berar pandits, who had marched with him to Chunar, sent 25,000 rupees; old Cantoo followed with £1000.

He needed consolation, as he came away from consultation with Law in Lincoln's Inn, or sadly compared the months of Archbishop Laud's impeachment with the years of his own. Once or twice the self-control on which he prided himself broke down. Once very early on, when Adam was arguing that his Benares narrative had doctored dates, and in an audible whisper Hastings said 'it is false'. 'I was provoked', says his note, 'by a gross

WARREN HASTINGS, 1795, BY ROMNEY

expression, accompanied by an insolence of gesture, to interrupt him.' But in general this self-discipline never relaxed. In 1790, when parliament was dissolved and the very continuance of his trial was at stake, his diary has this self-reproach, 'suffered myself to be too much moved to-day by the anxieties of my friends'.

Had he known how long it was to be, said his first petition, he would have pleaded guilty. And when after three years the managers closed their case, he once more rehearsed his grievances, his pen recovering for almost the last time the stately march of his Indian prime. He dwelt again on the denial of a chartered British liberty, of speedy justice; the loss of his witnesses; the ruin of his fortunes. Would he, for instance, be allowed to use the sworn statement of Colonel Eaton, who had died since, by far his strongest evidence for the disaffection of Chait Sing? He pointed to the sheer necessities of that time; to his success, when warring against two European powers and all India, as compared with Cornwallis' present struggle to reduce the single State of Mysore. He was accused of ruining India; had Dundas, then, annually presented false accounts to the Commons? The managers were sent there to prove their charges, 'not to revile me', not to import an 'atrocious calumny' like Devi Singh. Burke had said his Indian testimonies came from hands 'yet warm with the thumbscrews', but was there any case in history of 'an injured people rising up voluntarily to bear false testimony in favour of a distant and prosecuted oppressor'?

He was no orator, he said, in apologizing for reading from his notes. And once, when interrupted by Fox and Burke, broke out in almost an agony, — 'save me from this violence, I beseech you do not let me be interrupted. I cannot speak from the sudden impulse of my own mind.' There were many cries of 'go on'; as he did, to some purpose. 'To the Commons of England, in whose name I am arraigned for desolating the provinces of their dominion in India, I dare to reply that they are — the most flourishing of all the states in India. It was I who made them so. The valour of others acquired, I enlarged and gave shape and consistency to, the dominion which you hold there. I preserved it. I sent forth its armies with an effectual but an economical hand, through unknown and hostile regions, to the support of your other possessions. . . . I maintained the wars which were of your formation, or of that of others, not of mine. . . . When you cried out for peace, and your cries were heard by those who were the objects of it, I resisted this and every other species of counteraction by rising in my demands, and accomplished a peace, and I hope a lasting one, with one great state, and I at least afforded the efficient means by which a peace, if not so durable more seasonable at least, was accomplished with another. I gave you all; and you have rewarded me with confiscation, disgrace, and a life of impeachment.'

That was on June the 2nd, 1791. On the night of the 29th he moved to his new house at Daylesford, and slept there. One hundred and forty dozen of Madeira having preceded him, it was clear he meant to stay.

CHAPTER XXVII

The End of the Trial: 1791-95

THE rest of this year he spent mostly at home, with Baber and Mrs. Motte as their first guests. A burning hot summer that suited these Indians well, diversified by some weeks of sea-bathing at Margate. It did his heart good to read the tributes that had come from India. From Benares, that 'never did he break the glass-like minds of the lowly with the stone of violence'; from the Nuddea Brahmins, that 'he sought the right, and was judge of it'; from some obscure *zemindar*, that 'in the conduct that becomes a chief he had no equal'. And was not England coming round too? He kept a letter from the old Moravian bookseller, James Hutton, — 'most dear, most honoured, and most injured of men . . . the shame I wished for your enemies is increasing, and ought not to be diminished'.

The fire of the impeachment had gone out. No more crowded days now, as when 164 peers had marched in at the opening, or 300 of the Commons attended to hear Fox on Benares. Though even in those days Fanny Burney overheard one of the legislators groaning, 'What a bore! When will it be over? Who is that? Yes, a pretty girl, Kitty.' The country seemed to have come round to that way of thinking. Galleries were nearly empty, over thirty peers rarely were present, no more 'cold collations' in dukes' boxes. Even in 1789 Fox discussed 'honourable retreat', and when the Commons censured Burke, Fox and Grey were for throwing it up. Only the possessed purpose of Burke, and Francis inspiring it, determined they should go on. With each obstacle he grew all the fiercer, persuaded that he was avenging the cause of all humanity, and that the vote of the Commons for impeachment was itself a verdict of guilt. Yet even he recognized that his party must be allowed to see a terminus, and in May 1790, when only three of the twenty-two charges had been dealt with, it was resolved to make a short selection of what remained.

Burke survived a second crisis, when it was settled that impeachment had not lapsed with the dissolution of parliament. Pitt and Dundas voted with him, against most of the legal stars, Erskine and Arden and the future Eldon, and carried the day. But if public enthusiasm were dead, only party energy could make these dead bones live. And the Whig party was temporarily destroyed. The Revolution sent Burke, Portland, and Elliot in one direction, Fox, Grey, and Francis in another. The managers met infrequently and coldly, as enemies. The King's displeasure had been marked from the first; gradually the royal princes went the same way. But these were only contributory causes. The impeachment foundered on the evidence and the merits.

For one thing, the managers' own witnesses gave the lie to their build-up of Hastings as a Nero, a ravening beast, a monster of cruelty. Colonel Gardner, who showed much sympathy for Chait Sing, said of Hastings 'a more amiable private character he had never known'. Colonel Achmuty, who disbelieved in the Begums' rebellion, added he did not believe Hastings 'would oppress anyone'. Major Gilpin, whose decency to the Begums won him much honour, knocked down the legend that the eunuchs had been scourged; 'no severities used but the confinement and irons'. And when it came to the witnesses for the defence, every ship brought officers ready to testify to the insurrection of Oudh. Colonel Duff had waited long on the trial, returned to India to fight a campaign with Cornwallis, and now was back again to say that Indians looked on the accused as 'a very great and very injured man'. But the weight of evidence, so intangible on the printed record, depends on the character of the witness, and in some few cases we can judge the great impression made on the court.

Of these the first was Shore, examined in June 1790. This literal and profoundly religious man was apprenticed, we have seen, in Francis' following, though he had since received the confidence of Hastings. Both Dundas and Cornwallis held the highest opinion of him, having him in mind as next Governor-General, which duly came about in 1792. His private letters took a severe line on Hastings' 'reprehensible indifference' about other men's profits, but were emphatic on his own incorruption.

He had also declined to take any official part in collecting Indian testimonials in Hastings' favour. This very independence demolished the revenue charges once for all. Hastings' measure of 1781, he deposed, had not deprived Council of its powers; his abolition of the Provincial Councils had been well justified; no Indian, he thought, should have the authority allowed to Gunga Govind Singh, yet he was as good as any Indian official. Asked in cross-examination whether, if Hastings were the cruel and corrupt figure of the accusation, he would continue on terms of friendship with him, the witness answered emphatically, 'I should hope not'.

In May 1792 young Markham was questioned for four days on end about what happened at Benares eleven years before. As Burke led the cross-examination, and most scandalously tried to use a letter written at Benares in the midst of the tragedy, and privately confided to him then by Markham's father, the court came to life again. That Chait Sing was no prince, that his disloyalty was glaring and his government a low tyranny, Markham's evidence seemed to prove. What most struck the audience, however, was his final tribute, given with a solemn emotion; that Hastings was never moved by thought of self, that 'he is the most virtuous man of the age in which he lives'. Popham's evidence a fortnight later on the same scenes was almost equally effective; Hastings was 'beloved and reverenced' by the peoples of India, — 'the man of all others I would wish to serve under'.

In April 1794 the court, more crowded than for three years past, at Hastings' request heard his successor as Governor-General. Cornwallis' criticism of the revenue abuses and the condition of Oudh had been freely exploited by the managers, but Hastings' counsel now extracted some substantial points. Hastings was 'much esteemed and respected' by Indians. His conduct of the great war had rendered 'essential services'. He did not believe that the Begums had been reduced to financial distress, nor that our treatment of them and Chait Sing had damaged the national character.

He was followed immediately by Larkins, late Accountant-General, whose integrity both Cornwallis and the Directors vouched for. He had come home rather pained by Hastings, who had left him in a long silence, possibly because his home had been broken up and Hastings had begged him to forgive his wife. But Burke's 11th report had cast on him, he complained to the Directors, some 'implacable reflections', and his present answers to Burke were resolute and most revealing. Hastings' financial character was the exact contrary of that represented in the charges ; he was 'perfectly careless as to the state of his own private fortune'. Every rupee of the presents received had been spent in the public service. Every detail that he, the witness, had furnished to the Company of these gifts and bond transactions, had been given by Hastings' instructions.

By 1794, then, hopes of acquittal were much brighter. His demeanour had 'hardened', Burke complained. True, his champion Thurlow no longer presided, having been dismissed by Pitt, his place as Chancellor being filled by Francis' friend Wedderburn, now Lord Loughborough, whom the diary instantly denounces as 'scandalously partial'. And, despite his protestations, the managers had been given another six months to prepare their final reply. This, and his desperate finances, almost broke down his endurance ; his coach horses had gone to sale at Tattersalls, and he hired a pair of 'job greys'. Twice this year he had violent scenes with Burke. Once when he was accused of printing a reply in Calcutta to some censure from the Directors, 'the assertion is false', he said, 'it is all of a piece with everything I have heard since the commencement of this trial by that authorized, licensed, — manager'. And again in the middle of Burke's positively last nine-day oration, he sprang up to deny that the Directors had ever ordered an enquiry on his treatment of the Begums ; 'a man's patience may be exhausted, I hear so many falsehoods'. Burke's mad temper boiled over ; 'this wicked wretch', he began amid cries of 'order', 'the ravings of this unhappy man, — he ought to be sent to Bridewell'.

But Burke was alone. His band of brothers were now his enemies. His home was desolate. His brother Richard died in the spring ; his adored son was coughing life away, and died in August. Sorrow drove him to frenzy. Declaring the poisoned Ganges had contaminated the Thames, his report on the conduct of the trial attacked the judges. When Hastings complained of these unparalleled delays, he vowed the managers suffered even more ; 'we have not got £90,000 of Rajah Nobkissen's money in our pockets'. His nine days in winding up were execrable. 'Filth and excrement' ; 'a night cellar among thieves' ; 'if the

prisoner is innocent, the Commons are guilty'; 'Hastings says
to Hannay, "You have sucked blood enough for yourself, now
suck blood for your neighbours"'. And so forth. In June, when
the House voted thanks to the managers, a motion was made to
exclude Burke, and the principal resolution was only carried by
50 votes against 21. It was his last appearance in the House he
had so often glorified.

Before that day the accused rode off to Daylesford. 'Joined
the hounds on my grey pony, to see three hares killed', says his
September diary, in an autumnal peace. For the great attack
was over, and next year would bring the verdict. That it would
go well, he was certain, for he had already asked the headmaster
of Westminster to give the school an extra holiday the following
April. Meantime they were busy domestically, getting ready for
the marriage of his stepson Charles Imhoff. The bride was
Charlotte Blunt, daughter of that rather jobbing Sir Charles to
whom Hastings had given an agency, now making one of the impeachment charges, for the army's interminable supply of bullocks.

The Lords' proceedings, from early March till the verdict on
April the 23rd, 1795, were dominated by Thurlow. He alone
seemed to have every document at his fingers' ends. Pointing
out that on fourteen charges no evidence was offered at all, he
concentrated on the critical matters; speaking on the financial
detail with specially notable effect. Mansfield (Hastings' schoolfellow Stormont) also carried weight. As an ex-Secretary of State,
his evidence had been decisive on the danger of French war in
1778; besides, having been a member of the Fox-North Cabinet,
he spoke with detachment. In fact, he voted 'guilty' on the
Nobkissen charge, which he thought indefensible. And having
missed only seven hours over seven years, he contributed to the
understanding, that only those peers should vote who had heard
a substantial part of the case; which at least helped to maintain
the Lords' traditional character of being an assembly of average
men. Nothing assuredly could be more average than the majority
of the twenty-nine who gave judgement; such as Morton, who
had never missed a sitting, Somers, Hawke, Boston, or Sandys.
The political level was raised by the Whigs Loughborough,
FitzWilliam, and Norfolk; by Thurlow, Sydney, and Leeds, all
ex-members of Pitt's Cabinet, and the Prince's friend Moira,
afterwards Marquess of Hastings and Governor-General. Old

Markham of York and two bishops voted, but only the able and anti-revolutionary Horsley of Rochester spoke on these proceedings. The great Lansdowne would not vote, not having attended often, but the most typical of English views was given by this most untypical of Prime Ministers. To apply our liberal panaceas to India, he argued, was 'downright nonsense'. Cornwallis was, like Hastings, an absolute ruler. We should only ask one question. 'Had he governed India to the satisfaction of the people? And had he improved the interest which his native country had in those distant possessions? These would have been the only questions which the late King of Prussia, the greatest and wisest man of the age, would have asked Mr. Hastings, if he had possessed so rich a dominion and so meritorious a servant.'

On St. George's Day, at 12.30, for the last time the Lords came to the Hall, those who were giving judgement wearing their robes; at 1.50 an acquittal was pronounced on every article. The largest figures against him were six on Chait Sing and the Begums, and five on the Nobkissen loan; on the alleged bribes of 1772–74, going back to Nuncumar, he was acquitted unanimously. As sentence was given, there was some slight clapping in the galleries. That afternoon he called to thank Thurlow, and later entertained at dinner his old and loyal friends, Caillaud, Sykes, Impey, Anderson, Baber, Auriol, Toone, D'Oyley, Thompson, Stephen Sulivan, and Scott, together with his counsel, his stepson, and his nephew, Tommy Woodman. How he could pay for dinner remained to be seen, not to mention the £100 he distributed among the court attendants.

Life had more zest in the next months. He dined at the Academy, and finished sitting for his portrait to Lemuel Abbot. On May the 22nd the Bengal Club entertained him at Willis' Rooms in King Street, where 500 sat down under the presidency of Marian. 'Mrs. H. in tears, was near fainting', says the diary: however, she stayed till four in the morning, and he till half-past five. Did the shouting and the wheels wake Philip Francis, in bed in St. James' Square? Letters of congratulation flowed in, for many months; from Lord Hood ('Victory, St. Helens'), James Boswell, Bengal officers, or Jane's brother, Henry Austen, nephew of his dear Philadelphia Hancock. From Lally Tollendal too, son of the Frenchman who had suffered death for over-daring in India; 'vous ne serez sûrement pas surpris que le fils du

General Lally soit accouru à votre porte'. When he reached Daylesford, there were the band and bell-ringers from Stow on the Wold. In July the D'Oyleys gave an 'elegant breakfast' in the New Forest, with a band playing on an island, fruits and ices, Hastings' picture decked in lilies and flanked by a scowling Thurlow, children distributing bouquets beribboned in letters of gold 'Virtue Triumphant'. But was it so?

For here, perhaps, we should essay to sum up the broad impression left by this most famous of British political trials. What in the end remains from those twenty volumes of parliamentary reports, eleven folio volumes of evidence, and three thousand pages of oratory from managers and counsel? from twenty years of agitation, all the malign mass of Francis, and the crusade of Burke? Where the bulk is so great, and the moralities so involved, no one view can offer more than material for judgement.

The charges, as drafted by Burke and Francis, were a tissue of bias, falsified history, and unproved innuendo. Their central theme, of a 'habitual evil intention', is refuted by unassailable truths. No such character could have won the affection of Indians then, or the outstanding respect of Indians since. Half the legends withered as the evidence proceeded. Two of the angriest details, for example, could hardly survive the simple facts; that Cornwallis had recommended a pension to Munny Begum for her services, and that he praised the virtues of the Oudh minister Hyder Beg, with whom Hastings was supposed to be in an unholy alliance against his master. Indeed, Cornwallis' reforms, Shore's political failure, Wellesley's Mahratta wars, all proved within a decade that Hastings had made a British Indian dominion with rare wisdom, and vindicated his policy in dealing with Indian States.

It was the managers' first purpose to brand him as soaked in corruption and the basest self-interest. His money doings were, as Thurlow admitted, 'the weak point of his character'. His rewards to his disciples, or those linked to him by political interest, were excessive. David Anderson combined the emoluments of absentee head of the Revenue Board and of agent to Scindia, — in all, £15,000 a year. Stephen Sulivan had not been six months judge-advocate when he received the opium contract, which he at once resold for £40,000. And though Pitt, like the soldiers, defended the agencies given to Belli and Auriol, the commissions allowed were princely, and the accountancy loose in the extreme.

As for the gifts taken privately and then carried to the Company's account, they were open to manifest abuse. The Directors were informed of the fact, but never the donor's identity, on Chait Sing's bribe. Middleton never heard of the Vizier's ten lacs till he reached England. Larkins was dependent for his knowledge of the gifts from revenue farmers on what Cantoo, or the Governor's *munshi*, chose to tell him. To borrow largely off a rogue like Nobkissen, and then use it as a set-off to his own claims on the Company, was a shocking way of doing a conceivably good thing.

Yet, apart from Larkins' unshaken evidence, it is clear as daylight that every disclosure was made, and even inaccuracies exposed, by Hastings himself. His defiance to hostile Directors, his airy candour when they were friends, were alike open and convincing; as Fox said, though in no friendly sense, on all money subjects there was something 'peculiarly magnificent' about him. He could have concealed all these gifts, he wrote contemptuously, — indeed, had originally meant to, — but the Vizier's gift was too big to hide. He brushed aside as unprofitable conjectures why he had sometimes taken bonds, or sometimes not, and the dates when he had endorsed them; his services had not merited this petty investigation. For his secrecy he had his reasons, in the state of emergency and a divided Council, but for the principle he never apologized; any opportunity to relieve the public necessities was legitimate. When all is said, every prop by which he could have masked peculation was knocked away by his own hand, and the true charge must be not corruption but an insensibility, a legacy of the India in which he had been bred.

Corruption thus disposed of, what remained were charges regarding policy, which the course of the trial really reduced to two, Chait Sing and the Begums of Oudh. Granted the emergency of 1781, the proved status of Chait Sing and his proved disaffection, at what point did Hastings depart from the path of justice? Was it in even meditating a fine of half a million, 'to draw from his guilt', as the Narrative says, 'the means of relief to the Company's distresses'? A fine never finally fixed, nor announced to the victim. Or did it stop short with a culpable political mistake, the arrest in his own capital of a prince whom he did not mean to depose? In any case, he passed the margins which could have made possible any retreat.

In Oudh it may be thought that there were elements of more deliberation and dishonesty, which bring it nearer to political crime. It was the view of Wheler, and most military men, that the Begums' guilt was certain, though Major Gilpin would have acquitted the younger one. And that Oudh passed through an upheaval, and that recruits from Oudh reached Chait Sing, seem tolerably certain. Yet we are left with two ugly facts. The British officers in Oudh service feathered their own nests without much scruple; the popular hatred of Hannay in particular cannot be doubted. Again, Hastings' representations, both at the time and in the early stages of his trial, distorted the truth. It seems established that both the resumption of the *jagirs*, and the seizure of the treasures, were initiated by Hastings, — not, as he often alleged, on the Vizier's suggestion — and forced through by British sepoys. 'Memory' Middleton's word leaves an impression that we cannot trust it; and when Thurlow argued that Hastings never meant to compel the Vizier, and was ignorant of the eunuchs' imprisonment, he asks too much of us.

Better to leave this matter with the accused's words of 1793. 'The imperious exigencies of public affairs often present to the servants of the State no alternative but the painful choice of contending evils. . . . Besieged, as at some times I was, by the hourly and clamorous importunities of every department of the military service, goaded at others with the cries of our then famished settlements on the coast of Coromandel, should I have deserved well, I do not say of my country, but of the common cause of suffering humanity, if I had punctiliously stood aloof from those means of supply which gratitude, or expectation, had enabled me to appropriate to the instant relief of such distresses?'

And the last word, perhaps, must be left at the hope he expressed to the court the same year, that 'my name at least shall not descend blasted with infamy to posterity, but be recorded with those of the many other victims of false opinion, some of higher worth, none of better intentions'.

He was acquitted. Even so, he must live. Six of his Indian friends, — Baber, Toone, Sumner, Middleton, Auriol, and Dallas — each lent him £2000 this year, while he borrowed another £3000 from Wombwell. And £17,000 had come in 1790–91 from Company servants in India. Most of this had doubtless gone, while all combined would nothing like meet his need. The trial had cost him £71,000, of which £40,000 were still outstanding, on a bond carrying 5 per cent interest. His total debts mounted at least to £85,000, including a heavy bill from Major Scott. Against this, the Company put his assets as worth £45,000, coming from the Daylesford estate, a valuable diamond, and shares in two East Indiamen. So even if he stripped himself bare, he would still owe 10s. in the £.

His ever-generous employers, he never ceased to say, owed him nothing; his claim was against the nation. His first step, therefore, taken against strong warning from his counsel, was to sound ministers, whether they would support a petition asking repayment of his costs. To which Pitt returned a merely formal reply, that he could not so advise His Majesty. Thereupon the Company chairman, Lushington, laid two proposals before a general court, that his law costs should be paid, and that he should also receive an annuity of £5000, which was the sum voted to Cornwallis. The debate was by no means unanimous. Some objected to the burden on the Company, some thought Hastings should have saved money in his years of office, Charles Grant voiced moral disapproval of his policies. Though both resolutions were accepted by ballot, over 200 proprietors voted in each minority.

One point delayed any decision, whether under recent legislation the Directors had the power to vote indemnification of costs from Indian revenues. Their legal advisers were divided, while by September they had the law officers' ruling, that neither annuity nor costs could be paid without assent from the Board of Control. Another court showed no advance. Many showed some weariness of the lengthy eulogies falling from Scott and young Impey; the influential Francis Baring was strong on the legal objections. Nor did Hastings' own attitude assist his friends. He showed resentment at the possibility of being given a smaller sum than Cornwallis, and an unwise letter to the court claimed the costs as his right, — 'this was less my trial than that of the East India Company and the British nation'. Their reference to the Board of Control has a black mark in his diary; 'my disappointment on Thursday caused me to lose my temper, and affected me the whole day'.

At last, in March 1796, agreement was reached between the Directors and Dundas. The Company was to award an annuity of £4000 for twenty-eight years, running retrospectively from his return in 1785 to the expiry of their present charter in 1813, besides a loan of £50,000 without interest. So he received a sum down of £42,000 for his annuity up to date. But henceforward £2000 each year would be kept back by the Company, in order to liquidate their loan, on which he lost some 4 per cent interest, while he must assign the Daylesford title-deeds as extra security. He estimated his personal expenditure at £3500 a year, 'rather below than exceeding the rank in life which my former station might have entitled me to assume', and he was liable for £1000 a year in interest on another £20,000 of debt. In short, unless more were done, bankruptcy would come nearer with every year.

No matter, he was acquitted, and set about printing, and handsomely binding for selected friends, a report of the Lords' debates and votes. His preface was stern. 'Bound to the stake during a period of nine long years', he had no claim on the Company, but a great one on the nation; 'it still exists against it'. Yet he rejoiced in the hope that, 'when the determined hour of his corporeal extinction arrives, he shall not wholly die but still live in the hearts of many'. And Daylesford was his, though indeed the chief cause of the ruin to which for the moment he shut his eyes.

So, with £42,000 paid over, they lived a full life in 1796. In May Marian gave a London ball. In June they went to the Lakes; inspected a carpet factory at Kidderminster and iron works near Bridgnorth; put up at the Bridgewater Arms at Manchester, 'dirty and imposing'; on to Coniston, sailed to Ambleside, and rode up Skiddaw. All this, with six horses and five servants, cost £220. Finally, they had a London excursion before Christmas, to the Westminster play, and to visit Madame Schwellenburg at Windsor.

They kept the feast at Daylesford, where all was well, except 'the gas of the new beer rising into the bedchamber'.

CHAPTER XXVIII

The Squire of Daylesford: 1796-1818

HENCEFORTH Daylesford was their only home. In 1797 he sold his Park Lane house to Lord Rosebery, actually at some profit, though Marian used £10,000 of the price as a marriage settlement for her son Charles. And at Daylesford he lived ten months, perhaps, on the average in every year, till his death a quarter of a century later.

For a house in ruins and a decayed estate of 650 acres, Mr. Knight had driven a stout bargain, asking over £11,000, besides an annuity of £100. But Hastings was not satisfied till he had recovered every acre of the ancestral manor. He bought back the advowson of the rectory, spent another £3100 on a fifty-acre farm, and went on till a last eleven acres in 1808 rounded off the whole. Then came the rebuilding. His architect was Samuel Pepys Cockerell, the Company's surveyor, whose brother Charles, late of Bengal, was one of his neighbours, living at the fine house of Sezincote. And by this year Cockerell's bills had topped £21,000, with another £3000 to his clerk of the works. With other special items, the total cost reached about £54,000.

Nothing could be too good for Daylesford. Its stone was the finest Cotswold, from quarries beyond Burford at Windrush and Barrington. Its wrought iron-work came from the Soho works at Birmingham, and Wedgwood tiles from Etruria. Skilled London craftsmen lodged in the village a whole year, picking out cornices and shutters in pink and rose and two shades of green, varnishing mahogany sashes, gilding leaves, grain, and honeysuckle. All the latest comforts were installed: a hot bath, plate glass, a Bramah water-closet, and a muffin stove.

Then came the making of the walks, groves, and prospects in which that age delighted. His solicitor found most exorbitant the bills of the landscape gardener : 'he said he had made a very reasonable bill, to which I answered that those who received, and those who paid, money often saw things in a very different light'. In fact, his bill for 1788–89 alone was over £480, for silver firs and spruce, Lombardy poplars, walnuts and hornbeam, almond and lilac, juniper and acacia, tamarisk and tulip trees, heliotrope and magnolias, peaches and apricots and nectarines. He sent for dwarf peach and mango from Bengal. His garden cost him about £150 a year, of which his Scottish gardener accounted for a third. On a London visit he would slip off to buy carnation plants in Chelsea, while to their last pages his diaries will record planting 'a circle of acorns' or 'hollies for the church close'.

The most strenuous outside work was making the lake, with bridge and islands and cascade. Great stones, 'the grey geese of Adelstrop', were hauled from a hill near by. Here he bathed among the swans; there was a fishpond too, stocked with tench from Malmesbury, to which one year he added a hundred brace of carp. But the lake was apt to leak, running away with expense for revetment. Now all was getting done, he had his daily round, '897 of my paces'. From the west door to the flower garden, 'across the great bridge, over the end of the pond, down to the bridge across the brook, back through the dark walk, — round the mount, and through the greenhouse'.

By the time of his acquittal, he had the house of his dreams. Set back a mile from the river, where the first Hastings house had stood, it rose where the valley was folded back into the rising hills. The great rooms on the first floor looked south-west, towards a distant view of the church of Stow on the Wold, high on the Fosse way. In the centre was his library. On the mantel-piece blue and white Wedgwood vases, and busts of 'Prinny' and the Duke of York. Banks' bust of himself was there too, over which he had a little dispute, for the sculptor had been sending bronze casts to India as a speculation. On the walls, filled in part by Persian silver chain-armour, was Zoffany's 'Cock Fight' at Lucknow, showing Wheler pale and languid, the effete Asof-ud-Daulah, and that dubious Captain Mordaunt who had once done Marian service; here, too, was Stubbs' equestrian portrait of himself, and some of Hodges' Indian views. There were ebony screens for candles on the painted card-tables, two globes, and a French clock; they added a grand piano later, costing £95.

Here were the miniatures of the Mogul painters, till poverty
obliged him to sell, and his large rambling library. All the stock
Indian memoirs, and most of the English; Coxe's *Walpole*,
Garrick, or Dodington; Roscoe on the *Medici*, Tillotson's sermons
and Atterbury's, Froissart and Puffendorf, many dictionaries; the
Complete Farmer, and the Delphin edition of Catullus, Tibullus,
and Propertius. All Miss Burney's novels, of course, and as time
went on Miss Edgeworth's and Walter Scott's.

Next came the picture-room, with green silk curtains and
ornaments in Indian silver. Here were the portraits of those who
had saved his good name or befriended him, Thurlow and Lord
Morton and the rest; near Marian's enamelled 'Holy Family'
was Hodges' painting of the storm, and 'the heroic fortitude of
Mrs. Hastings' (so the catalogue of 1799) at the rocks of Colgong.
The dining-room was solid, in mahogany chairs and wine-cooler
and sideboard. There was a small drawing-room, with fire-
screens painted by Mary Motte; here they drank tea, for which
Toone, now a director, saw to it that Marian received the best
Souchong. The motif of the great drawing-room was blue and
silver; pale-blue satin curtains with silver lace, blue silk cushions
on painted chairs. Its pride was the famous ivory furniture, sofas
and tables and screens.

We move one floor higher, past the high lamp and the window-
seat, where a golden pheasant gleams under glass. Here was his
plain dressing-room, with Indian bed and mahogany chests, and
Marian's bedroom with purple and green pattern on the white
ground carpet, then her dressing-room with curtains and bell-
ropes in pink. Next door came her boudoir, having more ivory
chairs and bookcase in satinwood, holding 'a choice collection
of the first authors'; her chessmen and écarté box, and Abbot's
portrait of Warren. On this floor, too, were the best bedrooms,
and those kept for the Imhoffs. Another flight led to eleven
more rooms, for bachelors and staff. Every other room in the
house was an Indian museum. Views of Calcutta and Alipur
and the Taj, in silver frames, old Sulivan's portrait in a place of
honour, Coote's skied on the second floor. It was rich in Chinese
wall-papers, and packed with china; Worcester in the main, but
a French service of poppy and cornflower design, a best tea-service
in rose and gold, with another in green and white Spode bought
not long before he died.

Wide stairs led down from the library, by the passage with thermometer and barometer and the estate map, to an ante-room sacred to Marian's gardening outfit, folding camp-stool, hoe and rake with mahogany handles. That took you towards large kitchen quarters, rooms for housekeeper, butler, and the rest, the still-room and cellars; so out to the walled court and the dairy, bakehouse, carpenter's shop, and laundry. And a spacious coal-shed; they used 167 tons in 1799. While the bell strikes in the clock tower, you may inspect the stabling for six carriages, twelve loose-boxes, and stalls for thirteen more.

That sort of house meant a large staff. From Patrick the butler, Howard head groom, Aitchison head gardener, and four more men, to the housekeeper Mrs. Dutton, Sally and Nancy and Peggy, and four other maids. He paid assessed taxes, even in the hard year of 1805, on seven men-servants, besides five garden labourers, one chariot and one 'sociable', eight carriage horses, ten farm horses, three dogs, and the hair-powder tax for four persons. He had ruled too long not to like things decently and in order. So he wrote out 'rules for the barn', or, again, 'coach horses to be walked every morning, chariot at the door every day'. Yet a very kindly master. Each New Year's Day brought gifts to the household; when Howard retired, he was pensioned with fifteen guineas a year. And there are small signs all the time of the consideration that had made Indians love him. This, for instance, on a visit to friends in Portman Square: '£1 in addition to 1 footman, to whom I had given £5 by mistake, which he returned'. Or again, Mrs. Dutton, still with him in 1812, had a nephew, corporal in the Buffs, badly wounded at Albuera, for whom he took immense pains to get a discharge. And when the country was racked after the peace by banks breaking and inflated prices, so that his servants suspected the local bank notes, he sent for notes to the Bank of England.

Daylesford was a minute hamlet, with hardly a hundred souls, and no resident clergyman, the only other man of substance being his own tenant, Farmer Bowles. Even if he had been not Warren Hastings but another man, he must give the lead and guard the flock, body and soul. Any casual page in his diary will show it. 'This evening the sheep-shearers had their customary entertainment . . . the maid servants went to church in the new cart. . . . Good Friday, we all went to church; day labourers invited to go, as part of the day's work; all went.' He set ground aside for a parish green, and built two cottages for widows, — at a cost of £341. Marian organized the village schoolchildren to knit stockings, and plait straw for bonnets. And Kingham, the larger village next door, comes into the picture; 'walked in the procession to the church with the friendly society', whose anniversary sermons he continued to attend.

All this time the war was raging, and neither he nor Daylesford must hang back. A memorandum for Dundas on the food supply in the event of invasion was followed up, during the starvation prices of 1800, with a more finished scheme. Based on his own famine machinery in India, it advocated vesting compulsory powers in a central body which, through local committees, would draw up statistics of grain in store, and compel delivery on the market. On the renewal of war in 1803, he was more active still, his own position being more assured, and Addington a minister of whom he much approved. He wrote to the Duke of York asking military employment for Charles Imhoff, that he might not be 'condemned, as I myself have been, to waste the last period of my life in inaction'. He urged young Elijah Impey not to be backward in offering his service, or it might bring reflections on his father. Then he turned to the village. 'Summoned all my day labourers, and received from all individually a declaration of their willingness to serve as Volunteers under the last Act for arming the country. I afterwards received the same from the parishioners at Farmer Bowles.' He sent off to Woodman for an old musket he had brought back from India forty years ago, and ordered six new ones from Birmingham; then he extracted his old Park Lane porter from Chelsea hospital, and set him to drill the parish 'on Kingham field'. But the lord-lieutenant did not smile on the separate existence of the Daylesford volunteers.

In the peaceful duties of the country gentlemen, his neighbours, he took his share. Now to a meeting of protest against enclosing a bridle-path, now to serve as commissioner for assessed taxes, or at a meeting of turnpike commissioners. He would ride to attend their club at Stow, possibly not with complete enjoyment; one note running, 'dined at the Stow Club, and rode home afterwards with Mr. Penyston. N.B. to order my horse next time at 7, or before.'

His days were full with his horses and farming. Marian's favourite Suliman and his own Arab had many offspring, and in the early years the fields and stables held over thirty horses, whose names — Anne the grey mare, Favourite the Galloway, or the farm mare Cowslip — fill his diaries and his letters to Thompson and D'Oyley. But the stud dwindled as he got poorer, and his Arabian was too old to make a good sire. Both he and Marian in fact developed an equal, almost a Brahmin, love of their cows, whose 'accomplishments and moral virtues' he seriously praised. Sad entries chronicle their misfortunes; 'Letty delivered of a dead calf', or 'the red Yorkshire died suddenly of a clover surfeit'.

He worked at Cotswold farming with the detailed energy he had once given to ruling Bengal. Perhaps his notes and sudden enthusiasms betray the amateur. 'The gestation of a cow', runs one sober note, 'is 300 days', while he and Marian would buy, without more ado, Welsh cattle they met casually on the high road. He carefully studied Humphry Davy's essays in agricultural chemistry; made notes on blight and mildew, or comparative costs of threshing by flail and machine. The unfortunate Bhutan cattle and shawl goats from India wilted and died in the Cotswold winters; he had more success with a hybrid barley-wheat, while after everything else out of doors became too much for him he busied himself with his chillies, bags of which he would send to old Indian friends who liked their curry hot.

On an average he had some 100 acres under arable, kept about 250 sheep, and 18 or 20 cows. At first he was always going the rounds. So 'rode to the meadows; Mrs. H.'s lucerne sowed. She sowed 7 rows with her own hands.' He records transplanting turnips, making 'a repository for potatoes', clearing timber for a new road giving better access to the church, or hanging hams. He notes an approved 'method of preserving eggs', in quick lime, salt, and cream of tartar. He had his manorial code; no gleaner must come on the ground till the crop was lifted. When he left home for any length of time, Farmer Bowles received his marching orders; 'giddy sheep to be killed'; prepare for planting larches; 'Spartwell' to be sowed with vetch, and 'Great Walter's hill' with oats. His diaries become increasingly heterogeneous. So three consecutive entries compare the temperature of London and Bristol water, list the peers present at his trial on a given morning, and proceed to 'mares of 1795 to be covered'. But they are mostly concerned with the powers that came nearest him now, health and the weather, seed-time and harvest, or with small domestic things; 'clock wound, 26 Sept', or a table of the hills on the Daylesford-London road.

Their neighbours came and went, Lady Reade who asked for a lock of his scanty hair, the Penystons of beautiful Cornewell, the Rushouts of Batsford who became Lord and Lady Newick. He would drive to dine with them on moonlight nights. Sometimes Indian guests were staying with Cockerell at Sezincote, or the Dillons had an assembly at Ditchley; up hill and down dale, over hard frozen roads, or through summer's glowing beeches. When the Impeys came to stay, they must see her brother Sir John Reade, and disport themselves; this in June 1801, 'at 10½ we all set out for Bibury races in Sir Elijah's coach; cold and windy: we returned at 9½ P.M.' More rarely he drove to Worcester, to cast his vote for the county member, which took from six in the morning till six at night. A life of peace, but peace dropping slow; a quarter of a century of 'my probationary life', he wrote to Baber, 'certainly not such as I had projected for myself'.

He was only sixty-three when he was acquitted, but some mainspring had broken. Never do we hear again that measured proportioned judgement. For a time he shrank from any further publicity. There was a project to get Marian naturalized, which it was thought wiser to postpone; Lord Abingdon offered him one of the Oxfordshire parliamentary seats, which he declined. A still clearer case came in 1796. His nephew Tommy Woodman having abandoned the law for holy orders, Hastings promised him the reversion of the Daylesford living whenever Dr. Brooks departed this life, whom he thought lazy, and who sometimes cut a service in dirty weather. But when old Woodman suggested his son might take the Hastings name, he met most vehement objection. It would have the effect, Warren wrote, of 'drawing back the public attention upon me, and of exciting suggestions, and even assertions, of the most malignant kind'. So the idea of 'Woodman-Hastings' had to wait till he was dead.

Nine years of abuse and strain had worn his endurance away. A hitch over Lord Rosebery's payment for the Park Lane house robbed him of his sleep. And Marian wrote despairingly to

Richard Johnson, now his banker, that he was harassed day and night by 'gloomy thoughts how he is to live'. He was getting old faster than he should. Now and then he had a return of his dysentery, for which his remedy was plain abstinence; 'eat boiled apple and rice for dinner with an inclination'. For Marian's sake he watched his health assiduously, borrowed Lady D'Oyley's 'remedy for languor', dosed his sore throats with port wine and Daffy's elixir. His regimen became almost fussy. When in London, his drinking water must be carried from a particular spring in Kensington Gardens. And he had rigorous ideas on infusing tea, which he meted out stringently; 'I use daily for breakfast 100 grains of tea, equal in the year to 6 lbs. 4 ozs.'

Much though he loved his countryside, its cold winters and springs appalled him. He comes from church 'frozen to the heart', or goes there 'clad in my fur gown'. He often alluded to the fever of 1782 as leaving some lasting weakness behind. And in 1800, when dining out in London, he had a first serious warning; 'a partial deprivation of my powers of speech and a torpid sensation in my right hand', lasting about a quarter of an hour.

As always, he worried himself about Marian's ailments and her legendary 'tender frame'. She was exacting in those ways. She would ask that the Woodmans' Surrey doctor, by whose advice she had profited, be sent for to Daylesford, and induce her husband to make hurried journeys when she caught a chill. He came to recognize that her constitution was excellent, when she gave it a chance. 'Mrs. H. much better', we hear after one of her migraines, 'but indulging her appetite at dinner and drinking three glasses of port wine . . . was seized with a deadly sickness'; or of another which, surely, she invited, by 'oysters at noon and porter at dinner'. He waited on her with absolute devotion in sickness and in health; may be found by her bed, reading the Good Friday service, or reading a novel aloud to wile away the long coach journey from London. His 'dear associate', as he once called her, was his all; he wrote with delight of her exuberant spirits and her beauty, the year before he died, as though they were back on the *Duke of Grafton*. There was something very beautiful, too, in his relation to his stepson Charles, to whom his letters end, as often as not, with praise of his mother, as 'handsomer than many that were born thirty years ago'. They were rarely separated, but when they were he wrote as of old; 'adieu, my beloved, may the Almighty bless and protect you. This is my morning and nightly prayer, and the wish ever present in my heart.'

He was absorbed into Marian's clan. In 1799 her second son Julius died in Bengal after creditable service, leaving an Indian spouse and three natural children. For two months Warren would not break the news to her. Very soon the eldest boy appeared in England, 'master FitzJulius', being fitted by a Berkeley Square tailor into blue coat and pantaloons. Bills for his dancing lessons, cricket bats, and persistently torn trousers, then for his schooling in Devonshire, mingle with more serious accounts, until he was sent back to Bengal to plant indigo. For the matter of that, contact was never broken between Marian and her first husband. She was godmother to a child of his second marriage, while at his dying request Charles went to Germany to meet his half-sisters and brothers. With the Chapusets, Marian's own family, the bonds were drawn closer still. Her indomitable old mother made her way, during the war, from Stuttgart to Daylesford, and though he could not understand a word of German, much impressed her son-in-law. For one of Marian's nephews he got an Indian cadetship, characteristically equipping him with a case of mathematical instruments and a set of the *Spectator*. But he turned out badly, a late diary noting 'sent home for embezzlement and desertion'. However, a series of his impecunious sisters compensated for this black sheep. First Louise, whom Warren got to love, 'talks English indefatigably and almost intelligibly', and who soon married his parson nephew, Thomas Woodman. Then Rosalie. A third, after his death, who married yet another Rector of Daylesford.

As compared with this, his own kith and kin very occasionally appear. Yet he was fond of his sister, whom he would visit at Ewell to talk over Tommy's career. She died in 1802; he got word of her illness at eight on a May morning, by nine was in a four-horse chaise for Ewell; after three days watching, 'I was present, saw her expire, closed her eyes, and took my everlasting leave of her'. Her husband lived till 1816. Of his Buchanan stepdaughters, Mrs. Findlay still went on, ever begging for an advance on her annuity and with some unproduceable husband in the background.

Outside the family, his visitors and correspondents in the first
Daylesford years were his Indian champions, Thompson and
Middleton, Baber with his trout rod, and Mrs. Motte. And the
houses he visited most were the D'Oyleys at Lymington, Osborne
at Melchett near Romsey, and the Impeys at Newick Park in
Sussex. The one marked exception was Bowood. Lansdowne,
most selective of men, had taken to him warmly, putting his bust
in the long low library where Franklin and Bentham and Dumont
had been honoured guests. A good many summers Warren
and Marian were there, or Lansdowne with young Henry Petty
came to Daylesford. But his Indian links were fast disappearing,
or ending in sorrow. Madame Vernet was gone, the Dutch lady
to whom he had proved his gratitude so long, and who wrote
'your bounty is the only support I have'. His Indian partisans
went soon, Ali Ibrahim Khan and Cantoo; Kamal-ud-Din, dead
insolvent. William Hodges, who had marched that dire night to
Chunar. Angry Colonel Pearse, his second in the duel; old Joe
Price, the ship captain. The young Mogul prince of whom he
had thought so much; his father Shah Allum, worse than dead,
outraged and blinded by the Rohillas. Larkins went in 1800,
Samuel Turner next year, and in 1804 his oldest friend, Francis
Sykes. Chapman wrecked himself at the gambling-table.
Thompson was left with a broken marriage and countless
children. D'Oyley's wife died, he threw money away in speculation, and went back to India to make more. Halhed had
losses too, and was rescued by loans from Hastings, till he got
work for the India Office. Markham died young. Hardly a
soul then was left of his band of disciples, except Palmer with his
Begum wife at Lucknow, Toone the director, and David Anderson
in Midlothian.

As old dependants died, he found new ones, showering kindness on his friends' children. And his bankrupt hand was open
as ever. The widowed sister of a subaltern, hacked to death in
Chait Sing's presence, sent thanks for help with her seven
children; the Reverend George Austen, for introducing one of
Jane's brothers to the Board of Admiralty. Young Francis Sykes,
from the unpromising address of Boulogne, confesses his pecca-
dilloes. Elijah Impey the younger, an Oxford don, was always at
Daylesford, or exchanging verses. Late in life Hastings told
Baber 'I do not feel for the miseries of the human species as I

ought to do. I am too much hardened to them.' But, like others who have written like that, he felt for all whom his eyes beheld in need of help. He sent £40 to the starving Spitalfields weavers, and subscribed to all sorts of good causes, the British and Foreign Bible Society and the Radcliffe Infirmary among them. As for the D'Oyley boys, or his god-daughter Marian Briscoe, he treated them like his own children. He was over seventy when he took on himself the guardianship of young John D'Oyley, whose schools he chose with anxious care, whose lessons he heard in the holidays, and whom he saved from expulsion when a 'rebellion' disrupted the Company's new college at Haileybury.

So the tenor of his life was gentle, not often broken before 1800 except by short flits to London each winter. There, having no house of his own, they would stay with the Imhoffs in Portugal Street, or, that failing, at many hotels; Nerot's or the York, the St. James' in Jermyn Street or Wake's in Brook Street. But there, too, he lived much in his old circle. There was Mrs. Wheler to see at Richmond, Toone in Mortimer Street, the Halheds in Charles Street, and Auriol off Grosvenor Square. Now and then he took Mrs. Motte to a play; once, with Charlotte Imhoff's mother Lady Blunt, stayed at Vauxhall till two in the morning. His church attendance was regular; in South Audley Street, or St. James', Piccadilly. But he called the road to London his road to ruin, returning to Daylesford to pore over his accounts.

His money affairs tormented him. Marian groaned over his casualness. He had sold some of his best Hodges pictures for a song, and could not be got to make a complete list of his debts and his creditors. It came, she thought, 'from knowing that he cannot extricate himself from his troubles'. He was always mislaying papers, and now without any Larkins or Thompson to find them; as he deplored himself, 'it is part of my nature, which increases with years, to be careless of all things'. But even the most elementary arithmetic showed they could not go on as they were. In 1799 he put his debts at £71,000; their joint income was about £4280, but this was reduced by fixed deductions — taxes, interest, and a payment to Marian's mother — to less than £3000; whereas their annual expenditure was nearly £4700. Marian still had about £22,000 of capital, though some was locked up by a Dutch banking-house failing, and some more which D'Oyley had put into Irish land. Part of Warren's private borrowings, from Middleton for instance, had been paid off, but there was still much owing to Scott, who had tabled fantastic charges of over £6000, for overland messengers during the crises of 1782–83.

We may anticipate and abridge the sequel. His first appeal to the Directors in 1799 succeeded to this extent, that they arranged that the £2000 deducted from his annuity should be invested in Company bonds, so accumulating with interest for liquidation of their loan. By 1804, of that £50,000 loan he had repaid £16,000, but how could he expect to live to clear off the whole? He spoke to Addington, Prime Minister now, of 'the horror I should feel to leave my wife destitute'; Castlereagh, president of the Board of Control, pledged government assent to whatever the Company proposed. The Directors were generous; waiving all future repayments, they assigned him his annuity of £4000 in full, antedating it to 1803.

But nothing seemed to do much good, for long, for this generous and most improvident pair. They still had to find interest of about £1300 a year on their borrowings, bankers' letters with warnings of his overdraft descended on Daylesford, it was only in 1810 that he got enough from Marian's estate to pay off Scott. He is found making a few hundred by sale of diamonds to Messrs. Rundle, Bridge & Co. of Ludgate Hill, and painfully seeking to recover from Frederick Stuart's executors what he had lent, in 'improvident kindness' as he said, forty years before. Nothing of this changed him. When Halhed lost some thousands in the French funds, Warren signed a bond for his debts. They thought nothing of ordering at one swoop 1500 each of beech, hornbeam, larch, and birch trees, while between one September and the May following they spent £1345 on jaunts to London, Dover, Margate, and Brighton.

That long shadow always lay across his path. Yet it was not this, we feel, that most clouded the day, but rather frustration, and a sense of rusting powers. 'If I live three years longer', he told his stepson, 'and live as I have done the last 6 or 7, I shall be disqualified for any conversation but upon pigs, turnips, and potatoes.' And how much he felt his total insignificance in public life was made painfully clear to his friends. To have governed 'the first and only valuable portion' of British India thirteen

years, and find himself so powerless, must be 'a mortifying reflection to a mind even less susceptible than mine'. One successor
after another, from Cornwallis to Wellesley, was rewarded or
ennobled, but his advice was never asked on questions of which
he knew more than any man living. Was there not, he murmured,
'some mysterious spell put upon me'? Hours slowly passing in
driving ten miles to dine with a country squire, and ten miles
home again in the cold, — of such 'ennui working on the
imagination', he once and again mildly complained.

Nevertheless, he schooled himself to be content, with hopes of
a name fully restored in days he would not live to see, and to be
grateful for all he was allowed of happiness. The evening prayer
he composed for his household gave thanks 'for whatsoever Thou
hast enabled us to do . . . which we can reflect upon with
satisfaction . . . we bless Thee for our being, for our reason, and
all the endowments and faculties of our souls and bodies'. But
'grant us, O Lord, that the sense of our unworthiness may always
keep us humble'.

Many times in these Daylesford diaries he wrote of his daily
and nightly consolations : first and always Marian's presence, the
scent of his lilacs and laburnum, the peace of his native hills. And
as time goes on they tell us that the long night of humiliation was
nearly gone.

CHAPTER XXIX

The End: 1797-1818

AGED 64-85

THE first beam came from that eccentric political reflector, the Prince of Wales. In 1797 he asked the Directors to give him a dinner, including Hastings in the list of guests to be commanded, — perhaps a demonstration of his displeasure with Pitt. A few weeks later he gave him two interviews, at which he spoke in a misty way of employment or honours. Yet the Prince was not so potent a friend as time and the destinies.

It was not merely that Burke died the same year, writing almost on his death-bed a shocking letter about Marian and 'her paramour'. Nor that Dundas himself was impeached for corruption in 1805, nor that Pitt and Fox both died the year after. Nor even that the verdict of acquittal responded, as it clearly did, to most public opinion. Greater causes, a whole world changing, brought new light and warmth to shine upon him. War and revolution demolished the party which had denounced him, put in the ascendant the qualities that defy danger and the men who used the strong medicine of power, and immersed British India in the epoch of Napoleon. Those who saved the State did not disdain the praise of a tested man of action. In 1801 he wrote to Nelson, of 'the love and veneration of your country', to which the admiral answered he could value no man's praise more highly, 'you that have been the chief of an Empire nearly as large as Europe must be a fair judge of merit'. The triumph of Wellesley over Tippu, his drastic handling of Oudh and the Carnatic, seemed to vindicate Hastings' claims for British supremacy, and justify his short-cuts to great ends. The memorable band of his political officers obeyed Hastings' vision of Britain as an Oriental power.

Many small signs suggested that the Whig vendetta was nearly dead, and the ban lifted on the exile. The Royal Society made him a member. He became a governor of Christ's Hospital. Royal personages followed the Prince's lead. His devotion to the King, whose representative he had always proudly claimed to be, was tested and approved; an engraving of Dr. Willis, who had cured the royal insanity, hung prominently at Daylesford, while in later attacks he was always copying out the daily bulletins. But he contrived to adjust this to the friendship of the Prince, who during 1800 entertained him both at Carlton House and Brighton. In fact, he promised to visit Daylesford, which he never did, for which the *émigré* princes, Orléans and Montpensier, made inadequate substitutes.

Their real friend among princes, and regular visitor, was 'Silly Billy', William Duke of Gloucester, the King's nephew. This simple kindly man dined with their Cotswold society, or would send his carriage in London to take the old man to the opera; and on many Sundays they walked together to St. George's, Hanover Square. It would be idle to think that he did not enjoy this royal notice as much as most men. Whenever he could, he attended the levee; more than once making a note of displeasure, 'went to the drawing-room, and was almost undistinguished by the Queen, being perhaps the last spoken to'. But he found the increasing deference of the Company even more grateful. Of which an early sign was a request from the chairman of 1801, the very able David Scott, for his observations on Wellesley's college for young civilians.

So he began to emerge again, and rejoiced. His former enemies, he wrote to D'Oyley, 'who were such only from the prevalence of party — have either become converts to a different opinion and feeling towards me, or softened into indifference, and the time is fast approaching when I may revive from public oblivion with the expiration of my natural existence'. A second lease of life seemed granted. They were seen at Brighton, and for longer spells in London, at Bath in 1804, and Margate in 1805. He would dine with Charles Imhoff in barracks, or attend the Westminster dinner at Willis' rooms. In 1808 he named and launched an East Indiaman *Warren Hastings* and, having once given up riding, took to it again on a roan pony, sent him by Thompson.

The year 1806, his seventy-fourth, may serve to illustrate this restoration. Leaving the Impeys, where they had spent Christmas, they moved on New Year's Day to Brighton; 'on the marine parade were stopped and graciously accosted by the Prince of Wales'. Next day, dinner at the Pavilion, 'the Prince leading Mrs. Hastings and Mrs. FitzHerbert'. They returned to London on the 4th, having taken 112 Park Street for four months, at thirteen guineas a week. On the 9th he followed the funeral procession of Nelson, which occupied eleven hours. Pitt was just dead, and he canvassed votes for Henry Petty, who came in for the vacant seat at Cambridge University, beating Althorp and Palmerston. In March he went to vote for Mr. Lygon at Worcester, coming back to London for some important interviews with the Prince and Lord Moira, of which more later. In April he sat to Beechey, for a portrait he was giving to the Duke of Gloucester, paying forty-five guineas for it. After a few months at home, in August they set off for Scotland, after a week on the road reaching the Andersons at St. Germains. In Edinburgh, to a banquet from the East India Club, and to a Presbyterian service, — 'heard nothing'. In September they journeyed back by the Lakes, riding sixteen miles round Borrowdale; and so, by Kendal, Preston, and Lichfield, home.

It was more a revival of spirit than bodily strength. We hear much of colds and chills, and a good deal of hemlock pills and opium. But he continued unforgetting. Pitt he had never forgiven, and when Dundas was impeached he vowed that, if his costs were paid, he would again petition for his own. When in 1806 a new Governor-General had to be found, he was triumphant when the Directors resisted Whig pressure for Francis or Lauderdale, only to sicken at the final choice of 'such a fellow as Lord Minto'. He thought of a formal protest; hurried home to rout out Gilbert Elliot's 'most insidious letter' to him of 1781, which protested that his dead brother, 'the person whom I loved most in the world', had taught him both respect and affection for the Governor. But, fearing Minto's 'active malignity' would endanger his friends, he grudgingly dropped his purpose; 'such was not my practice when my mind possessed the vigour which it now wants'.

Here he judged himself aright, for we cannot derive from his latter-day political views any reasoned opinions, or much to commend. On some points he thought much more like a Whig than the average Pittite. He had drawn up a scheme for gradual abolition of the slave trade. He supported Catholic emancipation. He disbelieved in the Orders in Council. He thought that our attack on Copenhagen 'merited reproach'. On Bonaparte and the war he departed widely from the beaten track; 'I rejoice that God has made him the avenger of the spoliation of Poland', this he repeated to all and sundry. He disliked 'invectives of contempt' for the Emperor of the French, nor did he approve of the proposed dismemberment of France. This latent sympathy in part came from his belief that a single authority was superior to party Cabinets, and that 'all the great movements of the political world receive their direction and consequences from individuals'. How wretched a thing was party oratory! 'that waste of words and time'.

His own bitter memories and heartfelt desires dictated such intervention as he made in domestic politics. When war broke out again, and Pitt with Fox and the Grenvilles combined to overthrow the government, he asked for an interview with Addington, to whom he read a most ill-judged memorandum; declaring the Commons did not represent the voice of the people, who were indignant at this 'savage attack' on the good King. Enough for him that Addington had listened kindly to his money troubles, and that his fall meant the return of Pitt. So again, when the ministry of All the Talents succeeded to Pitt, he approached the Prince and his representative in the new Cabinet, Moira, a Hastings like himself. It was too late now, he said, to ask what he once had hoped for, reappointment as Governor-General, or a seat on the Board of Control. But he claimed some reparation from the Commons, who had marked him out 'as a traitor to my country'; some fulfilment, too, of the 'expectations which your Royal Highness yourself has excited in the breast of the person in the world whose wishes I have ever preferred to my own'. The Prince courteously agreed that Marian was 'the most amiable of women', but referred him to Moira, who pointed out the very considerable obstacles. His colleagues, Fox and Windham for example, could hardly be asked to stultify their past. At that he drew back. He would accept a peerage from the Prince, never as a favour from men who had 'grossly wronged me'; better 'go down to the grave with the plain name of Warren Hastings'.

It is more profitable to glean some of his last thoughts on what he cared for most; 'I love India a little more than my own country'. There were the men whose applause he aspired to deserve, the body of Company servants against whom an odium had 'so ungratefully, as well as injustly, prevailed'. A death in their ranks would recall what he owed them. So, when he heard of Colonel Morgan's, who with Pearse had shut the Fort against Clavering, he remembered how, but for them, 'I might have had my government wrested from me by violence, or been reduced to maintain it by bloodshed'. Occasionally he presided at Bengal Club dinners, while from Toone or Anderson he got reassurance in opinions which he himself had instilled. Here was 'the first office under the British Empire', which he urged Moira to accept, giving an opening for doing 'more extensive good' than any other in the gift of the Crown, enabling a man to win 'the love and admiration of a grateful people through a long succession of ages'. It was the safety of India, or its strategic import, that appealed to him in the great war. When Bonaparte invaded Egypt, he pressed for the immediate seizure of Perim; even in 1814, he almost sprang from his chair at mention of the Persian Gulf. He was speaking to a young Lieutenant Hastings, R.N., a distant connection, who handed down what fell from this 'little old man, with a black velvet cap'; 'if I were the minister of the Czar, — I should endeavour to occupy Persia, — I should take Constantinople in the rear'.

On the training of the men of British race who were to serve India, and the spirit he would have that service show, he had much to say. Though he deplored Wellesley's arrogance, and doubted whether his successors could carry the centralized burden he bequeathed, he applauded his college at Calcutta. A much better idea, he thought, than the later scheme of Haileybury College, 'a tedious scholastic discipline in England'. The study of Persian must be obligatory, 'the medium of all political intercourse'; so must Urdu, supplemented by the respective vernacular in each Presidency. He recommended Sanskrit, not for utility, but as a key to 'rich stores of knowledge', which must 'excite in the breast of the British student a respect and benevolence' for the Indian people. Finally, 'long habits of labour at their desks' were a necessary foundation for public servants.

He put his finger firmly on his successors' mistakes, or any

2 C   389

wrong inflicted on Indian feeling. Minto was away from Calcutta too much. No Governor-General could control the machine, 'that does not do as I did, inspect the weekly or monthly details of every department'. He was horrified at orders forbidding sepoys to wear caste marks or symbols of their religion, while to give freedom of proselytising to Christian missions would invite a Moslem revolt. Our conquest of Ceylon was unjustified, if we did not regard 'the rights of the ancient inhabitants'. He took much exception to Adam Smith's criticism of Company rule, questioning whether 'professed and dignified statesmen' would do any better. Yet the present dual system, between a parliamentary Board of Control and the Directors, was 'radically bad'. What his own ideal would have been, hardly appears; except that he would have kept directors out of parliament, and given the Governor-General more extensive powers.

In a beechwood box, made from Daylesford trees, young Elijah Impey kept some of his old friend's advice on Indian mythology, with the speculations coming from his wide spasmodic reading. Hindu philosophy, he apparently believed, had directly influenced the thought of Rome, even reaching Britain by way of the Druids. We should think of the two peoples as 'once possessing the same principles of religion, and now partaking of the same government; that government extended — not by their subjugation, but by the conquest and expulsion of their former despotic and uncontrolled rulers'. In 1812 he sent the Marquess of Hastings (formerly Moira), the new Governor-General, some notes on the peoples of India, in sentiment exactly the same as his words in Council half a century ago. 'Among the natives of India there are men of as strong intellect, as sound integrity and honourable feelings, as any of this kingdom. I regret that they are not sufficiently noticed, sufficiently employed, nor respected so much as they deserve to be.' Hindus were 'gentle in intercourse, — and grateful for benefits conferred upon them'. Such would be the impression made on 'every generous mind which shall receive the first rudiments of official life in India'.

To the end he kept his faith in the superiority of mind to matter, the duty of obedience to a disciplined reason. 'Do what is right', he tells the young D'Oyleys, 'from the impulse of your own judgement . . . when you have received the answer which your reason dictated, make that answer your law.' His own mind certainly never became a closed book, nor was the old fire of curiosity extinct. He much admired Malthus' work on 'Population', but not in blindness; 'I am just come from a christening. From the look of the parents, and the correspondent expression of the rest of the congregation, it is evident that none of them had read Malthus.' He praised a very different book, that of Robert Owen on his New Lanark experiments, as bringing some hope in the darkness of industrial civilization. He is found visiting Lancaster's school in St. George's Fields, 'much pleased with it' says the diary, and explaining to the monitors Indian ways of teaching arithmetic. The boys looked healthy, but he thought the girls were 'plain, pale, and sickly'. He read with pleasure Madame de Staël's account of Pestalozzi's teaching, and listened gravely to Davy lecturing on geology. Political reviews he detested. 'I hate the Edinburgh reviewers', he told Baber, 'not because they are bad critics and wicked politicians, but because they are sneerers, a character that from my heart I abhor.'

He was loyal still to the classics he had read at Westminster, Lucan and Horace in particular; giving some volumes to the son of an old soldier protégé, with the hope he would read them regularly, 'if it be but five minutes every morning'. And his idea of what was suitable for D'Oyley's daughters was thoroughly orthodox; Shakespeare and Milton, Addison, an expurgated Prior, Paley, and Madame de Sévigné. He was pleased and proud about Mrs. Hancock's niece Jane Austen, especially liking the character of Elizabeth Bennett. As for Walter Scott, every inch of the Border 'is, to me, consecrated ground', though liking the *Lady of the Lake* much better than the 'unworthy character' of *Marmion*. His own verse-making went on, a solace when he could not sleep, but never rose above mediocrity. He had always loved words, using them magnificently in prose when his passion was roused. But his present little themes, such as the fall of his beech grove in a storm, just passed the time away.

As he approached seventy-five, we seem to find an old and weary man whose mind is exhausted. He was living on his past; glad to receive each April congratulations on the anniversary of his acquittal, to hear that his portrait hung in Wellesley's new Government House, or that Charles D'Oyley prospered. On public affairs his letters become casual and ill informed. Each day he lived more and more by, and for, his affections, 'the best part of me', 'those best gifts of heaven'. They guaranteed his hopes for eternity, for 'the perfected society of those I loved'; in sorrow for the dead he found 'the affinities of this world to the next'. He had thought on it for years, he said, 'implanted it upon my heart with a holy conviction, which is blended with my hopes of eternal felicity'. That love and trust called forth their like in response, had always been his faith; so says a sentence that he borrowed from Proverbs, and put into his verse:

> As in the pool face answers face,
> So doth the heart of man to man.

He spoke of death without repining, and as not far distant, telling Baber in 1810 to come again soon, 'I have not many years, if years, to spare'. Two years before he had 'abdicated' the farm to Marian, who was often riding before breakfast, while he had taken to a chair drawn by a pony. And the usual nuisances of years bothered him, chills caught in London hotels, deafness, and teeth. But Marian guarded him well, while his old simplicity of life rewarded him. He rose very early, ate a spare breakfast alone, and worked before meeting his guests, dined at five o'clock, avoided the sun but demanded fresh air. When alone, he would read aloud, or play picquet or backgammon with Marian, who always beat him; or she would sing, — *O whistle and I'll come to you, my lad*, being one song of those remembered. Her vitality delighted yet astonished him, for he was very tired; when she dropped him in the gig the far side of the beech grove to walk home, it was all he could manage.

Her future was the load on his mind. In 1808 his bankers refused him further credit, his annuity would expire in five years, he was asking Francis Baring to get it extended. When he redrafted his will, leaving everything to her, it was with a recommendation that she should sell Daylesford to improve her income.

The year 1811, in which the King of Rome was born and Albuera was fought, and Jane Austen published *Sense and Sensibility*, was about the last of his normal activities. He spent January at Harman's hotel in London, finished his sittings to Sir Thomas Lawrence, and ordered Mitford's Greek history and Miss Edgeworth's last novel. In April he was in London again, without Marian, staying with Halhed and attending the levee, while the Duke of Gloucester was as solicitous as ever. He had hardly settled down again at home before they were invited to the Regent's fête in June; 'Mrs. Hastings has decided that we must accept it'. So they went to Carlton House, staying from nine at night till six in the morning; the Speaker noticing how 'old Mr. Hastings' was leaning over a brass rail, looking at the select table, all the length of which ran a little stream with live gudgeon in it. In July came the wedding at Daylesford of Tommy Woodman and Louise Chapuset, at which he praises 'three pretty bridesmaids'. The very next day the mare bolted and threw them from the gig; 'the first serious accident in which we were participators since our marriage'. Country-house visits to Stoneleigh Abbey and Melchett, and one to Daylesford by the Duke of Gloucester, passed before they entrenched themselves for a hard snowy winter. He timed a letter to Baber so that he might receive it on October the 8th, 'the date of my first arrival in Bengal, at the vast distance of sixty-one years from this day . . . of no consequence in itself, but it is, or ought to be, of use to me in suppressing all rising emotions of complaint at the too perceptible symptoms of a defective hearing and enfeebled memory'.

1812 went on quietly, into a miserably wet summer, leaving him with a devastating cold, during which he grew, but quickly 'excised', a beard. They went in December to the Imhoffs, keeping his eightieth birthday with a small dinner of old friends, the Halheds, Toone, Mrs. Motte, and her brother Peter Touchet. Early in 1813 he presided again at the Bengal Club. But this year much greater happiness, and all unlooked for, shone upon him.

The Company's charter was due for renewal, and two burning questions, among many more, exercised Toone and the Indian interest: the continuation of its trading monopoly, and the freedom of action permissible for Christian missions. On March the 30th Hastings was summoned to give evidence before the Commons, who examined him for three hours and a half. 'All the members rose on my dismission', says his diary, 'with their heads uncovered'; 'by a sudden spontaneous impulse', he told his nephew. While Marian noted with proud exultation, 'this mark of respect is only shown to Kings and Princes'. In April the Lords paid him the same compliment.

His testimony was to the same effect as his letters fifty years

ago. The Indian peoples were 'as exempt from the worst propensities of human passion as any people upon the face of the
earth'; had they not shown their equity and gratitude when he
was impeached, and they could expect nothing at his hands?
'The lower order of British subjects' must not be allowed to settle
there; 'they will insult, plunder, and oppress the natives'.
Every Briton, as our books and our everyday conversation showed,
thought of himself as a sovereign, '*our* native subjects' ever in
their minds and on their lips.

This sudden almost canonization, and a gracious letter from
the Directors, went to his heart, coming after 'my hard beating'.
He could hardly speak of it without tears, 'the colours of my
setting sun are too vivid'. For Marian above all, of course, he
was glad, 'whose happiness so many years have bound to my
own'. In June his joy was redoubled when, with loud undergraduate cheers, he received from the University of Oxford the
honorary degree of doctor of civil law.

His name was, indeed, now a part of history, of the triumph of
Great Britain and her allies in the great war, and he was drawn
into the pageants in which the Regent gloried. Early in 1814,
on the Prime Minister's proposal, he was made a privy councillor.
Simultaneously the Company extended his annuity for the
remainder of his life, though they would not hear of his hope
that it might be assigned for Marian's also, or raised to the scale
given to Cornwallis. The interval between Elba and Waterloo
had arrived. In June he went to Oxford, staying in Magdalen,
to meet the allied sovereigns, dining with them twice in state.
On the 18th he was bidden to the Guildhall banquet, where the
Regent introduced him to the Czar and the King of Prussia, 'as
the most deserving and one of the worst used men in the Empire',
adding 'he shall yet be honoured as he deserves'. But that was
his way. On July the 7th he took the chair at the dinner given
to Wellington by 'the gentlemen of India'; some of the press
reported his voice was very feeble; however, he paid their
tribute to 'our own Indian-taught General', calling him the
instrument of 'moral retribution'. The rest of the month was
full, with the Queen's drawing-room, a dinner with the Directors
and response to the toast of 'Mr. Hastings and the government of
India', winding up with the Regent's fête till six in the morning;
after which he went home to give the whole parish a dinner, to

WARREN HASTINGS, 1811, BY SIR THOMAS LAWRENCE

celebrate the peace. With some reason he wrote that 'from these proofs of what I can endure, I think I shall last through another winter'.

Only his spirit had carried him through. He had two of his paralytic seizures the winter before, and the truth of the Wellington banquet comes out in his later note, 'I had taken a prescription in two doses to prevent the return of my spasms'. In fact, calling at Toone's the day after, he found his speech gone and one hand useless, as before. From this time onwards he speaks freely of these attacks, 'what my physicians are shy of calling a paralytic affection'; a train of thought, or connecting word, would escape him, and one letter a day was about all he could contrive. Except for a few days in London to urge an increase of his pension, and a month by the sea at Sandgate, he did not leave home in the year of Waterloo. His old sympathy with Napoleon, in part sentiment for fallen greatness, crops up again; he was sorry, he said, to see this country 'in the character of the jailor of Europe'. 'I cannot yet reconcile it to the importance which his destiny has attached to that of Europe, that he should end his career in a prison.'

1816 opened badly with a heavy catarrh that shook him more than any ailment since his fever of 1782. Though the impeachment had left one lasting result, a dread of seeing his name in print, the letters of the last two years are wonderfully serene, and his zest for all he valued, like his long memory for injuries, was hardly impaired. He was still exchanging verses with Halhed, and sometimes noted, with a flash of masterfulness again, what the British government was doing. In Lord Exmouth's attack on Algiers he thought we lost a chance of winning a lasting footing on that coast, 'which once held out the prize of empire to the great rivals of the world'. He printed a little pamphlet on one of his hobbies, safeguards against fire. And he was more ardent still about another on the Indian salt revenue, his own creation, the credit for which had been inadvertently given to Henry Vansittart. 'I am angry', the old man wrote, 'but I shall cool before I get to town.'

But the great achievement of 1816 was his restoration of Daylesford church, a work that gave him interest, exercise, and almost a new hold on life. It had to be done, both stone and woodwork being badly decayed. He began demolition on July the 8th, the first service in the restored church was held on December the 8th. Every stone, as taken out, was numbered and went back in its old place, the line of the Saxon foundation was carefully followed. Charlotte Imhoff saw to the choice of stained glass; wood for the new ceiling came from larches he had planted himself. A tablet, for which he redrew the design, declared its identity unchanged, 'sanctified by the prayers, rites, and oblations of its successive parochial members through a period exceeding 1,000 years', and ending 'for a thousand years in Thy sight are but as yesterday'. At the same time he set up a new gravestone for his grandfather, the Rector who had brought him up, dead now sixty-four years ago.

He had lived, and was to die, a communicant member of the Church of England. And there is nothing in his thousands of papers to impugn the reality of his faith. Yet all his Indian life, and some famous utterances, are there to show how steadily he honoured other religions, and that his mind put no man of good-will among the heretics. He wrote once to Baber that his religion was 'more strongly confirmed by a single exemplification of the influence of true devotion in a well formed mind, than by all the sermons of the Bishop of London'. Much the same moral, of individual conduct as the core, sounds in a draft sermon he wrote at Charlotte Imhoff's request, on the text 'the poor shall never cease out of the land'. After dwelling on the 'shame' of the poor law, which was then demoralizing southern England, he proceeded that the rich man 'must submit to the condition of the poor, that he may rise to an equality with them'; if, we must understand, he were to achieve their hardihood, humility, and courage.

On March the 1st, 1817, he left home for two months, on what was to be his last visit to London. For the last time he dined with his India club, 'my health drunk with marks of the most expressive kindness'. He showed all his old deference for the Crown. He dined with the Duke of Gloucester to meet the Regent, and offered the use of Daylesford to the Queen on her way to Bath.

In June he went to Cheltenham to see the Duke again, who lent him John Taylor's new book on *The Identity of Junius*, that is, with Philip Francis. This he read and analysed at length, concluding that this identification was out of the question. His mind ran much on India this year, as he followed the Marquess of Hastings' policy. He harked back to Hyder Ali's first attack on Mysore as illustrating 'how assiduous the people of India are — in detecting the talents, weaknesses, designs and propensities of their opponents'; to argue thence that the Mahrattas would never take the aggressive against a man of determination, but wait for 'a shabby Governor-General to cope with'. His own past flowed in on him when he heard rumours that Hastings might resign; 'if I were at his elbow, I would say to him "you have no right to quit your post for a sentiment of disgust, — no, not though shame (present shame) and dishonour should attend your resolution"'. That his mind still turned on his own good name with posterity, we may judge from an enquiry this autumn as to the best means of having medals struck, stamped with his profile.

The first months of 1818 went badly, with some difficulty in swallowing, and perpetual cough. And the loneliness of old age closed in. He had just heard of William Palmer's death, last of his kindergarten in India, and was soon to hear of John D'Oyley's. But his interest was as warm as ever in the next generation, and his benign endurance unflinching. 'I am wonderfully well,' he told young Impey, 'my sufferings such as at their worst I should be ashamed to mention in a tone of complaint.' Writing to Auriol in April he asked the last news of the day. 'There is no period in the longest duration of life, in which a man who possesses external feelings may not indulge the wish, that his own may last a little longer. Two objects vehemently occupy mine; one, to see the result of the Polar expedition, — the other, to know the destiny of the man who has preached the doctrine of assassination, and invited others to practice it for the gratification of his own vengeance on Mr. Canning.' Another letter that month breathed his old fierce anger, branding an author who had written rather tepidly about Chait Sing, and adding what he called 'a well attested anecdote', — the story that only Dundas' pressure that very morning had made Pitt vote wrong on the Benares charge.

Early in May, willingly or not, he let Marian leave for a month in London. To Halhed he wrote he had 'the conscious satisfaction of having throughout allowed a bias in favour of every wish and opinion of hers, in preference to my own'. When she was gone, he welcomed spring and 'its arrears of delight';

spent the first week rearranging his library; kept his diary carefully, noting that Marian had been warmly received by the royal family. His bed was moved downstairs, for even a walk in the garden tired him now. Late that month he mentions 'sensations as of the sounds of distant multitudes, — at times resembling slow music'. But he was well enough on the 31st to drive to church, and when Marian came home in early June, 'in perfect health and gaiety of spirits', they welcomed the Duke of Gloucester's proposal to visit them in July.

On the 13th of that month, a very sultry day, he drove about twilight over the Adelstrop hills, and as he got out of the coach on their return, staggered and half fell. The local surgeon bled him; a slipping bandage lost him more blood. His sufferings were grievous, and he wished to go; 'passed this day', he wrote on the 15th, 'unexpectedly and regretfully well'. On the 20th, the hideous difficulty of swallowing set in again, and that day he made the final entry in his forty years' diaries. On the 3rd of August he dictated a last appeal to the Company, to be delivered by Toone. The loss of his annuity, he said, must leave 'the dearest object of all my mortal concerns in a state of more than comparative indigence. This is not one to which she ought to be reduced, for she has been the virtual means of supporting the powers of life and action by which I was enabled to maintain their affairs in vigour, strength, credit, and respect.' He begged them to continue for her the reward conferred 'on my services and sufferings; the latter have been great, but not without their reward from my country'. Then he bade farewell to his honourable masters. 'My latest prayers shall be offered for their service; for the welfare of my beloved country, and for that also of the land whose interests were so long committed to my partial guardianship, and for which I feel a sentiment in my departing hours not alien from that which is due from every subject to his own.'

With inexhaustible patience, though only able to sip cold water, he lingered another three weeks, his voice firm, but only to bless those round him. At seven on the evening of August the 22nd, he drew a handkerchief over his face and died, and in September the last Hastings of Daylesford was buried in the village churchyard. Forty-six years later, the last known descendant of Carl and Marian Imhoff, a Eurasian, was laid in a pauper grave at Karachi.

The End

No monument was erected to Warren Hastings in the Abbey by parliament or Company, only a tablet set up by 'his beloved wife and disconsolate widow'. Perhaps he had written his own epitaph best, not only in the 'blood and wounds' of an empire, but in all that he wrought and wrote over the years. Better still, some may think, in the words inscribed in the book he gave Nesbitt Thompson, 'a man more sinned against than sinning'. Best of all, in the quotation he had long ago sent to Marian from the Gita :

Let the Motive be in the Deed, and not in the Event. Be not one whose Motive for Action is the Hope of Reward. — Wise Men, who have abandoned all thought of the fruit which is produced from their action, are freed from the Chain of Birth, and go to the Regions of Eternal Happiness.

SOURCES

MANUSCRIPT

1. BRITISH MUSEUM

   (a) The Hastings Papers which have been consulted may be classified as follows :

Bengal Council Proceedings, Secret

Add. 28,976-78. Oct. 1774–75.
    28,984. June onwards, 1776.
    28,992. First half of 1779.
    28,994. Jan.-June 1780.
    29,048. Mahratta War, 1780.

Other Official Proceedings

    29,069. Select Committee, 1761.
    29,072. Revenue department, 1777.
    29,076. Committee of Circuit, 1772.
    29,081. Council notes, 1775–80.
    29,082. Revenue department, 1775–79.
    29,103. Letters to Directors, 1774–76.
    29,112. Appeals from Hastings and Barwell.
    29,113. Appeals from the Majority.
    29,115. Letters to Residents (copies).
    29,118. Bombay and Central India, 1778.
    29,121. Oudh letters, 1784.

Early Bengal Papers

    29,096-99. 1757–63.
    29,209.
    29,198.

General Correspondence

    29,125-54. 1758–82 : 30 volumes.
    29,156-63. Sept. 1782–May 1784 : 8 volumes.
    29,166-77. Sept. 1784–1800 : 12 volumes.
    29,181. 1806.
    29,191. 1816–38.

Finance and Accounts

    29,226. Agents' accounts in England.
    29,227-31. Private accounts.

Personal Papers

    29,232. Family and old age.
    29,233. Essays.
    39,893. Prayers.
    39,903. Autobiography.
    41,607-8. Poems.

Sources

Diaries

29,212. Benares diary of 1773 (edited by C. C. Davies for the Royal
  Historical Society, 1948).

39,878-88. Diaries, 1778–1818.

Miscellaneous Papers

29,193. Miscellaneous correspondence.

29,201. 1784–85.

29,202. Special documents.

29,206. Mir Kasim; Indian testimonials.

29,218. Memoranda, 1765–1801.

29,236. Papers of T. S. Hancock, 1769–75.

39,871. 1775–1818.

39,872. Letters to E. B. Impey, 1800–1818.

39,873. Mrs. Hastings' correspondence.

39,876. Letter book, 1807–13.

39,890. Memoranda.

39,892. *Ib.*

41,606. Various.

Impeachment Papers

29,219.

29,221.

29,225.

Daylesford Papers

39,902. Farming.

41,609-10. Contents and inventories.

(b) *Other Collections*

16,259-61.⎫
16,263.   ⎬ Papers of Sir Elijah Impey.

34,287. Correspondence of Clavering and Francis.

34,686. Papers of Robert Palk.

38,398. ⎫
38,401. ⎪
        ⎬ Papers of Charles Jenkinson, first Earl of Liverpool.
38,405. ⎪
38,407-8.⎭

2. INDIA OFFICE LIBRARY (Office of Commonwealth Relations)

Eur. MSS.

E. 13-17, 19, 28.⎫
D. 18.   ⎪
                ⎬ Papers of Philip Francis.
F. 7 and 10.   ⎪
G. 4.   ⎭

Orme MSS., Various

10. Joseph Smith.

30. Madras, 1767–71.

41. Bengal, 1756–74.

43. Bengal, 1761–73.

91. Hosea letters.

166. Hosea and S. Middleton.

202. Orme letters, 1768–84.

Fowke MSS.

$\left.\begin{array}{l}\text{20-21.}\\\text{24.}\\\text{26-28.}\\\text{30.}\end{array}\right\}$ Papers of Joseph Fowke and his family.

Factory Records

Kasimbazaar, 12 and 13.

Madras

Select Committee Proceedings; range C, vol. 55.

Public; range 240, vol. 28.

Military; range 251, vols. 66 and 68.

Home Miscellaneous

Vols. 189, 207-8, 212-13, 230.

3. BODLEIAN LIBRARY

Papers of Laurence Sulivan.

4. HASTINGS LETTERS FROM PRIVATE COLLECTIONS

   (i) To George Vansittart; in the possession of Miss Vansittart Neale of Bisham Abbey.

   (ii) To Auriol; in the possession of Sir Henry Dashwood.

   (iii) Extracts from letters in the possession of the Reverend Sir Frederick Sykes, Miss A. M. Woodman Hastings of Twyning, and H. S. Rogers, Esq.

PRINTED

(a) *Official*

   Reports of Secret and Select Committees of the House of Commons, 1772–73 and 1782–83.

   Journals of the House of Lords.

   Parliamentary History.

   State Trials.

   History of the Trial of Warren Hastings (Debrett), 1796.

   Minutes of Evidence: 11 vols., 1788–94.

   Speeches of the Managers and Counsel in the Trial of Warren Hastings, ed. Bond, 1859.

   Fifth Report from the Select Committee of the House of Commons, 1812, ed. Firminger, 1917.

   Calendars of Persian Correspondence (Calcutta, 1925).

   Selections from — *State Papers in the Bombay Secretariat, Maratha Series,* ed. Forrest.

   Selections from — *State Papers in the Foreign Department of the Government of India,* ed. Forrest. (Cited as 'Selections'.)

   Selections from the State Papers of Warren Hastings, ed. Forrest.

(b) *Contemporary*

   Bolts, W. *Considerations on Indian Affairs.*

   Burke, Edmund. *Works* (Bohn edn., 1854) and *Correspondence* (1844).

   D'Arblay, Madame. (Fanny Burney): *Diary,* ed. Dobson.

   Fay, Eliza. *Original Letters from India,* ed. E. M. Forster, 1925.

   Forbes, James. *Oriental Memoirs,* 1834.

Sources

Grand, G. F. *Life of a Gentleman long resident in India*, ed. Firminger, 1910.

Hickey, William. *Memoirs*, ed. A. Spencer, 1913–25.

Hodges, William. *Travels in India*, 1793.

Holwell, J. Z. *Indian Tracts.*

Ives, E. *Voyage to India.*

Memoirs of the War in Asia, 1788.

Orme, R. *Military Transactions of the British Nation in Indostan.*

Scrafton, L. *Observations on Mr. Vansittart's Narrative.*

Vansittart, Henry. *Narrative of the Transactions in Bengal*, 1766.

Verelst, H. *Rise, Progress, and Present State of the English Government in Bengal*, 1772.

Wraxall, N. W. *Memoirs*, ed. Wheatley, 1884.

(c) *Modern Works*, embodying original documents

Bengal, Past and Present (Calcutta, 1907 onwards).

Beveridge, H. *Trial of Nanda Kumar.*

Busteed, H. E. *Echoes from old Calcutta*, 4th edn.

Cornwallis. *Correspondence.*

The Francis Letters.

Gleig. *Life of Warren Hastings.*

Grier, Sydney C. *Letters of Warren Hastings to his Wife.*

Hill, S. C. *Bengal in 1756–57.*

Historical MSS. Commission reports: on Palk, Abergavenny, Rutland, and Hastings papers.

Impey, E. B. *Memoirs of Sir Elijah Impey*, 1847.

Lawson, Sir Charles. *Private Life of Warren Hastings.*

Lindsay. *Lives of the Lindsays*, 1849.

Love, H. D. *Vestiges of Old Madras.*

Macartney, Lord. *Letters of*, ed. C. C. Davies.

Macpherson, Sir John. *Letters of Warren Hastings to*, ed. Dodwell.

Macpherson, W. C. *Soldiering in India.*

Magnus, Sir Philip. *Edmund Burke.*

Malcolm, Sir J. *Life of Clive.*

Mill, James. *History of India*, ed. Wilson.

Minto. *Life and Letters of Gilbert Elliot, 1st Earl*, 1874.

Notes and Queries, vol. 154: Letters to Baber.

Parkes and Merivale. *Memoirs of Sir Philip Francis.*

Rumbold, E. *Vindication of Sir Thomas Rumbold*, 1868.

Strachey, Sir John. *The Rohilla War.*

Sutherland, L. S. *The East India Company in Eighteenth Century Politics.*

Weizman, S. *Warren Hastings and Philip Francis.*

(d) *Other printed Authorities*

Ascoli. *Early Revenue History of Bengal.*

Aspinall. *Cornwallis in Bengal.*

Bannerjee. *Early Land Revenue System in Bengal and Bihar.*

Cambridge History of India, vols. iv and v.

Chatterji. *Mir Qasim*, 1935.

Curzon. *British Government in India.*

Davies, A. M. *Warren Hastings.*

Davies, C. C. *Warren Hastings and Oudh.*
DasGupta. *The Central Authority in British India 1774–84.*
Dodwell. *Dupleix and Clive.*
Foster, Sir William. *The East India House,* and *John Company.*
Furber, H. *Henry Dundas,* and *John Company at Work.*
Grant Duff. *History of the Mahrattas.*
Hastings, G. W. *Warren Hastings.*
Kincaid and Parasnis. *History of the Maratha People.*
Philips, C. H. *The East India Company, 1784–1834.*
Ramsbotham, R. B. *Studies in the Land Revenue History of Bengal.*
Sarkar. *History of the Mogul Empire.*
Stephen. *Nuncumar and Impey.*
Teignmouth. *Life of John Shore.*
Wilks. *History of Mysore.*
Wyllie. *Sir Eyre Coote.*

NOTES

Chapter I—YOUTH: 1732–50

Daylesford and the Hastings, to 1660. Nash, *History of Worcestershire*; Book of Fees; Cal. Inq. P.M., 33, Ed. i; *ib.* 5, Ed. iii; Feet of Fines, Oxfordshire, p. 211; Cal. Patent Rolls, 1459 and 1467; *Records of Worcestershire Quarter Sessions*; Will of John Hastings, 1545, Worcester Consistory, transcripts, vol. 5; Will of Simon Hastings, 1622, Barrington 30; Inq. P.M. 1629 and 1638; Will of Susan Hastings, 1642, Worcester Consistory.

Boyhood. Family Wills—of Rev. Penyston Hastings, 1752, Searle, 174; of Howard Hastings and Thomas Warren, Add. 29,232.

His foster-mother. W. H. accounts, Add. 29,227; C. Ellis to W. H., 1785, *ib.* 29,168.

Chapter II—THE INDIAN SCENE: 1750–56

Autobiography, Add. 39,903.

Chapter III—THE FALL AND RECOVERY OF BENGAL: 1752–57

Factory records, I.O.
Hill's *Bengal in 1756–7*, and *Three Frenchmen in India*.
P. 21.   Madame Vernet; Add. 29,209, f. 196; Grier, 51.
P. 22.   Nobkissen and Indian intermediaries; Beveridge, 244; Hallward, *William Bolts*, 48.

Chapter IV—TRIAL AND ERROR: JULY 1757–OCTOBER 1760

P. 27.   Scrafton; Add. 29,132 and 29,126.
P. 28.   Clive-Hastings letters, Add. 29,131 *passim.*
P. 35.   H. on Mir Jaffir, Add. 29,096.
P. 37.   Treaty with Mir Kasim; Select Committee, 1772, 1st report; Forrest, *Clive*, ii, 213; Dodwell, *Dupleix and Clive*, 205.
P. 38.   Abdication of Mir Jaffir; Add. 29,198 ('transactions at Morshedebad'); Vansittart i; Caillaud, *Narrative of what happened in Bengal in 1760* (1764).

Chapter V—HENRY VANSITTART AND MIR KASIM: 1760–64

Hastings-Vansittart letters; Add. 29,098 and 29,132; 39,903 ('my official history').

Private trade; Verelst, 46 and 182.
P. 41.   Memorandum of 1765; Monckton Jones, 155.

P. 45. Troubles at Patna; *Cal. Persian Corr.*, i; Firminger, *Three Surgeons of Patna*.

P. 47. Arrest of Nuncumar; 'Selections', iii, appendix; *Bengal, P. and P.*, xvi; Add. 29,198, f. 14.

P. 49. Patna massacre; *Bengal, P. and P.*, xli.

P. 52. Clive and Sulivan; besides her definitive *East India Company*, see Sutherland's articles in *E.H.R.*, 1934 and 1947, and Malcolm, ii *passim*.

Chapter VI—UNEMPLOYED: 1765-69

Hastings' accounts; Add. 29,227.

P. 56. The chair of Persian; Add. 29,202.

P. 57. For date of his memorandum of 1766, see Weizman, 51 and 367, and Baber's letter of Oct. 1780, Add. 29,146.

P. 58. Nuncumar and Mahomed Reza Khan; Sel. Committee, 1773, 3rd report; Barwell letters in *Bengal, P. and P.*, viii-xi; Sykes to H., Nov. '79, Add. 29,144.

P. 59. On the Burkes, see Magnus, and Wecter, *Burke and his Kinsmen*.

P. 62. The Imhoffs; Grier, also appendix in her *The Great Proconsul*, and K. L. Murray, *Beloved Marian*.

Chapter VII—MADRAS: 1769-72

Madras MSS., as on p. 402.

Dodwell, *The Nabobs of Madras*.

Orme's correspondence; with Joseph Smith, O.V. 10; with Du Pré, *ib.* 30.

P. 65. Du Pré as Governor; Palk papers *passim*.

P. 67. Hancock papers, Add. 29,236; his letters from Hastings, *ib.* 29,125.

P. 70. Hastings' relations with the Nabob; Add. 29,126, letters to Sulivan and Peregrine Cust; *ib.* 29,129, to Scott, Oct. '83.

P. 75. Bengal under Verelst and Cartier; *Bengal, P. and P.*, ii (Pearse's account); *ib.* x and xii (Barwell).

P. 76. Sir G. Colebrooke; *Thraliana*, i, 335; Orme, O.V. 202; Namier, *Structure of Politics*.

P. 77. Fowke-Hastings letters, Add. 29,132-33.

Chapter VIII—BENGAL: 1772-74

P. 79. Calcutta; *Bengal, P. and P.*, xiv-xv; Busteed; *Hartley House*.

P. 81. John Graham; Orme MSS., O.V. 166; H. to Sykes, Dec. '72, Add. 29,125.

P. 85. H. on *banyans*; to G. Vansittart, March '76; Add. 29,128.

P. 85. H. on contracts; *Home Miscell.*, 212, May '75.

P. 86. H. on dispossessed proprietors; *ib.* 207, Oct. '76; despatch of 3 Nov. '72, appendix to Hunter, *Annals of Rural Bengal*.

P. 88. The Imhoffs in Bengal; Hancock letters, Add. 29,236; *ib.* 29,227, ff. 144, 206; *Bengal, P. and P.*, xxxiii; Busteed.

Notes

P. 89. Sulivan and Colebrooke; Sutherland in *Economic History Review*, 1936; *Letters of George Dempster*; Fortescue, *Letters of George III*, ii, 407.

P. 91. Sykes to H., Jan. '73, Add. 29,133, and Feb. '74, *ib.* 29,134.

Chapter IX—Reform of the State : 1772-74

P. 92. Mahomed Reza Khan; Monckton Jones, 190; Ironside, Dec. '73, Orme MSS., O.V. 41; H. to Sulivan, Jan. '80, Add. 29,128.

P. 94. Charges against Nuncumar; Hallward, *William Bolts*; H. to S. Middleton, July '73, Add. 29,125; Sel. Committee, 1773, 3rd report.

P. 96. Rajballabh; Nuncumar to H., June '72, Add. 29,133.

P. 98. Over-assessment of revenue; Orme MSS., O.V. 166; Francis MSS., Eur. E.28; Ramsbotham, 63.

P. 100. H. to Barwell on free trade; Add. 29,125, June '74.

P. 102. Provincial councils and service salaries; H. to J. Woodhouse, Jan. '74, Add. 29,127; Monckton Jones, 252; Palk, 231.

P. 106. Nomination as Governor-General; Sykes, Caillaud, and Sulivan letters, Add. 29,133; Jenkinson to Clavering, Dec. '76, Francis MSS.

P. 107. Fear of Nuncumar; H.'s letters, March to July '73, Add. 29,125 and 29,134.

Chapter X—Northern India and the Rohilla War

Origins; Strachey; Verelst, appendix; Secret Committee, '82, 5th report.

P. 112. First refusal to intervene; Orme MSS., O.V. 167.

P. 113. Benares conference; besides *Diary*, edited by C. C. Davies, *Cal. Persian Corr.*; Barker to H., Sept. '73, Add. 29,134; H. to Palk, March '74, Add. 34,686.

P. 116. Council vote for rejection; Macleane to Sulivan, Jan. '74, Bodleian MSS., Eng. hist., c. 271.

P. 118. Pearse's view; *Bengal, P. and P.*, ii.

P. 119. Hastings-Middleton letters; Add. 29,135.

Chapter XI—The Conspiracy: I. 1774 and 'The New Gentlemen'

P. 122. H.'s loans to F. Stuart and Belli; Add. 29,227, f. 480, *ib.* 29,232, f. 13.

P. 122. Sale of diamonds; *ib.* 39,902.

P. 125. Burke's changing view of H.; Burke, *Corr.*, i, 428; Magnus, 75; A. M. Davies, 151.

P. 128. Francis and Clive; Francis MSS., Eur. F.7, and Weizman, 217 and 295.

P. 128. Francis and Burke; F. to Ellis, Nov. '74, F. MSS., 49, and Strachey to F., Jan. '75, *ib.* 56.

P. 129. Joseph Fowke; Fowke MSS., 20; Parkes and Merivale, ii, 161.

P. 130. Sir Robert Chambers; C. to North, April '75, Add. 38,398; C. to Jenkinson, '78, *ib.* 38,401.

P. 131. Macpherson's news; Sept. '74, Add. 29,135.

P. 171.   Francis' letters; Weizman, 284 *seq.*; also F. to Fowke, 19 Sept. '76, Francis MSS., 49, and to Barrington, 16 Sept. *ib.* 47.

Chapter XIV—The Home Front: 1775–77

Miss Sutherland's study on the East India Company (published after this chapter was written) for the subject as a whole.

P. 173.   H. to Palk, Dec. '74, Add. 29,127.

P. 174.   Macleane's activities; Mackenzie to Francis, Dec. '75, Francis MSS., 56; *Bengal, P. and P.*, xvii; Dropmore papers (Hist. MSS. Commission), ii, 298; Sulivan to H., 1 April '76, Add. 29,137.

P. 175.   The Rockingham party; J. Stewart to H., Feb. '76, *ib.*

P. 176.   Jenkinson to Clavering, Dec. '76, Francis MSS., 51.

P. 176.   H.'s option when to resign; Pechell to H., 7 June '78, Add. 29,141.

P. 177.   H.'s breach with Vansittart; H. to V., March '77, *ib.* 29,128; Feb. '82 and Nov. '83, *ib.* 29,129; Pechell to H., Jan. '81, *ib.* 29,147.

P. 179.   Stewart to H., May '77, *ib.* 29,138.

Chapter XV—Years of Decision: 1776–78

P. 180.   H. to Vansittart, 24 Nov. '76, Vansittart-Neale MSS.

P. 182.   Impey on Francis; July '78, Add. 16,259.

P. 182.   Chambers to Jenkinson, July '78, Add. 38,401.

P. 183.   Baber's view of Marian; 22 Nov. '76, Vansittart-Neale MSS.

P. 184.   The Mahratta danger; Hannay to H., March '77, Add. 29,138; G. Farmer to H., Nov. '77, *ib.* 29,139; Forrest, *Maratha Series*, i; Grant Duff, ii, 70.

P. 185.   Condition of Oudh; Middleton and Hannay to H., Add. 29,138-40 *passim*; Goddard, Orme MSS., O.V. 91.

P. 186.   Resignation crisis; Barwell papers, *Bengal, P. and P.*, xvii; Sel. Committee, '82, 9th report; Francis' note of 16 June '78, Francis MSS., 48; H. to Dunning, 28 June '77, Add. 29,128.

P. 190.   Wheler's outlook; Elliot to H., 7 Dec. '77, Add. 29,139.

P. 192.   Hastings' loans to Kamal-ud-Din, etc.; Add. 29,229, f. 73 ('bad debts' still in 1789).

P. 193.   Sulivan to Hastings, 21 Dec. '78, *ib.* 29,142.

Chapter XVI—The Mahratta War: 1777–79

P. 194.   European troops in India; H. to Coote, Nov. '79, *ib.* 29,115.

P. 195.   Ragoba's projected *jagir*; Secret Committee, 1782, 6th report.

P. 196.   Orders to Bombay; H. to Hornby, Jan. '78, Add. 29,118.

P. 197.   Goddard's march; H. to Impey, 11 June and 4 July '78, *ib.* 16,261.

P. 198.   Alliance with Mysore? H. to Rumbold, 6 June '78, *ib.* 29,115; DasGupta, 60.

P. 198.   Francis to Farrer, April '78, Francis MSS., 51; cf. (Franciscan) *Authentic Narrative of the present Maratta War* (1781).

P. 199.   Elliot's last letters; to H., 31 July and 2 Aug., Add. 29,141.

P. 201.   Coote on Indian artillery; to H., Oct. '79, Add. 29,144.

Notes

P. 239. Money dealings with Barwell and Impey; accounts 1783–84, Add. 29,226.

P. 242. The contracts and agencies; Minutes of Trial *passim*; *Speeches*; *Trial* (Debrett), part viii; Fowke MSS., 27, April '84.

Chapter XX—THE GREAT WAR : 1780–82

P. 247. The Nizam's hostility; Hollond to H., Oct. '80, Add. 29,146.

P. 247. Condition of Delhi; Polier's account, *Bengal, P. and P.*, viii; Muir and Hannay, autumn '78, to H., Add. 29,141.

P. 251. Popham's project; P. to H., Dec. '80, *ib.* 29,146.

P. 252. Suffering of British prisoners; Bristow's narrative in *Captives of Tippu*, ed. A. W. Lawrence; *Lives of the Lindsays*, vol. iii; Wilks, ii, 26.

P. 254. Surrender of Gwalior; Muir to H., May '81, Add. 29,149; Gleig, ii, 379, 459.

P. 257. Popham on H. as a general; Thompson to H., *Bengal, P. and P.*, xx, July 1803.

P. 258. Bonds handed to Larkins; L. to H., March '88, Add. 29,171.

Chapter XXI—A BLACK HALF YEAR : CHAIT SING AND THE BEGUMS OF OUDH : 1781–82

In general; Davies, *W. H. and Oudh*; Select Committee, '82, 2nd report; H.'s *Benares Narrative*; *Trial*; P. E. Roberts in *Cambridge History of India*.

P. 260. Earlier reports against Chait Sing; Graham, '77–'78, Add. 29,139 and *ib.* 29,141; Coote, Dec. '79, *ib.* 29,144; Scott, Nov. '80, *ib.* 29,146; Markham's evidence at trial.

P. 261. His links with Francis and Clavering; Beveridge, 297; Fowke MSS., Eur. E.6.

P. 261. British officers' evidence; Sel. Committee, 2nd report; Balfour to H., Aug. '81; Gardner's evidence to H. of Commons, *Home Miscell.*, 230.

P. 262. H.'s remark to Johnson; J. to Impey, May '82, Add. 16,263.

P. 263. The massacre; Wade's evidence, Add. 29,221.

P. 264. Condition of Oudh; 2nd report, *ut supra*; evidence of Hannay (in 'Selections'), Osborne in Minutes of Trial, 1665; Cumming to H., 17 Sept., Add. 29,150.

P. 265. The flight to Chunar; Anderson's note, 21 Aug., *ib.*; H. to Wheler, 22 Aug., Add. 38,408.

P. 266. Blair's evidence; Minutes, 1777.

P. 268. H. on safety of Chait Sing's family; Minutes, 1644; to Impey, 6 Oct., *Home Miscell.*, 230.

P. 269. Unauthorized message to Poona; Macartney, etc. to H., 11 Sept., Add. 29,150; Goddard to H., 2 Dec., *ib.* 29,152.

P. 273. Official version on seizure of treasure; Bengal Secret letter, 11 Feb. '82, Sel. Committee, 10th report.

P. 274. Guarantee to Fyzullah Khan; Barwell letters, *Bengal, P. and P.*, xvii; Sel. Committee, 8th report.

Notes

P. 324. Directors' letter, 16 March '84, Add. 29,201; Hastings to Pitt, 11 Dec. '84, Bodleian MSS., Eng. hist., c. 271.

P. 326. H. to Directors ('never sent'), Jan. '85, Add. 29,167.

Chapter XXV—From One Exile to Another: 1785–86

P. 329. Marian in England; accounts, Add. 29,226 and 29,229; Scott's letters, *ib.* 29,166-68.

P. 332. H.'s first month at home; diary, *ib.* 39,879; Dundas to H., 17 Aug., *ib.* 29,168.

P. 334. H.'s fortune; accounts, Add. 29,229; Woodman's evidence, 25 May '93, at trial.

P. 335. Dundas' policy; Furber, 37; Philips, 38-49.

P. 336. H. to Thurlow, Dec. '85, Add. 29,169.

P. 337. His recommendations to Cornwallis; May '86, *ib.* 29,129.

P. 338. Burke's tactics; Burke, *Corr.*, iii, 38; Magnus, 147.

P. 340. Appearance before the Commons; diary, Add. 39,880; Minutes, 371; Rutland papers, iii; Gleig, iii, 289.

P. 341. Gilpin's evidence; *Home Miscell.*, 230.

P. 342. Opinion that charges will collapse; Rutland papers, *ut supra*; Auckland, i, 371; H. Walpole, *Letters*, xiii, 378-81.

Chapter XXVI—Nine Years' Persecution: 1786–95

P. 343. Wilberforce and 'the Saints'; Rutland, iii; Minutes, 109; Wraxall, iv, 339; Holland Rose, *Pitt*, 233.

P. 344. Francis' activity; Weizman, 182-8; *Windham Papers*, i, 85; *The Francis Letters*, ii, 369.

P. 346. Archbishop Markham's advice; n.d., Add. 29,169.

P. 347. Lord Hood and Pitt's speech; *ib.* 29,219; Minto, i, 133.

P. 349. Defence before the Lords; L.J., 28 Nov. '87.

P. 350. Opening of trial; *Trial* (Debrett); D'Arblay, *Diary*; Minto, i, 193; Hawkins Browne to J. Nicholls, 13 Feb., Add. 29,171.

P. 351. 'Common gazing-stock'; Add. 29,225.

P. 353. On Pitt's enmity; April '91, *ib.* 29,172.

P. 355. Burke on Shore's appointment; to F. Baring, Oct. '92, *ib.* 29,172.

P. 356. Devi Sing; Ramsbotham, 20; Shore's minute, Nov. '83, Add. 29,202; Paterson to Chapman, Sept. '89, *ib.* 29,171; Mill (ed. Wilson), v, 108, 200.

P. 357. Sheridan on the Begums; Gibbon's *Letters*, ii, 172; H. to Thompson, July '88, in S. A. Strong, *Critical Essays*.

P. 358. H. on Chait Sing; Add. 29,219, f. 61.

P. 358. Indian testimonials and help; *Bengal, P. and P.*, xviii; Add. 29,172.

Chapter XXVII—The End of the Trial: 1791–95

P. 361. Whigs for a retreat; Trevelyan, *Grey*, 25; Burke, *Corr.*, iii, 86, 127; Fox, *Memorials*, ii, 357; Prior, *Burke*, 286.

P. 362. Evidence of Gardner, Gilpin, and Duff; *Trial*, pt. i, 26, 62, pt. vi, 46; Minutes, 1971; Add. 29,219, May '88.

INDEX

415

Index

THE END

PRINTED BY R. & R. CLARK, LTD., EDINBURGH